HUMAN RIGHTS
AND BASIC NEEDS
IN THE AMERICAS

HUMAN RIGHTS AND BASIC NEEDS IN THE AMERICAS

Edited by Margaret E. Crahan

Woodstock Theological Center

GEORGETOWN UNIVERSITY PRESS
Washington, D.C.

Copyright © 1982 by Georgetown University Press

ISBN: 0-87840-402-3 (paperback)
        0-87840-403-1 (hardcover)

Printed in the United States of America

Library of Congress Cataloging in Publication Data
Main entry under title:

Human rights and basic needs in the Americas.

　　1. Civil rights—Latin America—Addresses, essays,
lectures.　　2. Latin America—Economic conditions—
1945-　　　—Addresses, essays, lectures.　　3. Latin
America—National security—Addresses, essays, lectures.
4. Economic assistance, American—Latin America—
Addresses, essays, lectures.　　I. Crahan, Margaret E.
JC599.L3H79　　　323.4′098　　　82-6211
ISBN 0-87840-403-1　　　　　　AACR2
ISBN 0-87840-402-3 (pbk.)

TABLE OF CONTENTS

PART III
United States Policies

PREFACE

This work and a companion volume, *Human Rights in the Americas: The Struggle for Consensus*, edited by Alfred T. Hennelly and John P. Langan are the products of a research project initiated in 1977 by the Woodstock Theological Center, located in Washington, D.C. Established in 1974 by the Maryland and New York Provinces of the Society of Jesus to stimulate interdisciplinary reflection on contemporary human problems, the Center has undertaken a wide variety of projects and published a series of studies dealing with personal values and public policy, ethics and nuclear strategy, religious freedom, social change, and ethical issues in foreign policy.

A key concern of the Woodstock Center has been issues of justice that have international ramifications. No human problem transcends national boundaries to the degree that violations of human rights do, not only in terms of the causes, but also in the search for solutions. The emergence of human rights as a prime criterion of U.S. foreign policy in the 1970s raised complex questions of definition, emphasis, strategy, and objectives. The tendency, for example, in the United States to emphasize violations of civil and political rights to a greater extent than social, economic, and cultural rights raised questions about the intentions and scope of U.S. human rights policies. Domestic challenges concerning the value of strong human rights stances in achieving national objectives, together with international questioning of U.S. understanding of the relationship between violations of the two sets of rights, prompted the initiation of the Woodstock project. This effort was undertaken to establish major political and economic factors affecting observance and to help clarify the normative, theological, and philosophical bases of human rights in the Americas. It was intended to provide both interested professionals and concerned citizens with a better understanding of the reasons for human rights violations and some insights into how they could be reduced.

In early 1977 consultations were held by the Woodstock Center with policymakers, human rights activists, and scholars in order to obtain suggestions for the conceptualization and organization of the project. Specialists from Latin America and elsewhere were asked to recommend research priorities, modes of analysis, and the most useful formats for the dissemination of the results. This began a dialogue aimed at refining and broadening the project that was to continue throughout the course of the work.

Of particular value were meetings held in Santo Domingo, Dominican Republic, in June 1978 and Bogotá, Colombia, in December of the same year, as well as in Washington in April 1979. They provided not only input for the Woodstock project, but also the stimulus for a number of other human rights activities. In the fall of 1977 a core of ten scholars representing the fields of economics, ethics, history, law, philosophy, political science, sociology, and theology began research on the theoretical bases of definitions of human rights and their implications for human rights observance in various cultural traditions in the Americas, focusing on the Anglo-American, Marxist, and Judaeo-Christian traditions. Analysis of historical, political, and economic factors contributing to violations was also begun.

Subsequently, additional scholars were incorporated into the project to cover specific aspects of the overall topic. These individuals examined the economic models underlying basic needs strategies in specific Latin American countries, as well as in some international financial institutions. In addition, the impact of private international capital flows on the fulfillment of basic needs was analyzed. The role of U.S. bilateral assistance in promoting the satisfaction of basic needs and the impact of the Carter administration's policies on general human rights observance in the Americas were also examined. Reflections on legal and philosophic issues raised in countries in which there were substantial violations were contributed by individuals who experienced them firsthand (see Chapters 3 and 9 in *Human Rights in the Americas: The Struggle for Consensus*). Seminars and meetings from 1978 to 1980 resulted in the incorporation of additional contributors who presented perspectives not covered by the core group.

An integral part of the research and writing was the critique of work-in-progress at seminars, conferences, and consultations. From January to June 1979 a series of six seminars focused on the moral and political implications of policy alternatives relating to basic needs strategies. These meetings involved government officials, human rights advocates, and other specialists in lively debates that one participant described as raising critical issues that had not been previously raised in discussions among some of the same individuals.

Twenty-five scholars gathered at Woodstock in January 1980 to critique papers dealing with political, intellectual, and cultural barriers to the recognition of social and economic rights, the relationship of the exercise of civil and political rights to the securing of social, economic, and cultural rights, and the broadening of normative traditions to give equal weight to social and economic, as well as to civil and political rights. The conference also explored the concept of community necessary to secure the full spectrum of rights and the problem of how to protect the rights of the individual without endorsing excessive individualism. Conclusions from these discussions flowed into analyses of the resources of the liberal, Marxist, and Judaeo-Christian traditions for dealing with conflict in a creative way. They also informed exchanges on how history and contemporary circumstances shape the impact of these traditions on human rights observance. The various threads of these exchanges were brought together in an exploration of whether or not there was sufficient convergence in the three traditions to provide a foundation for a coordinated defense of human rights. These discussions were used as the basis for revisions of the Woodstock papers prior to their being circulated to an even broader group of specialists throughout the Americas.

In March 1980, seven non-Woodstock specialists gathered to critique papers analyzing political, military, and economic factors affecting human rights and basic needs in the Americas. They focused on national and international structures of power and their impact on rights, emphasizing the basic character of states that violate civil and political rights and impede the satisfaction of basic needs. The role of the United States in rights observance throughout the Americas was also evaluated. After this meeting some 14 essays were circulated to government officials, lawyers, labor leaders, members of Congress, church representatives, human rights advocates, journalists, educators, and scholars in the United States and abroad. This was done in preparation for a three-day conference of some 60 specialists at Woodstock in May 1980.

This meeting served not only to assess the conclusions of the project up to that point, but also to disseminate human rights information and stimulate network building. Discussions covered the full scope of the project, ranging from shared values across cultures that can be used to promote the observance of human rights to exchanges on what specific strategies have proven effective in the defense of rights. Emphasis was on exploring the policy implications of the research presented. The discussions revealed a substantial lack of information about current developments and resources in the protection of human rights, particularly in countries with serious rights problems. While no panaceas were offered, some progress was made in refining existing strategies for the promotion of civil and political, as well as social and economic rights.

These meetings, as well as extensive networking with Latin American colleagues, were funded largely by a grant from the Inter-American Foundation to the Corporación Integral para el Desarrollo Cultural y Social (CODECAL), a nonprofit organization based in Bogotá, Colombia, that promotes education for human rights. A substantial portion of the research and writing was funded by a grant from the U.S. Agency for

International Development (AID) under Section 116(e) of the International Development and Food Assistance Act of 1977. This legislation was introduced by Congressman Donald M. Fraser to promote studies and programs to encourage increased adherence to civil and political rights as set forth in the Universal Declaration of Human Rights. Assistance from the Beirne Foundation was especially valuable in facilitating the dissemination both in this country and abroad of studies produced during the course of the project. Throughout, the Maryland and New York Provinces of the Society of Jesus provided substantial financial backing, as well as unflagging moral support.

An incalculable contribution was made by those individuals, too numerous to mention, who participated in the Woodstock seminars, consultations, and conferences. To the Latin Americans who attended the various meetings and critiqued early drafts of the essays that constitute the present volume, and its companion, *Human Rights in the Americas: The Struggle for Consensus*, we owe a deep debt of gratitude. Their contributions resulted in improvements in both books, and also generated valuable suggestions for new directions in human rights work at Woodstock and elsewhere.

Several Latin Americans spent extended periods of time at Woodstock during the course of the project, generously sharing with us their knowledge and expertise. These include Marcello de Carvalho Azevedo from Brazil and Patricio Cariola and Santiago Larraín from Chile. In addition, Frank Ivern of Spain provided a breadth of perspective that was very welcome.

Jaime Díaz, Director of CODECAL, not only shared with us his own insights, but put us in touch with a good number of other human rights specialists laboring throughout Latin America. Beyond this he greatly assisted the project by shouldering a variety of administrative burdens.

Special thanks are due to Roma Knee, Constantine Michalopoulos, Jonathan Silverstone, and Marilyn Zak of AID not only for their continuing support, but also for their thoughtful suggestions for increasing the utility of the project in various ways. The members of the project particularly appreciated their assistance in translating goals into reality.

A unique contribution was made to the project by José Zalaquett. As a fellow of the Woodstock Theological Center, Pepe brought to bear a keen analytical sense, honed by his work with the legal services department of the ecumenical Committee for Peace which functioned in Santiago de Chile in 1974 and 1975. He not only was able to bridge a multitude of disciplines, but also provided a valuable cross-national perspective. Overall, he helped mold the project intellectually and bring it to fruition.

The administrative burdens on the project co-directors, Margaret E. Crahan and Brian H. Smith, were lightened by the substantial assistance of Robert Mitchell, who served as Director of the Woodstock Center from 1976 to 1979, and Gerard Campbell, who succeeded him in September 1979. The realization of the project was also facilitated by the capable assistance of Suzanne Bash, Alice Halsema, Jude Howard, Tam Mehuron, Carol Merritt, Betty Mullen, and Arlene Sullivan.

Henry Bertels and the staff of the Woodstock Theological Center Library provided informed and courteous assistance at all stages of the project. Paz Cohen and Marcelo Montecino, in their patient and skillful work as translators for the conferences held in Washington, helped us and our colleagues to achieve understanding across languages and disciplines. Thanks are also due to Georgetown University for providing facilities for several of the conferences, and to Louis Sharp for special assistance in technical matters during the conferences.

The authors who contributed essays to this and the companion volume all displayed a commitment that went far beyond professional responsibility. Serious scholarship was infused with concern for developing effective strategies to improve human rights observance worldwide. In addition, many of the contributors gave generously of their time to critique the volumes as a whole. Sam Fitch and Jo Marie Griesgraber shared with us their valuable insights and made useful suggestions for the revision of a number of the chapters. Our friends and colleagues at the Center of Concern, especially Philip Land, gave wise counsel and support at many points in the process.

Three individuals made a special contribution to the Woodstock human rights project and to the production of the two books—Bernida Mickens, George Rogers, and Anna Sam. Not only did they work without stinting at a multitude of tasks, they did so with a *joie de vivre* that revived others when they were flagging.

A warm debt of gratitude is owed to all who participated in the Woodstock Theological Center's human rights project. From them we learned a great deal. They were also the source of many of the strengths of the two volumes. For not always realizing their highest expectations, the editor takes full responsibility.

Washington, D.C.   MARGARET E. CRAHAN

INTRODUCTION

The securing of rights was a prime rationale for the establishment of the United States as an independent nation. It also underlay the most searing internal conflict this country has ever experienced—the Civil War. In the twentieth century human rights issues have contributed to U.S. involvement in two world wars, as well as to efforts to establish mechanisms, such as the League of Nations and the United Nations, that would serve to promote civil and political, as well as social, economic, and cultural rights. Well before the 1970s rights were a leitmotif of U.S. domestic and foreign policy that was alternately emphasized and downplayed.

Assertion of human rights as a cornerstone of U.S. foreign policy in the post World War II period caused the United States to take an active role in the drafting of the Universal Declaration of Human Rights (1948) by the United Nations. [1] Since that time there has been a debate within this country's foreign policy establishment, as well as more generally, over the role of rights in molding U.S. relations with other nations. The most critical issue to emerge has been the degree to which rights' objectives or security issues should determine policy.

In the post-World War II period, Cold War attitudes tended to give low priority to human rights, while fear of interference by international bodies in U.S. domestic jurisdiction contributed to hesitation in signing human rights accords. In 1953 the Eisenhower administration, bowing to congressional and other pressures, agreed not to enter into any binding human rights agreements.

The invocation of human rights did not, however, disappear entirely as a foreign policy instrument during the Cold War. Rather it was used selectively as a propaganda weapon to criticize foes. After the making of U.S. foreign policy in the 1960s came under close scrutiny by Congress and the American public, primarily as a result of the war in Vietnam, the relative priority of security and human rights began to be intensely debated. Congressional norms for economic and military assistance, the policies of international financial institutions, and the nature of day-to-day diplomatic exchanges were affected. By the mid-1970s there was ample legislation supporting a strong U.S. stance on human rights internationally, occasioned in part by sharp increases in violations of civil and political rights in certain Latin American countries. [2]

The reluctance of the Nixon and Ford administrations to make human rights a prime criterion of U.S. foreign policy led Jimmy Carter to make it a keynote of his campaign for the presidency in 1976. The loss of moral authority by the Nixon and Ford administrations made promotion of human rights as the soul of a new foreign policy an astute political move. Carter demonstrated that it was not simply a campaign tactic when he expanded the Office of Human Rights and Humanitarian Affairs in the State Department and named Patricia Derian, a Mississippi civil rights advocate, to head it. Under her direction·the office became a full-fledged Bureau actively engaged in pressuring other countries to improve their human rights performance. Using the various legislative measures already enacted, the office sought to implement restrictions on aid and military sales to countries where rights violations abounded.

Resistance within the State Department bureaucracy, as well as elsewhere throughout the executive branch, to this departure from traditional diplomatic practice, was not long in coming. Debate within the Carter administration was accompanied by challenges from without, which escalated as the 1980 presidential election approached.

During the course of the campaign there was sharp criticism of the Carter administration's human rights policy, particularly on the grounds that it was contrary to U.S. security interests. It was charged that the policy had encouraged the overthrow of governments friendly to the United States, most notably in Iran and Nicaragua, and their replacement by anti-American forces. [3] It was further alleged that the policy had needlessly alienated a number of "moderately repressive regimes" whose friendship was necessary for international security and useful in international forums. Other critics faulted the policy because it was not applied in a more coherent and evenhanded fashion, arguing that countries of little strategic importance, such as those in Latin America, were more frequently the objects of U.S. pressures for improved human rights performance than those of greater strategic importance.

The election of Ronald Reagan has been seen as due in part to the impact of such criticisms. While Reagan has denied that his administration will abandon a commitment to human rights, persons connected with the new administration have asserted that security objectives should override human rights considerations. Secretary of State Alexander Haig, in his first press conference, announced, for example, that "international terrorism will take the place of human rights" as the chief priority of U.S. foreign policy. [4] The subsequent nomination of Ernest W. Lefever, a critic of the use by the United States of human rights standards or conditions in U.S. dealings with other nations, to be Assistant Secretary of State for Human Rights and Humanitarian Affairs, and the Reagan administration's moves to lift restrictions on economic and military aid to countries failing to meet rights criteria established by Congress, confirm the shift. While the Senate Foreign Relations Committee failed to approve the Lefever nomination, Congress has been more amenable to disassociating aid from human rights observance.

This swing away from human rights as a major criterion of U.S. foreign policy highlights enduring differences of opinion in the definition of U.S. foreign policy objectives and the means for achieving them. The primacy the Carter administration gave to human rights stimulated a strong reaction among those who give overriding importance to U.S. economic and military superiority. What the debate lacks is some indication that the choice is not between security and human rights but that the two are complementary.

The findings in the essays contained in this volume are useful in broadening the current debate, for they suggest that respect for the full spectrum of human rights is essential for national and international security. This conclusion is derived not only from the analysis contained in the respective essays, but also from the belief that human rights are priority claims inhering in persons or groups of persons and that the enjoyment of rights is directly related to the maintenance of social concord and human progress. Such enjoyment is clearly affected by the political, economic, and social character of the societies in which they are exercised, and to national and international structures which influence the development of these societies. Thus, the essays in this book focus on factors that influence the creation and maintenance of societies in which civil/political rights are respected and social, economic, and cultural rights fulfilled. Respect for the former is related to fulfillment of the latter, for without democratic participation in the setting of national and international economic, social, and cultural priorities and the allocation of resources, the likelihood of deprivation is increased. Likewise, failure to meet basic economic and social needs diminishes the individual's capacity to exercise civil and political rights. Hence violations of one set of rights are generally accompanied by violations of the other.

The concept of basic human needs is used in this volume to denominate, at a minimum, the physical requirements of life. It also includes the prerequisites of self-reliance and/or effective political and economic participation to insure the physical requirements of life. A basic human needs approach represents an effort to establish practical priorities for the implementation of human rights which will be acceptable across cultures. While some place greater emphasis on basic needs than on civil and political rights, and others reverse the priorities, the authors in this volume regard the two sets of rights as inextricably linked, requiring concurrent observance. The great weight of evidence indicating that political repression is often used to maintain systems that do not meet basic human needs reinforces that conviction. Hence the meeting of such needs provides a measure for assessing the legitimacy of the exercise of political, economic, and ideological power within societies.

The authors of this volume suggest that national and international security is enhanced by governments that respect civil and political rights, as well as social, economic, and cultural rights.[5] Further, the level of fulfillment of basic needs is linked to the breadth of democratic participation in setting national economic priorities and distributional policies.

Part I of this book, which focuses on political and military factors affecting human rights observance, argues that to emphasize security at the expense of rights both within nations and internationally is not conducive to long-range security. Threats to political stability are rooted in the denial of basic social and economic rights. Current efforts to meet these rights are examined in the second section, which analyzes the evolution of basic needs strategies to date and the problems impeding major advances. A principal conclusion is that no strategy will be successful without a strong commitment to rights on the part of the governing elite in the nations concerned. This reinforces the linkage between observance of civil and political rights and the satisfaction of basic needs found in the previous section.

Part III examines U.S. policy regarding international observance of human rights. Special attention is paid to limitations on the promotion of the fulfillment of basic needs by U.S. bilateral assistance programs channeled through the Agency of International Development. An analysis of the use of U.S. military aid to encourage Latin American armed forces to respect human rights, reveals little impact, either positive or negative, on the Latin American military. The limitations of economic and military aid programs are clearly spelled out, as are those affecting diplomatic efforts, particularly during the Carter administration.

The volume as a whole suggests that the achievement of security and the promotion of human rights are not antithetical, but that the development of a coherent human rights policy supportive of long-range hemispheric security requires substantially more analysis of the relationship of human rights violations to instability, as well as broad-based evaluations of the effectiveness of programs and strategies already employed by the U.S. government to promote human rights. Full political participation is necessary for guaranteeing the satisfaction of basic needs, while the meeting of basic needs increases the capacity for participation. Violations in one area are generally accompanied by violations in the other. Hence political repression is often a consequence of the failure to meet basic needs. While coercion may reduce pressures for change, there is no historical evidence that it is a long-term guarantee of stability. The emergence in the Americas of increasing numbers of authoritarian governments, which are founded on ideological justifications for a concentration of power in the hands of the military and which disregard the rule of the law, does not provide a secure base for hemispheric stability. Support for such regimes identifies the United States with governments having narrow popular bases whose repression is justified on the grounds that it is required to maintain the stability necessary for economic development. The experience of authoritarian regimes in Brazil, Argentina, Uruguay, and Chile reveals that growth is achieved at the cost of declines in real wages and an increasingly unequal distribution of income and wealth. The view that such governments contribute to U.S. security is short-sighted and ahistorical. Further, it identifies the United States with forces that have little moral respectability worldwide, thereby diminishing our own credibility. This hampers us in the competition with Communist powers, for only by establishing the political, economic, and moral superiority of the U.S. system can it be preserved.

Critics of human rights as a prime criterion of U.S. foreign policy argue strongly that authoritarian regimes exist because political cultures in many countries, particularly in the Third World, do not promote the development of democratic structures. In addition, they claim that such cultures lack institutions strong enough to channel and contain conflict, as well as nongovernmental institutions to "articulate and aggregate diverse interests and opinions in the society."[6] Without these, formal governmental institutions are not able to translate popular demands into public policy. This position regards political competition and conflict as detrimental to the body politic. Intermediary institutions between the people and the state are considered necessary since most citizens are presumed not to have the capacity or discipline to contribute usefully to governmental decision making. Such conceptions are profoundly exclusionary and have been used in Latin America to limit the admittedly arduous development of democratic participation.

Chapter 1 in this volume, "The State and the Individual in Latin America: An Historical Overview" indicates historical patterns of political and economic marginalization of the masses that have resulted from organic concepts of society which have accepted wide disparities among groups, particularly with respect to their satisfaction of socioeconomic needs and political rights. The requirements of controlling far-flung empires led Spain and Portugal to emphasize authoritarian forms of political and social control, although their impact was moderated by distance and local circumstances. The transformation of the colonies into republics in the early nineteenth century did not result in substantial broadening of political participation, but rather in the substitution of control by local elites for metropolitan control. Congresses and bureaucracies became the foci of elite competition, a situation that did not measurably change until the latter part of the century. Economic development, population growth, immigration, and other factors contributed to increased pressures on governments by the growing petit bourgeoisie and by workers. Popular coalitions were formed, although they were generally unstable and not able to maintain themselves in power over the long term. Political competition intensified in the face of the limited capacity of governments to provide substantial economic improvements for much of the population. Popular pressures for socioeconomic improvements escalated after 1945 and brought to power reformist governments that were generally limited by structural factors and political exigencies in their ability to meet demands. This tended to fuel societal conflict and to increase polarization, with both the left and right losing faith in reformist, developmentalist solutions to national problems. While socialist alternatives gained some support, rightist regimes with an organic view of society in which conflict was regarded as deleterious to progress appeared with more frequency. Military dominated authoritarian states were established in Brazil in 1964, Peru in 1968, Argentina in 1966 and 1976, Uruguay and Chile in 1973, and Bolivia in 1980. These, together with more traditional military dictatorships in Ecuador, Paraguay, Guatemala, Honduras, and El Salvador, contributed to widespread violations of human rights in the 1960s and 1970s.

A major development that contributed to the worsening of conditions was the systematic use of violations of civil and political rights by the state as a means of social control. This resulted, in part, from the development of ideological justifications for the overriding of constitutional guarantees and legal protections of rights.

Factors contributing to the emergence in the 1960s and 1970s of military regimes in Latin America that regarded themselves as more fit to govern and to achieve national goals than civilian politicians are described in Chapter 2, "The Evolution of the Military in Brazil, Chile, Peru, Venezuela, and Mexico: Implications for Human Rights." A prime cause for intervention was the severity of national political and economic crises, together with internal subversion and strong pressures for structural change. The armed forces had little regard for the capacity of civilian politicians to deal with such problems. This combined with general disenchantment with liberal democracy to stimulate loss of faith in civilian government and fear of popular participation. In some countries, such as Chile, there was a tradition within the armed forces, at least since the 1930s, of maintaining political neutrality and institutional distance from parties and administrations. Yet in the face of fundamental structural crises during the administration of the Socialist Salvador Allende (1970–1973), such traditions were undercut, partly by the dissemination of ideologies condoning alternative modes of behavior by the military, and partly by government attempts to co-opt officers. In countries such as Venezuela and Mexico, where officers occasionally held nonmilitary offices or were closely consulted by the civilian political leadership, civilian dominance was more readily accepted.

Frequently it is asserted that military professionalization decreases the likelihood of coups. It is true that bureaucratization of the armed forces, especially the imposition of a rational system of promotions and distribution of benefits, can defuse dissatisfaction among military personnel. However, the modernization of the military that professionalization promotes also encourages an increased sense of administrative capacity and technological expertise, which contributes to the belief that the military is able to solve national problems. Professionalization also tends to contribute to the greater ideological development of the officer corps.

While professionalization may not guarantee unity of opinion, it does contribute to greater politicization and to the questioning of prevailing political forms. European military advisers in Latin America from the 1890s to the 1940s contributed to the development of a world view that gave priority to the rights of the state over the rights of the individual in the pursuit of national security. Expanded educational facilities for the military and civic action programs during the post-World War II period, in part stimulated by the United States, directed the attention of the military to socioeconomic problems in their countries. They also stimulated a sense that it was the armed forces' duty to remedy them. The question was whether this could be accomplished without directly taking power. The apparent weaknesses of civilian governments and the spread of the doctrine of national security suggested that intervention was the only course.

National security ideology as it has developed in the Southern Cone of Latin America and its implications for human rights are examined in Chapter 3, "National Security Ideology and Human Rights," by Margaret E. Crahan. This ideology is a systemization of concepts of the state, war, national power, and national goals that places national security above personal security, the needs of the state before individual rights, and the judgment of a governing elite over the rule of law. It identifies the nation and state as one, with the military as the main instrument for the realization of national goals. The nation/state is regarded as a living organism with needs of its own that justify concentration of power in the state, particularly in the executive branch. Legislatures and the judiciary take secondary roles and are heavily influenced by the military. This obviously undercuts both popular sovereignty and the rule of law, leaving citizens with few of the traditional defenses of their rights. The prime concern of the state is guaranteeing national security through the elimination of societal conflict and subversion, even if this requires the unfettered exercise of state power by the armed forces and the police. Only in this way, it is believed, can the stability necessary for strong economic growth be guaranteed.

This helps explain the extent of rights violations in national security states such as Brazil, Uruguay, Argentina, and Chile. The elimination of the traditional legal defenses of rights also helps explain the flourishing of alternative mechanisms in defense of rights such as hunger strikes, basic educational programs, and international appeals, as well as the increased political activism of the Catholic Church. Human rights advocacy groups have proliferated throughout the Americas, challenging the political and economic policies of these governments as well as their ideological underpinnings. A prime means of accomplishing this has been the encouragement of scholarly analysis, along with the development of basic educational materials to inform and mobilize citizens within countries and without. The extent of support for such efforts reflects the narrowness of the political bases of national security regimes and suggests that unless they liberalize their policies and programs, as some have, their capacity to retain power is limited. Moreover, their futures are cloudy unless they can redeem the promises of economic improvement made to justify their exercise of power. To date, major socioeconomic improvements have not been realized for the bulk of the population in these countries.

Widespread poverty, underemployment and unemployment, together with maldistribution of wealth, continue in Latin America. Even in countries such as Argentina, Brazil, Chile, Mexico, and Venezuela, with substantial natural resources and industrial bases, there is a surprising proportion of the citizenry without adequate nutrition, housing, health care, and education. Factors contributing to this, as well as evaluations of national and international strategies for improvement, are examined in the Part II of this book. These include the conceptual assumptions of models of development which give rise to basic needs strategies, as well as an evaluation of actual basic needs strategies in six countries of varying political orientations. International factors such as capital flows and the stabilization policies of the International Monetary Fund (IMF) are also examined. While there remain a number of other national and international elements affecting the fulfillment of social and economic rights, the four chapters in this part detail some of the progress that has been made and the problems that remain.

John F. Weeks and Elizabeth W. Dore in Chapter 4, "Basic Needs: Journey of a Concept," stress that the obvious point of departure for devising such a strategy is establishing the causes of uneven development. They argue that this will provide the basis for realistic strategies. To do this, Weeks and Dore assert, requires defining poverty in absolute terms—using concrete standards of consumption. This places emphasis on redistribution as the most effective means of meeting basic needs rather than on income generation. In fact, by the late 1960s more and more development economists came to accept the position that the satisfaction of basic needs required redistribtuion of current income or wealth or both. Related to this is the thesis that in poor societies production of nonessential goods, with the possible exception of exports, should be limited in favor of the production of basic wage goods and services. This generally implies large-scale market intervention by the state in order to reorient the productive structure of an economy to supply the commodities required by the poor. The strategy is asserted in recognition of the experience of advanced capitalist countries, where despite nominally progressive tax structures, there is no evidence that indirect redistributive measures have any significant impact on the distribution of income and wealth, unless there is provision of income in kind. This position, however, does not necessarily mold the policies and programs of the major international financial organizations, including the World Bank and the Inter-American Development Bank. At these institutions, as well as in U.S. bilateral assistance programs, emphasis is generally on employment and income generation programs.

Weeks and Dore conclude that a successful basic needs strategy that would eliminate the worst symptoms of poverty requires considerable state intervention to ensure equitable distribution. The likelihood and capacity of a state to do this depends on the actual distribution of power in a society. If a governing elite is not committed to substantial redistribution, then any basic needs programs undertaken would have limited impact. Successful basic needs programs are, consequently, dependent on the political will of governing elites. The degree to which this reflects the wishes of the general populace, is, of course, determined by the level of democratic participation allowed and exercised within a country.

This is clearly seen in Chapter 5 where Dore and Weeks compare the fulfillment of basic needs in six diverse countries: "Economic Performance and Basic Needs: The Examples of Brazil, Chile, Mexico, Nicaragua, Peru, and Venezuela." In these middle-income countries the authors examined the level of per capita income, per capita calorie consumption, employment, purchasing power of blue-collar wages, life expectancy, infant mortality, as well as access to health care, sanitation, housing, and education. They found that neither high per capita income nor a rapid rate of growth necessarily results in increased satisfaction of basic needs. Two prime variables tend to determine the level of fulfillment of basic needs: 1) the actual commitment of a government to meeting basic needs, and 2) a more equal distribution of income. For example, in the early 1970s, although Chile had the slowest growth rate, it had the least unequal distribution of income and, until 1976, perhaps the best record of the six countries studied in satisfying basic needs. Mexico, second best in income distribution after Venezuela, had a fair record on basic needs. Brazil, with the most unequal distribution of income, had poor basic needs performance, although it experienced considerable growth beginning in the mid-1960s. Venezuela, with extremely unequal income distribution, demonstrated less progress in meeting basic needs than its resources would suggest.

The study shows that the level of fulfillment of basic needs is not high in any of the six countries and that, relative to other middle-income countries in the world, their overall performance is weak. Dore and Weeks conclude that rapid economic growth, relatively higher per capita income, and formal democracy do not guarantee improvements in the standard of living of the poor. Again, the level of a government's commitment to meeting basic needs appears to be the critical variable.

This conclusion is reinforced by John Willoughby's examination of the impact on basic needs of the growth of foreign investment and loans to Latin America. In Chapter 6, "International Capital Flows, Economic Growth, and Basic Needs" Willoughby concludes that the precise role that foreign capital plays in meeting basic needs in an underdeveloped country is ultimately dependent on internal factors in that country. Increases in production of basic commodities as a result of inflow of capital and limited improvements in the satisfaction of basic needs have occurred in both liberal (Venezuela) and authoritarian (Brazil) countries. In other authoritarian regimes (e.g., Chile and Argentina) with similar increases in foreign capital, there have been declines in the socioeconomic status of the poor.

Increased dependence on foreign capital presents some long-term dilemmas for these countries with regard to the future satisfaction of basic needs. To the degree that loans and foreign investment promote increased production of commodities, demand will also intensify and perhaps outstrip supply, thereby increasing social pressures. At the same time, dependence on foreign capital may impede pressures for the redistribution of income and improvement of working conditions. The ability of Latin American countries to deal with these contrary pressures does not appear to be substantial and hence there are continuing controls and intermittent repression of workers and other sectors of the society.

Such a situation helps explain New International Economic Order (NIEO) proposals for the forgiveness of debts, the easing of credit terms, and control of transnational corporations. These have not, however, received a very positive response from the developed nations. Channeling of loans and investments to countries that have a demonstrable commitment to improve the socioeconomic conditions of the poor could result in the stabilization of such countries with benefits for both those countries and their neighbors. Diminution of private loans and investment capital to countries not strongly committed to improved basic needs satisfaction could result in some positive changes in domestic economic priorities. Such efforts require the support of the governments and consumers in those countries supplying capital, particularly in order to influence private corporations and banks. This is a substantial challenge. Yet it is increasingly clear that economic problems in the advanced capitalist countries are related to patterns of capital outflow. A more coordinated policy focused on generally improving socioeconomic conditions worldwide would have benefits for both sides.

Escalating public and private debt in Third World countries has made them increasingly dependent on such international financial institutions as the IMF. The policies it follows and the programs it develops have become an important factor in the capacity of indebted countries to fulfill basic needs. In Chapter 7 these are analyzed by Richard E. Feinberg who examines "The International Monetary Fund and Basic Needs: The Impact of Stand-By Arrangements." This is a critical topic, given the fact that accusations have been made that IMF stabilization programs have negatively affected the satisfaction of basic needs in developing countries.

Feinberg concludes that the distributional impact of particular stabilization measures is not obvious. Some sectors of the population generally suffer, while others benefit. A critical variable is the objectives of the government implementing the program. Selective and targeted implementation can improve income distribution and hence the satisfaction of basic needs and government measures can be adopted to reduce the burden on the poor. For example, tax increases and budget cuts do assist the poorer segments of society. On the other hand, devaluation can raise the prices of imported foodstuffs, and removal of price controls can reduce real wages.

Since the poor have fewer resources to cushion the impact of stabilization programs, they will generally suffer more than the rich. This suggests that when stabilization programs are conceived, mechanisms to shift the burden of their impact to wealthier elements of a society should be included. The resistance of the advantaged would be strong, and since they are more likely to have greater influence on government decisions, it would be very difficult to overcome.

In the face of these and other problems, Feinberg recommends that the IMF focus more on the distributional impact of stabilization programs, in order to determine better their effect on income distribution and basic needs. Governments, if they wish, should be assisted in dealing with adverse distributional consequences of stabilization programs.

Given differences between World Bank and IMF policies that influence basic needs strategies, greater coordination between the two institutions should be attempted. This would require the IMF to give more attention to human capital formation and would allow for a more active public-sector role in supplying basic needs. The IMF should also revamp its policies to encourage countries to seek IMF assistance during the initial, more readily reversible stages of financial crises. Feinberg also suggests that the Fund should be more flexible in dealing with the negative consequences of adjustment measures for income distribution. In addition, the IMF should set deflationary targets more carefully, so that overshooting them would be less likely. Where possible, gradualism should be the policy rather than shock treatment.

Feinberg's recommendations clearly show the difficulty of making stabilization programs less onerous for the poor. They also indicate, however, that there are ways to do so. A substantial advance would be the IMF's using basic needs as a priority in developing new programs. Given increasing dependence on the IMF, particularly in Latin America, this would be a major contribution to improved satisfaction of basic needs in the area.

Strong concern for the promotion of social and economic rights abroad was expressed by President Carter in late 1977 when he indicated that U.S. foreign aid would be focused on meeting the needs of the poor, principally in low income countries. Two years later, the Foreign Assistance Act of 1979 mandated that development aid should be channeled to low income countries with a commitment to satisfying the basic needs of the poor. Issues arising in the course of implementing such directives are examined in Constantine Michalopoulos' study, "Basic Needs Strategy: Some Policy Implementation Issues of the U.S. Bilateral Assistance Program" (Chapter 8 of this volume). They include determining the optimum strategy for a particular developing country to achieve the satisfaction of basic needs, and setting the focus and mode of operations for specific assistance projects and programs. The relationship of assistance policy to other U.S. objectives and international economic policies must also be coordinated. Special attention is paid by Michalopoulos to the link between basic needs and U.S. human rights objectives, and the connection between basic needs and U.S. international trade policy.

Michalopoulos maps out the limitations of present policies in promoting the fulfillment of basic needs and offers some suggestion as to how to overcome them. As he sees it, the prime impediment is low levels of U.S. economic assistance that reduce the degree to which the United States can assist other countries in meeting basic needs.[7] Progress in meeting basic needs in developing countries would consequently require substantial increases in aid levels by the United States as well as by other developed countries. Present aid levels are, furthermore, too small to have major policy influence or impact on resource allocation within developing countries. Larger volumes of aid and higher concentration of resources would be useful but appear unlikely at present.

In addition, U.S. international economic policies in general, and trade policy in particular, need to be better coordinated with assistance policies in order to make the latter more effective. Development strategies should be reviewed and assessed so that they are well adapted to the particular conditions in each recipient country, as well as to various sectors within countries. The effectiveness of U.S. bilateral assistance would also be increased if it were more flexible with respect to specific forms of assistance. In addition, care should be taken not to limit impact by focusing only on basic needs sectors or projects.

With the limited resources available for bilateral assistance, careful selection of programs is necessary. Yet until recently evaluation of past programs was limited, in part because of lack of personnel. Michalopoulos argues that such evaluations are highly desirable. In addition, he urges more attention to both macroeconomic and microeconomic policy review. Related to this is the advisability of constant assessment of the relationship of bilateral assistance policies to U.S. human rights goals and other objectives. Changes in conditions from country to country and internal U.S. developments require continual fine tuning of U.S. bilateral assistance programs.

The effectiveness of cutting economic aid while upping military aid in achieving foreign policy objectives, including improved security, comes into sharp focus in "U.S.-Latin American Military Relations Since World War II: Implications for Human Rights." Here in Chapter 9 Brian H. Smith examines the principal policy objectives of U.S. military aid programs, indicating how these complemented or diverged from the development goals of the Latin American military. This analysis demonstrates that U.S. global strategic concerns have traditionally influenced U.S. military policy toward Latin America. Since World War II these have included the containment of Communism, the maintenance of close ties with Western allies, the enhancement of conditions favorable to U.S. private investment, and the promotion of U.S. access to raw materials and markets. Consideration of human rights criteria in determining military assistance flows, in part, from the U.S. preference for formal democracies in the Americas, a desire for limits on the sale of sophisticated weapons, and a desire that Latin American governments spend more of their budgets on economic development. The use of military assistance to promote democracy and U.S. human rights objectives has been controversial. In the 1980s it will be even more so.

Smith's examination of U.S.-Latin American military relations reveals that neither U.S. military assistance or military training has made the Latin American armed forces more apolitical or more respectful of democratic values. In addition, the rights priorities of Latin American military leaders diverge substantially from those of U.S. policymakers. This is unlikely to change, or to be affected substantially by the granting or withholding of U.S. military assistance. In addition, Smith concludes that there is no strong evidence that either the granting or withholding of such aid has measurably affected human rights practices. Stopping aid in the 1970s did, however, decrease the identification of the United States with governments that engage in gross violations of rights. This had positive international repercussions, particularly in the Third World.

Traditional security objectives did, nevertheless, continue to have major influence throughout the 1970s. These include protection of the hemisphere from Communism, maintenance of a favorable investment climate, access to raw materials and markets, and continued good relations with military allies throughout the Americas. In the last two years of the Carter administration these objectives were reasserted. In particular, preoccupation with possible damage to economic relations with Southern Cone countries and fear of Marxist inroads in the Caribbean Basin modified human rights objectives. U.S. pressure, especially on Argentina and Brazil, was reduced and steps were taken to reassure the military governments in those countries that the United States desired close, cooperative relations. Perhaps the most substantial change can be noted in Central America, where U.S. security assistance to the Salvadoran government, which has repeatedly been implicated in rights violations, was resumed, thus demonstrating the predominance of security over rights criteria in an administration that had heralded human rights as a keystone of policy. Under the Reagan administration, the shift from rights to security objectives in foreign policy became pronounced.

Oscillations in the weight given rights criteria and security objectives in recent U.S. foreign policy are chronicled in Chapter 10 by Lars Schoultz in, "The Carter Administration and Human Rights in Latin America." Comparing the Nixon-Ford years (1969–1976) to the Carter years (1977–1980) in terms of bilateral and multilateral U.S. diplomacy, military aid, economic assistance, and coordination with the private sector, Schoultz notes major departures during the Carter administration from traditional policies.

Strong human rights initiatives, especially during the late 1970s, did result in a lessening of U.S. involvement and identification with repressive governments. It is even possible, Schoultz posits, that several Latin American governments became less repressive sooner than they might have otherwise. However, the evidence also suggests that, by and large, violations result from a dynamic beyond Washington's control.

This is particularly true with respect Argentina, Brazil, Chile, and Uruguay, where strong authoritarian states exist. In countries such as Nicaragua, El Salvador, and Guatemala, U.S. pressures for improved observance of human rights coincided with upsurges in public opposition to existing regimes. As a consequence, U.S. initiatives appear to have encouraged moves to overthrow repressive governments, although they clearly did not cause them nor guarantee the outcome as some critics have alleged.

The most concrete contributions of the Carter administration to U.S. foreign policy were changes wrought in the governmental decision-making process. The opening up of this process to representatives of a broad range of human rights advocacy groups was a major development. Pressures from such sources will clearly continue during administrations less receptive to the utilization of rights criteria in determining foreign policy, and may even intensify. There is a good possibility of new coalitions being built, incorporating congressional critics of various aspects of U.S. policies.

Congressional initiatives during the 1970s left a body of legislation that mandates evaluation of human rights practices in allocating economic and military aid, in addition to affecting U.S. policies with respect to multilateral lending agencies. While these may be modified, it is unlikely that they will be eliminated entirely. There continue to be members of Congress who will concern themselves with promoting human rights internationally through congressional action. These individuals have worked effectively in the past, and will no doubt continue to work, with fiscal conservatives who desire to cut foreign aid across the board. In addition, Reagan administration proposals may very well prompt more intensive congressional review of the actual relationship between security interests and human rights observance in Latin America.

A substantial innovation during the Carter administration was the institutionalization of a human rights bureaucracy within the executive branch in response to congressional pressures. The former president's campaign commitment that human rights would be the soul of his foreign policy was given flesh primarily by the State Department's Bureau of Human Rights and Humanitarian Affairs. Spearheading the implementation of earlier initiatives, this Bureau led the way, although at times it left most of the executive branch behind.

The development of the human rights lobby, increased congressional activity in promoting humanitarian concerns in U.S. foreign policy, and the institutionalization of a human rights bureaucracy in the executive branch, all contributed to major changes in U.S. foreign policy in the 1970s. Doubtless, there will be additional changes in the 1980s that will reinforce some of these and reverse others. While many predict that human rights as a major component of U.S. foreign policy will diminish over the next few years, the nature and content of the current crises in the hemisphere, particularly in Central America, strongly suggest that human rights will continue to be a prime issue that the U.S. government will have to deal with.

Arguments that a strong U.S. human rights posture is contrary to U.S. security interests are not supported by the studies contained in this book. In fact, *Human Rights and Basic Needs in the Americas* offers the alternate view that without strong support for increased human rights observance, the United States will be contributing to the prolongation in power of repressive regimes with narrow political bases that will ultimately disintegrate. Anti-American hostility on the part of successor governments in these countries could pose real threats to U.S. security. This is not to suggest that regimes that engage in gross violations of human rights cannot endure for some time. In fact, recent years have seen the development of increasingly sophisticated means of social control by such governments that eliminate dependence on some of the more notorious violations of human rights such as torture. Furthermore, these governments are not unresponsive to both internal and external pressures for liberalization. Wherever that possibility exists, U.S. policy should encourage it. There is no evidence to suggest that military assistance and training make it more likely.

Assisting redemocratization is no easy task and requires thoroughgoing analysis of past U.S. policies and programs in an effort to make future efforts in promoting human rights more coherent and mutually supportive. This is essential with respect to coordinating various aspects of U.S. economic and security policies. Further, U.S. criticism of violations of civil and political rights must be rooted in an understanding of their socioeconomic roots and of the degree to which violations of civil and political rights flow from denial of social and economic rights. This is a task for all those concerned with devising a foreign policy that will ensure the stability that flows from justice. Hence it is incumbent on those committed to human rights that they redouble their efforts to make the strategies and policies they recommend well adapted to the realities and complexities of specific situations. In addition, there is considerable need for a much more extensive educational effort in the United States to inform the general public of national and international factors affecting human rights observance and their consequences for U.S. citizens. This requires broad coalitions not only of human rights organizations, but also of the media, together with educational, church, and labor groups, among others.

As the 1980s begin, the issue of human rights is very much in the forefront of the debate over U.S. foreign policy. Even if there are fewer pressures emanating from the United States for the improvement of human rights practices abroad, there is still the issue of what values the United States does champion. Our system will survive only so long as it is identified nationally and internationally as superior, not only in terms of the material benefits provided, but also in terms of the values it propounds. If U.S. foreign policy does not promote superior values, then it will have diminishing support both domestically and abroad. That is a prime threat to U.S. security. Hence human rights and security concerns are not antithetical, but rather critical components of any foreign policy that contributes to long-term peace and progress around the world.

Margaret E. Crahan

NOTES TO THE INTRODUCTION

1. The Universal Declaration of Human Rights is essentially a statement of principles intended to serve as a common standard for the promotion of the full spectrum of civil/political and social, economic, and cultural rights. In 1966 the United Nations General Assembly adopted a Covenant on Political and Civil Rights, as well as a Covenant on Economic, Social, and Cultural Rights, in order to make the principles expressed in the Universal Declaration binding treaty obligations. These Covenants, which did not come into force until 1976, specify exceptions, limitations, and restrictions on rights and aim at creating mechanisms to guarantee them internationally. Effective means have not, however, come into existence. The debates over the Covenants reflected the reluctance of nations, including the United States, to commit themselves to a system of international controls, as well as disagreements over the relative weight of civil/political rights and economic, social, and cultural rights. The latter flow, to a degree, from differences in values in societies having varied normative traditions and ideological orientations. (For explorations of these differences, see *Human Rights in the Americas: The Struggle for Consensus* [Georgetown University Press, Washington, D.C., 1982] In the present volume the Universal Declaration and the Covenants are regarded as expressions of a level of international consensus on criteria for human dignity and development.

2. During the 1970s the U.S. Congress and Department of State, the Inter-American Commission on Human Rights of the Organization of American States, and Amnesty International, among others, reported serious rights violations in the following countries: Argentina, Bolivia, Brazil, Chile, El Salvador, Guatemala, Haiti, Nicaragua, Paraguay, and Uruguay. The vast majority of Latin Americans live in these countries. Eight of these nations (Bolivia, Chile, El Salvador, Guatemala, Haiti, Nicaragua, Paraguay, and Uruguay) are signatories of the American Convention on Human Rights which entered into force on July 18, 1978. Barbados, Colombia, Costa Rica, the Dominican Republic, Ecuador, Grenada, Honduras, Jamaica, Panama, Peru, the United States, and Venezuela have also signed it. Together with the American Declaration of the Rights and Duties of Man proclaimed in

1948, it defines the rights of the individual in terms similar to the Universal Declaration of Human Rights. In addition, the American Declaration contains a list of duties of each individual. A comparable list of responsibilities of the states was not adopted. As is the case with most of the current constitutions of Latin American nations, emphasis is more on respect for civil and political rights than on the fulfillment of social, economic, and cultural rights.

3. Perhaps the most influential of these critiques was Jeane Kirkpatrick's "Dictatorships and Double Standards" (*Commentary* 68, 5 [November 1979]: 34–45), which was read and praised by the Republican presidential candidate, Ronald Reagan. After his election, President Reagan named Kirkpatrick, a professor of political science at Georgetown University, to be the U.S. Ambassador to the United Nations.

4. Secretary of State Alexander Haig, as quoted in Don Oberdorfer, "Haig Calls Terrorism Top Priority," *The Washington Post* (29 January 1981), p. A1.

5. Throughout this work, Brazil, Chile, Peru, Venezuela, pre-1979 Nicaragua, and Mexico serve as the principal basis for comparative analysis. These countries were chosen because they possess certain common characteristics as well as variations in political and economic forms, social composition, and resource bases. Brazil and Chile both have authoritarian military governments that tend to justify their human rights policies on the basis of a specific vision of national security. Both have opted for free market economies, although the Brazilian government attempts to maintain tighter controls than does Chile. Peru from 1968 until 1980 had a somewhat more progressive military government that made some unsuccessful attempts to reduce dependency on foreign capital and technology and increase worker participation in management. Nicaragua, until the summer of 1979, had been dominated for over 40 years by the Somoza family, buttressed by the National Guard. Political and economic structures were molded to conform to the personal objectives of the Somozas, which resulted in the alienation of a broad cross-section of Nicaraguan society. This was reinforced by frequent rights violations. Venezuela and Mexico both have civilian governments, the former being a multi-party, the latter a one-party dominant system. Oil revenues have stimulated substantial economic expansion in both countries, although major improvements in meeting basic needs have not resulted. Together these countries account for approximately 70 percent of the population of Latin America.

6. Kirkpatrick, p. 37.

7. Shortly after the Reagan administration took office, the new budget director, David A. Stockman, proposed cutting 1982 foreign aid by one-third. Cuts were projected in direct bilateral assistance to Third World countries, and in contributions to multilateral development banks and to international organizations such as UN agencies, the Food for Peace program, and the Peace Corps. The only area which was not to be slashed would be military aid. This precipitated an intense debate with foreign policy professionals, led by Secretary of State Alexander M. Haig, Jr. They

argued that Stockman's cuts would seriously weaken U.S. influence worldwide. While cuts of the size Stockman proposed were successfully resisted, overall there was a diminution of U.S. foreign aid. John M. Goshko, "Huge Cutback Proposed in Foreign Aid," *The Washington Post* (29 January 1981), p. A1, A3; John M. Goshko and Hobart Rowen, "Haig and U.S. Allies Thwart Stockman's Planned Aid Slash," *The Washington Post* (31 January 1981), p. A1.

MARGARET E. CRAHAN

1. The State and the Individual in Latin America: An Historical Overview

INTRODUCTION

Prior to the twentieth century there was a tendency in Latin America for the state not to impinge strongly upon the individual either positively or negatively, largely because it did not have the capability. As a consequence, those rights which required government action, such as access to education, were not satisfied for a substantial proportion of the population. On the other hand, rights that could be violated by government actions, such as freedom from arbitrary arrest, detention, or exile, were enjoyed by the majority of citizens. With the modernization of the state and the expansion of the resources available to it in the twentieth century, the impact of the state on the individual was augmented. The increasing emergence in the 1960s and 1970s of authoritarian states with access to modern technology, together with the high degree of social control imposed by these regimes, resulted in frequent violations of human rights. The origins of these states can be traced to the colonial heritage of Latin America, as well as to the historical experience of each country, including foreign political, military, and intellectual influences.

This chapter provides a synthetic overview of that heritage and experience, in order to specify some of the factors contributing to the nature of the contemporary state in Latin America and its impact on individual rights.[1] These include the concept of the state that was transferred to America in the colonial period and its modification over time. While in theory royal authority in Spain and Portugal was absolute, in practice both in the peninsula and the colonies there were substantial limitations because of distance, the lack or incompetence of personnel, and the frequency of exemptions from or disregard of regulations. Government was, in effect, a mediating instrument between the monarchy and competing elites, while the mass was largely beyond the purview of the state. As a consequence, the vast majority of individuals were able to enjoy rights to the degree that their status and means permitted. While rights were guaranteed in varying degrees to different groups within society, official protection or promotion of those rights was largely lacking. There was not the same evolution of individual rights that occurred in England and France, particularly during the seventeenth and eighteenth centuries. As a result, upon gaining independence in the early nineteenth century, most former Spanish subjects did not have a strong basis for the expansion of individual rights particularly through participation in government. Authority was transferred from the monarchy to American elites, who used control of the state to ensure the continuance of their privileged position within society. A similar pattern held true for Brazil when it became a republic in 1889.

Throughout the nineteenth century the state in Latin America reflected colonial patterns of theoretical concentration of power in the state with a substantial devolution of authority in practice. Elite domination and limited political participation continued, although the latter began to broaden as a result largely of economic expansion, immigration, and increased educational facilities. This was reflected in growing political pressures, particularly from the emerging middle class and organized workers during the latter part of the nineteenth and beginning of the twentieth centuries. The expansion of suffrage resulted in the creation of reformist, populist coalitions and parties which by the 1920s succeeded in taking power in some countries.

Populist coalitions, however, generally had relatively narrow bases that caused them to be unstable and easily fragmented. The most successful ones generally had a charismatic leader who served to override factional differences. These movements increased popular participation, but they often depended on authoritarian and paternalistic patterns of government which did not assure protection or enjoyment of rights for the bulk of the population. Competition for government benefits, particularly by the more advantaged, continued to dominate politics.

Restriction of socioeconomic rights in the face of economic growth, generated strong popular discontent which escalated after World War II. Reformist civilian governments were, by and large, unable to meet demands for the satisfaction of basic needs, and societal conflict increased. Critics of liberal democracy, as it had evolved in Latin America, became increasingly vocal. Those on the left called for the implantation of socialism, while critics on the right promoted authoritarianism and orthodox economic policies. The tradition of limited political participation based on partial enjoyment of civil and political as well as economic and social rights led to the triumph of the conservative option in a good number of countries, especially in South America. There highly authoritarian states dominated by the military emerged. They consolidated power at the expense of civil and political rights and implemented economic policies that restricted the fulfillment of basic needs by the lower classes.

I. COLONIAL HERITAGE

At the time of the conquest and colonization of America, Spain was undergoing a period of state building that modified existing political and economic structures as the result of demands generated by the development of mercantile commercialism. Some existing tendencies were reinforced, including royal absolutism, which had been evolving since the twelfth century and was accompanied by the articulation of the power of the aristocracy and urban merchants. The rise of absolutism, facilitated by the acquisition of an empire, combined to reinforce regionalism and elite competition, as well as to diminish pressures for more intensive economic development and exploitation of the peninsula. This in turn retarded the evolution of a modern Spanish state in which the concepts of political freedom and individual rights would have had increasing importance.

The conjunction of state-building and acquisition of empire stimulated the implantation in America of authoritarian, hierarchical societies based on the exploitation of land and the labor of the native population, and subsequently of enslaved Africans.[2] The Spanish colonies were conceived of as the personal possessions of Isabella, not of Spain, and were integrated into the administrative machinery of Castile, where laws, institutions, and customs allowed for less regional autonomy and individual rights than in some of the other peninsular kingdoms.[3] However, distance from the metropolis accomplished part of what *fueros* (exemptions from royal authority) did in Aragon and Leon: the provision of some defense against the arbitrary exercise of state authority.

The financial drain on the Spanish state of religious and dynastic wars in the sixteenth and seventeenth centuries contributed to the failure to develop a strong domestic economy, further limiting state-building and national integration in the peninsula. The decline of the physical and mental capacities of the seventeenth century Hapsburgs, Philip III (1598–1621), Philip IV (1621–1665), and Charles II (1665–1700), reinforced this and allowed for greater autonomy and flexibility in the colonies. This largely benefited the creole elite in Latin America which, consequently, was able to expand its authority over the lower classes and interpose itself between the masses and the monarchy.[4] Although legally prohibited from occupying senior colonial offices, they increasingly held those posts, promoting local rather than royal interests and filling, to a degree, the vacuum of power left by disinterested and incompetent peninsular officials.[5] It should be noted, however, that the creole elite did, at times, ally itself with peninsular elites for their mutual advantage.

The Spanish Empire in the New World was structured in a far more authoritarian fashion than the French and English possessions, although the impact was lessened by the development of ad hoc patterns of local control and the failure of the state to penetrate into large parts of the colonial hinterland. This pattern of organization was stronger still in Brazil. As a result, individualistic patterns of social, political, and economic control grew up that eventually contributed not only to the impulse toward independence, but also to the centralist-federalist conflicts that dominated such countries as Argentina, Mexico, and Colombia in the nineteenth century.[6] The implantation of authoritarian control from Spain hence coexisted with the development of strong tendencies toward regional autonomy and disregard for central authority. Both stimulated personalism in politics.

Both Spain and Portugal depended on their colonies to pay for growing bureaucracies, dynastic and religious wars, and lavish courts in Europe. So long as some benefits also accrued to the colonial elite, either through the normal functioning of the colonial relationship or by tacit disregard of it, allegiance to the metropolis was maintained. Contemporary legal thought, as well as theology and philosophy, together with the realities of imperial exploitation, contributed to a society in which substantial inequalities were sanctioned as the proper order of things. As one historian expressed it:

> The Spaniards recreated in the New World a version of the corporate society of the late Middle Ages. Hierarchically structured, it contained two kinds of associations: the primary estates and the functional corporations. The whites tended to dominate the latter. . . . One of the novel aspects of neo-medieval corporatism in the Indies was that the three primary estates were not the European trichotomy of the Church, the nobility, and the commoners. In America an informal racial trichotomy emerged consisting of the whites, the mixed groups, and the Indians-Negroes at the bottom of the social pyramid. It was the neo-medieval corporate character of the colonial society which enabled the Spaniards to find a place for the Indians. It was, however, an inferior place, for the only equality that the Spaniards were prepared to grant to the Indians was equality in the next world. Spaniards, Mestizos, and Indians were not equal, but they were organically interdependent. The Spaniards were the head of the body social. . . and the Indians and Negroes the arms and legs. English-American society in the seven-

teenth century, on the other hand, was moving away from the medieval corporate model toward equalitarianism and individualism. [7]

Inequalities in terms of property, status, and accomplishments were considered the result of imperfect human nature.

In the medieval concept, social inequality applied to individuals and groups within a society, but not to nations or races. However, the Spanish philosopher Juan Gines de Sepúlveda argued in the sixteenth century that certain races were inferior to others, thereby accepting the Aristotelian concept of natural servitude. As a consequence he posited that Spaniards were superior to the Indians "as adults are to children and as men are to women." He further insisted that enslavement of such peoples was justified by the natural order, albeit the superior race was obligated to see to their Christianization and civilizing. While his view was disputed, most notably by the Dominican priest Bartolomé de Las Casas, it was widely accepted not only in practice, but also in law and colonial institutions. Fear of Indian uprisings in the colonial period also contributed to their incorporation into the body politic in a restricted fashion without the same rights, privileges, and obligations as white subjects. The Indians were considered a separate commonwealth with their own laws and magistrates. [8]

Although this isolation did have some advantages, it served to confer inferior status on those considered racially inferior and limited political participation after independence. Mestizos and mulattoes, together with some impoverished Spaniards, constituted the *gente de razon*. They enjoyed some of the rights and obligations of a citizen, but were excluded from office unless they produced a document testifying falsely to the "purity" of their lineage. The group, as a whole, had no guaranteed rights to land and could be subjected to forced labor. There was, however, some limited social mobility and with economic development in the eighteenth century, a few gained entrance into an incipient middle sector or even the lowest levels of the elite. Such mobility did not mean, however, the extension of rights or privileges to new groups, but rather to certain individuals. [9]

The colonial period was to end with a highly stratified society. Substantial groups were deprived of the full benefits of citizenry, as well as of access to land and other sources of wealth to use as an economic base from which to initiate political claims on the newly independent republics. Beyond this, there were also a social legacy of degradation of the labor force, predominantly Indian and Negro, through slavery and debt peonage.

Moreover, the highly personalistic and absolutistic nature of the Spanish and Portuguese empires required that individuals or institutions be recognized and have the favor of the government for political participation. This situation reinforced the role of the monarch as ultimate arbiter and source of all authority—executive, legislative, and judicial. While officials were theoretically responsible to both their constituencies and the monarch, the latter attempted to exact greater allegiance. A bureaucracy arose to carry out the will of the monarch and provide benefits to royal supporters. Royal officials consequently focused on ad-hoc, specific, regulative, and distributive activities, rather than on long-range and more universal goals. This laid the basis for the development of clientelist and exclusionary patterns in governing in nineteenth and twentieth century Latin America. [10]

Demands, particularly by elites, inclined the Spanish monarchy toward colonial expansion rather than toward more intensive exploitation of peninsular resources, to which the crown had limited access. To deal with elite demands, complex administrative machinery was evolved to allocate national and imperial resources. This presaged somewhat the clientelist mechanisms developed in nineteenth and twentieth century Latin America with their orientation toward the mediation of conflicting claims, particularly by those most able to articulate them. It also encouraged circumvention of official procedures through the utilization of special access, personal contacts, and other means of influence to extract what was desired. What evolved was complex and often inefficient bureaucratic machinery aimed at particular goals rather than at universal ones, along with unofficial structures and a pattern of circumventing regulations. [11] Colonists and royal officials did not always ignore colonial laws but used them, selectively and astutely, to further their purposes. [12] This allowed for disregard of the law without implying disloyalty to the crown.

The additional belief that society was a functional corporate unit based upon scholastic natural law in which liberty was exercised within the corporate body permeated the republics established in early nineteenth century Latin America. This notion required a mediating instrumentality to deal with conflict and thus led to the conceptualization of a moderating power. During the colonial period the crown filled this role, and it was identified with the monarch's functions as lawgiver, executor, and adjudicator. This limited the possibilities for developing alternative avenues of political struggle and served to concentrate authority more fully in the monarch.

The moderating role of the crown reappeared in Simon Bolívar's constitution for Gran Columbia as the *Poder Moderador*, an authority over and above the executive, legislative, and judicial branches that would be called upon when there was marked abuse of authority by government or an irresolvable conflict within society. Implicit in this was lack of confidence, particularly among competing elites, in the ordinary processes of government and belief in an authority more enlightened, more honest, and more powerful than regular officials. This not only reinforced the tendency toward personalistic political leadership (*caudillismo*), but also contributed to belief in the mediating role of the military in twentieth century Latin America.

In addition, European law at the time of the discovery of America was "normatively diffuse and particularistic in application" and "so encumbered by religiosity and privilege as to forestall any but the most modest human rights developments." [13]

> Most importantly, in the middle ages, where the social organization of feudalism was concerned, no clear distinction was discernible between the "private person" and the "public individual." When this differentiation was made in the age of Reformation, the process of responding to the problem of political freedom was launched on an ideological plane. The private person sought not a new legal definition of his status as a public individual, and still less, political power. He sought assurance of his private existence: to be secure in the family unit by being unencumbered with excessive taxation and being left alone in religious (and therefore ideological) matters. Achieving this kind of accommodation between the "private person" and those in power entailed a crisis of political legitimacy growing out of two outmoded features of the traditional society. First, the essential norms and guiding principles of the older established legal order were anchored in transcendental standards— difficult to define and even harder to apply. Second, these systems generally lacked universal norms applicable to the whole society rather than to a few of its segments, estates or classes. [14]

From this we can trace the development of individual rights, primarily in France, England, and the latter's colonies in America, especially where centralized bureaucracy was effectively organized and used by elites. In particular, concessions in terms of rights involving legal and property protections were exacted. A comparable expansion of such rights did not occur in the Iberian peninsula and the Indies. The failure of the Spanish and Portuguese monarchies to consolidate power in centralized bureaucracies to the same degree as France and England limited the development of more universalistic goals for government, and diminished its role as an instrument of nonelites. The financial dependence of the Iberian monarchs on aristocratic and commercial elites meant, however, that the latter could exact some concessions. These constituted sectoral

privileges rather than the basis for the development of generalized individual rights. The dominant pattern in the Spanish and Portuguese
empires was to avoid or be exempted from state authority, rather than to
expand basic rights.

The penetration of Enlightenment thought, as well as the economic
development of the Iberian peninsula and the colonies, particularly in
the second half of the eighteenth century, augmented demands for self-
determination, freedom from onerous taxes and hence greater guarantees
of property, and more freedom of expression both in the political and
religious spheres. Some churchmen played a substantial role in promoting
the latter, going so far, in some cases, as to argue in favor of tyrannicide
which, during the reign of Charles III (1757–1788), contributed to
attacks on such special privileges as ecclesiastical immunity from
civil law.

However, neither in the Iberian peninsula nor in its colonies, did
there develop in the same fashion as in France, England, and their
colonies the inalienable rights to life, liberty, and property as part of a
process of protecting an area of individual activities from government
intervention. [15] In the former, society continued to be defined in an
organic fashion in which the individual's rights and duties were defined
by his or her position in the whole. This was reflected in a legal system
that provided for different punishments for the same crime. In the colonies
an Indian who stole could receive less severe punishment than a Spaniard,
because the former was considered to have less capacity to make moral
judgments and hence was less responsible. Such inequalities were expressions of Iberian paternalism that served to impede the incorporation
of Indians, Blacks, and mixed castes into the body politic.

The gaining of independence in the early nineteenth century did
not substantially modify the structure of colonial society, nor the political
isolation of the bulk of the population. Independence was actually the
outcome of the struggle to expand the autonomy and privileges of the
colonial elite within the imperial structure. It was stimulated, in part, by
the Industrial Revolution in Northern Europe, which encouraged the
search for large new markets and sources of raw materials in Spanish and
Portuguese America. Such interest encouraged colonial merchants and
manufacturers to define their interests in new ways. Disappointed by
Bourbon reforms [16] and suffering from the disruption caused by the
French Revolution and European warfare, discontent grew among the
colonial elite and increased the attraction for the objectives and language
of the Enlightenment and the French and American revolutions. Hence
the struggle was nominally for liberty, equality, and fraternity as in
France, and liberation from such colonial burdens as trade restrictions [17]
and taxation without representation as in the English colonies. Events,

particularly political instability in Spain and the subsequent attempted reassertion of royal absolutism, propelled the American leadership to take more radical steps than had been initially intended.

II. THE NEOCOLONIAL STATE (ca. 1820–1920)

In the former Spanish colonies the desire for stability and progress in the early years of the nineteenth century led to a search for a unifying factor, either in an individual (e.g., Portales in Chile, Bolívar in Gran Colombia, Iturbide in Mexico) or in a constitution, or both. [18] Neither was sufficient and political struggle intensified among those with some access to power. Hence there emerged personalistic leaders (*caudillos*) in many of the countries, frequent changes or modifications of constitutions, intra-elite conflicts, and chronic regional rivalries.

The process of integrating the countries economically and augmenting political participation was secondary to the competition for power among elites, with the conservatives, by and large, opting for a hierarchical, elitist state under the guise of a constitutional republic. Liberals generally favored somewhat broader, albeit limited, political participation. The failure of Spain to create a modern nation-state during the imperial period left the former colonies without a strong basis for doing so. Hence political structures continued to strongly reflect colonial patterns of particularistic goals, as well as elite domination and limited participation.

The special nature of the Iberian sense of history also contributed to American problems. Increasingly in the eighteenth century there had been an inclination in Spain to reject recent developments and harken back to the medieval era, as a glorious period of constitutionalism and representation. [19] This tendency to glorify a misperceived past can also be found in the present-day authoritarian states. It encourages dependence on models derived from historical experiences other than one's own. In the former Spanish colonies this meant the adoption of French and U.S. constitutional and governmental forms to overlay Iberian traditions and practices.

The result was the continuance of hierarchical structures dominated by a relatively small elite, despite some expansion within that group and other intermediary groups. Strong cleavages continued, and with the removal of the unifying principle of the Spanish crown (either as a source of loyalty or opposition), internal divisions increased, particularly as a result of disagreements over control of the state.

Mexico in the nineteenth century epitomized such conflicts in the struggles over the 1824 and 1857 constitutions, *La Reforma* (1854–1876), the French intervention (1862–1867), and the eventual emergence of Porfirio Díaz in 1876. The Mexican case is additionally illuminating because of the pressures generated by demographic and economic change which created popular demands for more open political, economic, social, and religious structures. Calls for democratization, however, generated considerable resistance among the elite who supported regimes that promised to control and channel change. Such was the Díaz regime (1876–1910), which disintegrated when the demands of excluded elements of the elite, together with those of the expanding petit bourgeoisie and some workers, could no longer be ignored.

The building up of pressures to broaden political and economic participation contributed to considerable instability in late nineteenth and early twenitieth century Latin America, where countries such as Bolivia had more than 100 presidential and constitutional changes. These did not involve the bulk of the population directly, [20] although they affected them by impeding economic development, political incorporation, and equal access to goods, services, and the law. In Argentina there was, in fact, no effective central authority until 1860. In this chaos, national symbols took the place of rational programs. The names of Bolívar, San Martín, and O'Higgins were frequently invoked; the Iberian heritage was extolled in the face of continued anti-Spanish feeling; and religious symbols were manipulated for political purposes. Similar efforts have been made in twentieth-century Latin America by governments—particularly authoritarian ones.

The striving for legitimation through these methods generated additional political competition, but also served to foster greater national identification. The frequent struggles tended to focus on issues that were discrete and rarely articulated, due, in part, to the relatively low level of political mobilization of a substantial proportion of the population. As the nineteenth century progressed, political competition, economic development, educational facilities, and immigration increased and, correspondingly, the number and range of problems or demands around which political conflict centered. Given the limited development of political, economic, and social structures, and the mounting claims on governments by increasingly differentiated social groups, the challenges to the state were substantial and were reflected in frequent changes of government. Escalating pressures brought forth calls for increased centralization of government machinery which contributed to the decline of the regional *caudillos* in favor of national ones. Brazil, having become the seat of the empire with the transfer of the royal family to America, escaped some of this. On the other hand, its enormous territorial extent resulted in strong regionalism and the maintenance of control by local leaders for a relatively long period. [21]

The economic policies of the new republics were aimed mainly at the extraction and distribution of resources as in the imperial period.

More emphasis was placed on increasing productivity, using traditional means, rather than on the development and exploitation of new resources or technological advances. Where the latter was done, it was often as a result of foreign investment, particularly from England, which tended to concentrate on infrastructure, production of exportable commodities, and banking. This promoted dependence on foreign capital and manufactured goods which served to foster neo-colonialism. Development was dependent development. [22]

The introduction of republican forms of government did result in certain shifts in the scope and channels of political struggle. Legislatures, when operative, became arenas for intra-elite conflict serving in some instances as a forum for compromise; sometimes, however, the tensions between modernizing and traditional elites broke out into open warfare, as in Chile in the 1890s. Congresses served symbolic rather than representational roles for the bulk of the population. But toward the end of the nineteenth century increasingly they became the focus for expanding suffrage as a part of an overall push to make political structures more responsive, particularly to the growing middle sectors. New political parties emerged out of this struggle, but they, too, reflected traditional patterns, frequently adhering to authoritarian, personalistic formulas. Such parties forged alliances among claimants for access to power and attempted to influence the distribution of benefits by governments through extension or modification of traditional patterns of patronage. Because they did not represent individuals united by like ideological orientation, their unity was somewhat ephemeral and disintegrated rapidly once they were in power.

In addition, the survival of oligarchic authority in modified form served to restrict the dissemination of power and resources, and maintained the gulf between the elite and the masses. The state continued to be dominated by the few whose power was ensured by control of economic resources. The restricted nature of political participation gave access to central power great importance. Control could only be maintained by limiting political rights, such as voting, and hence it was the battle over suffrage that dominated politics in the period 1890–1920 in many countries. As threats to the old order developed, fear of instability tended to encourage expansion and upgrading of the armed forces. This, however, did not guarantee that the military would serve as the guardian of the status quo, for increased professionalization prompted criticism of traditional ruling elites and development of the armed forces' own plans for national development. Both Chile and Brazil witnessed the attempted implementation of reformist programs by the military in the 1920s.

In nineteenth century Latin America liberal democracy was the stated ideal, but it often seemed to be the illusion of visionaries. Basic principles such as the division of powers clashed with authoritarian and personalist traditions. The rule of law suffered from this conflict and from the fact that courts and judges rarely penetrated into the rural areas and were frequently subject to direct and indirect pressures that undermined equal application of the law. [23] The representative system was frequently deemed impractical by ruling elites, because of the poverty and dispersion of the bulk of the population and the lack of resources and personnel to implement universal suffrage.

Some economic changes did result from the worldwide growth in trade and industry in the late nineteenth century which increased demand for Latin American products. This brought periodic prosperity to the area and contributed to improvements in the standard of living of the lower classes; it also attracted European immigrants. But there were negative consequences as well: cycles of boom and bust, maldistribution of income, and dependence on international market fluctuations. What evolved, by and large, were export economies heavily dependent on one or two staples at the mercy of fluctuations in demand or production. Hence, little advance was made toward economic sovereignty. The rise of new social strata was not, therefore, so much centered around the emergence of new modes of production in diversified economies as around coalitions of the somewhat advantaged for greater benefits.

By the turn of the century intra-elite struggle was occurring within the context of escalating demands for broadened political participation. The response to this varied considerably—from the reactionary to the reformist or populist, or a mix of all three. This promoted considerable political experimentation in the 1920s and 1930s which built on rather than eliminated authoritarian, personalistic, and paternalistic patterns and did little to destroy elite dominance.

The Catholic Church was heavily involved in these developments, given its preeminent role in society. As part of the elite, the church participated in intragroup strife, being identified in most countries with the more traditional conservative sectors. This prompted attacks by liberals that were aimed largely at stripping the church of its privileged position in society and curtailing its wealth. Initial moves in the nineteenth century to establish separation of church and state [24] were followed in countries such as Mexico by attempts to strip the church of its property and its special juridical status. [25] Conservatives inside and outside the church tended to believe that any attack on the church was a prelude to a leveling movement within the body politic. Impulses toward greater involvement in social problems were restrained, partially because of the impact of European events on the Latin American church via missionaries.

This included the introduction of antiliberal, antidemocratic, and anti-modern ideas derived particularly from France. [26]

Around the turn of the century the church began responding to certain challenges. By the 1920s new currents in European Catholic social thought that were reformist and activist led to the emergence of Catholic Action, the Young Christian Workers, and later of Christian Democratic parties. At the same time conservative movements such as integralism, Opus Dei, and Action Française were also being intro-duced. [27] These would play a role in the flowering of fascism in the 1930s and of authoritarian Latin American states in the 1970s.

During the nineteenth century the majority of Latin Americans were limited in their enjoyment of civil, political, social, and economic rights not as a result of positive government action, but because they lacked influence on official policies and actions. This was partially the result of the survival of colonial patterns within the new republics. The Wars of Independence were not revolutions, rather they represented a transfer of power from a metropolitan elite allied with some creoles to an American elite. Given the extractive nature of the colonial economy and the realities of the international market in the period, dependence on Spain was replaced by dependence on England, Germany, and later on the United States. Concentration of power, while theoretically less than under the monarchy, followed the ad hoc patterns of the colonial period. As populations grew and generated stronger demands, certain modifica-tions became necessary, but these did not radically change the concentra-tion of power nor the manner in which it was exercised. Government continued to benefit a small proportion of the population. Lacking broad-based support, the elites invoked traditional symbols and nationalist sentiment to legitimize the exercise of power. Substantial socioeconomic inequalities and political exclusion destroyed that sense of solidarity based on generalized attitudes, sentiments, and behavior necessary to transform social groups into a nation. This in turn contributed to the failure of states to emerge, except those dominated by particularistic goals. It also encouraged the military increasingly to regard itself as the only truly national institution, above partisanship and with the welfare of the nation at heart. As nonelites became more politically active, they required effective mechanisms of control. The mediating function of the state became more complex as the demands on it increased. No collective political identity was forged that overrode the sharp divisions of the social reality. The most successful attempts were those focused on a charismatic leader. The process was raised to a new level by individuals such as Getulio Vargas in Brazil and Juan Perón in Argentina in the 1930s and 1940s.

III. THE DEVELOPMENT OF THE
MODERN STATE (ca. 1920–1980)

Eventually, demands for political incorporation and reallocation of power by the urban working class, small businessmen, professionals, and others modified political structures to a greater degree than the Wars of Independence. These groups tended to follow traditional patterns of focusing on expanding access to benefits, broadening the bases of the collectivity without fully challenging the nature of centralized power, and modifying the allocation of resources. Such a strategy inclines groups toward intense, internal ideological and political conflicts that "often have little to do with restructuring the center or opening new avenues of participation in it."[28] Authoritarianism became an accepted response to the instability produced by pressures for change and conflict in the twentieth century.

Authoritarian regimes came to be regarded as modernizing ones to the degree that they brought greater efficiency and bureaucratic rationality to the distribution of benefits. Political parties were often extensions of clientilistic networks rather than broad-based movements. With limited popular support, governments made use of ascriptive symbols or values to appeal to different ethnic, religious, and subnational communities.

There was, however, some limitation of traditional elite control. New cliques grew up, some based on access to military force and others on populist appeals. The Peronist movement in Argentina originally contained both. Substantial cleavages within society, however, militated against the retention of power by these elements over the long term.

It has been argued that the tendency, particularly from the 1930s to the 1960s, to oscillate between limited democracy and authoritarian regimes is partially related to the rate of economic change.[29] During periods of steady growth, elective governments appeared with greater frequency (e.g., the late 1940s). When the growth rate either speeded up or slowed down substantially, governments considered more capable of stimulating or controlling change were favored.

What has become evident in recent decades is that the fading of colonial and neocolonial forms has not necessarily resulted in the emergence of democratic states. Rather there has been an increasing tendency toward the emergence of states that incorporate the tradition of centralized bureaucracies as mediating instrumenalities, with a technocratic, non-personalistic approach to policy making and problem solving. In order to hold sway over societies with deep cleavages resulting from socioeconomic disparities, manipulation, coercion, and sometimes repression are used. The combination of these elements has resulted in the emergence of new forms of authoritarianism in Latin America.

The most common explanation offered for the appearance of authoritarian regimes in Latin America is the chaos caused by contradictions between the needs of dependent capitalism and escalating pressures for democratization in the post-World War II period.[30] This position posits that the roots of these regimes can be found in the disintegration of oligarchic domination in the early decades of the twentieth century, largely as a result of the limitations of export-oriented economies based primarily on agriculture and mining. This analysis emphasizes the subsequent failure of import substitution strategies to respond adequately to the demands of the increasingly vocal and politicized middle and lower classes for greater economic benefits.

Instability was heightened by growing competition between the disadvantaged and those who had benefited from the expansion of domestic industry and commerce. Marxist critiques of the status quo became more common at a time when the Cold War was intensifying worldwide. Anticommunist sentiment was fueled by growing United States preoccupation with Soviet expansion in the Western Hemisphere, particularly after the Castro revolution in Cuba in 1959. United States economic and military aid, especially as channeled through the Alliance for Progress, aimed at promoting improved socioeconomic conditions that would undercut the appeal of socialism.

Beginning in the late 1950s Latin America underwent a further transformation as a result of increased penetration by monopoly capital particularly through the transnationals. Statistics are frequently cited indicating that a substantial percentage (40–50 percent) of the United States subsidiaries established in the area between 1958 and 1967 were local businesses that had been bought out. Economic expansion in this period provided for some sectoral improvements and an overall appearance of prosperity that stimulated pressures for redistribution of national wealth. Increased popular participation and the mobilization of urban workers revealed the limitations of existing political and economic structures, and raised the level of social conflict. As a result the existing political and economic systems were strongly challenged.

The reform-minded developmentalist approach in such countries as Argentina, Chile, and Peru in the 1950s and 1960s made them more dependent on outside capital, both as investment and aid, and more subject to international market forces. The objective of political democratization via capitalist development was not achieved and the expectations aroused by governmental promises remained unsatisfied. Increasing guerrilla activities reflected loss of faith in democratic means of political struggle, and greater polarization and conflict. This led to the growing appeal of radical solutions from both the right and the left.

Conservative forces tended to view the inability of reformist governments markedly to improve socioeconomic conditions as a demonstration of the inadequacies of liberal democracy and the bankruptcy of politicians and parties. The growth of the left and the emergence of radical guerrilla groups in Uruguay, Argentina, Brazil, Venezuela, Peru, and elsewhere in the 1960s were considered the result of the failure of civilian governments to prevent Marxist subversives from capitalizing on widespread popular discontent. During the 1950s and 1960s the left did gain some strength. Its most notable success was in Chile, where it took power via elections in 1970. In that country, as well as elsewhere, the left reflected the traditional weaknesses of populist coalitions, frequently fragmenting over internal differences.

Both the left and the right shared a belief in the need to restructure society in order to resolve the problems of chronic poverty, limited economic growth, and escalating political conflict. Progressives emphasized increased state control of the economy to ensure more equitable distribution of the benefits of economic development. The right promoted increased state power to implement orthodox economic policies emphasizing capital accumulation for investment. This, they believed, would promote growth and thus eventually benefit the whole population. Initially, however, real wages tended to decline and unemployment to increase, markedly affecting the capacity of the lower classes to fulfill their basic needs. [31]

Control of opposition to such policies particularly by labor unions and certain political parties required expansion of state authority and its exercise in a coercive fashion. Fear of political and economic chaos and the desire for stern measures to promote economic development had been growing within the military in the post-World War II period. As structural crises deepened, particularly in those countries which were undergoing rapid economic change (e.g., Brazil, Argentina, and Chile), the armed forces intervened to stabilize their countries in order to promote economic growth. The regimes they imposed gave priority to the guaranteeing of national security through the concentration of power in the executive branch of government and the implementation of economic policies that emphasized market mechanisms and the imposition of devaluation, floating exchange rates, reduction of tariffs, elimination of import and price controls, as well as reduction of public welfare programs. The most concrete expression of these policies has been in the national security states of Brazil, Uruguay, Chile, and Argentina. [32] Once the armed forces took power in Brazil in 1964, in Uruguay and Chile in 1973, and in Argentina in 1976, they moved quickly to exclude the popular sectors from political, social, and economic participation and obtain at least the passive acceptance, if not the support, of middle sectors. The upper classes were to be incorporated into a hegemonic nucleus with the military. The violation of civil/political rights and the decline of the condition of the poor were viewed as justified by the need to restructure society in order to release its natural growth potential.

According to the proponents of national security states, genuine rights cannot be violated because conflict between the legitimate objectives of individuals, groups, and the state does not exist. Hence the violations cited by national and international human rights organizations are not valid. In addition, class conflict is regarded as illegitimate and contrary to the ideal of organic national unity. To accomplish national destiny, all power must be accorded a state controlled by an enlightened elite. It is the special responsibility of this group to expand national power through economic development and without regard for majority rule, which is considered incapable of expressing the will of the nation and subject to oscillations that deflect from achieving the national destiny. Healthy civil society is hierarchical, disciplined, and organized in a unitary fashion without debilitating political competition. The origins of this particular version of the state derive from the Hispanic heritage of Latin America and the latter's historical evolution, together with some stimuli from Europe and the United States. [33]

Recent analyses suggest that the appearance of new forms of authoritarian states in Latin America are the result of a complex interplay of economic and political factors whose ramifications are not yet fully established. [34] These include the timing and nature of industrialization and the manner of insertion into the international economy. The size and variety of the national resource base and the extent of diversification of the economy affect the degree of dependency on foreign capital and technology, and hence the measure of sovereignty and stability. Where critical economic problems exist there is a tendency for the professional military to perceive itself as the most effective means of transcending them. Given the limited nature of incorporation of popular sectors into the body politic in most Latin American countries, the capacity for the bulk of the populace to deter military intervention is limited. Where the civilian political leadership has been discredited, their ability to mobilize popular support is somewhat negligible. The strengthening of popular forces, over the past 60 to 70 years in Latin America, has not been sufficient to overcome recourse to authoritarian means by those intent on impeding redistribution of national wealth, whether to protect their own privileged position or to carry out their strategy for national development.

CONCLUSION

The Iberian heritage of Latin America bred an organic concept of society in which wide disparities among groups were accepted, particularly their access to socioeconomic necessities and civil/political rights. The realities of colonial exploitation and the nature of the Latin American economy resulted in highly inegalitarian societies developing under the theoretical control of hierarchical, authoritarian states.

Even in areas where the state apparatus was not capable of penetrating, ad hoc methods of socioeconomic and political control evolved which, by and large, sanctioned domination by a small elite. The political and legal heritage of the Iberian peninsula tended to reinforce this. Positive guarantees of civil and political rights were limited largely to the upper echelons of society, who were regarded as morally more responsible than other groups who had limited rights commensurate with their capacity and place in society as a whole. Christian emphasis on the respective responsibilities and obligations of various sectors encouraged patriarchal and paternalistic relationships which in the nineteenth and twentieth centuries were reflected in the prevalence of caudillism and clientelism.

The gaining of independence represented, to a considerable degree, the transfer of power from a metropolitan elite to an American elite. The adoption of republican forms and constitutions occurred in a milieu where colonial characteristics survived, including authoritarianism, personalism, and unequal application of the law. Social transformation and economic development did not substantially modify traditional patterns until the latter part of the nineteenth century and the beginning of the twentieth. While social struggle increased, traditional elites were, by and large, able to maintain control into the twentieth century. By then, however, industrialization, urbanization, immigration, and other phenomena revealed the limited capacities of neocolonial states to deal with these socioeconomic pressures.

Constraints on the emergence of popular governments continued to exist, however—among them authoritarianism, personalism, and dependent economic development. The failure of limited democracies in the pre- and post-World War II period to maintain stability in the face of mounting popular pressures to satisfy socioeconomic needs helped bring to power military governments that promised strong economic growth, as well as an end to instability and subversion. Such governments have had their most authoritarian expression in the national security state, with its scant regard for human rights.

The historical experience of Latin America suggests that neither traditional, reformist, developmentalist, nor new authoritarian solutions succeed in guaranteeing basic rights. The implication is that only when governments are fully responsive to the needs of all their citizens will substantial progress be made. To do this the full enjoyment of the right to take part in government directly or through freely chosen representatives is essential.

NOTES TO CHAPTER 1

1. Political, military, and intellectual influences from Europe and the United States will be dealt with in Chapters 2, 3, 9, and 10 of this volume.

2. Juan J. Linz, "Early State Building and Late Peripheral Nationalisms against the State: The Case of Spain," in S. N. Eisenstadt and Stein Rokkan, eds., *Building States and Nations: Models, Analyses and Data Resources,* (Beverly Hills: Sage Publications, 1973), p. 37. For further discussion of the evolution of the Spanish state see José Cepeda Adán, *En torno al concepto del estado en los Reyes Catolicos* (Madrid: Consejo Superior de Investigaciones Científicas, Escuela de Historia Moderna, 1956); José Antonio Maravall, "The Origins of the Modern State," *Journal of World History* 6 (1961): 789–808; Jaime Vicens Vives, "Estructura administrativa estatal en los siglos XVI y XVII," *Rapports: Onzième Congrès International des Sciences Historiques* (Göteborg: Almqvist and Wiksell, 1960): IV, 1–24.

3. The classic study on the implications of the integration of the colonies into the Crown of Castile is Juan Manzano Manzano, *La incorporación de las Indias a la corona de Castilla* (Madrid: Ediciones Cultura Hispánica, 1948).

4. Creoles were Spaniards born in America.

5. This was even true of church officials appointed to royal posts, a practice followed by Spain and Portugal since clerics were considered less likely to identify and cooperate with local elites to the detriment of royal interests. One of the few studies available testing this presumption demonstrates that approximately 70 percent of the Peruvian and Chilean episcopacy were engaged in economic pursuits that tied them to the secular elite in the colonies or peninsula or both. Elizabeth Wilkes Dore, "The Training of an Elite: The Bishops of Peru and Chile in the Colonial Era," M.S. 1973.

6. For an examination of the interplay of settlement patterns and the limitations of colonial control in the peripheral areas of the empire, together with political theories they generated, see José Luis Romero's, *A History of Argentine Political Thought* (Stanford, Calif.: Stanford University Press, 1968).

7. John Leddy Phelan, *The Kingdom of Quito in the Seventeenth Century: Bureaucratic Politics in the Spanish Empire* (Madison: University of Wisconsin Press, 1967), pp. 57–58.

8. Ibid., pp. 56–58.

9. David A. Brading, *Miners and Merchants in Bourbon Mexico, 1763–1810* (Cambridge: Cambridge University Press, 1971), p. 23.

10. While there has been considerable debate about the precise definition of clientelism in the Latin American context, it is generally used to depict a pattern of exchange relationships between individuals and groups of unequal status. More specifically, it refers to "a tendency to rely on the activation of diffuse primary relationships in order to accomplish assorted social, economic, and political goals; and, most important, a posture of personal dependency on superiors in the status hierarchy." The full flowering of clientelism, according to the political scientist Robert Kaufman, "expressed concretely in landlord-peasant relationships, local elite autonomy, and caudillo movements—became possible only after the collapse of imperial bureaucratic authority in the nineteenth century." Robert R. Kaufman, "Corporatism, Clientelism, and Partisan Conflict: A Study of Seven Latin American Countries," in James M. Malloy, ed., *Authoritarianism and Corporatism in Latin America* (Pittsburgh: University of Pittsburg Press, 1977), p. 113.

11. For the specific consequences of this, see John Leddy Phelan, "Authority and Flexibility in the Spanish Imperial Bureaucracy," *Administrative Science Quarterly,* 5 (June 1960): 47–65.

12. Constance Ann Crowder Carter, "Law and Society in Colonial Mexico: Audiencia Judges in Mexican Society from the Tello de Sandoval Visita General, 1543–1547," (Ph.D. dissertation, Columbia University, 1971), p. 143.

13. Richard P. Claude, "The Classical Model of Human Rights Development," in Richard P. Claude, ed., *Comparative Human Rights* (Baltimore: The Johns Hopkins University Press, 1976), p. 11.

14. Ibid.

15. Ibid., pp. 23–24.

16. When the Bourbons came to power in Spain, at the outset of the eighteenth century their response to growing dissatisfaction in the colonies was to reform political and economic structures, in order to make colonial government more responsive to the monarchy's needs, as well as to criticisms from the colonial elite. Particular attention was paid to liberalization of the mercantilist system in order to stimulate economic activity and hence profits and tax revenues. This was part of an effort to make Spain less dependent on Northern European financiers to whom the crown had increasingly turned for loans since the sixteenth century. The Bourbon reforms concentrated on attempts to generate new income from the colonies through intensified exploitation of new and old mineral deposits and the expansion of production of certain agricultural commodities. Efforts were also made to reduce illegal trade and commerce, while allowing greater freedom via approved channels. Increasing prosperity in some portions of the empire helped expand the monarchy's base for imperial control—the colonial elite. It also increased the latter's demands for greater participation in government and economic benefits. As long as the crown responded to these groups, they helped stabilize it; when it did not or could not, they often became passive or withdrew support.

17. Free trade to the creole merchant did not mean the same as it did for the North American. It implied freedom for all Spanish merchant interests within the monopolistic structure rather than freedom from it, John Lynch, *Spanish Colonial Administration, 1782–1810: The Intendant System in the Viceroyalty of the Rio de la Plata* (London: Athlone Press, 1958), p. 12.

18. The mainland Spanish colonies achieved their independence by the mid-1820s, while the Dominican Republic did not do so until 1844. Cuba and Puerto Rico remained colonies until 1898. The transfer of the seat of the Portuguese monarchy to Brazil in 1811 after the Napoleonic invasion of the Iberian Peninsula helped postpone the establishment of the Brazilian Republic until 1889.

19. Richard Herr, *The Eighteenth-Century Revolution in Spain* (Princeton, N.J.: Princeton University Press, 1969), pp. 341; 347; 440–441.

20. Changes in government continue to be perceived by many Bolivians as having little relation to them. When asked to comment on the naming of a new president by the military in the summer of 1981, Victoria Suxo, an Aymara Indian woman, succinctly summarized a general feeling by saying, "Life here is a little sad. . . we do not earn much money. We get no help from any president." Edward Schumacher, "For the Bolivian Peasant, Politics Are Remote," *The New York Times,* 8 September 1981, p. A12.

21. For an analysis of this, see Alfred Stepan, "The Continuing Problem of Brazilian Integration: The Monarchical and Republican Periods," in Frederick B. Pike, ed., *Latin American History, Select Problems: Identity, Integration and Nationhood* (New York: Harcourt, Brace & World, 1969), pp. 259–296.

22. For an analysis of this, see Stanley J. Stein and Barbara H. Stein, *The Colonial Heritage of Latin America: Essays on Economic Dependence in Perspective* (New York: Oxford University Press, 1970) and Celso Furtado, *Development and Underdevelopment* (Berkeley: University of California Press, 1962), Chapter 2. For summaries of recent theoretical developments and some critiques of dependency theory, see Fernando Enrique Cardoso, "The Consumption of Dependency Theory in the United States," *Latin American Research Review,* 12, 3 (1977: 7–25 and David Roy, "The Dependency Model of Latin American Development: Three Basic Fallacies." *Journal of Interamerican Studies,* 15, 1 (February 1977): 4–20.

23. An excellent description of the inefficacy of the law in protecting Indian rights to land guaranteed by colonial grants is contained in John Womack, *Zapata and the Mexican Revolution* (New York: Random House, 1970). Of note is the fact that frustration with partisan judiciaries helped generate support for the overthrow of Díaz. Participation in the Revolution of 1910–1917 did not, hovever, result in securing Indian lands, but rather brought to power a new elite coalition which continued policies of exclusion.

24. A catalogue of such struggles is contained in J. Lloyd Mecham's *Church and State in Latin America: A History of Politico-Ecclesiastical Relations* (Chapel Hill: University of North Carolina Press, 1966).

25. Restrictions on the holding of property, other than that required

for specific religious purposes, resulted in the sale of a large number of ecclesiastical landed estates. These were, by and large, purchased by the oligarchy or by upwardly mobile members of the petit bourgeoisie. It caused the church to come into possession of substantial liquid assets which served to transform it into one of the principal sources of capital in late nineteenth century Mexico.

26. Claude Pomerleau, "The Missionary Dimension of the Latin American Church: A Study of French Diocesan Clergy from 1963–1971" (Ph.D. dissertation, University of Denver, n.d.), pp. 1–14.

27. For origins and nature of these movements, see Chapter 3, notes 23 and 24.

28. S. N. Eisenstadt, "Traditional Patrimonialism and Modern Neo-Patrimonialism," M.S., 1972, p. 171.

29. James C. Strause and Richard P. Claude hypothesize that "the greater the level of political stability, social development, and economic development per capita, the more civil and political rights are expressed and made available; but the more rapid the rates of economic development, the less civil liberties and political rights are expressed and made available." James C. Strause and Richard P. Claude, "Empirical Comparative Rights Research: Some Preliminary Tests of Development Hypothesis," in Claude, ed., *Comparative Human Rights,* p. 54.

30. Vicaría de Solidaridad del Arzobispado de Santiago de Chile, *Estudios sobre la doctrina de la seguridad nacional y régimen militar* (Santiago de Chile: Arzobispado de Santiago de Chile, 1977), pp. 6–10, 73–74; Aldo Büntig, "The Churches of Latin America in Confrontation with the State and the Ideology of National Security: The Reality and Its Causes," *Pro Mundi Vita,* 71 (March–April, 1978): 1–36; Genaro Arriagada et al., *Las fuerzas armadas en la sociedad civil (Alemania, USA, URSS, y América Latina)* (Santiago de Chile: Centro de Investigaciones Socioeconómicas, 1978), pp. 153–156, 191, 220–21; Roberto Calvo, "The Church and the Doctrine of National Security," *Journal of Interamerican Studies and World Affairs,* 21, 1 (February 1979): 69–88. José Comblin, *The Church and the National Security State* (Maryknoll, N.Y.: Orbis Books, 1979), pp. 56–63; Tomás Amadeo Vasconi, *Gran capital y militarización en América Latina* (Mexico: Ediciones Era, S.A., 1978), pp. 18–25; David Collier, ed., *The New Authoritarianism in Latin America* (Princeton, N.J.: Princeton University Press, 1979).

31. Alejandro Foxley, "Stabilization Policies and Their Effects on Employment and Income Distribution," paper presented at the Brookings Institution Conference on Economic Stabilization Policies in Less Developed Countries, Washington, D.C., 25 October 1979, pp. 23–24; 31.

32. For detailed analysis of the origins and ideology of these national security states, see Chapters 2 and 3 in this volume.

33. For detailed examinations of the contribution of Latin American, European, and U.S. sources to the emergence of national security states, see Chapters 2, 3, and 9 in this volume.

34. Perhaps the most influential such study is Guillermo A. O'Donnell's *Modernization and Bureaucratic Authoritarianism* (Berkeley: University of California Institute of International Studies, 1973), pp. vii; 51. O'Donnell argues that there is a "marked 'elective affinity' between contemporary South American situations of high modernization with bureaucratic-authoritarianism." He further states that "in contemporary South America, the higher and lower levels of modernization are associated with non-democratic political systems, while political democracies are found at the intermediate levels of modernization." O'Donnell offers this argument to challenge the assumption that more stable democratic structures occur in countries undergoing considerable economic growth. This underlying presumption of 1960s development theory tended to place the blame for failure to achieve political democracy on people rather than structures. O'Donnell also criticizes the presumption of evolutionary progress on the grounds that the only way it could be valid were if the causal processes operating today were similar to those that brought about earlier democracies. He concludes that:

> First, the higher levels of contemporary South American modernization are not associated with political democracies. Second, the Argentine and Brazilian bureaucratic-authoritarian systems can hardly be conceived as having increased the probabilities of establishment and consolidation of political democracies in these countries. Third, until much more solid and better focused evidence is brought forth, there are no reasons to believe that the chances of survival of the existing South American political democracies are significantly higher than those of their breakdown in an authoritarian direction. Fourth, as modernization proceeds, there is an indeterminate but considerable probability that such authoritarian breakdowns will fall within the "bureaucratic" category. . . . Fifth, the basic paradigm and its underlying assumption of equivalence of causal processes are not supported by the South American cases (p. 114).

For refinements of O'Donnell's thesis by himself and other scholars, see Collier.

MARGARET E. CRAHAN

2. The Evolution of the Military in Brazil, Chile, Peru, Venezuela, and Mexico: Implications for Human Rights

INTRODUCTION

The overthrow of elected civilian governments in Brazil, Argentina, Peru, Bolivia, Uruguay, Chile, Ecuador, and the Dominican Republic in the 1960s and 1970s generally initiated periods of widespread human rights violations. In Brazil, Argentina, Uruguay, and Chile the military have retained power and indicated they intend to maintain control for as long as they deem necessary to fully reconstruct—morally, institutionally, and materially—their countries.[1] Their goal is not the traditional one of imposing order and then returning to the barracks, but rather the implantation of new structures to foster their nations' economic and political potential. Such action is directed at remedying what the military regard as the prime failure of civilian government: to provide the nation with strong direction, to diminish domestic conflict, to maintain high levels of honesty and competency in government, and to transcend partisan politics.

Military intervention has been a constant in Latin American history, in the Spanish and Portuguese colonies there was a strong tendency to mingle civilian and military authority, as well as ecclesiastical, in an effort to maintain order in far-flung possessions and ensure that metropolitan authority would supersede local autonomy. The actual struggle for independence and its aftermath reinforced the heritage of military involvement in politics, with civilian elites turning to armies to resolve regional, constitutional, and other conflicts. In addition, the military came to inherit some of the traditional mediating functions of the crown. The incorporation of a Moderating Power in the 1821 Constitution of Gran Colombia by Simon Bolívar demonstrated belief among the creole elite in the necessity of a power above and beyond those normally specified by republican forms of government. Its purpose was to intercede when normal governmental authority failed. Despite attempts to establish non-military instruments for conflict resolution that could be called upon when the executive, legislative, judicial branches of government were deadlocked, it was the army that was most frequently sought out.

This heritage has contributed to the frequency of military interventions up to the present. It was reinforced in the 1960s and 1970s by a deepening sense of national crisis, generally characterized by increased political polarization, subversion, and escalating economic problems, such as inflation, worsening balance of trade, and rapidly growing foreign debt. These problems developed against a backdrop of post-World War II international political and economic readjustments, including the Cold War and growing popular pressures for greater economic and political participation. Not surprisingly, the latter came to be linked with the former, and domestic subversion was regarded as the result of the manipulation of the dispossessed by radicals, principally Marxists. In Latin America, the Cold War threat was defined in terms not so much of external attack, but of internal subversion.

In the face of repeated failures by civilian governments to eliminate guerrilla threats, terrorism, and internal strife, or achieve substantial economic progress, the armed forces in a number of countries came to regard themselves as the only instrument capable of eliminating barriers to the realization of a more stable and prosperous order. Elements within the military came to believe that the power of the state had to be augmented and the armed forces allowed unrestricted authority in matters of national security. Given the fact that national security was defined to encompass virtually all aspects of community and individual life, adoption of this criterion was usually accompanied by large-scale restrictions and violations of human rights.

Confidence in their capacity to govern better than civilian politicians was rooted in the limitations of the latter and encouraged by military professionalization. As early as the 1890s European military missions stimulated some Latin American officers to regard themselves as the only effective protectors of national interests in times of crisis. Foreign advisers also contributed to the disparagement of civilian politicians and Western democracy. The United States, England, and France came to be regarded as decadent and incapable of effectively resisting the inroads of secularism and Marxism. In countries such as Brazil, Argentina, Uruguay, Chile, and Peru these views stimulated the abandonment by the armed forces of the principle of the subordination of the military to civilian power. They also led to attempts to transform society in accordance with principles derived from the experience of the armed forces.

It is the purpose of this essay to explore the nature of this experience, in an effort to identify factors that encourage the establishment of military regimes in which a high degree of repression leads to the violation of human rights. The countries to be examined reflect considerable variety in terms of political and economic evolution, as well as present tendencies. Brazil and Chile have military regimes which espouse national security ideology and have records of large-scale human rights violations. [2] Peru until July 1980 had a military government molded, in part, by some of the same ideological currents as Brazil and Chile, but which took a less obviously repressive and more flexible path, utilizing since 1968 the rhetoric of revolution and some redistributive reforms to diminish the growth of discontent and subversion. Venezuela's and Mexico's civilian governments maintain a high degree of social control via sophisticated blends of cooptation, political manipulation, and distribution of governmental services and benefits, the latter facilitated by substantial oil revenues. Power in Mexico is exercised principally through an integrating, corporative single-party system refined repeatedly since the 1920s. Venezuela has a two-party dominant multi-party system that utilizes negotiation, compromise, and the distribution of benefits to promote stability. These countries were chosen for the diversity of their historical development, resources, and present political and economic structures in an effort to identify those elements that explain the imposition of long-term authoritarian military rule and substantial human rights violations.

This study suggests several factors that combine to encourage or discourage intervention by the armed forces. These include the severity of the political and economic crisis in their countries, the extent of internal subversion and pressures for structural changes, and a determination of the capacity of the incumbent civilian government. How objectively the latter is evaluated is influenced by generalized attitudes within the armed forces toward civilian politicians and traditional political forms and behavior.

These attitudes are molded, in good measure, by the nature of civilian-military interaction and relations over time, as well as by the expectations each has of the other. If, in attempting to deal with crises, civilian governments become dependent on the military, the latter are encouraged to believe in their superior capacity to govern. Attempts by civilian administrations to involve the armed forces in government can also be construed by the military as threats to its institutional autonomy and integrity, particularly in countries where military isolation has been traditional. In countries where civilian-military relations are more intimate, the courting and cooptation of offices is generally not regarded as a threat to institutional autonomy.

The nature of the professionalization of a military establishment also influences the inclination to intervene, as well as the orientation of the regime thus established.[3] The type and extent of exposure to foreign military training and the attitudes encouraged are also significant. Foreign military advisers can be the transmitters of ideological currents that reinforce beliefs generated by the specific historical evolution of the military. Where ideology and experience encourage authoritarian responses to challenges to the established order, human rights violations often occur.

I. BRAZIL

The institutional development of the Brazilian army was quite limited prior to the Paraguayan War (1865–1870). This conflict clearly indicated the need for greater military training, as well as for more commitment of men and materiel to allow the army to discharge its constitutional responsibilities to defend Brazil against external attack and maintain internal order. Since 1870 Brazil has not been seriously threatened by a foreign war, but frequent uprisings and rebellions have made internal security a concern.

From the end of the Paraguayan War through the establishment of the Republic in 1889, Brazilian army officers reflected two divergent concepts of themselves. One view was held by those who had come up through the ranks, another by those who had graduated from military school where they were exposed to European intellectual currents. The former accepted military intervention in politics to strengthen the army institutionally and benefit themselves personally in terms of power and prestige. The latter regarded themselves as "armed civilians" and believed that industrialization would open up an era of progress that would eliminate the need for armies. Before the military could disappear, however, it was necessary to strengthen and reform it, so that it could contribute to national development.[4] Up to the 1880s, however, civilian officials did not share this view, and the role of the army was limited. As a consequence, the officers corps tended to turn inwards, developing a view of themselves as self-sacrificing and superior to politicians whom they regarded as frequently corrupt, venal, and lacking in patriotism. This encouraged the military to assist in terminating the empire and in establishing a republic in 1889, in which it initially participated. The vicissitudes of governing, however, eventually led the officers to withdraw.[5]

Direct involvement in government did, however, sharpen the desire of the military to increase its capacity to contribute to and benefit from national development, particularly in the economic and technological spheres. This, in turn, stimulated interest in more sophisticated training, which was also encouraged by the modernization in the pre-World War I period of the army of Brazil's traditional rival, Argentina. Hence, beginning in 1910 officers were sent to Europe to serve in the Prussian army. It was not, however, until 1919 that European military missions began arriving on a regular basis. While German, Belgian, and French officers were all involved, the last predominated. [6]

Exposure to European military missions raised the level of professionalization and hence institutional identification and pride. It encouraged the belief within the officer corps that they represented the only truly national institution, characterized by a high order of patriotism, above partisan politics and personal aggrandizement. This sense of superiority compensated the military for what they felt was a general lack of government support and even occasional public disparagement. They could thus ascribe their weaknesses to the politicians, rather than to themselves. [7] The professionalization of the Brazilian army succeeded in accomplishing two objectives: it decreased personalism in favor of promotion on the basis of merit and strengthened the position that the military should not govern. In fact, it was not until 1964 that the Brazilian armed forces arrogated state power to themselves for an indeterminate period. European military missions and the kind of professionalization they encouraged did, nevertheless, stimulate a growing sense within the armed forces of their capacity to direct the nation, as well as ideas about the way it should be done. The latter grew out of exposure to European political thought and models that were in many cases rooted in critiques of democracy.

Foreign military advisers also argued strongly for a national draft to strengthen the Brazilian army. It was adopted in 1916 after two decades of debate. The draft was justified, partially, on the grounds that it would contribute to national development and progress by raising the physical and intellectual level of recruits, who would thereupon return to their communities and pass on their newly acquired skills and civic virtues. This, in turn, would contribute to the demise of regional political bosses who were seen by a good number of army officers as a barrier to the realization of Brazil's potential and the consequent improvement of the well-being of the population in general.

The potential contribution of widespread military training to national development was conceived of as enormous by its supporters. As one of them phrased it:

> The nation, that is, the remade people under middle-class leadership, would be the army; and the army, reformed, restructured, redirected, would be the nation. . . . The officer was the priest of the cult of the nation, and as such should flee from political ambition and

involvement. The officer would be the regenerator and disciplinarian, the middle-class would govern and direct. [8]

There are interesting similarities between this view and that of the officers who took power in 1964. For example, the emphasis is on the realization of Brazilian greatness through the regeneration of the citizenry aided by the military, as well as an underlying frustration with the traditional political leadership and its alleged particularistic goals; and most notably by the identification of the army with the nation, and the quasi-messianic role of the officer. As priest of the cult of the nation, the officer held superior authority on moral grounds. This encouraged a belief in the infallibility and neutrality of the military, as was the case with the traditional Moderating Power.

Brazil, Argentina, Uruguay, and Chile today tend to use this same position to justify absolute governmental authority and obedience to it by the populace. It also underlies their expectation that the Catholic Church and its ministers will be their natural allies and helps explain their pique when this is not always the case. There is, nevertheless, a major difference between the view quoted and current military thinking in those countries. In the early part of the century most officers believed the political role of the army consisted in supporting and molding civilian government rather than directly wielding power.

While the Brazilian army did experiment with direct political action on the national level, most notably via the *tenntes* movement in the 1920s, the general view remained that professional military establishments best left government in the hands of civilians. Such sentiments coexisted with increased involvement in politics on all levels, including state and local. The latter was promoted by the establishment in the 1920s of military installations in most states. Expansion of their presence throughout Brazil augmented the army's awareness of the extent of the country's problems and helped generate interest in attempting to eradicate them. Internal reforms were undertaken to make the military more efficient and technically skilled. This encouraged greater consideration and debate within the armed forces about national goals and the means to achieve them. The 1920s and 1930s were, as a consequence, a period of considerable ferment within the Brazilian military.

Expansion and modernization of the army increased self-esteem and encouraged military prejudice against civilian politicians, particularly in the face of corruption and periodic disorders. Technological and other training suggested that the military could if it wished, solve national problems more efficiently, finding remedies in science and technology, rather than in political debates. The inclination of the military was increasingly away from democratic participation in governmental decision making to hierarchically structured corporate societies in which substantial inequities were accepted. This view, already strong during the colonial period, was encouraged by French and German advisors. The military, regarding itself as the most patriotic, self-sacrificing, and efficient national institution, would naturally occupy a preeminent position, both politically and morally.

Resistance to the direct exercise of power within the military continued to be relatively strong, however, and contributed to the downfall in 1930 of the military officer turned president, Washington Luiz. The subesquent installation of Getulio Vargas as chief executive with some military support reflects the armed forces' very real ambivalence. Vargas' chief of staff, Pedro A. de Góes Monteiro, a regular army officer, advocated an independent political stance for the army, in order for it to avoid being manipulated by civilian political interests. In addition, he strongly reflected the growing nationalism and interest in developmental goals common in those Latin American military establishments that were undergoing modernization. Góes constantly promoted patriotism and encouraged national regeneration through improving education, both technical and moral, building highways and railroads for strategic and economic purposes, and collaborating with private industry for national defense purposes.[9] Realization of Brazil's greatness was intimately linked in Góes' mind with modernization of the army, while national security was to be the end result of economic development.[10]

The development of an independent political stance by the Brazilian army was regarded in the 1930s and 1940s as a means of avoiding conflicts based on partisan political allegiances, in contrast to Venezuela where, in the same period, officers tended to align themselves with a specific party bloc. In Brazil a prohibition against involvement in partisan politics was formally sanctioned in 1939 on the grounds that it was necessary to maintain military discipline. Anyone who deviated was to be punished severely.[11] Up to 1964 the Brazilian military continued to resist the idea of governing on a long-term basis.

Institutional identification and a broader world view in the officer corps was encouraged during World War II by the presence of a 20,000-man expeditionary force fighting with the Allies in Italy. This was further stimulated by the establishment of an Escola Superior de Guerra (ESG) in 1949.[12] Over the next 23 years, the war college trained close to 2,000 students, three-fifths of them civilians. The curriculum focused on three areas: the theory and historical experience of war, which was not limited to actual warfare; preparation for command posts and general staff administration; and intelligence gathering. The first provided the greatest opportunity for the emergence of a national security ideology. Nine of

40 weeks were spent in theoretical studies, while the remainder was devoted to analysis of national problems and possible solutions. The dissemination of the content of these courses to the civilian elite was made possible through actual attendance at the ESG or through short courses held in various cities throughout Brazil. [13] By 1976 it was estimated that more than 25,000 civilians had been reached in this way. [14]

> Civilians who participate in the courses of the ESG are consciously understood to represent elites and consider themselves honored. They are selected by recommendation and come from many fields of influence and decision-making: government, politics, science, business, law, education, or other professions. The ESG clearly aims at inculcating a significant segment of the present and future leadership of the country in the meaning of national security as the college understands it. [15]

Such understanding is molded by a sense of having inherited the role of champion of Western, Catholic civilization, at the very time when it is being strongly attacked by atheistic Communism. Anti-Communism and anti-Marxism are strong. While support for democracy is continually reiterated, it is redefined to emphasize the superiority of state power over individual rights and the rule of law. [16] Defense of Christianity is sometimes used to justify extreme action, although the institutional identification of the army and the Catholic Church has diminished. In some cases, as in the Archdiocese of São Paulo, the church is the source of considerable criticism and opposition to the military government.

Both domestic and international criticism are regarded by the military as inspired by Marxists and others opposed to a developmental model that emphasizes free play of market forces together with considerable direct governmental intervention in industrial development, monetary policy, and planning. Substantial growth rates are sought largely through high levels of investment—both foreign and domestic—encouraged by government incentives. In this fashion it is hoped that sufficient resources will be generated to allow the government to provide more social services, while at the same time increasing salaries in the private sector to permit greater purchasing power across the board.

At the ESG economic development is seen as the basis for the nation's security and the means to involve the entire population in the realization of the nation's destiny as a world power and defender of Western civilization. However, strong arguments have been made that the most substantial limitations on the accomplishment of these goals stem precisely from the tendency of the Brazilian developmental model to reinforce existing socioeconomic disparities. [17] Given the military's restriction of broad-based political participation, pressures for modifying the economic model to allow for greater distributive equity have not been very effective. The response of the military to such pressures, which recently have been coming from a cross-section of Brazilian society, is to continue strongly regulating political participation.

To reestablish stability in the 1960s the military leadership sought to eliminate traditional vehicles of political and economic competition within society through the suppression or control of political parties, politicians, and unions, together with the repression or elimination of those who would protest. After taking power in 1964, the military declared states of siege and emergency which allowed them to rule by decree or institutional acts which superseded existing laws and the constitution. These were used to suspend the political rights of a good number of civilian politicians, to restructure and tame the Congress, to create an official party and a mild opposition, and to grant exceptional powers to the security forces.

Overall, such actions were not entirely successful in curbing civilian opposition nor in silencing the critics of the regime within the ranks of the military. As early as 1964–65 strains developed between the military and civilian initiators of the coup. These tensions were partly the result of the failure of the generals to turn the government over to their civilian supporters, as expected by some. Others were generated by the offended nationalism of those who objected to economic policies, designed to attract foreign investment, that involved considerable concessions to foreign interests. Such policies, plus the rise in purchasing capacity of the upper 25 to 30 percent of the population that stimulated a strong demand for imported goods, contributed to an escalating foreign debt whose reduction was a prime justification for the 1964 coup.

Opposition to these and other policies led to the formation of new political groups among workers, students, churchpeople, professionals, and others. The government responded to dissent with purges of universities, labor unions, and the national and state governments, together with the deprivation of individual political rights. Strikes, protests, and demonstrations prompted strong response, including increased surveillance of dissident organizations and individuals. Government losses in the 1965 gubernatorial elections encouraged the military to undertake further political restructuring. All existing political parties were suppressed and two new ones were created: the progoverment Aliança Renovadora Nacional (ARENA) and the Movimento Democrático Brasileiro (MDB), representing the approved opposition. Political protests were outlawed as threats to national security

During the presidency of General Arturo da Costa e Silva (1967–1969), guerrilla forces attempted to overthrow the military regime.

This, together with continued nonviolent protests and denunciations of state terror by some members of congress, led to a substantial increase in repression and eventually the promulgation of Institutional Act #5 in December 1968. It dissolved congress, suspended habeas corpus for all those accused of subversion (which was broadly interpreted), and limited other civil and political rights. Torture of political prisoners continued, as well as other extralegal activities by the armed forces and police. By the early 1970s both violent and nonviolent dissent had been suppressed at considerable cost to human rights.

The 1970s have, however, witnessed the recuperation and strengthening of the conservative, moderate, and progressive opposition. Failure of the government to sustain growth, a decline in real wages for a majority of the population, growing distaste for heavy-handed repression even among the supporters of the regime, together with international pressures, helped coalesce the opposition and diminish civilian support for the military. Attempts to generate popular support for the government and its policies through strong appeals to nationalism have not been notably successful.

Some positive results have flowed from the government's social security system (INPS), housing programs, such as the National Housing Bank (BNH), and the campaign to eliminate illiteracy (MOBRAL). Initiation of these programs, however, has added to pressures on the government for even greater social services. Attempts to expand public services through the Program for Social Integration (PIS), Project for National Integration (PIN), Program of Assistance to the Rural Worker (PRORURAL), and Program of Land Redistribution and of Stimulus to the Agrarian Economy of the North and Northeast (PROTERRA) have not generated widespread popular support, in large measure because of their limited impact.[18] Such efforts have also not succeeded in eliminating the government's dependence on force, although the military has generally abandoned heavy-handed repressive measures for more sophisticated means of social control. In fact, the government in 1978 and 1979 allowed the return of several thousand political exiles who have added to the ferment already underway in the Brazilian body politic. While some liberalization has occurred, the government continues to impose strict political controls on labor unions, political parties, and the press, and continues to limit political participation.

All this the military considers necessary to contain the pressures generated by limited popular participation in government and by difficult socioeconomic conditions. Despite the failure of the growth model of development to achieve major inroads on poverty, and despite rising inflation and foreign debt, the government reaffirmed its commitment to it in 1979 by turning to some of those individuals who were involved in its original formulation and implementation in the 1960s. At the same time government efforts are continuing to undercut criticism of Brazil's dependence on foreign investment, loans, and technology. These include attempts to stimulate nationalist feeling by presenting Brazil as a leader of the nonaligned, declaring its independence of U.S. foreign policy, and developing its own nuclear potential and arms industry. Talk of democracy by the military leadership has increased, but it continues to be defined in terms of a controlled, corporate society in which the military will be the ultimate arbiter of national goals and the common good.

II. CHILE

The first military school in Latin America was established in Chile in 1817. It was not, however, until the 1880s that a modern professional army began emerging. In the aftermath of the struggle for independence, civilian control of the military was a prime objective of the conservative leader Diego Portales, who, as a cabinet minister in the 1890s, stimulated creation of a civilian militia to counterbalance the regular army. While there were brief uprisings in 1851 and 1859, overall the army did not engage in direct political intervention, partly because of institutional weaknesses and lack of clearly enunciated, coherent goals. In addition, foreign wars in 1837–1839 and 1879–1883, together with the military subjugation of the indigenous population, drained energies that might have sought other outlets.

The War of the Pacific (1879–1883), like the Paraguayan War for the Brazilians, revealed the limitations of the Chilean army and stimulated a desire for modernization. Victory over Peru and Bolivia in 1883 and fear of retaliation made Chile even more eager to strengthen its armed forces. As in Argentina and Brazil, Chile turned to Europe for military advisers and in 1885 arranged for Captain Emil Körner, a Prussian officer, to teach courses at the Academia Militar in artillery, infantry, cartography, military history, and tactics. He helped establish the Academia de Guerra in 1886. Over the next quarter century a modern, well-equipped, and educated army was created in Chile.

The purpose of this school was to provide officers with scientific and technical instruction in the first two years of training; nontechnical subjects were added in the last year. The latter included Chilean military history, Latin American geography, international law, and world history. This curriculum built a coherent, standardized world view among the military, and exposed them to European political thought. The latter provided arguments to justify the army's intervention in 1891 in the conflict between President José Manuel Balmaceda and congress, although the officer corps split, some supporting the former while Körner and his followers backed the congress.

After the defeat of the Balmaceda forces, Körner and his allies purged the army of their opponents, and the Prussian became Chief of the General Staff. In this position he insisted on the importation of German armaments and advisers who not only taught at the Academia de Guerra and Escuela Militar, but also served on active duty. Chilean officers who had studied in Germany in the early part of the twentieth century generally dominated command positions. In 1906 Körner succeeded in having the army reorganized along the lines of the German Imperial Army. The lack of trained officers to fill a good number of staff positions meant filling some posts with incompetents who had political connections; this aroused discontent within the army. [19]

Generalized resentment of certain aspects of the modernization program, together with criticism of civilian politicians, led to the formation in 1907 of the secret Liga Militar. This organization worked for a more rational military promotion system, increased salaries and other benefits, larger budgets, and overall improvement of the situation of the army. Possible solutions for Chilean socioeconomic problems were also discussed. This helped make the officer corps more consciously critical of ineffective, corrupt civilian governments. An economic slump in post-World War I Chile heightened the military's contempt for civilian politicians and increased their tendency to consider the possibility of intervening. Much of the criticism focused on the continuing dominance of the executive by a torpid congress. In order to strengthen the executive branch and reorganize the legislature, President Arturo Alessandri Palma in 1924 called upon the army to supervise congressional elections in an effort to ensure the victory of reform-minded deputies. Such military involvement in politics was widely criticized and helped precipitate Alessandri's resignation in September of that year. He was succeeded by a group of officers who believed that the military was the national institution best equipped to accomplish national regeneration.

Because of opposition both inside and outside the army to military government, Alessandri was able to resume the presidency in March of 1925. The involvement of elements of the officer corps, led by Lieutenant Colonels Carlos Ibañez del Campo and Marmaduke Grove Vallejo, continued, however, during the rest of his tenure and that of the ineffectual conservative President Emiliano Figueroa Larraín. The constitution promulgated in September 1925 showed evidence of military influence in its strengthening of the executive, fiscal reform, and certain progressive labor and welfare provisions. These reforms aimed at creating a docile, skilled working class, and were similar to the program of Spanish modernists in the same period. [20] Military reform did not prevent the armed forces from forcibly putting down labor unrest in Iquique in May–June 1925 and later that year in Antofagasta and Tarapaca.

While there were some differences within the military over the nature and degree of its involvement in politics, there was a general sense that when the armed forces judged civilian government incapable of maintaining stability and promoting progress, then it was the military's duty to step in. Ibañez del Campo, the most prominent of the officers, sharply criticized members of the Chilean legislature "of irresponsibility and lack of concern for national needs." These, he claimed, made the people "susceptible to extreme leftist propaganda." He also disputed "the right of senators and deputies to criticize the army, in or out of congressional session." [21] Implicit in this was a sense of the moral superiority of the military, whose greater concern for the populace put them above criticism, a characteristic shared by the officers who staged the coup of September 1973. Ibañez and his colleagues also had a vision of the military as the ultimate guardian of the country's destiny and its last recourse, not only in the face of external threat but also in confronting the chaos accompanying periods of rapid change. [22]

In 1927 Ibañez del Campo, a distinguished graduate of the Academia de Guerra who had also trained in Germany, took over the presidency. He believed firmly in the capacity of technology to solve Chile's socio-economic problems. Progress in the economic sphere was accompanied by a curtailing of political rights on the part of an authoritarian government that lacked confidence in liberal democratic solutions to Chile's problems.

After Ibañez's exit from office in July 1931, fellow officers continued to intervene, elevating Marmaduke Grove to the presidency. The difficulties of direct political involvement in the 1924–1932 period generated self-doubt within the military and loss of prestige and discouraged intervention for the next 40 years. The attitudinal and ideological base remained, however, for such a step. [23]

A review of the contents of the Chilean army journal, *Memorial del Ejército de Chile*, from 1930–1932 tends to confirm this. While most articles were devoted to technical subjects, certain ones gave a prominent role to the army in the social and intellectual development of the citizen and emphasized the necessity of the union of state, industry, and military for successful national development. They also praised a disciplined work force that was obedient to the nation's leadership and demonstrated a spirit of sacrifice. European, particularly French, views of the special responsibilities of the officer to society were also promoted. [24]

During the 1940s the challenges presented first by facism and then by communism resulted in some muting of military criticism of liberal democracy. Nevertheless, army publications accused it of contributing to moral laxness, lack of intellectual rigour, deleterious social leveling, and a general decay in civic virtues. While this was not a major theme, it was a recurrent one. [25] There also appeared in this period more interest in military history and a tendency to harken back to periods of alleged Chilean greatness and tranquility.

With the decline in economic growth in the late 1940s and early 1950s, doubts about the capacity of civilian governments to promote national development increased. Civilian control of the military was questioned within the armed forces and some disaffected officers began to organize discussion groups. Interest in geopolitics and the works of Argentine, Brazilian, and European national security theorists surfaced. [26] Studies of economic development which focused on models that strongly emphasized growth were disseminated in military journals. Beginning in the mid-1960s publications by Chilean officers concerning geopolitics increased. [27]

Other publications attacked socialist reform programs, particularly as the possibility of a Marxist takeover of the government through the electoral process became more real in the 1960s. Thirty years earlier, Communist participation in the Popular Front electoral coalition of President Pedro Aguirre Cerda generated considerable hostility among certain elements of the military, even though the Communist Party refused representation in the cabinet. Fear of Marxism contributed to an attempted coup in June 1939, led by officers who were influenced by Italian fascism. [28] With the emergence of the Cold War in the post-World War II period, anti-Marxist attitudes among Chilean officers enjoyed a resurgence as they did in Argentina and Brazil. This was accompanied by a tendency to reevaluate fascism more positively, ascribing events in Europe to the weakness of unstable leaders (Hitler and Mussolini). There is no hard evidence that these views were held by a majority of military men, but they were present among an influential number. [29]

Some anti-Marxist officers allied themselves in the late 1940s with the civilian constituted Acción Chilena Anticomunista and unsuccessfully laid plans for a coup in the fall of 1948 that was aimed at installing a government that would totally uproot Communism and impose the calm regarded as necessary for unfettered economic development. Civilian and military supporters of anti-Communism did succeed in having the Law for Defense of Democracy, which suppressed the Communist Party, passed in that year. [30]

The organization in Santiago of the military lodges Por Una Mañana Auspiciosa (PUMA) in 1952 and La Línea Recta in 1955 were further expressions of strong anti-Communism and belief in the necessity of authoritarian government to realize Chilean national potential. The program of the latter included:

> establishment of a type of corporate state, the need for anti-Communist legislation, of labor reorganization into "vertical syndicates" of owners and workers by economic activity, suppression of the right to strike of workers in public utilities and producers of primary necessities and mandatory arbitration of labor disputes by the state. . . . [31]

These objectives are quite similar to those of the Chilean military men who took power in September 1973, the major difference being the refusal of the former to take political control into their own hands. That such views were not yet dominant is evidenced as late as 1970 by the fact that the military resisted intervening to prevent Salvador Allende from assuming the presidency, in spite of internal and external pressures.

When they did act in 1973, it was after having lost confidence in the capacity of a civilian government to maintain stability while accomplishing substantial socioeconomic reforms. Only after Chilean society entered into a severe crisis did military intervention occur. This challenges the frequent conclusion that Augusto Pinochet and his allies acted simply in response to bourgeoisie pressures and in pursuit of their limited interests. Quite obviously, the military and the bourgeoisie, as did other groups, desired a return to a calmer era. Since support for civilian government was far stronger among the middle and upper classes than support for authoritarian military government, it was only after Chile entered into a period of severe political and economic crisis that civilian acceptance of military intervention grew. [32]

The military does not act simply in response to pressures from the bourgeoisie. The armed forces decide to intervene or not on the basis of their own analysis of the nation's political and economic health, although they share some of the same views as the bourgeoisie. In the Chilean case, action by the military was precipitated by the conclusion that the situation was out of control and highly damaging to the country. Conditions under the Unidad Popular (UP) government tended to confirm the armed forces' prejudices regarding civilian politicians and highlighted the weaknesses they attributed to liberal democracy. Since the chief. critics of civilian government and traditional democratic forms were the conservative officers, this gave them an edge in assuming ideological and practical leadership. Frustration with elected governments and with participatory democracy was common within the professional military and surfaced repeatedly, most notably in the 1890s and 1920s. High levels of instability during Allende's tenure caused it to burst forth once again with a vengeance. This helps explain why the military forces that took power in September 1973 were not inclined to relinquish it once order was restored, as some civilian politicians had expected.

The Chilean case suggests that relatively strong traditions of democratic participation and civilian government are not sufficient barriers to military intervention unless governments have a fair degree of success in mediating competing socioeconomic and political claims within society. Where that capacity is severely diminished because of administrative weaknesses, structural impediments, domestic political polarization, or international pressures, the possibility of a coup increases. A sense of generalized crisis within society can override those aspects of military professionalism that discourage direct political action by the armed forces. While professionalization does discourage intervention, it also encourages the armed forces to trust in their capacity to succeed where civilians, who are thought to lack the same level of commitment, loyalty to the country, experience in command, and organizational efficiency, have failed.

Where geopolitics and national security theory provide ideological justifications for the imposition of hierarchical, authoritarian military government on a more than temporary basis, the likelihood of intervention is even greater. This suggests that the proximate cause of authoritarian military governments is profound systemic crises within society. It is even more likely where elements within the military believe that the armed forces are the only means of national salvation and regeneration.

In a society with as strong a tradition of civilian government as Chile, however, the extent of crisis must be substantial. One of the prime stimuli to the Chilean political crisis was the attempt of the Unidad Popular government to construct a socialist order in the face of a highly competitive party system rooted in a populace whose ideological positions had remained fairly constant since the 1950s. Even after two years under Allende, the March 1973 congressional elections showed no major shifts in the distribution of conservative, moderate, and left support. The stability of political allegiances in Chile flowed, in part, from the fact that most of the major parties or coalitions had cross-class support, although certain groups were more heavily represented in specific parties than in others.[33] In the 1964 and 1970 presidential election significant numbers of working class voters could be found voting for conservative candidates, and up to 1970 it was the Chilean lower class that was most open to military involvement in politics.[34] This was partially due to substantial differences in income and status within the Chilean working class resulting from the uneven development of the industrial, commercial, and service sectors.[35] Basing their recruitment and mobilization efforts principally on the unions which, due to legal restrictions in the 1960s, represented only 20 percent of the industrial work force, leftist parties in Chile never really gained a broad and cohesive base of working-class electoral support. Moreover, Christian Democrats made inroads into the working class through their social welfare programs initiated during the Frei administration (1964–1970). Privileged blue collar and white collar employees did not give strong support to the Unidad Popular government. Agitation by copper miners, in fact, contributed to Allende's undoing. Among the Allende government's chief problems was that it "not only threatened a small group of wealthy individuals. It also threatened a host of middle and even working class groups that were in a relatively privileged position within an economy of scarce resources."[36] Inflation, substantial declines in real wages, and unemployment under Pinochet are not likely, however, to generate support for military government among these same workers.

The Unidad Popular government was a tenuous coalition of political parties without an integrated political base. This placed limits on the possibility of mobilizing support for substantial change. The very nature of the governmental apparatus undercut reform efforts under Allende since the bureaucracy traditionally did not marshal resources effectively to accomplish the administration's stated goals. Moreover opposition parties, especially the Christian Democrats, were well entrenched in key sectors of the bureaucracy. Nor was the UP equally responsive or accessible to the rising expectations of various groups or individuals that it encouraged.[37] Failure by Allende at the outset of his term to consolidate his power and impose his programmatic objectives on the bureaucracy limited his administration's capacity to respond to the popular pressures it generated. The probability of his being able to do so without a majority of popular as well as congressional support was slight.

In the face of these and other problems, Allende felt impelled to seek support from the armed forces through a policy of cultivation and cooptation, thereby legitimizing greater involvement by the military in government than his civilian predecessors had encouraged. In his attempts to generate loyalty to himself and support for his programs, Allende undercut the role of the Ministry of National Defense in maintaining civilian control over the armed forces. In his search for approval for his programs, he frequently alluded to the responsibilities of the military in national development. These efforts prompted criticism within the army, navy, and air force of the blurring of the lines between the civilian and military spheres. But military men generally accepted Allende's frequent praise more readily than that of leftist parties and publications. Socialist and Communist attempts to win allies among the troops were strongly resented.

Preoccupation within the armed forces over too close an identification with the Allende government (based either on constitutional grounds, or opposition to the objectives and programs of the UP, or a combination of these) was heightened in September 1972 when Allende specifically called on the military to assist in the political and socioeconomic transformation of the country. This attempt to increase the identification of the armed forces with the UP government was pursued further in October 1972 by the naming of officers to high government posts traditionally held by civilians. Such action encouraged the impression that the government could not maintain control without the military, while the increasingly stymied UP administration confirmed military prejudices about the competency and altruism of civilian politicians and the weaknesses of democracy. Allende's attempt to cultivate the armed forces weakened barriers to military intervention and generated intense debate within the officer corps that helped conservatives to clarify and disseminate their positions.[38] The sense that the military's institutional unity and integrity were being undermined by the Unidad Popular government grew and was seen as a threat not only to the military as an institution, but also to the nation.

The ferment generated by Allende's policies toward the military appears to have contributed to the insistence of Pinochet and his allies that their intervention was not politically motivated. While this may be difficult to accept, it is logical if one accepts their definition of politics as being the pursuit of narrow interests to the detriment of the national good. The resulting polarization and disorder, whatever its causes, helped undercut the armed forces' acceptance of civilian rule to the extent that a critical mass of officers lost faith in civilian dominance of the military and became convinced of the need for a new form of government. This loss of faith is comparable to that which preceded the coups in Brazil in 1964 and Peru in 1968.

Hostility toward civilian politicians and parties contributed to the severity of the repression in the aftermath of the September 1973 coup and helps explain why it was not confined to leftist parties and politicians. The disintegration of belief in civilian dominated democratic governments also helps explain the resistance to pressures for a return to civilian rule and the determination of the junta to restructure the Chilean political system to provide for greater centralized control and stability. Rapid changes and generalized social ferment from 1970–1973 fed suspicions among the military that their country was being subverted. The anti-Marxism of some officers made Allende's faltering government appear to be part of an international conspiracy to destroy basic Chilean values. Individuals perceived to be engaged in the subversion of the country, even if only indirectly, were readily designated enemies without the protection of the law. This resulted in wholesale violations of the rights of those who were simply opposed to military government.

Non-intervention by the Chilean armed forces from the 1930s to the 1970s does not mean that they were apolitical. [39] In fact, the period was one of considerable politicization and ideological development within the Chilean military. Because of the traditional isolation of the military within society, this was not readily apparent. However, when crisis enveloped the country in the early 1970s these developments stimulated the Chilean military to direct political action.

While officers, who favored intervention, found some support among civilians, they did not take power at their behest; rather they acted primarily out of military motives rooted in discussions over the political role of the armed forces which had been underway since the nineteenth century. Debate over this issue intensified as the sense of crisis under Allende mounted, further politicizing the military.

Societal crisis in Chile in 1973 was more acute than in Brazil in 1964, thus the higher level of repression in the immediate post-coup period. Distrust and hostility toward political parties and leaders was also greater and contributed to the more exclusionary nature of the Chilean military regime. The ideology of Pinochet and his closest colleagues was not as highly refined as that of the Brazilians and consequently, to date, the Chilean regime has been somewhat less flexible and imaginative in exercising control. There has also been less experimentation with development models. In both countries, however, government economic policies have resulted in increasing maldistribution of income and declines in real wages. Protests against these have led to violations of civil and political rights, although in Brazil there is currently more space for political organizing and protest than in Chile.

III. PERU

While the military men who took power in Peru in October 1968 shared some of the same attitudes as their counterparts in Brazil and Chile, including a sense of pervading national crisis and a loss of faith in civilian politicians and parties, their objectives and actions differed substantially. The institutional development of the Peruvian armed forces emphasized the social responsibility of the military and the need for more distributive justice as a means of neutralizing subversion. The individual backgrounds of many Peruvian officers, together with their professional experiences, made them less insulated from civilians and made them more interested in the socioeconomic problems of the large indigenous population. The exposure of senior officers to a fairly sophisticated political, economic, and social analysis of the Peruvian reality at the Center for Military Instruction (CIMP), beginning in 1948, and after 1950 at the Center for Higher Military Studies (CAEM), also helped.

In addition, Peru did not suffer the same degree of political conflict as did Brazil prior to 1964 and Chile from 1970–1973, in part because a large share of its population was not politically active. The Peruvian officers who took power in 1968 regarded themselves as revolutionaries engaged in the transformation of their society, albeit gradually, so that socioeconomic disparties would not provide fertile ground for subversion. [40]

Military dominated governments appeared with some frequency in twentieth century Peru, including 1919–1933, 1939–1945, 1948–1962, as well as 1968–1980. During the nineteenth century, however, the Peruvian military was anything but dominant. The depth of its institutional weaknesses were sharply revealed by its defeat by Chile in the War of the Pacific (1879–1883). By the end of the century the Peruvian army was suffering from a crisis of confidence, reinforced by difficult political and economic conditions within the country.

Rather than responding positively to requests for resources to build a professional military establishment, Nicolás de Piérola, head of state from 1895–1899, sought to limit its growth. Faced with unstable domestic conditions, he was fearful of military insurrection. The regular army was reduced to 2,000, given a limited budget for arms purchases, and restricted in promotions and salary increases. Although improved economic conditions under Piérola led to salary increases for government employees of from 15 to 50 percent, the armed forces did not share in them. As part of the effort to reinforce civilian control, a French army mission began training programs in Peru in 1896. It was felt that this would not only improve the technical skills and administrative ability of officers, but also discourage any tendencies to intervene directly in politics.

The Peruvian experience in the nineteenth century contrasts with that of Brazil and Chile in the same period. Defeated by Chile in the War of the Pacific, the Peruvian army had less capacity to exact civilian support than did their more successful Chilean and Brazilian counterparts. In addition, while Piérola's determination to rein in the army resembled Portales' efforts in Chile, it occurred 60 years later, when the military in both Chile and Brazil were successfully expanding their role in society and even directly participating in government. The impulse toward greater professionalization was shared by all, however, and prompted Peru to use foreign military advisers.

Foreign advisers were also sought, in part, as a reaction to the build-up of the Chilean army by Emile Körner and by consequent fears of possible aggression from the South. French officers were chosen partially because of a sense that their defeat by the Germans in the 1880s would make them more preoccupied with devising defense strategies against the Prussian-trained Chileans. In addition, certain elements of the ideology of the French officer corps were in tune with Peruvian inclinations. French military conservatism and tendency to view officers as "priests of the fatherland" devoid of any personal interest struck responsive chords in the Andean country. Scant monetary recompense was considered confirmation of an officer's altruism, particularly since materialism was on the rise in both France and Peru.

Assignments to isolated outposts under difficult living conditions were sought to demonstrate a higher level of patriotism than civilians possessed. Rural experience also provided officers with the chance to acquaint themselves with the local population and its problems, in some cases to a greater degree than civilian officials. The antiliberal, antirepublican, proclerical, and anti-Semitic attitudes of some French officers found resonance among certain of their Peruvian counterparts and further contributed to military elitism. [41] Contact with the French military reinforced the Peruvian army's sense that the military was the ultimate champion of national honor and promoter of the country's greatness. This was accompanied by an increasing sense of superiority over politicians and a general contempt for politics. While this discouraged direct military involvement in political affairs, it did not contribute to their depoliticization. Instead, it encouraged disdain for elections, legislatures, courts, and other elements of the democratic process as inferior to the military mode of command. These attitudes were comparable to those which developed within the Brazilan and Chilean military.

Similarly, when threats of political chaos were perceived, the Peruvian armed forces were not entirely unwilling to intervene to restore order and instruct the nation in what they deemed proper civic behavior. [42] As a consequence, the military came to be seen as the guarantors of stability during periods of turmoil and ultimately as the last resort in the face of problems which appeared to overwhelm civilian authorities.

Such was the case of Augusto Leguía, who gained power in 1919. He subsequently was elected president twice with military cooperation. Leguía was not so much the creature of the military as its occasional ally and patron. From 1919 to 1930 he encouraged inter- and intraservice rivalry and used the Guardia Civil as a counterweight to the regular army. Like Piérola, Leguía limited the size of the armed forces, as well as salaries, promotions, budgets, and privileges in order to maintain supreme authority in the manner of the Spanish monarchy of the colonial period. The playing off of one service against another, or of one officer against another, was a favorite tactic of Leguía which generated considerable tension, even within the military high command. Disaffection among more junior officers over the close identification of certain senior officers with Leguía helped bring about his fall in 1930 and the emergence of Lieutenant Colonel Luis M. Sánchez Cerro and other junior officers.

Tensions within the officer corps remained unresolved, however, fueled by generalized societal tensions. As a result, 1930 was a year of sporadic military uprisings, with five juntas in quick succession, and an attempt by insurgent forces to establish a government in Arequipa. Sánchez Cerro and his allies were ultimately able to consolidate their power and install him as president in December of 1931.

Fear among conservative elements of Sánchez Cerro's mildly reformist tendencies contributed to his assassination in 1933 and the taking of power by General Oscar Benavides. His chief objective was to stamp out all challenges to the existing socioeconomic order. To accomplish this Benavides increased and concentrated the powers of the presidency and imported an Italian police mission to create assault units to repress dissent. Benavides was attracted to fascism because of Mussolini's accomplishments, and he believed Italy's experience offered solutions for disorder and lack of economic progress in Peru. Dissident elements within the army, together with civilian opponents, failed to oust Benavides in 1939 or to prevent the government from subsequently being turned over to his ally Dr. Manuel Prado Ugarteche that same year. [43]

From 1939 until the election of Fernando Belaúnde Terry in 1963 the armed forces were involved in various ways in governing Peru, although there was no unanimity within the military over its proper role. Training at the Center for Military Instruction and at the Center for Higher Military Studies increasingly involved the study of national socioeconomic problems. CAEM, in particular, exposed senior officers to international social science literature in a one-year course on contemporary political, economic, and social questions. In addition, in the 1950s and 1960s Peruvian officers went abroad to study not only military, but also nonmilitary subjects. By 1970, 87 percent of the army generals on active duty were CAEM graduates, as were 30 percent of upper echelon Air Force officers and 46 percent of top Navy personnel promoted from 1965 to 1971. [44]

According to the founder of CAEM, General José del Carmen Marín, the prime purpose of the institution was to assist the state in achieving Peru's national potential through planned development. [45] An additional objective was to establish how best the Peruvian military could defend the nation's sovereignty. This involved devising ways to increase the country's political and economic independence, particularly from the United States. A nonaligned foreign policy was considered essential, and after 1968 Peru increased its openness toward Communist countries while promoting regional autonomy within South America. Such steps were seen as necessary to reduce dependence on a specific superpower and to diversify economic relations. It was hoped that this would result in a spurt of economic growth whose benefits would stay within Peru and fund programs to reduce socioeconomic inequities. This, in turn, it was believed, would diminish discontent and the threat of subversion.[46]

Like their counterparts in Brazil and Chile, Peruvian officers in the 1950s and 1960s saw their country entering a period of crisis leading to chaos that could be exploited by the radical left. The Peruvian military, however, due in part to more diverse socioeconomic studies and a lesser degree of isolation than the Brazilian and Chilean military from civilian society came to have a more complex perception of their national reality. In addition, a greater exposure to humanistic elements of Catholic social thought reinforced the officers' sense of social responsibility.[47] Their concern for land and tax reform and worker participation reflected a rather different view of the causes of subversion than that of their Brazilian and Chilean counterparts.

Nevertheless, the Peruvian armed forces still share certain of the attitudes and beliefs of their Brazilian and Chilean colleagues, including strong anti-Communism, lack of confidence in civilian politicians and parties, and belief in the capacity of the military to solve critical socioeconomic and political problems with technical skills. The administration of the reformist President Fernando Belaunde Terry from 1963 to 1968 did not succeed in overcoming opposition to moderate reforms; its corruption and inefficiency only confirmed these sentiments. Military concern over U.S. economic and political influence, heightened by discord over the negotiations for the nationalization of the International Petroleum Corporation holdings at La Brea and Parinas, further reduced confidence in traditional political elites.[48]

On the first anniversary of the military takeover of October 3, 1968, President Juan Velasco Alvarado contrasted the bankruptcy of civilian politicians with the probity, commitment, and capacity of Peru's armed forces. He argued strongly for the legitimacy of the military government on the grounds that it was a direct response to the needs of the people. He also held that the restoration of stability and elimination of violence had earned the government more popular support than its civilian predecessors. This, he believed, had helped restore the confidence of private investors, both domestic and foreign.[49]

Limitations inherent in the Peruvian economy and weaknesses in the regime's economic planning, however, proved to be major constraints on the realization of the military's goals. In order to undercut the traditional economic elite and reduce dependence on foreign capital, the government by 1975 had taken over approximately 50 percent of basic industrial investment. This placed considerable strain on public revenues and encouraged foreign borrowing. In addition, while the government repeatedly reassured private domestic and foreign investors of its commitment to a mixed economy by providing tax incentives, concessions, and other means to stimulate private investment, success in this area was limited. [50]

Between 1969 and 1974 a substantial portion of large landholdings were taken over by the government for the purposes of redistribution. Laws dealing with water rights were adopted in order to facilitate agrarian reform. Profit sharing and participation in management decisions were also introduced in some sectors of the economy, including mining, fishing, and telecommunications. The social security system was upgraded to increase retirement, health, and accident benefits for those previously covered, as well as new groups such as domestic servants. New labor laws improved job security. Overall, however, income was not substantially redistributed and benefits flowing from government reforms generally helped the already advantaged. [51]

Studies of the agrarian reform program have concluded, for example, that it would result in less than one percent redistribution of income and that one-fifth of the rural population would receive three-fourths of the land. Inflation and other factors caused the increased income of peasants to be transferred relatively rapidly to the commercial and industrial sectors. In general, the pattern was repeated with respect to industrial reforms, with only one percent of the workers in this sector benefiting, and these were the most skilled. [52]

Hence the reforms of the military government had limited impact on the large number of very poor. With the adoption of conservative fiscal policies under the presidency of General Francisco Morales Bermúdez beginning in 1976, partially as a result of pressures from the International Monetary Fund and private lenders, improvements for lower and middle class Peruvians further diminished. [53] The general economic situation further suffered from lower than projected national income from oil, copper, and fishing.

Increased criticism of the government in the late 1970s made the military feel unappreciated, and they began to blame opposition on traditional economic elites, both national and international. The military reacted by turning in upon itself, mounting propaganda campaigns to promote its policies, and by repressing the opposition, although not to the extent of Brazil and Chile. Throughout it insisted that only the armed forces had the capacity, patriotism, and altruism to ameliorate Peru's deeply rooted political and socioeconomic problems, even though there was an increasing desire within the military to retire from direct political involvement.

Since the military repeatedly stated that its objective was the creation of an open social democracy, the question of participation was a critical one. The tendency of the military toward aloofness, isolation, and concentration of power in the hands of an exclusive group all militated against this goal. Rule by degrees drafted by military advisers emphasized the paternalistic rather than popular nature of the government. Efforts to generate broad-based support via such mechanisms as SINAMOS bear more resemblance to corporatist hierarchical views of society than democratic ones. [54]

Such efforts were heavily influenced by the government's desire to undercut traditional political and economic actors including the oligarchy, political parties, economic interest groups, labor unions, and the media. The military leadership thought this would facilitate the transformation of society by eliminating barriers to the realization of national potential. The judiciary, educational system, peasant organizations, and bureaucracy were all revamped as part of the restructuring. Of all the traditional institutions, only the Catholic Church escaped criticism, in good measure because it was perceived as an ally and, by and large, supported the military.

Underlying these attempts to create new social groupings within society was a corporatist view of society derived from the medieval Iberian and Spanish colonial experience, together with Catholic views generated in response to eighteenth and nineteenth century political and economic developments in Europe. These same sources helped mold Vargás' Estado Novo in Brazil in the late 1930s, as well as the views of some in the Pinochet government in Chile.

Throughout there was a strong sense of the military as an institution transcending individual interests. In spite of cross-class criticism, the military continued to hold that its actions since 1968 constituted a revolution characterized by "justice, freedom, work, participation, solidarity, creativity, honesty and respect for human dignity." [55] It was a process admittedly based on gradualism for fear that otherwise the forces of prerevolutionary capitalism or Communist statism would triumph.

This opposition not only to Communism, but also to certain forms of capitalism, distinguishes the Peruvian military government from Brazil's and Chile's. The Peruvian model was regarded by its creators as humanist, socialist, Christian, solidary, pluralist, democractic, and participatory. [56] Unfortunately, the changes implemented have not contributed substantially to the creation of an equitable society. In fact, there has been some regression, particularly in terms of the fulfillment of basic needs.

The authoritarianism and paternalism of the military regime that dominated Peru from October 1968 to the summer of 1980 limited popular participation and circumscribed the impact of pressures for more substantial redistributive policies. International economic factors and scarce resources combined with bureaucratic and technological deficiencies to reveal the limits of the military's capacity to solve Peru's economic problems. The confidence that flowed not only from the nature of the army's training in the 1950s and 1960s, but also from the elitism inculcated by professionalization, eventually weakened.

Perhaps the most serious barrier to the transformation of Peru that the military encountered when it took power in 1968 was the tension between the military as government and the military as institution. This impeded the transfer of power to the functional representative groups that the government conceived of as the basis for implementing substantial change. While some officers within the government seem to have wanted to incorporate such organizations into the process of governing, the military as an institution never acquiesced. [57] The government did not, as a consequence, build a viable base, and, not willing to impose the level of repression used in Brazil and Chile, the military eventually returned power to traditional civilian politicians through elections in May 1980.

The historical experience of the Peruvian military tended to isolate it less from the civilian population and its needs than did that of the Brazilian and Chilean armed forces. This was indicated when during the 1960s campaigns against rural guerrillas, the local populations frequently displayed more trust in the army. French military missions and military education in Peru also were rooted in a more humanistic view of society than the Prussian views which influenced the Chileans. While the Peruvian military shared a strong concern for national security, it attempted some balance of redistributive policies and popular participation with the promotion of economic growth. While societal instability was no more acceptable to the Peruvian military, than to the Brazilian and Chilean, its elimination was seen principally in the eradication of social and economic inequalities, rather than in the eradication of subversives. Since the government took social and economic reform as it prime objectives, it enjoyed some popular support and felt less threatened by opposition. When it failed to make major progress toward its goals, and disagreements about government policies threatened the unity of the military as an institution, withdrawal from power seemed more and more a desirable option. This does not suggest, however, that the military is content with civilian government, nor will remain so, particularly if the current civilian government of Fernando Belaunde Terry does not succeed in stimulating economic development and in controlling dissent.

IV. VENEZUELA

In the Venezuelan case, it has been argued that professionalization has been one of three factors that have helped keep the armed forces from intervening directly in politics since 1958. The other two are presidential leadership and civilian political oversight.[58] A review of the evolution of the Venezuelan military suggests that as in Brazil, Chile, and Peru, professionalization and civilian leadership together with oversight can serve variously both to encourage and to discourage direct political action by the military. The critical element appears to be the conjunction of a sense of crisis within society that threatens not only the military as an institution, but also its vision of the nation it is committed to defend. Venezuela, like the other countries examined in this chapter, has experienced a long history of military involvement in politics. What distinguishes it from the others is the more intimate mingling of military and civilian elites in governments dominated by one or the other. Hence the aloofness of the military, and accompanying depreciation for civilian politicians and for political parties, is not as strong as in Brazil, Chile, and Peru, although it is not entirely absent.

Since Venezuela was the source of a good portion of the independence forces of Simon Bolívar, the country emerged from the colonial period with a substantial army and officer corps. This contributed to a fairly strong military presence in the early republic. Once independence had been gained, however, disintegration and a loss of discipline set in. In an attempt to arrest this, a military school was founded by General José Antonio Paez, who dominated Venezuela from 1830 to 1848. Paez's additional efforts to subordinate the army to the authority of the central government were not well received and precipitated some local uprisings. Military dissatisfaction, together with the growing disenchantment of civilian elites with his economic policies, led eventually to a shift in 1848 from Paez's Conservative government to a Liberal one headed by General José Tadeo Monagas, whose government was marked by repression, corruption, and constant turmoil.[59] The absence of unity and institutional identity in the army was evidenced in the 1850s and 1860s by the involvement of officers and troops on all sides of regional, party, and personalistic struggles. The Federal War from 1859 to 1863 resulted in the fragmenting of the armed forces into regional, caudillistic armies with narrow goals. Such tendencies did not entirely disappear until the first decade of the twentieth century.

Chronic instability in late nineteenth century Venezuela stimulated the search for a strong leader who could bring order out of chaos. Such was General Antonio Guzmán Blanco, who dominated the country from 1870 to 1888. Guzmán was fairly successful in suppressing regional leaders and their armed supporters and in establishing sufficient order to allow for economic growth and the strengthening of the authority of central government. The coalition of civilian and military leaders he forged at the outset of his regime eventually disintegrated, and he was followed by a series of relatively weak military and civilian leaders who presided over a country afflicted with periodic military uprisings and civil strife. By 1897 the country was mired in a civil war that was won by the Army of the Liberal Restoration led, in the main, by young officers from the Andean region. In October 1899 they established a government they characterized as one of the new men, ideals, and methods, headed by Cípriano Castro. [60]

The idealism of certain of the officers, including Lieutenant General Juan Vicente Gómez, was not to be given free rein under Castro, who failed to bring about promised socioeconomic and political reforms and whose fiscal mismanagement led to foreign intervention to collect debts. Castro did, however, contribute to the establishment of a stronger central government, particularly by defeating a coalition of regional armies in 1901. He also ordered the creation of a general staff for the army which forced local armies either to incorporate themselves into the regular army or be suppressed. This resulted in the creation of the first truly national army.

Castro's successor, General Juan Vicente Gómez, who dominated Venezuela from 1908 to 1935, promoted the professionalization of the armed forces through the opening in 1910 of an Academia Militar which produced a core of trained officers loyal to the central government, rather than to regional caudillos. Prussian-trained Chilean officers staffed the Academia, beginning in 1913, and also supervised the reorganization of the general staff. Subsequently, Venezuela engaged a series of foreign military advisers from Belgium, Germany, and France. Officers were also sent to Peru, Chile, Argentina, Europe, and the United States. The foreign influences that the Venezuelan military were exposed to were hence somewhat more varied than in Brazil, Chile, or Peru. Overall, in the period prior to 1950 the French and Peruvians had the strongest influence.

Up to 1940, over 75 percent of Venezuelan army officers came from the Andean region, an area that also tended to be heavily represented in the upper echelons of the government bureaucracy. This encouraged the identification of military and civilian elites. During Gómez's period, the predominance of Andeans was resented by officers whose professional training emphasized promotions based on merit rather than clientelism.

Discontent with Gómez's promotion policies, combined with dismay over general socioeconomic conditions, encouraged reform-minded officers to join study groups with his civilian opponents. Discussions focused on such international events as the Mexican and Russian Revolutions, as well as World War I, and their implications for Venezuela. These encounters led to the drafting of programs calling for broad-based socioeconomic reforms in Venezuela in order to ensure a vital democracy. Emphasis was placed on more nationalistic policies of economic development and fairer distribution of its benefits.

In April 1928 a coalition of students, intellectuals, and workers was joined by cadets from the Academia Militar and some progressive officers in an unsuccessful uprising. The objectives of the military participants resembled those of the *tenentes* in Brazil in the early 1920s and of Carlos Ibañez and Marmaduke Grove in Chile later in the decade. The Venezuelan officers were galvanized by dissatisfaction with the domination of less merit-oriented, poorly educated older officers, and by the government's failure to respond to popular pressures for improvements in living conditions. These reformist elements believed that the traditional ruling elite had to be replaced by a more open one if national stability was to be ensured.

A strong impetus for the professionalization of the officers' corps was provided by General Eleazar López Contreras, Gómez's Minister of War, who succeeded him as president in 1935. López Contreras emphasized advanced training for officers, including study abroad in Italy, Chile, Argentina, Peru, Ecuador, and the United States, particularly to learn how to use the sophisticated weaponry that was increasingly being imported. The Academia Militar was reorganized, and separate military and naval academies were established. A national guard was created and the direct political role of the armed forces diminished. Officers were appointed to fewer cabinet posts and state governorships under López Contreras than under his predecessors. [61]

There was some political liberalization under López Contreras that resulted in a resurgence of party activities and a reduction in press censorship. Even these modest advances annoyed conservative forces which caused López Contreras to seek to ensure military support. Hence there were improvements in salaries and other benefits, together with attention to better training and upgrading of military facilities. These measures did not, however, eliminate the resentment of the younger officers at the continuing domination of holdovers from the Gómez period.

Political liberalization in Venezuela continued during the presidency of General Isaias Medina Angarita (1941–1945), who allowed for even greater press freedom and reduced the arrest and expulsion of political opponents. Medina believed in the separation of the military and civilian spheres and allowed a broad spectrum of political parties, including the Communist Party, to function. Emphasis was on promoting modernization through nationalistic economic policies as reflected in the Petroleum Reform Law of 1943.

The armed forces received more advanced training with the expansion of facilities in Venezuela and continued opportunities for study abroad. Salaries improved somewhat and promotions and fringe benefits were more available. Such actions did not, however, eliminate either discontent or the generational cleavages that pitted younger, better trained officers against older, less technically skilled ones. The attempts of López Contreras and Medina Angarita to restrict the actions of the armed forces to external defense and the maintenance of internal stability were not successful, and on October 18, 1945 a coup was led by junior officers and their reformist civilian allies. They were also joined by certain conservative elements within the military who had been alienated by Medina's reforms and his failure to accord them a greater role in political decision making. [62]

The intervention was justified by its leadership as an attempt to end abuses of power by both Medina and civilian political interests, particularly the Acción Democrática Party (AD), which was accused of irresponsibly stimulating civil turmoil and seeking power solely for the benefit of its leadership. Medina was accused of being overly influenced by the AD to the detriment of national wellbeing and the institutional integrity of the armed forces. The administration was also charged with allowing foreign capital too large a share of the Venezuelan economy and of failing to subordinate economic planning to nationalist criteria. [63]

Spearheading the coup was the Unión Patriótica Militar (UPM), constituted largely of junior officers who were highly critical of what they regarded as the failure of past governments and the military to utilize Venezuela's considerable economic resources to improve the condition of the bulk of the population and make Venezuela a world power. There was a strong sense that a wholesale reform of existing structures was needed, together with the elimination of incompetence, corruption, and cronyism within the civilian and military bureaucracies. The involvement of both civilian and military elites in government made it less easy for reformist Venezuelan officers to ascribe national problems exclusively to politicians. It also lessened military isolation and disdain for civilian government.

The Unión Patriótica Militar called for the establishment of a democratic government based on free and direct voting, and the drafting of a constitution that would give expression to the national will. Special interests would no longer dominate and military reforms were to go hand-in-hand with civil regeneration. The coup leadership disclaimed political ambitions and styled itself as apolitical.

These sentiments were cogently expressed in the charter of the UPM. Patterned on the lodges that had existed in Argentina, Chile, and Peru since the 1920s, the organization was divided into cells that functioned as study groups. Members were bound together by loyalty to the country. Exposure to the Peruvian military helped reinforce the sense that the military was the only institution capable of controlled reform that would reduce the possibilities of subversion. French advisers inculcated considerable self-esteem in Venezuelan officers and a strong sense that they had special responsibilities for eliminating societal inequalities. Study in the United States suggested to some that a more democratic system would be of benefit to the armed forces. [64]

The government that replaced Medina included both military and civilian reformers, the latter drawn largely from the left wing of the AD, who regarded themselves as dedicated primarily to the welfare of urban and rural workers and as harbingers of a new political order in which personalism and regionalism would be eliminated. In spite of some progress, democratic civilian government was not established on a firm basis, and the period from 1945 to 1948 witnessed continued heavy military involvement in politics, as well as civilian interference in the armed forces. Tensions between civilians and the military ran high particularly over attempts by the AD to proselytize within the barracks. The resentment thus generated resembled the backlash to attempts by certain elements of Unidad Popular to win adherents among the Chilean military from 1970 to 1973. Such overt attempts to capture the loyalties of military men have traditionally had negative results and are generally the source of considerable tension. Although the intimacy between the civilian and military elites bred by the mixed nature of Venezuelan government from 1945 to 1948 did cause officers to identify themselves with one or another sector of the various political parties, a good number of officers were uncomfortable with this pattern and suspicious that it would increase civilian interference in the armed forces.

Fears of eroding institutional autonomy, and internal conflict stemming from party rivalries, together with increasing opposition, largely economic, to the AD from a cross section of Venezuelan society, caused the military to conclude by 1948 that the AD-dominated government of Romulo Gallegos should be replaced. [65] A junta composed of Lieutenant Colonels Carlos Delgado Chalbaud, Marcos Pérez Jiménez, and Luis Felipe Llovera Paez thereupon assumed control in order to ensure "the security and safety of the whole nation and to seek the final establishment of social peace in Venezuela." [66]

Chalbaud had been trained at the St. Cyr Military Academy in France and served in a French engineering regiment during the 1930s. Subsequently, he attended the U.S. General Staff School at Fort Leavenworth, Kansas. Both Pérez Jiménez and Llovera Paez had extensive advanced training in Peru. [67] Given the French influence on Peruvian military training, the respective backgrounds of the junta members were complementary.

The junta and their supporters were convinced that the Venezuelan government could be made to function as efficiently and competently as they felt the military did. Given the corruption and discord that flourished from 1945 to 1948, the new government claimed it would need time to install a more honest, stable government. Hence the junta did not move quickly to restore civilian government. Dislike for the AD served to forge links between the junta and adherents of the Unión Republicana Democrática (URD) and Comité de Organización Política Electoral Independiente (COPEI), who accepted posts in the administration. From 1948 to 1950, however, the junta appears to have consulted the military high command more frequently than civilian political leaders.

By 1950 Marcos Pérez Jiménez emerged as the dominant figure within the junta and was able to maintain himself as president until 1958. Pérez Jiménez's vision of Venezuela emphasized its potential for leadership in Latin America because of its history, economic wealth, and geographic, demographic, economic, and social situation. The purpose of the state was the harmonious unification of all Venezuelans in order to achieve national objectives that transcended partisan interests. The armed forces were to have a principal role in national development and the protection of the moral and material patrimony. Their efforts, as well as those of all Venezuelans, were to be aimed at achieving the transformation of the country through the moral, intellectual, and physical rejuvenation of all Venezuelans. This, Pérez Jiménez believed, would result in the realization of Venezuela's national destiny, which, however, he did not clearly define. [68]

Elements of Pérez Jiménez's new national ideal resemble the geopolitical thinking of proponents of national security ideology. Belief in the nation as a living organism and in the corporate state is common to both, as is the tendency to identify the nation, state, and armed forces. The concept of an integrating state harmoniously incorporating all Venezuelans reminds one of the national security state in which societal conflict is anathema. The unification of the whole populace in the pursuit of national interests rather than partisan ones suggests that the state has goals which can supersede individual rights. Frustration with and denigration of civilian politicians, resulting in their eventual repression, was also common; but even the extensive violations of civil and political rights under Pérez Jiménez, were never as great as in post-1968 Brazil or post-1973 Chile, partly because Pérez Jiménez was bound by the Venezuelan tradition of greater military-civilian contact and cooperation. Even closer to certain elements of contemporary national security ideology, as it has developed in the Southern Cone of Latin America, were the thought and writings of Pérez Jiménez's allies Rafael Pinzón, his legal advisor, and Laureano Vallenilla Lanz, son of one of Venezuela's leading positivists. Their works offered biological, sociological, historical, and geopolitical justifications for the type of paternalistic dictatorship that Pérez Jiménez imposed on Venezuela. [69]

In line with the stated goal of judging Venezuelan democracy by its practical accomplishments rather than by its origins or methods, Pérez Jiménez embarked on a program of large-scale public works and the stimulation of industrial and commercial growth. Since government revenues were growing as a result of increased oil production, substantial funds were available for public projects. Little attention was paid to stimulating agriculture, however, and as a consequence substantial numbers of peasants migrated in this period to urban areas, particularly Caracas, where they crowded into slums known as *ranchos*. Seven hundred thousand immigrants from Italy, Spain, and Portugal were attracted to Venezuela in the 1950s by visions of economic opportunity. They, too, concentrated in the capital. By 1957, when the worldwide oil boom began subsiding, Pérez Jiménez's government was financially overextended. It also faced considerable antagonism from individuals in all classes who felt that the government had not fulfilled its promises of greater prosperity and less corruption. The outlawing of political parties, purportedly to free the country from the chaos of partisan conflicts so that national energies could be more fully focused on economic development, generated considerable opposition.

As criticism increased so did government repression, which in turn reduced divisions within the opposition. Gradually, a coalition of party leaders, urban and rural workers, intellectuals, students, and professionals came together with some disaffected elements of the military. Their prime object of criticism was the Ministry of Interior Relations, which had engaged in substantial violations of civil and political rights. [70] The brutality and corruption of some of the 5,000 employees of its subdivision, Seguridad Nacional, alienated the Catholic Church as well as sectors of the military from the Pérez Jiménez regime.

In May 1957 the Archbishop of Caracas, Monsignor Rafael Arias Blanco, published a pastoral letter criticizing the Pérez Jiménez government for squandering the material resources of the country and not improving the condition of workers. [71] This action by Arias, together with that of like-minded clerics, resulted in arrests and other harassment. Given the conservatism of the Venezuelan church up to that time, it reflects the degree to which the Pérez Jiménez regime had angered even traditional elements.

Sectors of the Navy, Air Force, and National Guard had also been progressively alienated since they were less favored by Pérez Jiménez than the Army. Young officers of all services felt their preparation was superior to that of Pérez Jiménez's generation; in addition, surveillance of officers by Seguridad Nacional was particularly resented.[72] Most irritating of all perhaps was the growing sense of damage to military prestige and institutional integrity caused by the financial corruption and venality of the Pérez Jiménez regime. His civilian and military allies were condemned for trampling on popular sovereignty in their greed for wealth and power. A call for free elections and opposition to the candidacy of Pérez Jiménez became rallying cries. The Armed Forces were specifically called upon to restore democracy so that individual rights would be respected.[73]

In response, Pérez Jiménez announced a plebiscite for December 15, 1957 in which he was the only candidate. The Junta Patriótica urged abstention and students in Caracas mounted protests. The 2,374,790 to 364,182 vote was trumpeted by the government as a strong vote of confidence and Pérez Jiménez claimed the presidency for five more years.[74]

Such actions did not prevent a civilian supported military coup from toppling Pérez Jiménez on January 25, 1958. The fourth junta to govern Venezuela in 12 years thereupon took power. The December plebiscite was declared void and free elections promised by the end of the year. Political parties were allowed to resume their activities and political exiles returned from abroad. Seguridad Nacional was eliminated. A new electoral law enfranchised illiterates and provided for universal adult suffrage and a secret ballot. In November 1958 campaigning began for the December election. Romulo Betancourt, the Acción Democrática candidate, won and assumed the presidency on February 13, 1959.

The fact that the regime of Pérez Jiménez was a personalistic one with ultimately limited support from the armed forces, helps explain his removal from office by his fellow officers. The difficulties of governing in the interim convinced a good number of them of the wisdom of their planned withdrawal. Throughout 1958 the junta was criticized for lack of planning and poor administration, as well as for resorting to short-term solutions and ad hoc responses to popular pressures.[75] Reduction of repression resulted in an upsurge of sometimes violent political activities. The disbanding of Seguridad Nacional caused some former security police to turn to crime.[76] The Junta Patriótica, therefore, bent its major efforts toward maintaining a reasonable degree of calm in a volatile political atmosphere.

The junta also concentrated on discouraging coups aimed at disrupting the transference of power to a civilian government. One of their chief preoccupations was containing civilian agitation that might prompt a counter coup. In an attempt to reduce the influence of the allies of Pérez Jiménez, the General Staff was replaced by a joint staff, and each service was given administrative and fiscal autonomy under the jurisdiction of the Ministry of Defense. In order to encourage support for the junta, military salaries and fringe benefits were increased. Both the Navy and the Air Force were represented in the junta and officers who were committed to respecting constitutional limitations on military activities were promoted. These steps, nevertheless, did not prevent an ultimatum being served on the junta by General Jesús Maria Castro León in July 1958. It criticized the government for failing to maintain order, control the Communists, eliminate corruption and laxity in the bureaucracy, restrict labor, decrease unemployment, limit the activities of the AD, and present a better image of Venezuela internationally. [77] Memories of the damage done to the military by Pérez Jiménez's regime were sufficiently strong, together with a real commitment to a return to civilian rule, to defuse the potential coup. Since 1958 civilian government has been consolidated in Venezuela.

While the Venezuelan military has technically returned to the barracks, it is not isolated from politics and it continues to be consulted extensively by the civilian political leadership. Senior officers, both before and after retirement, have benefited substantially from government posts. Furthermore, while the proportion of the national budget devoted to the armed forces has not significantly increased, the growth in the budget itself has resulted in substantial increases in military salaries and benefits, as well as the expansion of purchases of arms and other equipment.

Continuing nonintervention by the military depends, in good measure, on the performance of civilian administration, particularly in managing economic development and responding to popular demands for greater equity in the distribution of its benefits. Skyrocketing oil revenues beginning in 1973 raised expectations of considerable socioeconomic progress which, to a considerable degree, have not been met. Runaway inflation has contributed to a decline in real wages affecting both the working and middle classes. Government efforts to alleviate poverty through programs in housing, health care, education, employment, and the provision of basic foodstuffs have met with only mixed success, due, in part, to the size of the task and deficient methods.

The tripartite presidential commission composed of business, labor, and government representatives established in the late 1970s to advise on setting economic priorities has not had a major impact on improving the condition of the poor. While subsidized low interest loans have been made available for small and medium sized industries that are intended to be labor intensive, most government investment has flowed into large industrial complexes that are capital intensive.

So long as high rates of growth fueled by oil revenues are maintained, Venezuela has the potential for making some progress toward greater fulfillment of the basic needs of its population. However, increased imports, inflation, and a rapidly expanding external debt threaten this. The social welfare programs that do exist have not made major advances, and Venezuelan government estimates continue to categorize one-half of the population as at or below subsistence levels. [78]

Economic plans for the development of projected large-scale industries are in question, in view of lack of progress in developing markets, especially in Central America and the Caribbean. Revelations of rampant corruption during recent administrations, particularly that of Carlos Andrés Pérez (1974–1979), have contributed to an increasing sense of the venality of civilian politicians. If the present administration of Luis Herrera Campins does not reduce corruption and more effectively respond to popular pressures for socioeconomic reform, the possibilities for increased political conflict are good. While the military continues to display confidence in civilian government, a generalized crisis could prompt them to intervene directly once more.

The experience of the Venezuelan military in government before 1958 has discouraged direct intervention since then. The considerable access of officers to the upper echelons of the civilian bureaucracy and the tradition of consultation have also tended to reassure the armed forces that their views are being taken into consideration. The extrication of the military from politics in Venezuela in 1958 was not as complete as in certain other countries. The need for the military to intervene to achieve its objectives is hence not as great.

While civil and political rights in Venezuela since 1958 have been more respected than in many other Latin American countries, social and economic rights have fared less well in spite of economic growth due to oil revenues. Lack of a strong commitment on the part of the government to redistributive policies has resulted in only limited progress in basic needs. This points up the fact that the lower classes have not been able to substantially affect economic policies in their favor through the exercise of such rights as voting. The existence of a formal democracy in Venezuela has not, therefore, guaranteed the fulfillment of social and economic rights for a substantial proportion of the population.

V. MEXICO

The evolution of the Mexican military diverges in several respects from that of Brazil, Chile, Peru, and Venezuela. The nineteenth century did not witness the emergence of a national military establishment that had its own identity and worldview. Nor was there the same interest toward the end of the century in foreign military missions to assist in the modernization and professionalization of the armed forces. The Mexican Revolution (1910–1917) was fought largely by nonprofessional armies organized on the basis of regional and personal loyalties. By 1940 the federal government had consolidated its authority over the military, ensuring civilian domination up to the present. This was part of the process of incorporating major interest groups into a political system dominated by a single party whose strategy for gaining support focused on cooptation and manipulation. Nevertheless, when traditional means of social control falter, Mexican political elites turn to the military to eliminate turmoil. Hence the role of the armed forces within Mexican society has been contingent on the degree to which civilian political and economic structures have dealt successfully with pressures for change.

Soldiers in nineteenth century Mexico and up through the Revolution were generally recruited by force; this contributed to the general populace's fear of and lack of esteem for the military. The struggle for independence (1810–1821) and the war of La Reforma (1855–1860) were fought by such troops, who depended more on surprise and attrition than on formal tactics for victory. Nor were officers provided with training which encouraged a sense of group identification or a shared ideology. As a consequence, they remained open to varied, and sometimes opposing, political currents within Mexican society. Uprisings and rebellions against central and state governments were often resolved by negotiation rather than military means, and only the war with the United States (1846–1848) and the French intervention (1862–1867) resulted in full-scale battles.

While these conflicts did help build nationalism, they did not result in the creation of a regular army. It was not until the era of Porfirio Díaz (1876–1911) that a federal army was created.[79] Even then, personal loyalties to one's commander counted more than nationalism and institutional identification. This helps explain the heavily personalistic nature of the forces that participated in the 1910–1917 conflict.

Unlike the situation in Brazil, Chile, Peru, and Venezuela, concern for the professionalization of the Mexican military did not become strong until the 1920s. It arose principally out of the desire of civilian administrations to ensure a disciplined armed forces that did not threaten it. Hence, the 1920s saw the expansion of higher educational facilities, including the Colegio Militar which provided training for officers from all services. Specialized schools followed, such as the Escuela Médico Militar, Escuela Militar de Transmisiones, Escuela de Ingenieros Militares, Escuela de Materiales de Guerra, Escuela de Aplicación, and the Escuela Superior de Guerra.

By the 1960s the Colegio Militar was graduating between 220 and 290 cadets a year. [80] In 1973 92.8 percent of the commandants of military zones were graduates of the Colegio Militar and 75 percent of the Escuela Superior de Guerra. Only 3.5 percent had no advanced studies. [81] Moreover, after 1961 increasing numbers of Mexican officers went abroad to study in Germany, the United States, Argentina, Chile, France, Italy, Switzerland, and the Canal Zone, but the great majority received their preparation in Mexico. [82]

Training emphasized the subordination of the military to civilian control and its role as a support of the government. As a consequence, the major responsibilities of the military since the 1920s have been the maintenance of internal order in Mexico and assistance in carrying out government objectives and programs. Well before the emphasis on civic action by the armed forces in other Latin American countries in the 1960s, the Mexican military was participating in the implementation of government social welfare programs. Initially, these emphasized improving transportation, communication, and educational facilities. Today in some rural areas officers are used to administer public works and agricultural and health programs. Such activities have increased in recent years in an effort to counteract criticism of the military resulting from such actions as the killing of reportedly over 300 students and other protesters in Mexico City's Plaza of the Three Cultures in the summer of 1968.

There is, however, a strong preference within the civilian and military bureaucracies for not using force to maintain social control. Negotiation, compromise, cooptation, and manipulation have been principal tools of the Mexican political system and these have had reasonable success. The subordination of the military to civilian control was not, however, easily achieved. In fact, it tended to dominate civil-military relations up to 1940.

In the 1920s as the revolutionary leadership sought to consolidate their power through the creation of new political structures, efforts were undertaken to establish the primacy of the central government. In particular, regional and personalistic loyalties were deemphasized in favor of institutional ones. This included deemphasizing traditional patterns of military leadership. Internal reform of the army reduced the number of generals (as many as one per 335 soldiers), imposed stricter discipline, and emphasized loyalty to the nation. Training was restructured to increase technical skills, and some military cadets studied abroad. Frequent rotation of zone commanders limited the possibilities of their building regional bases to promote personal ambitions.

The creation of the Partido Nacional Revolucionario in the late 1920s as the prime forum for political struggle within Mexico further diminished the impact of the military leadership, just as the evolution of a government bureaucracy alongside the party's limited the capacity of the armed forces for direct political action and relegated them to the status of another interest group.

The most thoroughgoing limitation of the role of the military occurred during the presidency of Lázaro Cárdenas (1934–1940). The promotion of workers' organizations, such as the Confederación de Trabajadores de Mexico (CTM) and the Confederación Nacional Campesina (CNC) greatly expanded support for the government. Their incorporation into the official party, the renamed Partido Revolucionario Mexicano (PRM), and insertion into the bureaucracy, served to create a new political context in which an expanded civilian elite with a growing popular base controlled the state apparatus. Cárdenas' objective was to build a broad base of support that would reduce challenges to his power by narrow interests. This caused him frequently to describe the armed forces in his public pronouncements as the soldiers and lower echelon officers rather than commandants. Militias were also encouraged, particularly in rural areas. The expansion of the power of the federal government, due in large part to Mexican economic growth, increased its supremacy over the military. The integration of a broad spectrum of functional and interest groups into the party and government bureaucracy reduced the likelihood of their supporting military intervention. The incorporation of the military meant that attempted coups would have limited support within the army, as happened in 1938.

The 1940 elections were the last in which a military man was chosen president of Mexico. Indeed, General Manuel Avila Camacho (1940–1946), Cárdenas' Secretary of Defense, had made his career primarily in the bureaucracy. When Camacho was declared the winner over General Juan Almazán, an anti-Communist, pro-foreign investment candidate, the latter threatened revolt, but did not succeed in winning sufficient support to undertake it. [83]

In the post-World War II period, demands by Mexican workers for a greater share of the benefits of economic growth resulted in strikes and other job actions. The situation was aggravated by a postwar slump in demand for Mexican products. The tendency under President Miguel Alemán (1946–1952), Mexico's first postrevolutionary civilian president, was to use the army, as well as the police, to suppress these protests.

Alemán continued cooperative security policies with the United States, initiated during World War II, signing a Reciprocal Assistance

Treaty in 1947. There was, however, both civilian and military resistance to a more intimate relationship with the United States and direct military assistance was refused. This was in contrast to the increasing closeness of the Brazilian, Chilean, Peruvian, and Venezuelan armed forces with their U.S. counterparts at the time. Proximity to the United States and historic suspicion of its intentions made Mexico more cautious about aid from its northern neighbor. As a consequence of this, the Mexican military did not receive the foreign assistance that stimulated the expansion and modernization of the armed forces particularly in Brazil, Chile, and Peru.

Alemán's successor, Adolfo Ruiz Cortines (1952–1958), presided over a declining economy that provoked labor unrest. Unlike Alemán, Ruiz Cortines was less inclined to use force in response, although he did call out the military against students and other protesters. They were also used, at times, to replace striking workers. Dependence on the armed forces continued under Adolfo López Mateos (1958–1964), during whose presidency the army used violence to end some strikes. López Mateos increased military dependence on the federal government by promoting improved benefits for military men and their families, including the establishment of a social security system for the armed forces in 1961.

Under Gustavo Díaz Ordaz (1964–1970), military personnel were again used to break up strikes and other protests, sometimes violently when police forces failed. With the outbreak of guerrilla activity, particularly in the western coastal state of Guerrero, the army was increasingly called up. There was some expansion of the army's political role as a result of increasing fears of subversion. Military intelligence gathering and surveillance of civilians were expanded. The greater dependence of the civilian bureaucracy on the military allowed the latter to increase its input to governmental decision making.

The administration of Luis Echeverría (1970–1976) adhered, in general, to previous policies of cultivating and co-opting the military, as well as using it when nonviolent means of conflict resolution failed. In part, because of opposition generated by some of Echeverría's economic and foreign policies, he was concerned about maintaining the support of the armed forces, and during his administration military benefits were increased. In addition, there was renewed emphasis on civic action by the military, particularly in rural areas. This was in conjunction with other efforts of the government to implement socioeconomic reforms that would defuse popular pressures. There was also increased attention paid to building national unity via the reconciliation of class interests within the corporate state structure. [84]

Economic problems such as inflation, a decline in real wages, a worsening balance of trade, and an increasing foreign debt limited the impact of these efforts. As opposition to the government grew, both the army and police forces were used to dissolve demonstrations, detain opponents, and control labor and students on a regular basis through surveillance and intelligence gathering. The decreasing efficacy of the government's strategy of negotiation, compromise, cooptation, and manipulation in the face of a more complex society increased the role of the military, although there continued to be a strong preference for means other than force to maintain stability. [85]

Since the early 1960s the Mexican military has, in fact, been regularly employed to reinforce the civilian government's ability to control dissent. As in Peru, social and economic inequalities are considered a prime stimulus of discord. This belief was enhanced by U.S. military training, which emphasized reform as a prime means of averting revolutions like Cuba's in 1959. [86] Hence Mexican troops were assigned to public works, medical, and other welfare projects. These included the Plan Acuario, which distributed potable water to communities in the north central part of the country during dry seasons. By 1970, 1,500 communities were being served. The Plan Verde was aimed at replanting deforested areas and was accompanied by efforts to control forest fires. Military medical personnel were involved in plans to control epidemics and respond to natural disasters. A literacy campaign focused on instruction for nonliterate recruits and the peasant population; new schools were constructed and others repaired. Sports programs, particularly for youths, were established and equipment provided. Clothing and basic foodstuffs were distributed and roads and medical facilities were constructed in certain areas, especially if there was guerrilla activity. In recent years the various programs have been coordinated through social action brigades and regional development plans. [87]

Mexico has found that these programs contribute to greater unity and discipline among the troops. Repeated emphasis on the soldier as servant of the people has encouraged a sense of being an instrument of a civilian state. But it also has stimulated a feeling of paternalism which causes some soldiers to distinguish themselves from those they are assisting. This has reinforced the military's sense of having a unique and critical role in society. [88]

In general, the social welfare efforts of the Mexican military have contributed to the maintenance of order and stability, and hence of internal security. Yet since 1968 civic action and the traditional strategies of the civilian bureaucracy and leadership have obviously not been sufficient to control rising discontent over socioeconomic conditions. To date the military has worked closely with civilian politicians to maintain public order, and the latter have been spared the depreciation common in Brazil, Chile, and Peru.

While rumors of possible coups against civilian presidents have circulated in recent years, none are known to have been actually attempted. Presidential authority over the armed forces is strong and greater than that of João Goulart in Brazil in 1964, Fernando Belaúnde Terry in Peru in 1968, and Salvador Allende in Chile in 1973. Civilian domination of the Mexican armed forces is assisted by their clientelist nature. Promotions tend to be made according to personal, group, or generational alliances, and advance is generally tied to how well one conforms to and cooperates with the military and civilian bureaucracies. While emphasis is also on technical skills and achievements, the civilian leadership has more influence than they ever had in the more institutionally autonomous militaries in Brazil, Chile, and Peru. The permeation of the civilian and military leadership and bureaucracies in Mexico is also greater than in Venezuela.

A further element contributing to cooperation between the civilian and military elites is the fact that the armed forces are expected to provide the central bureaucracy, especially the Presidency and Secretary of the Interior, with political information concerning the areas in which they are based. Regional military commanders have also, at times, been used by disaffected local groups as channels of communication with the central government when the local civil officials were not regarded as responsive. Army commandants have, occasionally, replaced state governors or intervened at the behest of the president in local political disputes. There are also instances of local officials consulting regional military officers on nonmilitary decisions. Moreover, while the number of cabinet or upper echelon executive branch positions held by officers has diminished, they have not disappeared. In addition, military men continue to serve in congress. In recent years these have increasingly been lieutenant colonels and below. [89] Such activities reinforce military support for existing political structures and leadership.

By 1970, the influence of those officers who had participated in the 1910–1917 struggle had waned in favor of younger generations of officers. From 1970 to 1975 alone, 354 generals retired. In this same period constitutional restrictions on the army were also reduced, permitting more direct political involvement. In addition, the size of the standing army was increased by 60 percent, with lesser gains by the air force and navy. [90] This has permitted the creation of new command posts for distribution to presidential allies. The generous social welfare system of the armed forces has also been expanded. [91] Another new development has been the emergence of paramilitary groups. There is evidence that these groups have incorporated some military men and receive training by the army. The Military Police, the Federal Judicial Military Police, and the Federal Security Police allegedly cooperated in 1976 in the creation of such an organization, the Brigada Blanca, in contravention of the Mexican constitution.[92] Operating in secrecy, the Brigada Blanca engages in intelligence gathering, as well as in the suppression of dissent in extralegal fashion. Such groups have not, however, been as active as their counterparts in Argentina and Brazil.

These developments suggest qualitative changes within the Mexican military. In the aftermath of the Revolution, military men as individuals exercised political power directly through the holding of high office, including the presidency as well as cabinet posts. As the corporatist Mexican political system was molded from 1920 to 1940, the military was increasingly treated as just one of a number of political supports of a regime under growing civilian dominance. Particularly after 1940 the Mexican military underwent a process of bureaucratization that helped decrease political involvement in the interventionist sense. By 1960, however, it was evident that when the civilian leadership faltered, the armed forces, and especially the army, would be used to fill the power vacuum. In the last 20 years the specific means of social control have been refined and today include a mix of civic action programs, intelligence gathering, and direct and indirect repression. While civilian dominance continues, the insertion of the military into the governing apparatus has made the civilian political leadership more dependent on it. It is likely that if societal unrest increases, the armed forces will augment their role within the political system.

A prime stimulus for this would be escalating civil disorder and guerrilla activitities, as a result of worsening socioeconomic conditions within Mexico. This is a distinct possibility as even the size of the oil revenues since 1973 has not substantially reduced inequalities and, in fact, income distribution has worsened.[93] Mexico's enormous foreign debt, exacerbated by increasing imports of manufactured goods, as well as foodstuffs, has resulted in protests from a broad spectrum of the population, including the military. The economic squeeze has affected both troops and officers, resulting in work stoppages, resignations, and milder protests.[94]

This suggests that greater efforts will have to be made to improve the economic status of the armed forces. It does not appear, however, to indicate the type of discontent that could lead to a military coup. Rather, the military continues to identify its interests with the political elite. The Mexican military does not seem to regard the existing Mexican political system as bankrupt as did the Brazilian, Chilean, and Peruvian military prior to their respective coups. The incorporation of the Mexican military into the system seems to have diminished that likelihood up to the present. Furthermore, as in Venezuela, oil revenues have resulted in major increases in the Mexican military budget, a factor likely to increase the acquiescence of the armed forces to continued civilian dominance.[95]

The original strategy of the Mexican revolutionary leadership to integrate the armed forces into political structures, as refined by Cárdenas and his successors, continues to mold civilian-military relations. Not having developed a great deal of institutional autonomy prior to the early implementation of this policy, the Mexican army generally regarded it as beneficial rather than as threatening. This contrasts with the negative reactions of the Brazilian and Chilean military to Goulart's and Allende's attempts at cultivation and cooptation of the armed forces. Greater institutional autonomy and pride in their neutrality in partisan political matters caused a good number of Brazilian and Chilean officers to regard Goulart's and Allende's efforts as threats to their professional integrity and the institutional unity of the military.

The growing dependence of the Mexican civilian leadership on the military to maintain public order and accomplish the objectives of the state, however, does contain within it the possibility that as in Brazil and Chile the government will come to be regarded as weaker and less competent than the military. Furthermore, if the Mexican civilian leadership is increasingly ineffective in dealing not only with the pressures generated by poverty, but also with middle and upper class preoccupations with inflation, foreign dept, corruption, and other problems, it may turn more to the military to control dissent. As a consequence, stabilization of economic conditions and increased fulfillment of basic needs[96] are critical issues for the preservation of existing levels of enjoyment of civil and political rights in Mexico.

CONCLUSION

This comparison of the evolution of the military in Brazil, Chile, Peru, Venezuela, and Mexico is an attempt to identify some factors which have contributed to the violation of human rights in those countries. This is not, in any sense, an exhaustive study of all causes, but rather a schematic overview of the development of the armed forces in five countries in order to see whether there is any connection between the nature and behavior of the military and the observance or nonobservance of both civil and political, as well as social and economic rights. The focus of this chapter has been largely on national rather than international factors. This should not be interpreted as implying that the latter have any lesser weight, simply that these factors are beyond the scope of the present study.

Review of developments in Brazil, Chile, Peru, Venezuela, and Mexico suggests that human rights violations increase under military governments, particularly in those whose ideology offers justifications for the exercise of state power relatively unrestricted by constitutions and law, or by popular participation in government. The emergence in Latin America in the 1960s and 1970s of military regimes that regarded themselves as more fit to govern and achieve their nation's destiny than civilian governments has meant that the armed forces in a number of countries have retained power on a long-term basis in an effort to restructure the political system in their countries, in order to eliminate instability and promote economic growth. This was to be accomplished by the creation of hierarchically ordered, corporate societies in which conflict and discontent were eliminated, thereby allowing for a redirecting of attention and energies toward national development. Such restructuring and hostility to political and economic competition encouraged repression and rights violations. The enormity of the task, and contradictions inherent in the means, have resulted in 18 years of military rule in Brazil, close to 12 in Peru, and 8 in Chile.

In each of these countries the military was prompted to turn out elected civilian officials and take power as a result of loss of confidence in the existing governments and, in particular, in their capacity to respond to escalating pressures for remedying socioeconomic problems and to demands by the poor for the fulfillment of basic needs. Given the military's responsibility for maintaining internal order, officers were particularly concerned by the growth of dissent, guerrilla activities, terrorism, and civil disturbances. The sense of generalized crisis within these countries encouraged an increasing disposition among officers to regard themselves as the only ones capable of restoring stability and/or realizing their country's economic potential and, hence, international role. To accomplish this, society would be disciplined and extraordinary controls imposed, justified by the promise of realizing the nation's potential.

Rapid change in Latin America since World War II imposed severe strains on existing governmental structures, and often resulted in fewer civil liberties and political rights being assured as well as in growing disparities in the enjoyment of social, economic, and cultural rights. In countries where the population was organized, at least to a degree, in parties, labor unions, professional, and other groups, the possibilities of protest were greater, and both the apparent and real threat to the existing order were felt more sharply by those entrusted with defending it. This was the situation in Brazil and Chile. Where substantial portions of the population were unorganized, conflict was less apparent, although this did not necessarily discourage intervention by a military imbued with a strong sense of responsibility for national welfare as in Peru. There the military's own analyses of economic and social conditions, and resentment of the oligarchy as well as of the country's dependence on the United States, reinforced the inclination toward intervention.

The experience of these three countries suggests that worsening socioeconomic conditions in Venezuela and Mexico and partial or ineffectual responses by their governments could contribute to the type of crisis atmosphere that encouraged the Brazilian, Chilean, and Peruvian military to stage coups. Counterbalancing this is the fact that the armed forces in the former countries have traditionally had more intimate and cooperative relations with civilian politicians. Furthermore, economic conditions in Venezuela and Mexico are more positive than in pre-coup Brazil, Peru, and Chile.

Examination of past military interventions in the countries studied suggests there is a genuine sense of patriotism and commitment to change within the armed forces, although the definition of the latter and the means to achieve it are disputed. There is generally a strong desire to encourage modernization, prompted in part by the military's own experience with and esteem for new technology. This is linked to a commitment to the development of the country's natural resources that has been a strong preoccupation among most of the military establishments since the 1920s and 1930s. While in the past coups have been engineered in part as a result of desires for internal reforms and generational discontent, such motives have receded in the recent past because the armed forces in most of these countries have become professionalized, with standardized criteria for advancement and improved benefits. In this respect professionalization has diminished some of the traditional motives for military intervention. At the same time it has provided other stimuli for taking power.

These include a stronger sense of corporate identity and ideological definition. Professionalization did not make the military apolitical in Brazil, Chile, and Peru. It only promoted the eschewing of partisan politics. In Venezuela and Mexico it did not even succeed in this. Professionalization and exposure to European military missions in the period 1890–1940 encouraged the military to believe themselves capable of governing their countries. Technical training, as well as more general study of economics, history, politics, and sociology, prompted the breaking down of the insulation of officers from general governmental concerns. This was further encouraged by involvement in civic action programs that were, in part, stimulated by U.S. pressures, beginning in the 1960s, for reforms to stabilize Latin America and protect against Communist inroads in the hemisphere. Such training and activities encouraged members of the armed forces to become more critical of civilian politicians, the sense of integrity of the former being deeply offended by corruption and demagoguery among the latter. Military efficiency and discipline inclined officers to be alienated by incompetent and corrupt bureaucracies. Such attitudes were encouraged by the greater institutional isolation from civilian leadership of the military in Brazil, Chile, and Peru than in Venezuela and Mexico. There the closeness of civilian-military relations appears to have, at least to date, neutralized the other tendency. [97]

Depreciation of civilian politicians and parties by Brazilian, Chilean, and Peruvian officers contributed to the development of their own ideology and its expression via military lodges, the curricula of war colleges, and the contents of military publications. Particularly in Brazil, Chile, Peru, and Venezuela there has been considerable ideological development within the armed forces. [98] The European orientation of South America in the nineteenth and first half of the twentieth century resulted in continuing exposure to Old World intellectual currents and absorption of major ideological developments. The geopolitical base of national security ideology in Brazil and Chile is one result. The particular formulations that have been developed in each country flow, however, from adaptations to particular historical, demographic, economic, political, and cultural circumstances.

Elements of geopolitical thought are also found in Venezuela and Mexico, where the ideological development of the military has not been as coherent and extensive as in the Southern Cone. Nor have generalized structural crises occurred in the post-World War II period with the force and frequency that they did in Brazil and Chile. The relatively limitless nature of state power inherent in the geopolitical thought of the Brazilian and Chilean military opens the way for substantial violations of civil and political rights in situations where social and economic inequalities breed ongoing protests of both a nonviolent and violent nature. While these military governments have stated their intention to reduce some disparities, their unwillingness to undertake substantial redistribution has limited progress and in some instances even led to regression. In these cases continued denial of social and economic rights is generally accompanied by repression of civil and political rights.

NOTES TO CHAPTER 2

1. Brazil, Argentina, Uruguay, and Chile are frequently categorized as national security states, as they share an ideological orientation that justifies extreme measures to eliminate political conflict and subversion. These regimes are also characterized by concentration of power in the executive branch of government dominated by the military. Legislatures, where they function, are circumscribed and the judiciary largely subor-

dinated to the executive. A high degree of social control is maintained, at times, by means of repression. This is done, ostensibly, in order to carry out government policies aimed at realizing national potential, particularly in the economic sphere. For an analysis of national security ideology and its implications for human rights, see Chapter 3.

2. For a recent survey of human rights violations in Latin America, see U.S. Department of State, *Country Reports on Human Rights Practices: Report Submitted to the Committee on Foreign Relations, U.S. Senate and Committee on Foreign Affairs, U.S. House of Representatives,* February 2, 1981 (Washington, D.C.: Government Printing Office, 1981).

3. "Professionalization," as used in this chapter, refers to the development of technical expertise, corporate identity, institutional autonomy, and bureaucratic norms, as well as attitudes and patterns of behavior. For a discussion of variations in definitions of military professionalization, see John Samuel Fitch, "The Political Impact of U.S. Military Aid to Latin America: Institutional and Individual Effects," *Armed Forces and Society,* 5, 3 (Spring 1979): 370.

4. Frank D. McCann, "Origins of the 'New Professionalism' of the Brazilian Military," *Journal of Interamerican Studies and World Affairs,* 21, 4 (November 1979): 508–509.

5. Ibid., pp. 507–510. See also William S. Dudley, "Professionalization and the Brazilian Military in the Late Nineteenth Century," in Brian Loveman and Thomas M. Davies, Jr., eds., *The Politics of Antipolitics: The Military in Latin America* (Lincoln: University of Nebraska Press, 1978), pp. 58–64; June Hahner, *Civil-Military Relations in Brazil, 1889–1898* (Columbia: University of South Carolina Press, 1969).

6. Frederick M. Nunn, "An Overview of the European Military Missions in Latin America," in Loveman and Davies, pp. 40–41.

7. Ibid.

8. Olavo Bilac as quoted in McCann, p. 513.

9. This same impulse was also present in the Argentine and Chilean armies in the 1930s. Brazil, however, is the one country to have eventually developed a substantial arms industry, although Argentina has also made progress in this direction. In the former, domestic production of arms occurred primarily since the military takeover of 1964 and was stimulated by the cutoff of U.S. arms sales resulting from U.S. human rights legislation.

10. Pedro A. de Góes Monteiro, *Relatório apresentado ao presidente da república dos Estados Unidos do Brasil* (Rio de Janeiro: Imprensa do Estado-Maior do Exército, 1935), pp. 22–24, 38–42; McCann, pp. 518–519.

11. Eurico G. Dutra, *Relatório apresentado ao presidente da república dos Estados Unidos do Brasil* (Rio de Janeiro: Imprensa do Estado-Maior do Exército, 1940), p. 22; McCann, pp. 519–520.

12. Alfred Stepan, in his *The Military in Politics: Changing Patterns in Brazil* (Princeton, N.J.: Princeton University Press, 1971), p. 244, points out that most of the officers participating in the 1964 coup had served in Italy. On the formation of the ESG see pp. 129, 174–178.

13. Ibid., pp. 175–177, 186, 246. See also Thomas G. Sanders, "Development and Security Are Linked by a Relationship of Mutual Causality," *American Universities Fieldstaff Reports,* XV, 3 (September 1971): 3–4.

14. Michael Burgess and Daniel Wolf, "Brazil: The 'Escola Superior de Guerra' and the Philosophy of the National Security State," MS, 1977.

15. Sanders, p. 4.

16. Antonio de Arruda et al., *Disenvolvimento Nacional* (Rio de Janeiro: Associacão do Diplomados da Escola Superior de Guerra, 1970), pp. 41–42.

17. For two elucidations of this view, see Albert Fishlow, "Brazil's Economic Miracle," and Peter Flynn, "The Brazilian Development Model: The Political Dimension," in Loveman and Davies, pp. 251–269. For an evaluation of Brazilian government strategies for the fulfillment of basic needs, see Chapter 5 of this volume.

18. Flynn, pp. 266–267.

19. Frederick M. Nunn, "Emil Körner and the Prussianization of the Chilean Army," in Loveman and Davies, pp. 72–78.

20. Diana Vélez, "Regeneration and Pacification: Modernization and the Agents of Social Control in Spain, 1895–1917" (Ph.D. dissertation, Princeton University, 1977).

21. Frederick M. Nunn, "The Military in Chilean Politics. 1924–1932," in Loveman and Davies, p. 131.

22. Ibid., pp. 125–132.

23. This fact was underestimated by such analysts as Alain Joxe, whose 1970 study *Las fuerzas armadas en el sistema político chileno* (Santiago: Editorial Universal) discounted the possibility of the type of military intervention that occurred in September 1973 in Chile.

24. Singled out for special mention was Hubert Lyautey's *Du Rôle Social de l'Officier.* Frederick M. Nunn, "New Thoughts on Military Intervention in Latin American Politics: The Chilean Case, 1973," *Journal of Latin American Studies,* 7, 2 (November 1975): 282–283.

25. Ibid., pp. 283–284.

26. Geopolitics is the study of the relationship between physical environment and politics. In nineteenth century Europe geography was increasingly used to explain the political and social environment. Geopolitical determinism became fashionable in Germany, where Fredrich Ratzel, under the influence of Darwinism, posited that the state is a living organism that must grow or die. Treitschke, who introduced the concept of *Lebensraum* (living space), propounded the view that a strong state may seize the territory necessary for a nation's natural growth. In Nationalist Socialist Germany Karl Haushafer disseminated Sir Halford John MacKinder's theory of a "heartland" central to world domination. These theorists were widely read and cited in Latin America. For further discussion of geopolitical thought and its relation to national security ideology in the Southern Cone, see Chapter 3.

27. Ibid., pp. 285–286.

28. Ibid., pp. 273–274 and Genaro Arriagada, "Ideology and Politics in the South American Military (Argentina, Brazil, Chile and Uruguay),"

paper presented at the Woodrow Wilson International Center for Scholars, Washington, D.C., 21 March 1979, p. 14.

29. Nunn, p. 274; Carlos M. Rama, "Los raices fascistas del actual régimen militar chileno," *Cuadernos Americanos,* 33, 192 (enero-febrero 1974): 7–26.

30. This law was repealed in 1958. Nunn, p. 275.

31. Ibid., p. 276.

32. Arturo Valenzuela, *The Breakdown of Democratic Regimes: Chile,* Volume IV of Juan J. Linz and Alfred Stepan, eds., *The Breakdown of Democratic Regimes* (Baltimore: The Johns Hopkins University Press, 1978), pp. 106–107.

33. A good analysis of these factors that challenges some traditional stereotypes regarding political behavior by class is Brian H. Smith and José Luis Rodríguez, "Comparative Working-Class Political Behavior: Chile, France, Italy," *American Behavioral Scientist,* 18, 1 (September 1974): 59–96. See also James W. Prothro and Patricio E. Chaparro, "Public Opinion and the Movement of Chilean Government to the Left, 1952–1972," *Journal of Politics,* 36 (February 1974): 2–43, and Thomas G. Sanders, "Military Government in Chile," in Loveman and Davies, pp. 270–287.

34. Nunn, p. 289.

35. Smith and Rodríguez, pp. 73–75.

36. Arturo Valenzuela, "Political Constraints to the Establishment of Socialism in Chile," in Arturo Valenzuela and J. Samuel Valenzuela eds., *Chile: Politics and Society* (New Brunswick, N.J.: Transaction, Inc., 1976), p. 9.

37. Peter S. Cleaves, *Bureaucratic Politics and Administration in Chile* (Berkeley: University of California, 1974), pp. 24–29, 315–321.

38. Nunn, pp. 292–303.

39. Frederick M. Nunn, "Military-Civilian Relations in Chile: The Legacy of the Golpe of 1973," *Inter-American Economic Affairs,* 29, 2 (Autumn 1975): 46.

40. Such themes appear repeatedly in the public pronouncements of General Juan Velasco Alvarado, who served as president from 1968–1976, and General Francisco Morales Bermúdez, who served from 1976 to 1980.

41. Victor Villanueva, "The Military in Peruvian Politics, 1919–1945," in Loveman and Davies, pp. 80–81.

42. Ibid., pp. 81–84; Nunn, "Overview," pp. 42–43. Approximately 75 French officers served in Peru from 1896 to 1940, while from 1916 to 1940 every Peruvian officer who reached the rank of general studied at some time in France. Dependence on French military missions declined as Peruvian training facilities gained in sophisticaton.

43. Villanueva, pp. 134–141.

44. Victor Villanueva, *El CAEM y la revolución de la Fuerza Armada* (Lima: Instituto de Estudios Peruanos, 1972), p. 50; and Luigi R. Einaudi, "Revolution from Within? Military Rule in Peru Since 1968," in David Chaplin, ed., *Peruvian Nationalism: A Corporatist Revolution* (New Brunswick, N.J.: Transaction Books, 1976), p. 404.

45. José del Carmen Marín A. "Prologo," in Edgardo Mercado Jarrín, *Seguridad, Política, Estrategia* (Lima: Imprenta del Ministerio de Guerra, 1974), p. ii.

46. For a Peruvian analysis of the requirements for national security that emphasizes a diversified economic base and a nonaligned foreign policy, together with regional cooperation that diverges from policies in Brazil and Chile, see Captain Raúl Parra Maza, "La Convivencia Pacífica de los Estados Americanos y el Desarrollo Integral: Evolución hacia un Sistema de Seguridad Colectiva," *Revista de Marina*, 356, 4 (julio-agosto 1975): 281–295. See also Einaudi, p. 406; and Abraham F. Lowenthal, "The Military Government in Peru, 1968–1974," in Loveman and Davies, p. 293. One of the chief proponents of this position is General Edgardo Mercado Jarrín, who served in the cabinets of both Presidents Juan Velasco Alvarado and Francisco Morales Bermúdez, and directed and taught at CAEM. For a general statement of his views, see his *Seguridad, Política, Estrategia.*

47. General Francisco Morales Bermúdez, who assumed the presidency in 1976, frequently expressed the Christian humanist position. This orientation has links to European social Catholicism as expressed by such individuals as the Belgian Catholic sociologist Frère L. J. Lebret, who lectured at CAEM in the 1950s.

48. An astute unravelling and analysis of the complex negotiations surrounding the IPC holdings is Richard Goodwin's "Letter from Peru," *The New Yorker* (17 May 1969): 41–109.

49. Juan Velasco Alvarado, "Speech, 1969," in Loveman and Davies, pp. 210–213.

50. The official policy was described as economic pluralism, a mix of state social, reformed private, and unreformed private property (generally small-scale companies). The relationship among them was never clearly specified and the precise nature of social property not clearly established.

51. Lowenthal, pp. 293–295.

52. Julio Cotler, "Concentration of Income and Political Authoritarianism in Peru," in Loveman and Davies, pp. 298–300.

53. For the impact on basic needs, see Chapter 5.

54. SINAMOS was an attempt to encourage some popular participation in economic and political decision making through education and community organizations based on economic groupings. It was intended to serve as a counterweight to traditional groups such as political parties and labor unions. While SINAMOS did help politicize some rural and urban workers, overall it failed to fully meet the government's objectives, in part because it was regarded as an instrument of control rather than of democratic participation. For an analysis of its decline, see Alfred Stepan, *The State and Society: Peru in Comparative Perspective* (Princeton, N.J.: Princeton University Press, 1978), pp. 314–315.

55. Francisco Morales Bermúdez, "Speech, 1976," in Loveman and Davies, p. 219.

56. Ibid., p. 218.

57. Stepan, p. 316.

58. Gene E. Bigler, "The Armed Forces and Patterns of Civil-Military Relations," in John D. Martz and David J. Myers, ed., *Venezuela: The Democratic Experience* (New York: Praeger, 1977), p. 114.

59. Winfield J. Burggraaff, *The Venezuelan Armed Forces in Politics, 1935–1959* (Columbia: University of Missouri Press, 1972), pp. 5–7.

60. Ibid., pp. 8–11.

61. Bigler, p. 116.

62. Ibid., and Burggraaff, pp. 33–56.

63. Ana Mercedes Pérez, *La verdad inédita: historia de la revolución de octubre* (Caracas, 1954), p. 94.

64. Burggraaff, pp. 55–59.

65. Ibid., pp. 76–78, 95–99, 109–111, 115. For a complementary view of the reasons for the removal of the government of Romulo Gallegos, see Daniel H. Levine, *Conflict and Political Change in Venezuela* (Princeton, N.J.: Princeton University Press, 1973), pp. 38–41.

66. Government of Venezuela, *Documentos oficiales relativos al movimiento militar del 24 de noviembre de 1948* (Caracas: Oficina Nacional de Información y Publicaciones, n.d.), p. 11.

67. Burggraaff, pp. 113–115.

68. Marcos Pérez Jiménez, *Venezuela Bajo el Nuevo Ideal Nacional: Realizaciones durante el Gobierno del Coronel Marcos Pérez Jiménez, 2 de diciembre de 1952–19 de abril de 1954* (Caracas: Publicación del Servicio Informativo Venezolano, 1954), pp. 129–132.

69. Laureano Vallenilla Lanz, *Escrito de memoria* (Caracas: Ediciones Garrido, 1967) and *Razones de proscrito* (Caracas: Ediciones Garrido, 1967). Pinzón is reputed to have written many of the documents describing the new national ideal of Pérez Jiménez.

70. Burggraaff, pp. 139–141.

71. José Umaña Bernal, *Testimonio de la Revolución en Venezuela* (Caracas: Tipografía Vargas, S.A., 1958), pp. 87–88; Levine, p. 45.

72. Burggraaff, pp. 151–153.

73. Bernal, pp. 138–139.

74. Burggraaff, pp. 147–149.

75. Ibid., pp. 170–174.

76. The problem of security forces turning to crime either while employed or after has developed in a number of countries, including Brazil, Argentina, and Guatemala.

77. Bernal, pp. 262–263 and Burggraaff, pp. 188–189.

78. Jeffrey A. Hart, "Industrialization and the Fulfillment of Basic Human Needs in Venezuela," paper presented at an Institute for World Order Colloquium, October, 1978, pp. 1–2, 15–16, 26, 36–41. Forthcoming in John G. Ruggie, ed., *Alternative Conceptions of World Order*. See also Chapter 5.

79. Jorge Alberto Lozoya, "Un guión para el estudio de los ejércitos mexicanos del siglo XIX," *Insignia*, 2, 26 (13 octubre 1976): 66–67.

80. Guillermo Boils, *Los militares y la política en Mexico, 1915/1974* (Mexico: Ediciones "El Caballito," 1975), pp. 108–111. While the Colegio

Militar was originally established in 1822 it was not until after the 1910 Revolution that it became something of a prerequisite for reaching a command position. For additional information on advanced training facilities, see Frederick C. Turner, "Mexico: las causas de la limitación militar," *Aportes* (Paris), 6 (octubre 1967): 60.

81. Boils, p. 99.

82. Jorge A. Lozoya, *El ejército mexicano (1911–1965)* (Mexico: El Colegio de Mexico, 1970), p. 126.

83. Boils, pp. 62–77.

84. Ibid., pp. 79–89.

85. For a description of some of the incidents in which the army has been used to repress students, intervene in elections, pacify the rural population, and break up strikes by industrial and communications workers since 1968, see David F. Ronfeldt, "The Mexican Army and Political Order since 1940," in Abraham F. Lowenthal, ed., *Arms and Politics in Latin America* (New York: Holmes and Meier, 1976), pp. 292–293.

86. By 1973, 28 percent of the commanders of military zones had studied in the United States and a substantial proportion of the remainder had participated in official exchanges, Boils, p. 165. Mexico had the lowest percentage (1.6 percent) of officers with some U.S. training in all Latin American from 1950–1978. In the same period Brazil had 3.3 percent, Chile 10.8 percent, Peru 14.3 percent, and Venezuela 173.4 percent (percentages over 100 represent multiple periods of U.S. training for the same individuals). John Samuel Fitch, "Human Rights and the International Military Education and Training Program," Congressional Research Service, Library of Congress, Washington, D.C., 27 February 1979, p. 8. U.S. aid to promote narcotics control has increasingly been used to train Mexican police and customs officials. Violations of civil and political rights by these individuals, particularly in rural areas, have been reported, e.g., Miguel Cabildo, "Un piloto estrella su avión para matar a sus torturadores," *Proceso,* 128 (16 abril 1979): 23–25.

87. Boils, pp. 130–134 and Ronfeldt, p. 293.

88. Boils, pp. 141–144. In 1968, 11 percent of the articles in the *Revista del Ejército y Fuerza Aérea* were on technical topics and in 1973, 17 percent. During the same period articles on Mexican economic, social, and political problems increased from 2 to 18 percent.

89. Ronfeldt, pp. 295–297.

90. José Reveles, "De sostén de la Constitución a puntal del sistema: entrevista con Ramiro Bautista," *Proceso,* 111 (18 diciembre 1978): 18 and 113 (1 enero 1979): 29.

91. Bautista as quoted in Reveles, p. 18.

92. Ibid., p. 21.

93. José Ayala et al., *Mexico, hoy* 2nd ed. (Mexico: Siglo XXI, 1979), pp. 19–94. See also Chapter 5 in this volume.

94. Bautista as quoted in Reveles, p. 21.

95. In 1979 Mexican defense expenditures were approximately $518,-000,000, a 40 percent increase over 1977. The International Institute for

Strategic Studies, London, "The Military Balance 1979/80: Latin America," *Air Force Magazine,* 62, 12 (December 1979): 118.

96. While some progress in meeting basic needs has been made in Mexico in recent years, it has not been commensurate with the resources available. See Chapter 5. For evidence of human rights violations in general reported by international organizations, see Carlos Marín, "Defensores de los Derechos Humanos: Solopamiento oficial de aprehensiones arbitrarias y tormentos en Mexico," *Proceso,* 114 (8 enero 1979): 9–14; and José Reveles, "Inquietud internacional: 24 parlamentarios británicos piden a JLP que investigue desapariciones," *Proceso,* 115 (15 enero 1979): 18–20.

97. Nunn, "Overview," pp. 38–40; Ronfeldt, pp. 299–301; Bautista as quoted in Reveles, p. 19.

98. Some specific ideological developments are explored in Chapter 3.

Margaret E. Crahan

3. National Security Ideology and Human Rights

INTRODUCTION

Since 1964 the armed forces have seized power in Brazil, Argentina, Uruguay, Chile, and Bolivia, alleging that the national security of their countries was in severe jeopardy. In so doing, the military adduced a unique definition of national security which was also used to justify widespread violations of civil and political, as well as social, economic, and cultural rights. Versions of this definition, in addition to elements of the ideological currents underlying it, can also be found in traditional military dictatorships, such as Paraguay and Guatemala, as well as in formal democracies, such as Peru, Ecuador, Colombia, and Venezuela. Flowing, in part, from the Iberian heritage and colonial experience of Latin America, the nature of military professionalization, and some tendencies in European and U.S. geopolitics, as well as Catholic social thought, national security ideology is a response to the political, economic, and social crises that occurred in Latin America in the post-World War II period.

Stimulated by concern over failure of existing political and economic structures to respond effectively to and control growing popular pressures for improved living conditions, the professional military in a number of countries sought in their own experience and understanding of the world an escape from the chronic instability engendered by underdevelopment and maldistribution of wealth. The nature of military professionalization, examined in the previous chapter, had a substantial impact on the policies they chose. The search also tended to focus on ideological currents that were rooted in a critique of liberal democracy and that claimed to possess remedies, albeit radical ones, for its weaknesses. National security ideology is most fully articulated among the armed forces in the Southern Cone, especially in Argentina, Brazil, Chile, and Uruguay. This chapter will examine its principal characteristics and intellectual origins, including European geopolitical thought, anti-Marxism, positivism, and some elements of conservative Catholic social thought. The nature of the state and the economic policies that national security ideology gives rise to will also be explored, in order to elucidate the implications for human rights.

The content of national security ideology, as well as the degree to which it has molded political and economic structures and policies varies somewhat from country to country, with its most sophisticated formulations occurring in Brazil and Argentina. But perhaps the greatest efforts to mold society and transform the state and the individual according to its tenets have been made in Chile and Uruguay. Such attempts have not been entirely successful.[1]

National security ideology as examined in this chapter is not an exact replication of it in any single context. Rather it is a synthesis of major characteristics that transcend national boundaries and have serious implications for human rights. Some variations will be noted from country to country in order to indicate the extent to which this ideology has evolved and been adapted to specific national conditions. Attention will be paid to the policy implications of this ideology, not only for national security states, but also for U.S. relations with these countries.

I. CHARACTERISTICS OF NATIONAL SECURITY IDEOLOGY

National security ideology should not be confused with the internationally accepted right of a nation to protect itself from external or internal attack. Rather it is a systematization of concepts of the state, war, national power, and national goals that places national security above personal security, the needs of the state before individual rights, and the judgment of a governing elite over the rule of law. Furthermore, it identifies the nation, state, and armed forces with one another and regards a challenge to one as a threat to the others. Under this rubric, criticism of military involvement in politics is regarded as unpatriotic and antinationalistic.

The direct involvement of the military, as an institution, in government is justified as the only means to achieve the nation's destiny, defined as the realization of the country's political and economic potential. The enormity of this task helps explain why the military, when it took power in Brazil in 1964, Uruguay and Chile in 1973, and Argentina in 1976, planned to remain in power indefinitely, in contrast to the traditional pattern of military intervention, in which power was relinquished once order was deemed to have been restored.

As the junta that overthrew the elected government of Salvador Allende in Chile in September 1973 affirmed in its *Declaration of Principles,* the armed forces were not placing a time limit on their exercise of power, given the necessity of reconstructing the country morally, institutionally, and materially. The junta further expressed the intention of infusing Chileans with a new civic mentality. This task was being undertaken in order to initiate a new era in which Chileans would have healthier political habits that would be conducive to social harmony and national development. The military had no intention of serving, as they phrased it, as a parenthesis between two partisan civilian administrations, nor of returning power to politicians who, they felt, had virtually destroyed the country.[2]

Such statements reflect a strong strain of messianism among the armed forces. This was inculcated, in part, by the nature of their professionalization which instilled a great deal of pride and confidence in the military as the most competent, efficient, and patriotic national institution. It also flowed from the belief, inherent in national security ideology, that their countries were the last bulwarks of Western civilization against the inroads of secularism, Marxism, and communism, given the decay of the Western European democracies and the United States. The officers who took power were the evangelists of a new, purer form of democracy that would reduce social conflict and hence create that level of stability they deemed necessary for rapid economic growth.

The model of development espoused by national security ideology emphasizes government intervention to stimulate domestic and foreign investments through such means as "devaluation of the currency, adoption of floating exchange rates, tariff reduction, abolition of import and price controls, and increases in the charges for public services to reflect their cost."[3] It is believed that this will eventually result in sufficient economic growth to raise the overall standard of living, thereby reducing unrest and the appeal of socialism. Civic peace would facilitate the achievement of the nation's economic and political potential, increasing its ability to withstand external and internal threats to its security.

Such thoroughgoing restructuring of societies in countries such as Argentina, Uruguay, and Chile, with relatively strong traditions of political and economic participation, requires considerable coercion. As a consequence, the advent of these regimes resulted in substantial violations of civil and political rights. Political parties, unions, and professional associations, together with urban and rural popular movements, were generally restricted or suppressed. Legislatures were reconstituted, suspended, or abolished. Press censorship was initiated and freedom of association curtailed. Opponents were often jailed without due process.

Violations of the physical integrity of persons by torture or execution abounded.

Limitation of civil and political rights was required to control the unrest caused by the national security states' economic policies. The adoption of models of development emphasizing monetary stability, capital accumulation, and high growth rates necessitated restricting popular claims for more equitable distribution of national wealth. While the policies imposed have resulted in growth in some countries, most notably in Brazil, it has been accompanied by worsening income distribution, decline in real wages, escalating foreign debt, and other phenomena which have had a deleterious effect on the fulfillment of basic social and economic rights.[4] Hence the national security regimes generally have not been successful in defusing popular pressures for economic improvement.

Given the fact that a major justification used by the armed forces for the overthrow of civilian governments is the promise of economic regeneration, the national security states are today the objects of considerable criticism, even from some of their original supporters;[5] the response has ranged from increased coercion to some liberalization. The latter has been aimed at increasing the legitimacy of military government and defusing domestic and international criticism. Fluctuations between repression and liberalization have given rise to substantial debates over the degree to which political openings reflect actual progress in redemocratization and over what the proper response of critics, including rights advocates, should be. While this chapter does not provide specific recommendations for such cases, it is based on the belief that effective redemocratization strategies[6] will be devised only when the origins and nature of national security ideology and its implications for human rights are broadly understood throughout the Americas.

II. INTELLECTUAL ORIGINS OF NATIONAL SECURITY IDEOLOGY [7]

Geopolitics. Geopolitics[8] is defined by one of its most influential proponents in Latin America, Jorge Atencio, as "the science that studies the influence of geographic factors in the life and evolution of states, in order to extract conclusions of a political character." He also considers it a guide for statesmen in devising domestic and international policies for the state and the military in the preparation of national defense and the formulation of security measures. Most importantly, Atencio believes geopolitics can assist in deducing how national objectives can best be achieved.[9]

Early geopolitical formulations were disseminated through German military missions in Argentina and Chile in the latter part of the nineteenth and beginning of the twentieth centuries. They encouraged the belief that, "in the life of nations man's relation to space finds its ultimate expression in war; for states struggle with each other in order to win space. This lust for space and more space is . . . the inevitable consequence of the biological fact that the State itself is a living organism."[10] This concept of the state encouraged the conviction that it had needs that transcended those of the individual. States came to be viewed as locked in constant struggle to achieve their national destinies, with those impeding the achievement of national potential classified as enemies, whether they were states or individuals.[11] Constant warfare became the norm and national survival the prize at stake. World Wars I and II were offered as evidence of this. Since then, according to Atencio, the focus of the struggle has changed from conflicts between states to internal subversion.[12]

The lack of serious threats of international warfare in the Southern Cone of Latin America since the nineteenth century and the development of guerrilla movements in the 1950s and 1960s, seemed to confirm Atencio's position. In addition, geopolitics' emphasis on the necessity of geographic integration and infrastructural development for economic progress echoed a long-standing sentiment among the armed forces.[13]

Anti-Marxism.   The responsibility of the military became not just the defeat of the enemy, but also the strengthening of the nation by physically and economically integrating it and mobilizing popular energies for development.[14] The chief impediment to this in the modern world was internal subversion initiated by international communism to destroy Western democracy and the capitalist system. This meant total war and, hence, an effective response had to use a broad range of political, economic, psychosocial, and military tactics.[15] National leadership must be given extraordinary powers to deal with the threat of subversion.

The idea that the denial of political participation and of social and economic justice contribute to subversion is largely rejected by national security ideology which prefers to see international communism as the cause, aided by inefficient, incompetent, and corrupt civilian governments. It is imperative, consequently, that governments be in the hands of those whose loyalty to the nation transcends personal or group interests. This was precisely how the military defined itself. Thus, only under the direction of the armed forces could governments defeat Marxism and end the threat to national security.[16]

Partisan politics, strikes, inter- and intra-group conflict are regarded as Marxist inspired. This inclines national security states to categorize as subversive those organizations whose strategies have traditionally been based on competition, including political parties and unions. Conflict, even in the legitimate exercise of rights, is regarded as inimicable to security. Hence

> because there are numerous causes which may generate a conflict, security tends to be all-embracing, seeking to control all foreseeable situations. At the beginning, the military fought armed extremists, but since this was not sufficient to achieve "total security," not only are the Marxist political parties proscribed, but also those parties which are "easy prey" for the Marxists—in the case of Chile, the radical parties and the Christian Democrats. This, however, is still not enough. Total security becomes like a snowball rolling downhill, continually growing in size with those who are "infiltrated" by Marxism. Union members and professionals are added to the proscribed parties, and finally the Church itself. In their search for total security regimes end by marginalizing the majority of a society which will never be secure enough for those in power.[17]

Under such conditions the ability of the ordinary citizen to enjoy civil and political rights and full social and economic needs is circumscribed.

Although a good number of analysts of national security ideology ascribe its anti-Marxism to Cold War attitudes imported from the United States in the 1950s and 1960s, the evidence shows that it was strong within the armed forces in the Southern Cone as far back as the 1920s.[18] Even in Chile, where the military accepted the election of a Socialist president, Salvador Allende, in 1970, anti-Marxism was a constant within the military.[19] This attitude spread throughout the armed forces and beyond during the 1960s and early 1970s, fueled by fear of socialist transformation of political and economic structures.

Military anti-Marxism in national security regimes has not, however, obviated pragmatic foreign policy decisions, particularly in Argentina and Brazil. Nationalism, anti-U.S. sentiment, and economic necessity, among other factors, have contributed to the expansion of trade with the Soviet bloc, cooperation with socialist members of the nonaligned movement, and occasional sharp disagreements with the United States. Anti-Marxism, in fact, has had more bearing on domestic matters than on foreign policy in national security regimes.

Conservative Catholic Social Thought. The tradition of anti-Marxism within Catholicism reinforced that of the military and led the latter to presume that the church would be a natural ally in accomplishing national security objectives. While there has been some support from conservative Catholic elements, in general repression and worsening conditions for the poor have served to alienate the church from the military, particularly in Brazil and Chile, and to a lesser extent in Argentina and Uruguay. Tension has also developed over the claims of the national security states to be promoting a Christian humanist concept of man and of society, even when engaged in violations of human rights. Frequent references by military leaders to Catholic teaching on the individual, family, common good, natural law, private property, subsidiarity,[20] and Marxism are all part of an attempt to legitimate their government. Such efforts have increasingly been challenged by church officials as perversions of actual Catholic social thought. Nevertheless, there is some convergence between national security ideology and conservative strains of Catholicism.[21]

These include versions of Catholic social thought that posit a hierarchically structured organic society in which the government determines what is conducive to the well-being of the nation. Such thinking is also critical of the free play of democratic forces within society and of popular sovereignty. The ideal is to have participation channelled through nonpolitical groupings representing workers, professionals, students, and others.[22]

This orientation finds one of its chief expressions in Latin American integralism,[23] which has been heavily influenced by some of the same currents of European Catholic social thought that gave rise in the 1920s and 1930s to Opus Dei in Spain and Action Française in France.[24] These groups shared a desire to remold modern society according to an idealized version of medieval Christianity in which social harmony was thought to have reigned. They also supported a strong central government and a hierarchically structured society. In the 1950s an organization known as Cité Catholique, which shared a similar orientation, appeared among the French military. It regarded liberalism, socialism, and communism as the principal sources of modern problems. Members of the Cité Catholique were dissatisfied with democracy and parliamentary government, considering them to be dangerously weak in the face of Marxist subversion. They justified psychological warfare and torture as necessary means of overcoming this threat and preserving national security. The primacy of the dignity of the person in Catholic social thought was largely discounted in such formulations.[25]

In 1960 groups linked to the Cité Catholique were established in Buenos Aires and Caracas. The ideas they promoted subsequently influenced the orientation of Societies for the Defense of Tradition, Family, and Property (TPF) in Brazil and Chile. These groups supported the

1964 military coup in Brazil and the 1973 one in Chile. In Argentina, members of the Buenos Aires Ciudad Católica were heavily represented in the government of General Juan Carlos Onganía (1966–1970). TPF schools were opened and were run jointly by French exiles from the Organisation de l'Armée Secrète. Periodicals such as *Itinéraires* in Argentina, *Permanences* and *Hora Presente* in Brazil, and *Tizona* in Chile helped disseminate integralist concepts.[26] The Catholic Universities of São Paulo, Santiago, and Valparaiso all had groups espousing the basic tenets of conservative Catholic thought, including integralism.

Catholic integralists participated in Brazilian, Argentinian, and Chilean politics as early as the 1920s, and hence by the 1960s integralism had been fairly widely disseminated. In Chile, Jaime Guzmán, a student leader at the Catholic University in Santiago, organized integralist groups in the 1960s. They frequently attacked Christian Democratic socioeconomic reforms during the presidency of Eduardo Frei Montalva (1964–1970) as confiscatory and socialist. Claiming that modern society was decaying under the weight of materialism and egoism, the Chilean integralists called for a strengthening of the presidency and the reorganization of society into functional groups or *gremios*. This was intended to eliminate the need for political parties, unions, and special interest groups, and the political and economic conflicts they gave rise to.

Such views were shared by a good number of the officers who led the September 1973 military coup, including General Augusto Pinochet. Guzmán and some of his fellow integralists, in fact, played major roles in the drafting of the junta's March 1974 *Declaration of Principles* and the national constitution adopted in September 1980. Integralists have also inserted themselves into those areas of the Chilean government which they regard as highly influential in molding civic attitudes. These include communications and public relations, the National Secretariat for Women, and the National Secretariat for Youth.[27] These organizations, together with business, professional, and labor *gremios,* are intended to replace political parties and unions and promote a harmonious, organic society that will achieve the stability necessary for substantial economic development.

Such corporate visions of society tend to diminish the rights of the individual by making them subordinate to the ends of the state. The concept of subsidiarity in the national security states is not used so much to promote greater popular participation, as originally intended in Catholic thought, but rather to allow for greater social control by government. It is also misused to justify turning over substantial economic decisionmaking to private interests, thereby reducing the possibilities of fulfilling the social and economic rights of the lower classes.[28]

Disenchantment with Democracy.   A principal rationale offered by the armed forces for the establishment of national security regimes is the inefficiency, incompetence, and corruption of the governments they overturned and the weakness of liberal democracy in the face of Marxism. Traditional versions of participatory democracy, individual rights, and legal guarantees are regarded as undercutting government in the total war against internal subversion. The military in national security states has condemned harshly the use of rights claims by "audacious" minorities purportedly to gain benefits from the state at the expense of national well-being. Competition for government benefits by traditional interest groups and political parties is seen as contrary to general national interests, as is the idea that national objectives should be determined by universal suffrage. Majority rule is defective in that it gives influence in government to the masses, which are incapable of making decisions conducive to the realization of national potential, a task, it is argued, best left to the state. Government should be accorded exceptional powers and placed in the hands of those with the expertise to devise policies that will exploit a country's potential. Legitimacy for such governments comes not from votes, but from their accomplishments.[29]

The deeply rooted traditional military disdain for civilian politicians has a long history, springing in part, from the armed forces sense of integrity and patriotism, but also from their discipline, efficiency, and technological expertise. "Members of the professional officer corps in Argentina, Bolivia, Brazil, Chile, Paraguay, and Peru blamed social disorder, economic collapse, and professional shortcomings on civilians and their politics long before the Cold War, Castro, and Che Guevara."[30] Such attitudes were encouraged by European military missions and reinforced by the relative isolation of the military in society and the reality of the limitations of civilian governments. After European military missions were phased out in the late 1930s and early 1940s, the establishment or expansion of war colleges in most of these countries helped nurture an increasing sense of the armed forces' capacity to solve national problems and lead their countries to greatness. U.S. encouragement in the 1960s of military involvement in civic action programs further stimulated such attitudes.[31]

Advanced social science and technological training, together with their actual application, revealed the complexity of the political, economic, and social problems facing Latin American countries. This further helped "undermine the credibility of solutions advanced by political parties, thereby weakening the claim of civilian leadership to sole legitimacy."[32] It also inclined the military, which had also been exposed to positivist philosophies,[33] to seek out what were regarded as neutral solutions to national problems. Such solutions would transcend the limitations of partisan political ones. This would end ideological struggle and ultimately allow societies to reach "a natural equilibrium with no structural contradictions." [34] This is a direct challenge to the Marxist tenet that political and economic change can only be achieved within the context of class struggle. It is, in sum, a technocratic authoritarian answer [35] to perceived weaknesses of participatory democracy in dealing with the problems of underdevelopment and Marxist subversion.

Military distrust of civilian politicians and politics was augmented in Brazil, Argentina, and Chile by attempts by civilian administrations to convince officers to take partisan political positions, as well as increase their identification with particular governments. Such efforts during the presidencies of João Goulart (1961–1964) in Brazil and Salvador Allende (1970–1973) in Chile were resented by some sectors of the military as compromising their professional integrity and political neutrality. In each case, anti-Marxism, a strong preference for gradual rather than rapid social change, and fear of turmoil increased the number of officers foreseeing damage to the military as an institution. The perception of elected civilian governments as threatening the survival of the institutional integrity of the military helped increase support for the overthrow of constitutional governments by the armed forces.

III. THE NATIONAL SECURITY STATE [36]

Convinced that they were the only bulwark against national disintegration, the armed forces—when they took power in Brazil in 1964, in Uruguay and Chile in 1973, and in Argentina in 1976—regarded themselves as the only legitimate representatives of national interests. As such, it was incumbent on them to mold a state capable of creating a powerful nation. [37] As the guardians of national interests, the military considered themselves above political competition and, as a consequence, rejected allegations that they represented the interests of certain economic groups or social classes. Instead, they saw themselves as operating autonomously and independently of politics and special interests in the pursuit of the common good, which explains the belief in their moral right to lead their countries and the outrage they felt when institutions, such as the Catholic Church, accused them of immorality as a result of human rights violations.

The armed forces in such regimes frequently identify themselves as the saviors of their nations which were in danger of being destroyed by misuse of state power by civilian politicians.[38] Under the military, state and nation are increasingly identified with each other, with the state being the incarnation of the nation and the national spirit.[39] Reflecting the influence of geopolitics, the military regards the state as the institutionalized expression of the nation, with government the apparatus through which state power is exercised. The supreme expression of state power is the armed forces and hence any criticism of them is an attack on the state and nation. [40] With the concept of the state absorbed into that of the nation as a living organism, national objectives emanate from the essence of the nation rather than from popular consensus. The state specifies them, and conflict is regarded as a threat to national unity and hence national security. [41]

The principal task of the national security state is to organize the population to achieve national objectives, [42] the instrument being national power used by the state to organize society to carry out the will of the state. Such power is political, economic, military, and psychosocial. The latter focuses on transmitters of culture and values, such as the church and the media. [43] Factors constituting national power include:

> territory, population, national character of the population, national spirit, renewable and nonrenewable natural resources, industrial capacity, capacity for scientific and technological development, military might, form of government, popular support, economic policy, quality of diplomacy, education and culture, communications systems, internal legislation, and sovereignty. Essentially, they are the same elements which make up the state. [44]

All are to be employed to accomplish national objectives.

These elements also contribute to the consolidation and institutionalization of what is categorized as authentic social power. This is regarded as the most efficient instrument for constructing a technological society in which those with the greatest knowledge prevail. According to national security ideology, the result is a true participatory society, for in it an enlightened elite leads a populace organized into corporate units in the pursuit of the betterment of all. Such an accomplishment, however, requires groups, such as *gremios,* that serve to make the people more technologically and less ideologically oriented. Coalitions of *gremios* also facilitate the social organization of the country. Only in this way can social power be independent and depoliticized, and hence effective in attaining national objectives by aiding groups within society to achieve their specific goals. In this instance the state performs a subsidiary function by removing obstacles and deficiencies that impede the achievement of the common good of a truly free society. [45]

The concepts in national security ideology of the organic state, governmental decisionmaking by narrow elites, and subsidiarity are profoundly exclusionary. In particular, they tend to bar those sectors of society previously organized and politically mobilized, since societal conflict is attributed to them. These organizations are frequently suppressed, their leadership jailed or exiled, and the exercise of such rights as freedom of association and free expression impeded. These actions are generally more common during the initial period of consolidation of power. Later, in the face of the regime's desire for increased legitimization through popular support, some openness has, in fact, developed, particularly in Brazil, and to a lesser extent in Chile, Argentina, and Uruguay.

The reorganization of society under the aegis of national security states has not progressed very far, and patterns of political and social participation similar to pre-coup ones continue to be present, even though traditional parties and other groups may have disappeared. In their stead, there has been a proliferation of new groups stimulated, in part, by repression. These include human rights organizations, workers' groups, and grass roots church communities, among others. They constitute prime challenges to the national security state and its underlying ideology. Hence they have become targets for repression by the state. [46]

IV. SECURITY AND DEVELOPMENT

In national security ideology, development is regarded as a political, economic, psychosocial, and military process that increases national power, so that external and internal security is ensured. The link between national security and development is not of recent vintage. It was made by the military as early as the nineteenth century and more frequently beginning in the 1920s. In the latter period military officers often called for governments that would lead in modernizing their countries' economic infrastructure and in expanding industrialization. Only in this way, they argued, would their countries be sufficiently strong to maintain and defend their national sovereignty and independence. [47] Furthermore, the armed forces stood ready to assist civilian governments in this effort, and the 1920s and 1930s witnessed the growth of military involvement in communications, transportation, and industry. A good number of the coups that occurred in this period were justified by the failure of civilian governments to see to the strategic needs of the nation.

By the 1960s the concept of development in national security ideology required the mobilization of entire countries in the national project, that is, the achievement of national objectives. [48] To do this it was thought necessary to introduce new technology, stimulate industrial growth and exports, encourage capital accumulation for investment, and mobilize material and human resources more fully. [49] The state had to encourage greater economic competition through allowing relatively free play of market forces. Only in this fashion, it was argued, would individual freedom and the common good be achieved and poverty, together with the social disorder that accompanied it, be eliminated. The state did, however, have to carefully regulate monetary policy, wages, prices, and the quality of products. While foreign investment was to be encouraged, government should see that international monopolies did not damage national interests. Extremes of wealth and poverty were to be avoided through public provision of some educational, health, and housing assistance where necessary. [50]

Brazil, with its substantial economic resources, best reflects the strengths and weaknesses of the development policies of national security states. As the economist Albert Fishlow has stated:

> A market system oriented toward maximum growth, and unencumbered by popular wishes, will almost inevitably emphasize profits at the expense of wages, will almost inevitably tolerate monopoly gains and prevent labor from organizing, will almost inevitably subsidize investment and attract foreign capital to exploit especially favorable opportunities. In such circumstances, excesses occur, and have occurred. [51]

Styling the Brazilian model as authoritarian capitalism, Fishlow notes that giving priority to rapid economic growth has produced worsening income distribution and hence the need for a repressive political system and, specifically, a controlled labor sector. Brazilian planners themselves have, at times, acknowledged the negative consequences of:

> strategies which favor growth at the expense of a more equitable pattern of distribution, relying, if at all, on some form of "trickle-down" mechanism to satisfy distributive demands. For example, Dr. Mario Henrique Simonsen, director of MOBRAL, the Brazilian literacy movement, in a recent paper was unambiguously clear that the Brazilian development philosophy is one which "establishes as a basic priority the accelerated growth of the GNP, accepting as a short-term liability the corollary of an appreciable imbalance between individual rates of income. . . . " Speaking with evident satisfaction of an established, government-controlled system of wage adjustment, he explained that in the first place, it has served to simplify and pacify wage-claim negotiations; these are no longer resolved by rounds of strikes and other forms of collective pressure, but simply by rapid mathematical calculations. . . . [52]

Faith in technical solutions is a hallmark of national security ideology, as is the necessity of having a relatively closed political system in which power is centralized in the hands of a hegemonic elite, which dominates the apparatus of the state. The closed nature of the political system in Brazil has, nevertheless, been modified somewhat since the early 1970s as a result of pressures not only from outside the government, but also from within.

Sharp challenges by nationalist officers and technicians who oppose widespread foreign penetration of the economy occurred in 1967–1969 under the leadership of General Afonso Augusto de Albuquerque Lima, and again some ten years later. Such critics charged that Brazilian national security was not being promoted by policies which made the country more dependent economically on international capital and that stimulated worsening income distribution, declines in real wages, and escalating foreign debt. The defenders of the intensive promotion of growth won out, however, in struggles that occurred largely within the upper echelons of the regime. Independent worker organizations, which have grown substantially in recent years, have little direct say in such decisions and continue to be the objects of repression. They, as well as some independent political and professional groups together with the Catholic Church, have spearheaded the movement for redemocratization. Their growing strength has resulted in some liberalization. Repression continues to be used, however, as a means of imposing government policies.

In Chile, after the military coup of September 1973, economic planning was largely in the hands of technicians, including some U.S. economists from the University of Chicago, who favored orthodox economic policies including devaluation, floating exchange rates, tariff reduction, elimination of import and price controls, and wage controls. Government provision of social services was reduced. The burden of such policies fell predominantly on the working class with declines in real wages and rising unemployment. The government did provide some food and employment programs to ameliorate this situation, but they were not adequate. Decreased income and hence demand reduced inflation from 1973 levels. There has also been an upsurge in foreign loans and investment which has stimulated some sectors of the economy.[53]

As in Brazil, criticism of the government's economic model has been widespread, even within the Chilean military. The reasons have been similar to those in Brazil: objections to the denationalization of Chilean businesses, fear of rising foreign debt, and concern over social costs. Repression of the labor sector has been a constant, although workers have managed to escape total control. Industries aimed at the domestic market (e.g., textiles, appliances) have suffered because of declines in real wages.[54] Such factors were repeatedly criticized by the Air Force's General Gustavo Leigh Guzmán, who eventually was forced out of the ruling junta.

A recent analysis of the economic policies implemented by the national security regimes in Chile, Brazil, Argentina, and Uruguay has concluded that their application resulted, in all four cases, in real wages falling 30 to 40 percent as well as a decline in the income share of the poor. There was, in contrast, a significant gain for the wealthiest 20 percent. In addition, in Argentina and Chile these policies contributed to recessions, declines in the Gross Domestic Product (GDP), and substantial unemployment. [55] The costs of such policies fell predominantly on the lower and lower middle classes. The domestic tensions which this has produced challenge the thesis that such economic policies promote internal security. Hence the prime justification for the economic models used by the national security states has been undercut. Though there have been advances in some economic indicators, the promises of stability, harmony, and the achievement of national well-being have not been realized.

V. IMPLICATIONS FOR HUMAN RIGHTS

The emergence of national security regimes in the 1960s and 1970s in the Southern Cone of Latin America resulted in widespread violations of civil and political rights. The enjoyment of social and economic rights, particularly by the lower classes, also suffered. This was the result of the coming to power of military men imbued with a concept of national security in which their definition of the needs of the nation superseded the rights and needs of individual persons.

While national security regimes in Brazil, Uruguay, Chile, and Argentina did reduce certain barriers to economic development, it was at considerable social and political cost. In particular, the trend toward greater political participation on the part of the masses was arrested and, consequently, their ability to obtain a just share of national wealth was constrained. While traditional forms of political dissent were suppressed, the evidence suggests that political polarization increased. In their zeal to preserve their vision of Western capitalism and democracy, the national security states resorted to extra-legal and unconstitutional means that discredited their cause and undercut the legal bases of their societies. [56] There could be no greater threat to the security of these nations. Furthermore, the policies and actions of these states, in the name of capitalist growth and a purer form of democracy, have alienated substantial numbers of citizens, making them more receptive to such alternatives as socialism.

All this resulted, in large measure, from the military's distrust of participatory democracy and civilian government. This sentiment, which the armed forces traditionally harbored, was heightened by partisan political conflict in the face of increasing structural crises in post-World War II Latin America. Frustration and disquiet within the officer corps was reinforced by exposure to colleagues who espoused ideologies that were rooted in critiques of traditional politics and promised solutions to national difficulties that augmented the role of the military in national life. Officers who championed national security ideology had the advantage of clearly defined positions that sharply questioned civilian domination of the military.

Intervention was, in large measure, the result of generalized belief within the armed forces that their nations were in grave danger of succumbing to chaos and that there was no viable option other than for the military to take power. Those who spearheaded the coups in Brazil in 1964, Uruguay and Chile in 1973, and Argentina in 1976 were, in that sense, acting out of nationalist rather than personal motives. In this respect the professionalization of the military which was initiated in the nineteenth century was successful. Furthermore, the military may very well have been the most unified and efficient institution in their countries. Problems arose from the attempts to restructure society in order to eliminate the ferment and conflict which resulted from social and economic inequalities. In such a situation, long-term stability can be achieved only if there is sufficient improvement in living conditions to reduce pressures from the disadvantaged. Imposition of order from above, without major social and economic reforms, can only be maintained by coercion and repression which result in large-scale violations of rights. This has been the case in the national security states.

Violations of civil and political rights have resulted specifically from the concept of the nation/state as a living organism with its own needs rather than as an instrument to satisfy the needs of the people. Identification of the state and the nation reinforces the authority of the state and conflicts with the idea that sovereignty resides in the people. As a consequence, individual rights and democratic processes tend to be superseded by the objectives of the governing elite. Disagreements over these objectives and the means to achieve them are regarded as antithetical to the realization of the common good. This is defined in national security ideology as the sum of individual good. As traditionally conceived, however, individuals and collectivities are not only the object of common good, but also contribute to it. Consequently, common good is common "not only in its end (final cause) but . . . also in its origin (efficient cause): hence the systematic marginalization of broad sectors of society is a complete negation of the common good." [57] Furthermore, it "encompasses all the good that society can transmit and that reverts to the person through justice. In order to be realized, the common good entails and requires recognition of the fundamental rights of the person.

It therefore embraces right, justice, liberty, and material prosperity." [58] The concept of common good in national security ideology contributes to widespread violations of human rights, because it does not require democratic participation in government. Furthermore, it undermines the belief that rights inhere in the individual. [59]

While not all proponents of nation security ideology would assert, as has the Brazilian General Argus Lima, that freedom and human rights derive from the state and are bestowed by it on individuals as privileges, the concept of human rights in national security ideology is a diminished one. [60] Rights, it is posited, must be restricted for the common good, to combat terrorism, or because the level of development does not permit their full enjoyment. [61] The latter does not simply refer to limitations imposed by scarce national resources, but also to those required by government economic strategies. Challenges to models of development are consequently seen as contrary to the government's efforts to fulfill social and economic rights, and hence are not considered a legitimate exercise of the right of political protest. Such factors have contributed to violations of freedom of opinion and expression, of peaceful assembly and association, and of the right to take part in government either directly or through representatives. [62]

Concentration of power in the hands of the armed forces, imbued with the belief that there are no limits to the means that can be used to eliminate subversion, defined so broadly as to include nonviolent dissent and general opposition to a government, has also resulted in violations of civil and political rights. Most notable has been the extent of deprivation of life, liberty, and security of person. [63] Since under national security ideology countries are regarded as locked in constant internal warfare, peacetime restrictions on government authority are generally lifted via the imposition of states of siege or emergency. These allow for the disregard of rights such as habeas corpus, while the belief that no quarter must be given the enemy sanctions torture, assassinations, and generalized repression. The enemy is defined not as those who are actively seeking to overthrow the government by violence, but as anyone whom the government decides is subverting the state. In contemporary Brazil, Chile, Argentina, and Uruguay, this has at times included even those individuals attempting to change government by peaceful means, as well as those simply opposed to government policies.

Those who take up arms to change existing political and economic structures are accorded no rights whatsoever. The rationale is that such individuals do not deserve the benefits of citizenry, because they have acted contrary to the common good of society and consequently are worse than common criminals. [64] To accord them legal protections would be for governments to violate natural law by acting contrary to the fundamental rights of a nation, which has rights as a living organism. This helps explain the spread of rights violations, especially those relating to the physical integrity of the person in national security states, and the hostility with which international pressures on behalf of political prisoners are greeted. A mentality of giving no quarter predominates, justifying extralegal actions by governments or the invoking of states of emergency or siege. Under these conditions there is no such thing as political prisoners or prisoners of conscience, and legal protections have scant impact.

Furthermore, concentration of power in the hands of the executive branch of government has tended to undercut the judiciary, which has sometimes been disregarded entirely in favor of military courts. Purges of the ranks of the judges, arrests or expulsions from the country of lawyers who defend political prisoners, secret trials, and other violations of the right to free trial have been encouraged by the concept of executive power in national security ideology. In 1977 in Uruguay, for example, Institutional Act #8 eliminated the autonomy of the judiciary and made it dependent on the executive. Nine years earlier, Institutional Act #5 in Brazil attempted something similar, in addition to dissolving congress and imposing other restrictions on representative government. This practice of ruling by means of institutional acts and similar instruments circumvents the rule of law and representative government. [65]

Dominated by a concept of total war and inclined to disregard legal limitations, the armed forces and police in national security states often ignore the right to privacy through unauthorized searches, surveillance, censorship of mails, and similar activities. Frequently, such actions are directed against leaders of political organizations, labor unions, and professional and student groups. In addition, limitations on freedom of association, including severe restrictions on the number of persons that can gather for anything other than purely social purposes, hamper the full expression of the political will of the citizenry.

CONCLUSION

In sum, the emergence of national security ideology and its implementation via military dominated states in the Southern Cone has had negative consequences for human rights. In addition, these regimes have not succeeded in substantially achieving their own stated goals. In the political sphere, for example, concentration of power in the state has led to excesses which have increased distrust of authority. In the economic sphere, their policies have increased denationalization of local business and increased international dependency, thereby substantially decreasing national sovereignty. In the social sphere, the ideal of a harmonious society appears farther away, given the increase in class antagonisms. In the cultural sphere, a new era of censorship and indoctrination has been initiated, although repression has stimulated considerable intellectual and cultural vitality among the opposition and within exile communities. In the religious sphere, the Catholic Church, which traditionally had been a conservative bulwark of the status quo, has become more progressive and alienated from the governing elite. Finally, in the judicial sphere, national security ideology places the state above the law, which strikes at a fundamental basis for order in society. This is a substantial challenge to the legitimacy of the national security state.

These consequences arise from some intrinsic weaknesses in national security ideology. Only in theory can the state and the nation be identified. Nor are the sources of national security to be found in the exercise of state power, but rather in the peoples' judgment that government is responsive to their needs. The level of repression that has been used belies the claims that the state is acting in accord with natural law. Nor is loyalty to one's nation to be confused with loyalty to the state, for the former can exist without the latter, which can be legitimately withheld by the people.

The abandonment of popular participation in governmental decision making in favor of elite determination has cast the military in the role of enforcer. To maintain control, the armed forces have frequently acted illegally, disregarding laws, at the same time that they expect a high level of observance from the populace. National security states are therefore widely regarded as arbitrary, causing both their opponents and supporters to seek ways to circumvent regulations. This further contributes to the appearance of illegitimacy. If this is combined with the continuing failure of these regimes to improve substantially the welfare of the people, the inclination of the citizenry to defend the state against internal or external challenges is decreased. Such a situation facilitates the penetration of critical ideologies.

Devoid of broad-based popular support, increasingly challenged as illegitimate and contrary to the well-being of the citizenry, these states must ultimately use coercion and repression to stay in power. This further weakens the ties between the state and civil society, and makes these governments more dependent on the manipulation of symbols, public opinion, the media, and educational and cultural institutions. As the people increasingly distrust such institutions, they give more credence to opposition opinions.

The proliferation of alternative sources of information confirms this and has helped reinforce the growth of opposition organizations, whether they be workers' organizations, new political groups, student associations, or Christian base communities. The failure of the *gremios* in Chile, government supported political parties in Brazil, and official workers' organizations in all the national security states to attract broad-based support and participation has been one of the major setbacks of these governments. The limited capacity of the national security states to mobilize popular support for their programs and policies impedes realization of national objectives. These states have, consequently, extremely narrow bases which over the long term threaten their stability. Concern over this problem has given rise to much of the criticism from within the military. National unity has not been achieved, polarization continues, and internal security is unattained.

Overall, the promises of political and economic stability and realization of national potential made by the military in Brazil, Argentina, Uruguay, and Chile have not been realized. The potential for societal conflict has been increased. The problems which the military initially set out to resolve continue to dog them, encouraging critics, military and otherwise, to urge a return to civilian government. These pressures would appear to be growing, suggesting that the military may eventually withdraw with its integrity badly damaged and a large residue of animosity from the civilian populace. If the military does not retire from government, and political, economic, and social conditions in these countries do not markedly improve, then the possibility of internal subversion increases. Hence national security states have not realized their principal goal.

Nor has the threat of Communism been eliminated. This is largely due to the fact that to defeat Communism requires the offering of a morally superior ideology. The justification of violations of human rights as a means to an end in national security ideology undercuts any claims to moral superiority. The failure of national security regimes to establish their moral authority and civic concord is not conducive to hemispheric security.

U.S. policymakers should take this into account when determining the nature of relations with national security states. There is no convincing evidence that identification with these governments increases U.S. security. History does suggest, however, that U.S. support of repressive governments provides anti-U.S. forces with ammunition to discredit this country's commitment to democracy and freedom.[66] Support of national security states is, consequently, not conducive to the short- or long-term interests of the United States.

NOTES TO CHAPTER 3

1. The defeat in a national plebiscite in late 1980 of a new Uruguayan constitution that would have institutionalized the role of the military in government and accorded a National Security Council extraordinary powers, reflected strong popular resistance to the legitimization of the current authoritarian regime. The voter outcome apparently took the military by surprise and precipitated some reevaluation of the government's political options. In Chile, a September 1980 plebiscite on a new constitution resulted in reportedly 65 percent of the voters approving a document that embodied a less radical version of the national security state. Edward Schumacher, "Uruguay Brass, Now Tarnished, Begin to Snipe at Each Other," *The New York Times,* 28 December 1980, p. E8, and "Uruguayans Tense as Military, Outvoted, Ponders Future," *The New York Times,* 14 January 1981, p. A2; Charles A. Krause, "Chilean Students Protest Plebiscite: Thousands Denounce Pinochet Eve of Vote on His Charter," *The Washington Post* 11 September 1980, p. A26, and "Pinochet Wins Overwhelming Vote on New Constitution," *The Washington Post,* 12 September 1980, p. A22; "Chile Gets to Vote But Not to Choose," *The New York Times,* 17 September 1980, p. E3.

2. Junta de Gobierno, Chile, *Declaración de los Principios del Gobierno de Chile* (Santiago de Chile: Editora Nacional Gabriela Mistral, 1974), pp. 28–29.

3. David Collier, ed., *The New Authoritarianism in Latin America* (Princeton, N.J.: Princeton University Press, 1979), pp. 401–402.

4. For analyses of the impact of such economic policies on basic needs, see Chapters 4, 5, 6, and 7 of this volume.

5. Criticism has also come from inside the military. In Brazil, periodic debates over economic policies have divided the armed forces, as well as alienated some of the regime's civilian supporters. On December 26, 1980, for example, a former Chief of Staff of the armed forces, General José Maria de Andrada, was briefly put under house arrest for criticizing the government for not following more nationalist policies with respect to the operations of multinationals in Brazil. Similar complaints were voiced in the late 1960s by General Afonso Augusto de Albuquerque Lima, representing a good number of other officers and technocrats. They objected especially to the increasing penetration of the Brazilian economy by foreign interests. "Brazilian Ex-Staff Chief Detained," *The New York Times,* 27 December 1980, p. 5; Peter Flynn, "The Brazilian Development Model: The Political Dimension," in Brian Loveman and Thomas M. Davies, Jr., eds., *The Politics of Antipolitics: The Military in Latin America* (Lincoln: University of Nebraska Press, 1978), pp. 262–264.

6. The construction of such strategies must be based on a comprehensive understanding of both the domestic and international factors that have contributed to the emergence of authoritarian states in Latin America. A recent comparative study of such regimes in Latin America concludes that these include:

the problems associated with different phases of industrialization; the rise of transnational corporations and the internationalization of production; differences among countries in the long-term prosperity of the primary product export sector; short-term fluctuations in the prosperity of this sector; the scope of the resources that the state is able to derive from taxing this sector; the growing political importance of certain social sectors and social roles, such as the popular sector, technocrats, and "nationals" within each country who are closely tied to transnational corporations; the emergence of "new professionalism" in the military and of new military ideologies about intervention in politics; the nature of the earlier political incorporation of important class groups in society, for instance, the urban popular sector and industrialists; the closely related issues of the degree to which social conflict is mitigated by the existence of multi-class, integrative parties and the degree of effective state control of organized labor; the political strength of the popular sector (which may be affected by the nature of the incorporation, but which is also shaped by other factors); U.S. intervention; the revolutionary and counterrevolutionary reaction to the Cuban revolution; military competition among Latin American nations; differences among countries in political ideology and political culture; political leadership, and the presence (or absence) of deliberative "preemptive" political action that leads to political compromises that help to mitigate the crises that tend to trigger the rise of authoritarianism; and a pattern of "tentativeness" of Latin American political institutions that makes regime change more likely to occur in the context of crises.

David Collier, "The Bureaucratic Authoritarian Model: Synthesis and Priorities for Future Research," in Collier, pp. 377–378.

7. For the historical context out of which national security ideology flowed, see Chapters 1 and 2 of this volume.

8. It is asserted by José Comblin in *The Church and the National Security State* (Maryknoll, N.Y.: Orbis Books, 1979), p. 70 that geopolitical theory was introduced into Latin America by the United States in the post-World War II period. One of its chief proponents, the Argentine Jorge Atencio, disagrees. He claims that works by the Germans R. Hennig and L. Korholz, including *Introducción a la Geopolítica,* which were published and distributed to the Argentine Army and Navy by the Escuela de Guerra Naval in 1941, were critical in spreading geopolitical thought. Also important were works by Emilio R. Isola and Angel Carlos Berra, including *Introducción a la Geopolítica Argentina,* and Julio Londono's *Geopolítica de Colombia.* While U.S. strategic theorists were increasingly read by the Latin American military in the post-World War II period, the influence of European thought in their ideological formation appears greater. The sources cited by proponents of national security ideology are overwhelmingly German, French, and Latin American.

Even in the 1960s, when the ties between the United States and Latin

American military were close, French military literature, particularly that concerning the Algerian War (1951–1962) appeared to have been more influential. Works by Colonel Roger Trinquier and the novelist, Jean Larteguy (e.g., *The Centurions* and *The Praetorians*), were widely distributed in Argentina and Brazil. They continue to be cited today. While this does not deny the impact of U.S. Cold War attitudes and security policies, it does suggest that the transmission of geopolitical thought to Latin America and the emergence of national security ideology was a complex process that developed over time and had a variety of sources. Jorge E. Atencio, *¿Qué es la geopolítica?* (Buenos Aires: Ediciones Pleamar, 1965), pp. 10, 66–73; Genaro Arriagada, "Ideology and Politics in the South American Military (Argentina, Brazil, Chile and Uruguay)," paper presented at the Woodrow Wilson International Center for Scholars, Washington, D.C., 21 March 1979, pp. 15–17.

9. Atencio, p. 41.

10. Arriagada, p. 24.

11. The influence of such concepts is particularly clear in General Augusto Pinochet Ugarte's work, *Geopolítica,* 2nd ed. (Santiago de Chile: Andres Bello, 1974), written while he was a professor of geopolitics at the Academia Militar. Pinochet led the military coup that overthrew the government of Salvador Allende in September 1973 and eventually established himself as president of the country.

12. Atencio, p. 12.

13. See Chapter 2. This thinking is reflected in the works of some of the major national security theorists in the Southern Cone, including the Argentine general, Juan E. Guglialmelli, editor of the military journal *Estrategia;* the Brazilian generals, José A. Amaral Gurgel and Golbery do Coutu e Silva; as well as General Agustín Toro Dávila, a Chilean. See Juan E. Guglialmelli, "Economía, Poder Militar y Seguridad Nacional," *Estrategia,* 51 (marzo-abril 1978): 7–26; Golbery do Coutu e Silva, *Geopolítica de Brasil,* 2d ed. (Rio de Janeiro: Editorial José Olympio, 1967); José A. Amaral Gurgel, *Segurança e democracia* (Río de Janeiro: Livraria José Olympio, 1976); Agustín Toro Dávila, *La seguridad nacional* (Santiago de Chile: Universidad de Chile, 1976). For a comparative analysis of the evolution of geopolitical thought in Latin America, see John Child, "Geopolitical Thinking in Latin America," *Latin American Research Review,* 14, 2 (1979): 89–111.

14. Arriagada, p. 16.

15. Ibid., pp. 8–9, 16. Psychosocial means include propaganda, indoctrination, and control of those institutions that were transmitters of values, e.g., the family and schools.

16. General Augusto Pinochet, "Mensaje dirigido al pais," Santiago de Chile, 11 septiembre 1976, pp. i–iii. While the Peruvian military which overthrew President Fernando Belaúnde Terry in October 1968 was exposed to European geopolitics and adhered to some elements of national security ideology, there are differences between its views and those in Brazil, Argentina, Chile, and Uruguay. Specifically, the elimination of subversion was

linked directly to the reduction of political, economic, and social inequalities. Hence from 1968 to 1976 the Peruvian armed forces undertook a series of redistributive reforms. Both domestic and international factors impeded their success and by 1976 the military returned to relatively orthodox economic policies and in 1980 allowed a return to civilian government under Fernando Belaúnde Terry. General Edgardo Mercado Jarrín, *Seguridad, Política, Estrategia* (Lima: Imprenta del Ministerio de Guerra, 1974), p. 220; Luigi R. Einaudi, "Revolution from Within? Military Rule in Peru Since 1968," in David Chaplin, ed., *Peruvian Nationalism: A Corporatist Revolution* (New Brunswick, N.J.: Transaction Books, 1976), pp. 404–410; Victor Villanueva, *El CAEM y la revolución de la Fuerza Armada* (Lima: Instituto de Estudio Peruanos, 1972) and *Nueva Mentalidad Militar en el Peru* (Buenos Aires: Editorial Replanteo, 1969).

17. Robert Calvo, "The Church and the Doctrine of National Security," *Journal of Interamerican Studies and World Affairs,* 21, 1 (February, 1979): 84.

18. See Chapter 2.

19. Arriagada, p. 14; Frederick M. Nunn, "Military-Civilian Relations in Chile: The Legacy of the Golpe of 1973," *Inter-American Economic Affairs,* 29, 2 (Autumn 1975): 56–57.

20. The principle of subsidiarity was officially enunciated by Pius XI in the encyclical *Quadragesimo anno.* It posits that functions that can be performed by individuals or small collectivities within society should not be transferred to larger collectivities, e.g., the state. It foresees a felicitous social order in countries where a hierarchical order exists among various intermediary organizations. It is based on the belief that nineteenth century liberalism had led society to the point of being composed largely by individual members and the state. Intermediate bodies to care for juridical and economic needs were lacking. As a result either market forces dominated or the state had to intervene. The solution lay in the formation of vocational or functional groups as subsidiary organizations.

21. Vicaría de Solidaridad del Arzobispado de Santiago de Chile, *Estudios sobre la doctrina de la seguridad y régimen militar* (Santiago de Chile: Arzobispado de Chile, 1977), pp. 61–64.

22. Ibid., pp. 59–64; Genaro Arriagada et al., *Las fuerzas armadas en la sociedad civil Alemania, USA, URSS, y América Latina* (Santiago de Chile: Centro de Investigaciones Socioeconómicas, 1978), pp. 206–207.

23. Integralism emerged strongly in late nineteenth century Europe, stimulated by fear of modern trends in Catholic social thought as well as in secular society. Claiming to be protectors of the purity of the faith, as well as traditional social values, the integralists harkened back to an ideal vision of medieval society where Christendom was one. Emphasizing a harmonious, hierarchical society in which groups within society are incorporated into the whole as units, Latin American integralism makes use of the concept of functional intermediary groups found in subsidiarity. Latin American integralism was also influenced by the writings of the Spanish dictator Primo de Rivera and the experience of Mussolini's Italy.

24. Opus Dei is a Catholic organization founded in Spain in 1928 by Monsignor José Maria Escriva de Balaguer to combat secularism by encouraging spirituality among lay people, particularly professionals. Since that time it has spread throughout Europe, Africa, Asia, and the Americas. Membership is open to men and women and emphasis is placed on educational activities and social welfare work. Opus Dei is noted for promoting conservative political, economic, and religious views, at the same time encouraging pragmatism in daily life. The organization is thought to be strong among the military in Latin America, as well as among technocrats. Action Française was established in 1898 in France during the Dreyfus Affair. Its purpose was to combat the republic and reestablish the monarchy, together with the purported social and religious harmony of France's past so that the country could prosper. Its proponents asserted that national interest had primacy in moral matters. It spread rapidly among Catholic intellectuals as well as conservative clergy, and attracted a good number of activist young people in France, Belgium, and elsewhere. In December 1926 it was condemned by the Holy See as contrary to doctrine and lost support throughout the 1930s and 1940s. Its political views, however, influenced later organizations such as the Cité Catholique which gained strength in the 1950s and 1960s among the military and conservative civilians, who favored stronger prosecution of the war in Algeria and a restructuring of the state to increase its authority.

25. Comblin, p. 85; Centro de Estudios para el Desarrollo e Integración de América Latina (CEDIAL), *Seguridad Nacional y Temas Conexos: Comentario a la Bibliografía Disponible en América Latina,* n.d., p. 45; Jorge Valdes Tapia, "The National Security Doctrine and the Military Fascism in Latin America," MS, 1976, pp. V: 67–68.

26. CEDIAL, pp. 46–47.

27. Thomas G. Sanders, "Military Government in Chile," in Brian Loveman and Thomas M. Davies, Jr., eds., *The Politics of Antipolitics: The Military in Latin America* (Lincoln: University of Nebraska Press, 1978), pp. 272–275.

28. Arriagada, p. 208; Vicaría, p. 62.

29. Augusto Pinochet, "Mensaje dirigido al país," 11 de septiembre de 1976.

30. Frederick M. Nunn, "The Military in Chilean Politics, 1924–1932," in Loveman and Davies, p. 40.

31. See Chapters 2 and 9.

32. Einaudi, p. 412.

33. Positivism is a system of philosophy devised by the Frenchman Auguste Comte, which was introduced into Latin America around the middle of the nineteenth century. It divided history into three stages: the theological, metaphysical, and positivist, the hallmarks of which were, respectively: superstition, abstract principles, and reality and progress. Science, statistics, sociology, and political economy were regarded as prime instruments for social and material progress. Influenced by social darwinism, it tended to blame political freedom for civil disorder and advocated government by an elite.

Positivism was particularly influential on the Brazilian army in the nineteenth century as a result of its introduction into the curriculum of the military school in Rio de Janeiro by Benjamin Constant de Magalhaes. It served to encourage army support for the 1889 republican revolt. Positivists also influenced the Argentine, Uruguayan, and Chilean military, as well as civilian elites in these and other countries (e.g., Mexico).

34. Aldo Büntig, "The Churches of Latin America in Confrontation with the State and the Ideology of National Security: The Reality and Its Causes," *Pro Mundi Vita,* 71 (March-April 1978): 13.

35. Guillermo O'Donnell, an Argentine political scientist, styles it "a type of authoritarianism characterized by a self-avowedly technocratic, bureaucratic, non-personalistic approach to policy making and problem solving." For an elucidation of this model, see his "Tensions in the Bureaucratic-Authoritarian State and the Question of Democracy," in Collier, pp. 291–294. Modifications of this model are offered by Fernando Enrique Cardoso in "On the Characterization of Authoritarian Regimes in Latin America," pp. 34–38, and Robert R. Kaufman in "Industrial Change and Authoritarian Rule in Latin America: A Concrete Review of the Bureaucratic-Authoritarian Model," pp. 244–253 in the same volume. All agree, however, that it is applicable to contemporary Argentina, Brazil, Chile, and Uruguay.

36. The concept of the state presented here is that which is described in national security ideology rather than fully implemented in reality. The characteristics explained, however, are present, to greater or lesser degree, in Argentina, Brazil, Chile, and Uruguay, where they have had substantial impact on human rights observance.

37. Guglialmelli, p. i. See also Amaral Gurgel, *Segurança e democracia;* Junta de Gobierno, Chile, *Declaración de Principios;* Junta de Gobierno, Argentina, "Acta de Proclamación," *La Opinión,* Buenos Aires, 25 March 1976.

38. Junta de Gobierno, Chile, *Declaración de Principios* and Junta de Gobierno, Argentina, "Acta de Proclamación."

39. Pinochet, *Geopolítica,* pp. 16, 68.

40. Ejército Argentino, *Reglamento: Conducción para las fuerzas terrestres, 1979,* p. 295; Guglialmelli, p. 9; Junta de Gobierno, Chile, *Acta Constitucional, Decreto Ley 1,* septiembre 1973.

41. Pinochet, *Geopolítica,* p. 153; Arriagada, p. 200, Vicaría, pp. 53–55.

42. Guglialmelli, p. 25. According to Brazilian national security theorists, there are both permanent and current national objectives. The former include territorial integrity, sovereignty, progress, national integration, democracy, and social peace. The latter are those determined by contemporary circumstances. Thomas G. Sanders, "Development and Security Are Linked by a Relationship of Mutual Causality," *American Universities Field Staff East Coast South American Series,* 15, 3 (September 1971): 6.

43. Amaral Gurgel, p. 83, 113–119; Pinochet, *Geopolítica,* p. 153; Golbery, p. 160.

44. Calvo, pp. 76–77; see also Guglialmelli, p. 8.

45. Junta de Gobierno, Chile, pp. 17–18, 27–32; Golbery, p. 104.

46. Büntig, p. 4.

47. CEDIAL, pp. 15–16; Frank D. McCann, "Origins of the 'New Professionalism' of the Brazilian Military," *Journal of Interamerican Studies and World Affairs,* 21, 4 (November 1979): 505–520; Peter Snow, "Desarrollo económico y seguridad nacional en el régimen militar Argentino," *Estudios Internacionales (Santiago/Buenos Aires),* (20 December 1972): 67–75; Augusto Varas and Felipe Aguero, *El desarrollo doctrinario de las fuerzas amadas Chilenas* (Santiago de Chile: Facultad Latinoamericana de Ciencias Sociales, n.d.), pp. 1–27.

48. Guglialmelli, pp. 7–8.

49. Antonio de Arruda *et al., Desenvolvimento Nacional* (Rio de Janeiro: Associaçio do Diplomados da Escola Superior de Guerra, 1970), pp. 40–42.

50. Emilio Sanfuentes Vergara, "El rol del estado en una sociedad libre," *Seguridad Nacional* (septiembre-octubre 1976): 110–114.

51. Albert Fishlow, "Brazil's Economic Miracle," in Loveman and Davies, p. 256.

52. Peter Flynn, "The Brazilian Development Model: The Political Dimension," in Loveman and Davies, pp. 258–259.

53. Sanders, "Military Government," pp. 275–281.

54. Ibid., p. 281; Vicaría, p. 76; Büntig, p. 20.

55. Alejandro Foxley, "Stabilization Policies and Their Effects on Employment and Income Distribution," paper presented at the Brookings Institution Conference on Economic Stabilization Policies in Less Developed Countries, Washington, D.C., 25 October 1979, pp. 23–24, 31.

56. For an analysis of the negative consequences of national security states for the rule of law and social order, see Hernán Montealegre Klenner, *La seguridad del Estado y los derechos humanos* (Santiago de Chile: Academia de Humanismo Christiano, 1979) and "The Security of the State and Human Rights," in Alfred Hennelly, S.J. and John Langan, S.J., eds., *Human Rights in the Americas: The Struggle for Consensus* (Washington, D.C.: Georgetown University Press, 1982).

57. Büntig, p. 30.

58. Calvo, p. 83. For a more extensive discussion of this, see Ignacio Ellacuría, "Human Rights in a Divided Society," in Hennelly and Langan.

59. On this point, see John Langan, S.J., "Defining Human Rights: A Revision of the Liberal Tradition," in Hennelly and Langan.

60. General Argus Lima, *Jornal do Brasil* (Rio de Janeiro), 9 November 1976, p. 13. The Chilean military junta asserted in 1974 that human rights must be redefined so that their exercise would not result in democratic excesses. Junta de Gobierno, Chile, pp. 26–27.

61. Jorge Figueroa Calderón, "El Terrorismo y los Derechos Humanos," Colegio Interamericano de Defensa, Washington, D.C., April 1979, p. 21.

62. These rights are specified in the Universal Declaration of Human Rights (Articles 19, 20, 21). For the extent of such violations in Latin America, see *Country Reports on Human Rights Practices,* submitted annually since 1977 to Congress by the State Department, as well as the annual

reports of Amnesty International and those of the Inter-American Commission on Human Rights of the Organization of American States, together with the latter's country reports. For the fulfillment of social and economic rights as a criterion for models of development, see Drew Christiansen, S.J., "Basic Needs: Criterion for the Legitimacy of Development," in Hennelly and Langan.

63. In Chile, for example, in the first month after the September 11, 1973 coup, an estimated 45,000 persons were arrested. Some of these were executed without trial, while others were tortured. Six months later, 10,000 Chileans were still detained, many without charges. Between September 1973 and September 1975, one out of every 100 Chileans was detained by security forces. An estimated 60,000 eventually went into exile (Sanders, pp. 282–283). Among violations of the integrity of the person, the upsurge of disappearances of citizens is a serious development. See U.S. House of Representatives, Subcommittee on International Organizations of the Committee on Foreign Affairs, *Hearings on Human Rights and the Phenomenon of Disappearances, September 20, 25 and October 18, 1979* (Washington, D.C.: Government Printing Office, 1979).

64. Calderón, pp. 1–2; 5; 24.

65. Montealegre, *Seguridad del Estado,* pp. 11–13.

66. Stanley Hoffman, "Wrong on Rights," *The New York Times,* 31 December 1980, p. A15.

PART II

Economic Factors Affecting Basic Needs

JOHN F. WEEKS AND ELIZABETH W. DORE

4. Basic Needs: Journey of a Concept

INTRODUCTION

Development economics as a field of scientific inquiry addresses itself to perhaps the most qualitatively complex phenomenon of the social world —the vast, indeed staggering, uneven development of the world's societies with regard to an individual's ability to produce the physical requirements of existence. The complexity is made all the more difficult to analyze by the fact that analysis is inexorably enmeshed in ideologies which reflect the material fact that uneven development—between countries and within countries—is advantageous to certain groups. An obvious point of departure for scientific inquiry is to pose the question of what might be the cause of this uneven development, and, as part of the answer, what forces generated it and maintain it. On the basis of this a strategy for solution could begin to be formulated.

In general, development economics in the neoclassical tradition has not proceeded in this manner, but rather moved immediately to the question of solutions. To the extent that causes were and are considered, uneven development has been treated as its own cause. That is, countries are poor because they lack capital, skilled labor, infrastructure, or efficient administrative capacity. This, of course, is rather like explaining that a child is malnourished because it does not eat enough. While it implies a rather straightforward solution (to eat), little is revealed about why this solution was not effected previously.

This approach arises out of the political explosiveness of attempts to explain causality. One might say that neoclassical theory begins by defining as secondary how the existing state of affairs came into being, and concentrates on how to improve it. Whether such an approach can generate useful solutions is at the heart of the Basic Human Needs (BHN) literature. Whatever its innovative features, the BHN "strategy" posits that the causes of uneven development—poverty in the underdeveloped countries specifically—are of little practical importance. The difficulties in turning the BHN concept into a "strategy" derive precisely from a lack of attention to the causes of poverty. Only through a serious consideration of causality can the BHN strategy be of any practical significance. This emerges clearly in the implementational literature, where there is strong evidence of a retreat from the original formulation of the BHN strategy.

Basic needs strategy represents a response to the generally perceived failure of the trickle-down strategy which was explicit or implicit in the development literature of the 1950s and 1960s. Perhaps more accurately called an optimistic anticipation strategy, it was based on the belief that rapid economic growth must eventually reach its way down the economic pyramid to affect even the poorest. There is now a growing consensus that, in general, this has not been the case.[1] Some basic needs strategies are, in fact, quite close to the trickle-down hypothesis.

I. THE GENESIS OF THE BASIC NEEDS CONCEPT AND THE QUESTION OF MEASUREMENT

While the term "basic needs"[2] is of relatively recent currency,[3] it can be traced back to the debate over whether poverty is an absolute or relative phenomenon, which took the form of a dispute over the measurement of poverty. Here the question of measurement encompassed major theoretical and even philosophical issues. At issue was whether poverty is merely an aspect of income distribution and the poor are those at the lower end of the distribution. It is important to note that there is a difference between inequality and poverty; and major conceptual as well as practical confusion results from defining the poor merely in terms of distribution. To do this turns poverty into a purely definitional and quantitative concept. If poverty and inequality are defined as one, then one of the causes of poverty is the existence of inequality.[4]

Another conceptual problem arises in the distinction between a definition and a measure of poverty. There is a clear absolute descriptive content to aspects of poverty: e.g. child mortality, life expectancy, access to certain services (education, health, water, etc.), which could be called definitional. What is somewhat arbitrary is drawing a poverty line; and also relating levels of "human welfare" to certain poverty characteristics. This latter is a question of measurement. While defining poverty and describing its characteristics is clearly quite different from saying something about relative poverty or income distribution, in drawing welfare implications from these characteristics, or in deciding on a poverty line, one tends to be pushed back to the relativist position which frequently reflects the societal norms.

The first attempt to measure poverty in a rigorous way was by

Rowntree in his study of York, England, in 1901.[5] He offered the concept of "primary poverty," which characterized a family if it lacked the income to satisfy "merely physical efficiency." The important aspect of this approach tended to be lost in subsequent debate over whether it is possible to determine minimum nutritional requirements with precision. The significance of Rowntree's concept is not so much in its biological approach, but in its treatment of poverty as something which exists independently of its measurement. A person suffers poverty if his or her food consumption is below what is necessary to maintain health, normal efficiency, and vigor. In this approach, poverty is not merely a reflection of a conceptual category, but exists whether or not it is conceptualized correctly. This is the sense in which we use the term "absolute poverty," which could also be called "material poverty."

Subsequent criticism of Rowntree's and others' work coalesced around defining poverty as a relative phenomenon. It was argued that poverty can be defined operationally only in relative terms,[6] and usually this is done by designating some portion of the lower end of income distribution as the poor. Poverty is merely a reflection of a concept or definition, and does not exist independently of the way in which it is measured. The pros and cons of the debate over measurements tend to veil the basic issue, namely, is poverty something which exists because it is conceptualized, or does its existence call forth a concept by which it can be analyzed?

The critics of absolute poverty have correctly pointed out the mistakes made in trying to measure in the fashion of Rowntree. It probably is true that a concept like the "minimum cost diet" is useless. One chases a will-o'-the-wisp if one tries to measure the absolute level of income which would allow a minimally nutritious diet. This implies that a strategy to eliminate poverty based merely on raising incomes of the poor is probably resting on weak theoretical ground. Between that income and the minimally nutritious diet lie dietary habits and ignorance of the nutritional values of foods.[7] However, the indeterminancy involved in no way affects the fact that people do have biologically determined needs, and the further fact that a significant portion of the world's population suffers from these biological needs not being met at a sufficiently high level. Malnutrition remains a material phenomenon, an aspect of reality, whether or not it can be closely estimated by income.[8]

Thus, if we sweep away the cloud of confusion generated by criticisms of attempts to measure absolute poverty (as valid as these criticisms may be), the conclusion that there remains an absolute element in poverty which must somehow be captured if we are to proceed scientifically seems not only correct but essential.[9] Going beyond nutrition to the five basic needs—food, health, education, water and sanitation, and shelter—it is obvious that physical hardship to the point of death results from absolute deprivation of any one of these. [10] Further, the relationship between deprivation of basic needs and death has been statistically verified. [11]

The problem in establishing an absolute measure of poverty lies in the fact that human beings do not merely subsist, but subsist in a social context. Thus human needs, as opposed to nonhuman needs, are not in reality determined by biological necessity alone, and, therefore, cannot be so defined conceptually. This does not mean that the biological component is irrelevant, but it is always enmeshed in a social context of values and societal norms. [12] This complexity is precisely what leads some writers to conclude that any attempt to measure subsistence (for want of a better term) is arbitrary. Such a position is clearly unscientific since it implicitly treats the variation in social norms themselves as arbitrary. And as Amartya Sen points out, "for the social scientist studying poverty the conventions of a society are matters of fact and not of value judgement." [13]

It might seem that measuring poverty relatively is merely a matter of convenience, but the "convenience" gained involves serious consequences. As pointed out, it makes poverty a definitional matter, rather than a real phenomenon. By definition it confuses poverty and inequality, merging them into one. [14] If one defines the poor as that portion of the population at the bottom of income distribution, then inequality, having served to define poverty, cannot be used as part of the explanation of its existence. [15] This, in effect, rules out an entire school of analysis which explains both the existence and perpetuation of poverty in part in terms of the income inequalities in society. [16] It becomes impossible to speak of poverty *and* inequality, since they are the same thing in this view. This is a major limitation, for it suggests 1) that poverty is purely quantitative in essence, and 2) that inequality necessarily implies poverty.

The latter implication is clearly wrong. Extreme inequality is certainly a contributing factor to poverty, since it reflects patterns of political power which limit the access of the politically weak to basic necessities of life. However, few would argue that complete equality of income and wealth distribution is a precondition for eliminating poverty. [17] Ironically, defining the poor in terms of income distribution can lead to ignoring distribution altogether. Since this approach implies that poverty is only a quantitative phenomenon, the solution it offers is the growth of the incomes of the poor. This growth can either be relative (through redistribution), an increase in the incomes of the poor while leaving the incomes of other strata unaffected, or part of a general increase (growth of all incomes). Since all three have the same effect—increasing the incomes of the poor—there are no obvious grounds for choosing one over the other. Since it is frequently stressed in the basic needs literature that there are severe political constraints on redistribution, this is generally put aside in favor of the other possible strategies. [18]

In summary, viewing poverty as a material phenomenon implies measuring it absolutely. Such measurement has a biological component, but cannot be conceptualized outside specific societal norms, themselves subjects of scientific investigation. This approach implies that poverty is qualitatively different from nonpoverty, and analytically cannot be reduced merely to a question of incomes. This qualitative difference has two aspects. With regard to the condition of being poor, quantitative differences in income at some objectively determinable point (or range) involve qualitative differences in living standards, primarily indicated by one's health and vitality. With regard to causes, absolute poverty is the result of specific social mechanisms which either affect the poor in a manner different from the rest of society, or which are the result of the lack of development of the entire economic system: e.g., some African economics. The BN development approach or strategy arises from such a view of poverty. The alternative approach to poverty is to define it purely relatively—in terms of income distribution.

While these two ways of measuring poverty in fact represent two distinct concepts and two separate outlooks, they are frequently confused. The concept of absolute poverty is part of a concern for improving the quality of life of the poor; while the concept of relative poverty is concerned with reducing the income gap between the rich and the poor. Therefore the BN strategy consists in defining poverty in concrete terms —in terms of certain standards, or lack of them, of consumption. Thus, incomes are no longer the definitive method of tackling poverty; or at least they are a means rather than an end.

II. BASIC NEEDS: TWO POSITIONS WITHIN THE SAME TERMINOLOGY

Growth with Redistribution vs. Redistribution.   Since the late 1960s, there has emerged within the development literature, both academic and policy-oriented, a new emphasis on distributional questions. Up until about 1965, a bibliography on income distribution by Western economists would have been quite short. [19] Perhaps the first international agency report to reflect the growing concern with distribution was the ILO employment mission volume on Colombia. [20] The report, despite its vagueness and weak empirical basis, was probably one of the most politically progressive, perhaps even radical, ever published under the auspices of an international agency. The central theme of the report was that the unemployment and poverty problem in Colombia could not be significantly reduced in the absence of land reform and major income redistribution. While many of the concrete policy recommendations had a familiar ring, reminiscent of the days before the new emphasis on distribution, the overall impact of the report was to generate debate over equality and inequality. Despite the emphasis on distribution—or because of it—the report clearly treated poverty as a problem synonymous with inequality, which could be solved through income generation, predicated on redistribution. Indeed, the analysis of the report had almost a Keynesian flavor—redistribution of income would incline the structure of effective demand toward more "labor-intensive"[21] commodities, which would generate greater employment for a given level of national income.[22]

In a subsequent ILO employment mission report on Kenya one finds suggestions of what subsequently developed into the BN strategy.[23] In fact, this report, considerably less influential than that on Colombia, also contains elements of the "growth with redistribution" strategy. While the Colombia report had argued that redistribution was the policy measure by which unemployment and poverty would be eliminated, in the Kenya report the opposite was argued. The Kenya report did stress the distribution-employment link in terms similar to the Colombia report, but placed more emphasis on a strategy of redistributing or redirecting *current investment* rather than current income. In this strategy, current investment would be directed to productive projects which would lead to faster growth of incomes at the bottom of income distribution. This strategy represented a significant step back from the radical social changes at least implied by the Colombia report. By reversing casuality from redistribution-employment and poverty reduction to employment and poverty reduction-redistribution, the need for significant changes in current distribution of income and assets, and therefore, implicitly, in the status quo was potentially eliminated.

This theme, through growth there would be redistribution, was elaborated in a volume written under the auspices of the IBRD ("World Bank"), published in 1974.[24] What had been part of a strategy which also included some redistribution of current assets and incomes in the case of the Kenya report, now stood on its own as an alternative to such redistribution. All but insignificant redistributions of current income and assets (called radical and static redistributions) are rejected as either politically impossible, too expensive because of the compensation that would be required (in the case of assets), or damaging to productivity.[25] It concluded: "In these circumstances direct programs of investment support may provide the only mechanism for raising low incomes in a reasonable period of time."[26]

It is, however, quite open to question whether such a strategy could generate any significant gain for the poor, whether the time period be reasonable or unreasonable. Stewart and Streeten have argued cogently that a strategy which explicitly does not challenge the existing power relations in society, indeed makes a virtue of not doing so, can be confident that any changes it generates will be easily contained by the ruling classes.[27] In any case, it is not difficult to demonstrate that given investment rates in underdeveloped countries and the fact that most investment in any base year is relatively inflexible for reallocation, the amount of investment which could be redirected to the poor, assuming no opposition from the privileged, is marginal at best. Redistribution-with-growth seemed destined to live a short life. By 1977, even within the World Bank (the institution out of which it had emerged), there was pressure to abandon redistribution-with-growth in favor of the BN strategy. This was probably because there was little new in the strategy and its difference from the growth-oriented strategy of the 1950s and early 1960s was not obvious.[28]

One last point about redistribution with growth (RWG) is relevant to the discussion of the BN strategy. In the World Bank RWG volume and its supporting literature there is an unquestioning acceptance of the conclusion that it is possible to achieve incrementally a redistribution which would come asunder if introduced as a total package to be implemented in a short period of time. But it is not obvious that the privileged classes would look more favorably upon their privileges being slowly reduced. Indeed, it could be argued that incremental redistribution alerts the privileged to unpalatable changes without in any way reducing their power to resist them. Success with the strategy would seem to depend upon a strong element of *noblesse oblige*.

III. BASIC NEEDS AND THE BREAK WITH REDISTRIBUTION WITH GROWTH

There developed in the policy and academic literature on underdeveloped countries in the late 1960s a consensus that the process of growth in these countries had at best left economic inequalities untouched and at worst accentuated them to the point of explosiveness.[29] While redistribution-with-growth seemed superficially to address this problem, and some argue that the BN strategy represents "an evolution from abstract to concrete objectives"[30] in relation to RWG, in fact, the BN strategy represents a break with RWG. The World Bank RWG volume put forward a strategy that was a major step back from the emphasis on redistribution which had been emerging in the 1960s and was epitomized, however vaguely, in the Colombia report.

The BN concept, on the other hand, represents a shift toward a redistributionist position, insofar as any significant steps to implement the strategy must imply redistribution of current income or wealth or both. This is a controversial point, though not an original one. [31] One purpose in sifting through the BN literature is to demonstrate the implicit link between BN and redistribution. In this essay the term redistribution will always be used to mean redistribution of current income resources, and assets since it is a misnomer to speak of redistribution of future income and assets. Before something can be redistributed, it must be distributed, and before it can be distributed it must be produced.

In order to avoid degeneration into semantic debate or debate over what various sources "really mean" by a BN strategy, it is necessary to be clear about what the problem is that the BN strategy aspires to address. The strategy does not merely seek the elimination or reduction of poverty and its associated sufferings, for there are many strategies that attempt to do this. Rather, it is a strategy for reducing poverty in underdeveloped countries, constructed in light of certain generalizations (correct or incorrect) about the growth experience of such countries since World War II. The more important of these are summarized by Haq, though they are not necessarily his views:

> The proponents of basic needs contend that, in a poor society, the production of non-essential goods (apart from exports) should be tightly controlled; all incentives and market signals should be modified towards the production of basic wage goods and services; the state should stand ready for large-scale market intervention if the existing markets are a slave to the interests of the privileged groups. Without these further steps the increased income in the hands of the poor may largely evaporate into higher prices if corresponding supplies of basic wage goods are not readily available. The opponents of basic needs programs fear that such market interventions will often be inefficient, serve only the interests of the ruling elite, and are probably a soft-sell for communism. [32]

It is instructive to draw out the major elements of this definition which differs from what most writers mean by a basic needs strategy. The strategy requires major intervention by the state, not just in the redistribution of income, but directly in production, to supply the commodities required by the poor. This approach evokes strong reactions from those committed to a capitalist economy with little social welfare activity by the state. In Haq's summary the BN strategy is the underdeveloped country equivalent of the programs of the European social democratic parties, particularly the Scandinavian ones. [33]

This emphasis is not simply one possible approach to the BN

strategy, but the only one that allows for a BN strategy in any way unique. The BN strategy is not merely a way to combat poverty; it derives from certain judgments about the failure of previous strategies. One of these is that no significant reduction in poverty is possible as long as a strategy leaves the productive structure of the economy unchanged. [34]

The experience of advanced capitalist countries demonstrates this. Despite nominally progressive tax structures, there is no evidence that indirect redistributive measures have had any significant impact on the distribution of income and wealth. [35] There is general consensus among writers in the field of wealth and income distribution that the only cases of significant poverty reduction in advanced capitalist countries have been those characterized by major programs of state provision of income in kind—subsidized state-owned housing, medical care without user charges, free education, subsidized or rationed basic foods. [36] It should be noted that even in those countries where such direct state delivery of basic needs has greatly reduced absolute poverty (the Netherlands, Sweden, and Denmark), there has been surprisingly little impact on inequality. While related, inequality and poverty are distinct phenomena with certain causes unique to each and others shared in common. [37]

To the extent that the Basic Needs strategy keeps to the view that some direct state intervention, frequently involving delivery of basic necessities, is essential, it constitutes a coherent, recognizable program. To the extent that it equivocates on this, or even denies this aspect of the strategy, it becomes indistinguishable from previous strategies—"trickle down" and "redistribution from growth."

In general, writings emanating from the Policy Planning and Program Review Department of the World Bank have stressed the central role of direct state action in the BN policy package, though not always as clearly as Haq did in his 1977 paper "Basic Needs: A Progress Report," where he presents the views of proponents of the BN strategy. The policy and research papers of the department entrusted with developing a BN strategy repeatedly emphasize that unsatisfactory country performance in fulfilling the basic needs of the population is not, in general, the result of the low level of income in underdeveloped countries. Rather it is due to the structure of asset ownership, monopoly of political power by privileged classes, and state policies which result from that monopoly. The work of Streeten and Burki is clear on this point. [38] Closely related to this is the view that for all but the poorest countries, internal resources are more than sufficient to solve basic needs problems successfully within a reasonable period of time. [39] The World Bank has divided underdeveloped countries into two groups, middle income and low income, on the basis of per capita income. Virtually all Latin American countries fall into the former category. Included in these are all of those whose basic needs provision is analyzed in Chapter 5.

If it is the case that a large number of countries possess the necessary resources to eliminate the worst manifestations of poverty, the question naturally arises as to why this has not been done. While different positions are propounded within this department of the World Bank, its most radical expression is the view "that this is explained by the structure of economic and political power in underdeveloped countries." Sometimes the euphemistic term "political will" is used and the need for the "participation" of the poor is stressed. [40] Streeten and Haq argue that international assistance should be assured to those governments which demonstrate willingness to engage in political and economic reforms. [41] Such a recommendation may not seem too startling until one recalls the general aversion of the major donor institutions to the regime of Salvador Allende in Chile. This stress on the central importance of political and economic power and the necessity of reform is also present to a degree in the work of the OAS. [42]

Streeten has been quite clear in stressing that the BN strategy involves a partial break with the market-oriented commitments of neoclassical theory, which itself derives from value-laden concepts such as consumer sovereignty. This approach rejects the emphasis on income for the poor, which characterized RWG strategy, in favor of a more general emphasis upon access to BN goods and services. [43] An emphasis upon access or entitlements avoids the problem that relative price movements can reduce or eliminate the income gain of the poor, particularly if the supply response of basic necessity production is sluggish to increased effective demand. An emphasis upon access is explicit recognition of the intermediary role that income plays in the reproduction of the social unit. [44] Raising the income of a family is not the same thing as increasing its material welfare, unless one accepts all of the tenets of neoclassical consumer theory, e.g., rationality and perfect information.

Once the intermediary role of income is recognized—that income is a means and not the only available means—other ways of increasing access to BN goods and services present themselves. Rationing and direct state production and delivery are two alternative means, and Streeten suggests that the latter has a place in BN strategy. Direct state action of this type reduces the problems of 1) ignorance on the part of the poor of nutritional and other information, 2) possible relative price movements which would price the poor out of markets, and 3) the portion of the poor which at least in the short run is unemployable. All of these considerations require a strategy which breaks qualitatively with the reliance on the market mechanisms, so characteristic of previous strategies, though this break is likely to be limited quantitatively.

In summary, the BN strategy which originally emanated from the ILO and was further developed by the Policy Planning and Program Review Department of the World Bank, stresses the following elements: 1) supply management of basic necessities by the state; 2) major interventions in the markets for commodities to restrict production and consumption of nonessentials; and 3) redistribution of income, primarily, but not exclusively, to redirect state expenditure towards the poor.

And central to these elements is significant political change, as "[i]t is quite clear that a major restructuring of political and economic power relationships is a prerequisite for a BN strategy." [45] Such changes are also a prerequisite for successful application of foreign assistance. [46]

The BN strategy which calls for major economic and political restructuring may well represent the early views of the Policy Planning and Program Review Department of the World Bank. There are indications, however, that this department has retreated from this earlier and comparatively radical position, to embrace a BN strategy which is more consistent with that proposed by the other donor institutions, as well as more acceptable within the World Bank itself.

While a radical conceptualization of a BN strategy has emerged within the World Bank, it would be incorrect to construe this as the official position of the World Bank; it is not. The official position of the IBRD speaks of poverty, but not of basic needs; and the lending policies of the Bank tend to favor loans which are bankable (i.e., made on a commercial basis), rather than those which address basic needs. This orientation toward traditional lending policies is perhaps slowly changing as the Bank is moving in the direction of greater emphasis on loans to develop health, clean water, sanitation, and educational services.

IV. DOMINANT INTERPRETATION OF THE BN STRATEGY

In the previous section it was argued that the characteristic features of one interpretation of the BN strategy arise out of a recognition of the failure of previous strategies, and that they place major emphasis upon the role of the state. This indicates the necessity for major economic and political reforms in underdeveloped countries. [47]

This interpretation of the BN strategy is not prevalent among donor institutions. These institutions tend to reject major economic and political changes on the grounds that they are not feasible or are politically unacceptable. Instead, they present a BN strategy which represents no radical break with previous approaches to the elimination of poverty. This is explicitly recognized by Michael Crosswell of the Agency for International Development (AID), who holds that "it should be emphasized that policies for meeting basic needs are on the whole quite familiar," and what is unique is "providing a coherent framework" and concrete objectives for eliminating poverty.[48]

What is familiar is the emphasis on employment and income generation as the primary means of meeting basic needs. What Crosswell describes as new is an "integrated focus on both income and production—more specifically on the pattern of production and the distribution of income."[49] The dominant interpretation of the BN approach is to combine income generation with a concern for the composition of output.

The rationale for the emphasis on income generation is twofold. First, it is argued that the poor must be involved in more productive laboring activities since general growth must occur if the basic needs of a large portion of the population are to be met. This implies increases in income. Second, income generation and the market must be the primary mechanisms for the distribution of basic needs goods and services if production and allocation of resources are to be efficient, and if the poor can effectively exercise some degree of choice in the specific nature of the goods and services consumed. This focus on employment and income is combined with a concern for generating an adequate supply of basic necessities.[50]

It is not difficult to see that there are major problems inherent in this approach. Consider the question of timing. Assume for the sake of argument that it is possible without redistribution to generate an equitable pattern of growth in which the incomes of all the poor begin to rise, while at the same time the production of basic necessities increases. It is doubtful that anyone would be so optimistic as to argue that the two processes would move in perfect step. The first possibility is that the incomes of the poor would rise faster than the supply of basic necessities. In this case, excess effective demand would push up prices and in the short run make BN more accessible to the higher income groups. A second possibility, and one that is more hopeful, is that the supply of basic necessities will increase faster than the incomes of the poor, and the prices of the basic necessities will fall, giving the poor more access to them. However, unless supply and prices are controlled by the government it is generally held that it would be unlikely for prices to fall because of the downward inflexibility of prices if markets are not competitive, particularly at the wholesale level.

How then, is the supply of basic necessities to reach the poor? Crosswell suggests various theoretical possibilities. First, that the poor pay direct fees to cover the cost of basic services, as well as purchase food and housing at market rates.[51] This, of course, requires a synchronization which is virtually impossible in practice. Failing this, "to directly tax some portion of the income or output associated with more productive employment *of the poor* (emphasis added), and then use these revenues to finance services delivered at fees that are correspondingly less than costs." [52] That is, the poor shall pay, and if there are portions of the poor which cannot pay, tax the "better off" poor to cover costs. [53] This is in reality an effective demand strategy whereby basic needs will only be supplied if someone can pay for them.

The solution to the supply problem offered in the AID, ILO, and World Bank literature is some form of state intervention in the production and distribution of goods and services which are essential for the satisfaction of basic needs. This can take the form of active state intervention in the pricing system, subsidies, taxation, or state participation in the production and distribution of basic necessities. State intervention is not a simple solution, and perhaps primarily for political reasons the emphasis on supply management varies. Even the Policy Planning and Program Review Department of the World Bank has retreated considerably from its previous position of placing it at the heart of any BN approach.

V. CLARIFICATION OF A CONCEPT

The purpose of this chapter has been to clarify and place in context an idea or concept which has quickly come to dominate the discussion of development goals and policy, a concept that has been criticized for its vagueness. Basic needs strategy need not be vague, although it encompasses a definite worldview of development problems. This worldview has much in common with the social democratic critique of the operation of a capitalistic society.

To focus merely on basic needs, to raise a banner that proclaims them as the goal of development, is not very original. Every development strategy purports to have this goal, however indirectly. A strategy becomes a basic needs strategy or a redistribution with growth strategy, as opposed merely to having BN as a general goal, by virtue of the manner in which it pursues the solution of meeting basic needs. A strategy which concludes that basic needs will automatically be met by general economic growth is a growth strategy or a trickle-down strategy. A policy which redirects current investment to generate faster income increases for the poor in order to meet BN is an investment-reallocation (RWG) strategy, and so on. A basic needs approach is a strategy which includes as a large component the provision of fundamental necessities by direct state intervention in the economy, though not to the exclusion of economic growth. This requires redistribution of current income. [54] Once the distinction between goals and strategies is made clear, it is possible to assess particular policies and compare the advantages of different strategies. A successful strategy to satisfy basic needs and eliminate the worst symptoms of poverty requires considerable state intervention. Redistribution of resources by the state would be more equitable than that provided by the market. Consideration of the conditions under which this would be the case is beyond the scope of the present discussion. State action never occurs in isolation from the rest of society, and economic and social policies are the product of class relations in society, not merely of technical decisions. In circumstances in which a society is fundamentally inequitable and those benefiting most control the state, it is illogical to think that state action would do anything but reinforce inequalities. This, however, is not an argument against the position presented here, but points up the obvious: a basic needs strategy can be implemented only within certain political conditions.

CONCLUSIONS

It is widely accepted among multilateral lending institutions as well as by development economists that a major barrier to growth in underdeveloped countries is low labor productivity caused by a deficiency in human resources, such as skilled labor or an educated work force. To confront this pervasive problem, the goal of many programs and projects is to increase productivity. The basic needs strategy encompasses an explicit recognition that the satisfaction of basic needs, i.e., the provision of adequate nutrition, housing, water and sanitation, health care, and basic education, leads directly to the development of the human resources which are a prerequisite to economic growth.

Given the assumption that the satisfaction of basic needs is an investment in human capital and essential to increasing the productivity of the working population, it would seem advantageous to satisfy basic needs as efficiently and as quickly as possible. As a consequence, insofar as possible, ideological considerations must be cast aside and nonmarket measures be integrated with market mechanisms in the provision of basic needs. This implies that the state must be encouraged to play an active role in the organization, production, and distribution of those goods and services which are essential to the satisfaction of basic needs. This would facilitate the rapid provision of the basic necessities which would not only satisfy individual needs, but from a macroeconomic perspective, provide the foundations for the development of human capital and the corresponding increase in labor productivity which are essential to economic growth.

Direct provision of a portion of basic needs is frequently given only brief consideration on the grounds that such a policy would be politically unrealistic in most countries. Strategies which concentrate on increasing the incomes of the poor, combined with generating, through the market, an adequate supply of basic needs goods and services, are considered more politically acceptable. Nevertheless, the direct provision of basic needs has been suggested by some experienced policymakers, including former Deputy Assistant Secretary of State for Latin America Albert Fishlow, who argues that income generation policies have had insufficient impact on the poor, and that these need to be supplemented by a larger component of social provision programs. [55] This view will become increasingly influential as serious attempts are made to satisfy basic needs.

NOTES TO CHAPTER 4

1. The "trickle-down" hypothesis is dealt with explicitly by us in Chapter 5, "Economic Performance and Basic Needs in Six Latin American Countries." See also Marcelo Selowsky, "Balancing Trickle Down and Basic Needs Strategies: Income Distribution Issues in Large Middle-Income Countries with Special Reference to Latin America," World Bank Staff Working Paper No. 335 (Washington, D.C.: July 1979); and Montek S. Ahluwalia, "Growth and Poverty in Developing Countries," World Bank Staff Working Paper No. 309 (Revised), (Washington, D.C.: May 1979).

2. From this point on, we shall use the phrase "basic needs" (BN) rather than "basic human needs," which is redundant; no one in the literature seems concerned with other than human needs.

3. The BN concept was made a center of focus and debate for development agencies and social scientists by the International Labor Organization (ILO). There is some difference of opinion as to when and by whom the concept was first developed. International Labor Organization, *Employment, Growth and Basic Needs: A One-World Problem* (New York: Praeger, 1977). This is a report of a 1976 conference.

4. For a moral and ethical analysis of the essentially qualitative nature of poverty, see Drew Christiansen, S.J., "Basic Needs: Criterion for the Legitimacy of Development," in *Human Rights in the Americas: The Struggle for Consensus,* eds. Alfred Hennelly, S.J. and John Langan, S.J. (Washington, D.C.: Georgetown University Press, 1982).

5. S. Rowntree, *Poverty: A Study of Town Life* (London: Macmillan, 1901).

6. M. Orshansky, "How Poverty is Measured," *Monthly Labor Review* 92, 2 (February 1969): 37–41.

7. For a discussion of the many steps in the income-nutrition link, see John Weeks, "The Problem of Wage Policy with Special Reference to Africa," *Economic Bulletin of Ghana* 1, 1 (1971), 1–11.

8. This point is made by A. K. Sen, in "Three Notes on the Concept

of Poverty," World Employment Program Working Papers (January 1978), p. 5.

9. Ibid. See also A. K. Sen, "Poverty: An Ordinal Approach to Measurement," *Econometrica* 44, 2 (March 1976): 219–231.

10. Education may seem an exception to this, but is not. Given the level of the satisfaction of the other needs, increased education results in better health and longer life expectancy. See "The Relationship of Basic Needs to Growth, Income Distribution and Employment: The Case of Sri Lanka," IBRD, Policy Planning and Program Review Department (June 1978), pp. 11 ff.; Gilbert Brown and Shahid Javed Burki, "Sector Policies and Linkages in Meeting Basic Needs," IBRD, Policy Planning and Program Review Department, Basic Needs Paper No. 7 (February 1978), pp. 11 ff.

11. Time series data show a statistically significant positive relationship between the death rate and the price of rice in Sri Lanka, particularly in 1974. See IBRD, "The Relationship of Basic Needs to Growth. . . . The Case of Sri Lanka," p. 11 and Appendix.

12. Marx was one of the first social scientists explicitly to recognize this, and referred to human subsistence needs as having a "moral and social element." Karl Marx, *Capital* (London and Moscow: Lawrence and Wishart and Progress, 1970), 3 vols., I, Chapter 19.

13. Sen, "Three Notes," p. 13. Indeed, for a *social* scientist the conventions of society are always matters of scientific investigation, whatever is being studied.

14. See Richard I. Szal, "Poverty: Measurement and Analysis," World Employment Program Research Working Papers (October 1977), where the distinction is blurred.

15. Sen, 'Three Notes," p. 9.

16. Frances Stewart and Paul Streeten, "New Strategies for Development: Poverty, Income Distribution, and Growth," *Oxford Economic Papers* 28 (1978): 393.

17. In the BN literature, the Peoples Republic of China is frequently cited as a country in which poverty had largely been eliminated by 1976, but inequalities in income distribution remained. IBRD, Policy Planning and Program Review Department, "Basic Needs: An Issues Paper," (Washington, D.C.: March 21, 1977), p. 7.

18. The literature from USAID tends to shy away from suggesting anything redistributive because it is argued that it would be "politically quite difficult." In fact, one AID official has argued that the BN approach does not imply or require redistribution of income or assets. Michael Crosswell, "Basic Human Needs: A Development Planning Approach," AID Discussion paper No. 38 (Washington, D.C.: AID, October 1978), p. 35. The suggestions of the Policy Planning and Program Review Department of the IBRD and of the ILO more frequently stress the inevitability of some redistribution as an aspect of a BN strategy.

19. The qualifier Western is necessary. For example, considerable work was done in India in the 1950s and early 1960s on income and land distribution. Indian planning reflected this to some degree.

20. International Labor Organization, *Towards Full Employment* (Geneva: ILO, 1971). The mission was led by Dudley Seers.

21. This concept and its opposite, "capital-intensive," play starring roles in the BN strategy.

22. Partly as a result of the Colombia report, in the early 1970s a number of studies sought to test the income distribution-employment hypothesis. It is beyond the scope of this paper to review these results. See, for example, Richard Weisskoff, "A Multi-sector Simulation Model of Employment, Growth and Income Distribution in Puerto Rico," Yale University, Economic Growth Center, Discussion Paper No. 174 (March 1973); and William R. Cline, "Income Distribution and Economic Development: A Survey and Tests for Selected Latin American Cities," in Robert Ferber, ed., *Consumption and Income Distribution in Latin America* (Washington, D.C.: ECIEL, 1980).

23. ILO, *Employment, Incomes, and Equity* (Geneva: ILO, 1972).

24. H. B. Chenery et al., *Redistribution with Growth* (Oxford: Oxford University Press, 1974).

25. Ibid., Chapter 4.

26. Ibid., p. 81.

27. Stewart and Streeten, pp. 398 ff.

28. Deepak Lal makes this point, commenting, "The current concern with distributional issues amongst the international agencies and American development economists marks more their acknowledgment of *their* past neglect of what a number of Third World governments and many development economists have for a long time recognized to be a major area of concern (distribution and equity) than any 'new' insight into the development process." Deepak Lal, "Distribution and Development: A Review Article," *World Development* 4, 9 (1976): 736.

29. Pakistan was probably the most glaring example of the failure of the growth-now-distribute-later strategy. "Pakistan was the paradigm of rapid development with postponement of matters of distribution, especially regional distribution. The war provided dramatic evidence that time is not always available for this postponement." Cline, p. 205.

30. Paul Streeten and Shahid Javed Burki, "Basic Needs: Some Issues," *World Development* 6 (1978): 412.

31. A number of writers point this out: T. N. Srinivasan, "Development, Poverty, and Basic Needs: Some Issues" (Stanford Research Institute, MS, n.d.): 25; and E. William Colgazier, "Basic Human Needs as a Development Strategy," Colombo Plan (Washington, D.C.: November 1978) CC (78) OM STC–D/2, pp. 9, 29.

32. Mahbub al Haq, "Basic Needs: A Progress Report," IBRD, Policy Planning and Program Review Department (August 10, 1977), p. 6.

33. That is, it does not challenge the capitalist structure of the economic system, but seeks to modify its undesirable characteristics through intervention in markets and direct state provision of certain necessities.

34. Commenting on the Peruvian experience after 1968, Webb and Figueroa write:

What characterizes the present reforms in Peru is that they preserve the connection between production and distribution. . . . The structured transformations maintain the structure of the economy. . . . Whatever redistribution strategy which maintains the connection between production and distribution is clearly directed against the most poverty-stricken groups.

Richard Webb and Adolfo Figueroa, *Distribución del Ingreso en el Perú* (Lima: Instituto de Estudios Peruanos, 1975), p. 142.

35. See A. K. Atkinson, *The Distribution of Income and Wealth* (London: Penguin, 1973). This volume is a collection of studies surveying the pattern of wealth and income distribution in the United States, the United Kingdom, and a number of continental European countries.

36. Virtually all the Scandinavian countries, as well as the Netherlands and to a lesser extent the U.K., have all of these to some degree.

37. Sen, "Three Notes," p. 9. See also his influential lectures on inequality, A. K. Sen, *On Economic Inequality* (London, 1973).

38. Streeten and Burki.

39. "It is not so much the poverty of the middle income countries—for they have the resources to tackle their basic health problems—but the socio-economic conditions of the poorer segments of their populations and the structure of political power which limits their access to basic health facilities that explain persistent high rates of morbidity and mortality." John Simmons and Shahid Javed Burki, "The Performance of Middle-Income Countries on Basic Human Needs," IBRD, Discussion Draft (January 19, 1979), p. 31. "Middle-income countries" include 63 countries with per capita incomes of $260 to $3,900 in 1975, the lowest being Togo ($260) and the highest Israel ($3,920).

40. Ibid., p. vi; and "Basic Needs: An Issues Paper," IBRD, Policy Planning and Program Review Department (March 21, 1977): 12.

41. Paul Streeten and Mahbub al Haq, "International Implications for Donor Countries and Agencies of Meeting Basic Human Needs," Discussion Group on International Cooperation in Meeting BHN, Council on Foreign Relations, (February 21, 1978); see also Brown and Burki.

42. Juan Espinosa, *El Problema de la Pobreza en América Latina y la Nueva Política de Necesidades Básicas* (Washington, D.C.: Organization of American States, October 1978).

43. The following discussion is based on Paul Streeten, "The Distinctive Features of a Basic Needs Approach to Development: A Note," prepared for the Discussion Group on International Cooperation in Meeting BHN, Council on Foreign Relations (New York: November 15, 1977).

44. Sen, "Three Notes," p. 9.

45. Streeten and Burki, p. 414.

46. "The requirement for foreign assistance (to meet BN) should not be overemphasized at the cost of attention for the crucial internal changes that are needed before basic needs can be implemented with success," Shahid Javed Burki and Joris J. C. Voorhoeve, "Global Estimates for Meeting Basic

Needs: Background Paper," IBRD, Basic Needs Paper No. 1 (August 1977), p. 2. A somewhat contrary view is taken by Constantine Michalopolous in Chapter 8 of this volume, where income generation is stressed.

47. This emphasis on changing the structure of political and economic power has been pointed out by a number of writers. Indeed, some use this as a critique of the practicality of the BN strategy. See Colglazier, p. 9; and Srinivasan.

48. Crosswell, p. 3.

49. Ibid., p. 10.

50. The AID literature stresses that an adequate supply of basic necessities is a fundamental prerequisite for a basic needs strategy. They argue that it is to assure this adequate supply that half of AID's development assistance budget goes into agriculture, with the result that in most cases increased farm output means higher incomes for the poor as well as an increased supply of those goods on which the poor spend their income.

51. Ibid., p. 34.

52. Ibid., p. 35.

53. It is quite clear that Crosswell is not suggesting that all basic needs, goods, and services, especially health and education, be produced and distributed solely via the free market. He is presenting some possible alternatives which would minimize the burden on the state, which he argues in most countries has had great difficulties in generating revenue in order to use the fiscal system for purposes of redistribution. A relatively inflexible fiscal system as well as skill shortages in government administration are, of course, characteristics of underdevelopment. It is also true, however, that the market mechanism is underdeveloped. Consequently, the one that is more efficient, the government or the market, is not obvious in general.

54. There are parts of the world, especially Africa, where because of the pervasiveness of extreme absolute poverty, the opportunities for significant income redistribution are circumscribed. While even in these countries there is a role for the redistribution of current income, emphasis must be placed on increasing output in basic needs sectors at the same time as increasing the incomes of the poor. While there are important commonalities in the basic needs strategy, its specific features must be tailored to respond to the particular conditions of each country.

55. Albert Fishlow, "Who Benefits from Economic Development?: Comment," *American Economic Review* 70:1 (March 1980): 250–256.

ELIZABETH W. DORE AND JOHN F. WEEKS

5. Economic Performance and Basic Needs: The Examples of Brazil, Chile, Mexico, Nicaragua, Peru, and Venezuela

INTRODUCTION[1]

Access to the necessities of life by the mass of the population of a country is, in the first instance, dependent upon the productive capacity of the economy. In the literature on basic needs,[2] one finds a distinction between those countries which are at a level of development allowing for satisfaction of basic needs under present circumstances and those which are not.[3]

In this chapter, six Latin American countries (Brazil, Chile, Mexico, Nicaragua, Peru, and Venezuela) which fall into the World Bank's category of middle-income countries are analyzed.[4] In these countries, the level of per capita income, per capita calorie consumption, and other indicators suggest that the most extreme forms of poverty, malnutrition, and physical deprivation in general can be eliminated through appropriate policies and within a relatively short time frame. This places such countries in a different category, particularly with respect to policy options, from most of the countries of Africa and Asia.

That the elimination of the worst aspects of poverty is possible in these countries does not imply that this will occur. Redistribution of income, at least in the form of state expenditure, is required. Such redistribution would probably encounter serious political opposition. However, political opposition does not necessarily make the redistributional alternative impossible, and it would be arbitrary to eliminate it a priori.

This chapter first considers the macroeconomic performance of each of the six countries under review. This performance is related to what are called models of political and economic development. The macroeconomic performance is then compared to indicators of the manner in which economic growth has been distributed among the various sectors of the population. The general point to be made is that the benefits from economic growth can be distributed in different ways, and an impressive macroeconomic performance is quite consistent with poverty for a substantial portion of a country's population, or, at least, with indirect indications of substantial poverty. In the next section, indicators of material deprivation are examined (life expectancy, infant mortality, etc.). Insofar as possible, these are related to macroeconomic performance, though this is difficult since the data on material deprivation is considerably less accurate, frequent, and current than macroeconomic data.

I. MACROECONOMIC PERFORMANCE AND DISTRIBUTION

The six countries studied include Brazil and Mexico, the most populous in Latin America, and three populous countries, Peru, Venezuela, and Chile, as well as Nicaragua, one of the smallest in size and population. Together, they accounted for about 70 percent of the population of Latin America in the 1970s. In this section the economic performance of these six countries over the last 25 years is reviewed. A detailed consideration of each economy is not possible, however, and the discussion is limited to macroeconomic trends and general indicators of how economic growth has been distributed among the various sectors of the population and its impact on fulfillment of basic needs.

These countries represent political as well as economic diversity. Venezuela has a recent history of democratic institutions, while Mexico is characterized by a one-party system which tends to stifle opposition. Nicaragua had 40 years of single family rule until the summer of 1979, when a popular movement took control. Brazil has been governed since 1964 by an authoritarian military junta, while Peru was led from 1968 until mid-1980 by a reformist military dedicated to stimulating industrial development. The sixth country, Chile, has experienced in the recent past a variety of political regimes from democratic (1964–1970) to radical social democratic (1970–1973), to the current authoritarian military dictatorship. In terms of per capita income, in 1976 the six countries fell into two groups: Peru ($500), Nicaragua ($490), and Brazil ($525) on the one hand, and Mexico ($718), Chile ($736), and Venezuela ($1,032) on the other. (See Table 1, last line).[5] This basis of grouping the countries demonstrates how per capita income can be misleading as an indicator of development. Though Brazil's per capita income in 1976 was only 7 percent above that of Nicaragua, according

TABLE 1:   Indices of Constant Price GDP and Growth Rates, 1955-1977

	Peru	Mexico	Chile	Brazil	Venezuela	Nicaragua
1955	58.8	53.4	64.0	57.7	51.3	56.8
1956	61.5	56.2	64.4	59.5	56.8	56.7
1957	62.1	60.4	71.1	64.3	63.4	61.6
1958	64.2	63.2	73.8	69.3	64.2	61.8
1959	66.5	66.0	73.4	73.1	69.3	62.7
1960	72.5	70.9	78.3	80.2	70.2	63.7
1961	78.4	74.4	83.1	88.5	73.8	68.2
1962	85.7	77.9	87.3	93.1	80.5	75.4
1963	88.9	84.1	91.4	94.6	86.1	80.2
1964	95.9	93.9	95.2	97.3	94.4	89.5
1965	100.0	100.0	100.0	100.0	100.0	100.0
1966	105.3	106.9	107.0	105.1	102.3	103.1
1967	107.0	113.6	109.5	110.1	106.4	110.1
1968	107.7	122.9	112.7	120.4	112.1	111.7
1969	112.5	130.7	116.2	131.2	116.0	118.2
1970	122.7	140.7	120.4	143.7	121.8	124.2
1971	129.0	145.5	129.7	162.8	125.2	129.2
1972	136.5	156.0	129.6	181.2	129.7	133.7
1973	145.0	168.0	124.9	207.3	137.2	139.7
1974	154.9	177.5	132.0	227.5	143.4	158.1
1975	160.1	184.7	117.1	140.5	152.4	160.9
1976	165.0	187.5	121.9	262.0	164.4	170.9
1977	163.5	192.9	132.3	174.2	---	181.1
Growth rate, GDP	4.8%	6.0%	3.4%	7.3%	5.7%	5.4%
Growth rate, per capita income	1.9%	2.6%	1.1%	4.1%	2.6%	2.2%
Per capita income, 1976	$500	$718	$736	$525	$1,032	$490

Source: United Nations, *Monthly Bulletin of Statistics,* various issues;
United Nations, *Economic Bulletin for Latin America,* IX (1972); and Wilkie
and Reich, *Statistical Abstract of Latin America,* p. 239.

to an international source, Brazil was by most indicators the most industrialized economy in Latin America, and along with Mexico, the only
Latin American economy with major manufactured exports.

The share of manufacutring in gross domestic product does not
correctly capture the significance of the degree of industrialization of
the six countries. Venezuela (38 percent), Chile (40 percent), and
Peru (31 percent) all had higher or similar proportions than Mexico
and Brazil (30 percent each). [6] However, in the literature of international agencies the latter two countries are referred to as semi-
industrial, while the former three are not. This reflects a qualitative
judgment about the nature and potential of industry in Brazil and

Mexico. Increasingly over the last decade, Brazilian based industry has established itself as internationally competitive in a number of sectors, and to a lesser extent this is true for Mexico. This places the two countries in a qualitatively different category from Chile (at least up to 1974) and Peru, where manufacturing has been almost exclusively for the internal market. The relationship of these economies to the world market is also correspondingly different. Events in Chile since the military coup of September 1973, and the discovery of great oil and gas reserves in Mexico, significantly altered the situations in these countries, but as a first approximation we can differentiate between Brazil and Mexico, on the one hand, and Peru and Chile on the other, on the basis of the type of industrialization. [7]

Nicaragua and Venezuela both represent types of economies different from the others. Venezuela has an economy whose growth and structure have been conditioned by the domination of the petroleum sector. It is beyond the scope of this paper to analyze the particular dynamics of petroleum dominated economies, except to point out the most obvious characteristics. In economies where petroleum is of overwhelming significance, a tremendous portion of social wealth is generated on the basis of a tiny proportion of the labor force. As a consequence, the link between the petroleum economy and the rest of the economy is primarily on the expenditure side, usually state expenditure, and only weakly on the production side. For this reason, such economies have been characterized as experiencing expenditure-led growth. [8] Such growth tends to establish a pattern of sectoral profitability and thus investment incentives quite different from nonoil economies.

Nicaragua is the most underdeveloped country of the six, an underdevelopment far greater than its per capita income would indicate. In 1975–1976 manufacturing was only 21 percent of GNP, and just over 50 percent of manufacturing value added was accounted for by food processing, beverages, and tobacco. This reflects a very low level of industrial diversification, having greater similarity to the more industrialized African countries than to other Latin American countries. And while each of the countries under review is still in the process of agricultural transformation from precapitalist to capitalist social relations, this process began more recently in Nicaragua, though since 1979 it may be proceeding more rapidly than elsewhere.

In Table 1, the growth performance of each country is presented. The first point to note is that three of the six had similar growth rates from 1955 to 1965. Peru, Brazil, and Nicaragua experienced growth rates of GDP of 5.5 to 5.8 percent per annum. GDP grew a percentage point faster in Mexico and Venezuela, 6.5 percent and 6.9 percent, respectively. For Chile GDP growth was slowest, but still well above the

4.5 percent rate of population growth. From 1965 on the variation in growth rates of GDP increased sharply. While the ratio of the fastest to the slowest growth rate for 1955–1965 was 1:5 (Venezuela to Chile), for 1965 to 1977 it was 3:7 (Brazil to Chile). There are, however, some patterns within this diversity. From 1965 to 1971 Peru, Chile, Venezuela, and Nicaragua all grew at more or less the same rates, despite the great differences in the structures of the four economies. The table indicates that, taking the entire period for three of the six countries (Mexico, Brazil, Venezuela), growth was sufficiently rapid to provide considerable potential for the satisfaction of basic needs. Per capita income, at the minimum on index of resources available for satisfying basic needs, grew faster than 2.5 percent a year in each of these cases. In the case of Brazil, per capita income grew at a rate implying a doubling of per capita income in less than 20 years. Given this, even no change in the distribution of income would have resulted in a major improvement in the lot of the poor. In Peru and Nicaragua, per capita income grew more modestly, implying that, *ceteris paribus,* less improvement in the lot of the poor was possible within the existing distribution of income. In the case of Chile, income per head grew very slowly, though at roughly the same rate as in Peru and Nicaragua up to 1973, when aggregate GDP fell.

However, in each of these countries, in varying degrees, there were political forces operating not only to block a distribution of the increment in growth toward the poor, but also to direct the increment away from low income groups. Chile is the most extreme case. From 1955 (when the time series in Table 1 begins) until September 1973, the governments of Chile were democratically elected ones, either social democratic reformist (in the case of Allende's administration) or more conservative governments with a strong social democratic and socialist opposition (before 1970). In this political context organized labor, and to a lesser extent the peasantry, were able, to voice their interests to a significant degree through representative institutions. The poorest 20 percent of the Chilean population received the largest percentage of national income in the 1960s of any of the countries under review. (See Table 2. There is no distributional data available for Nicaragua). The organized political strength of the Chilean working class in particular probably moderated any tendencies in the economic system toward extremely regressive distributional shifts. [9] However, the violent coup of 1973 and subsequent repression qualitatively changed the political situation, destroying representative institutions and establishing a national security state. [10] Evidence presented below demonstrates the distributional consequences of this.

The case of Brazil is somewhat similar, though the coup of 1964

TABLE 2: Income Distribution by Population Quintiles in Five Latin American Countries

[Statistics give percentage of national income received by each quintile.]

Quintile	Peru		Mexico		Chile*	Brazil		Venezuela	
	1962 c	*1972 c*	*1963 a*	*1969 a*	*1968 a*	*1960 b*	*1970 b*	*1962 a*	*1971 c*
1st	3.0%	2.5%	3.7%	4.2%	4.8%	3.5%	2.8%	3.3%	2.7%
2nd	7.0	6.5	6.7	6.0	8.2	6.8	5.3	6.3	5.5
3rd	13.0	12.5	11.3	9.7	12.2	10.7	9.0	11.2	9.6
4th	21.5	20.5	19.6	16.9	19.0	16.9	15.6	20.2	16.8
5th	55.5	58.5	58.7	63.2	55.8	62.1	67.3	59.0	65.4
Highest 5%	26.0	33.0	29.1	37.8	31.0	39.9	44.8	27.2	40.5
Gini d	.56	.59	.54	.60	.51	.53	.62	.57	.61

*Comparative figures unavailable for Chile

a Household distribution

b Income recipient's distribution

c Economically active population distribution

d Coefficient of inequality

Source: Shail Jain, *Size Distribution of Income* (Washington, D.C.: World Bank, 1975) and R. Webb and A. Figuera, *La Distribución del Ingreso en el Perú* (Lima: IEP, 1977).

was not quite so brutal at the outset. Again, representative institutions were abolished, including the independent trade union movement. Much has been written about the "economic miracle" in Brazil after the military coup, with the implication that the military regime bought about a dramatic surge of economic growth. However, the rate of economic growth in Brazil from 1955 to the coup was one of the highest in Latin America (6 percent annually), and while higher afterwards (8 percent annually), the difference is substantial but not dramatic. [11] If one thinks that the military dictatorship was instrumental in accelerating growth, it is instructive to compare what GDP would have been, had growth proceeded at the precoup rate. In such a counterfactual circumstance, the index for 1977 would have been about 16 percent below the actual figure. [12] What this suggests is that the most dramatic consequences of the "miracle" were not in aggregate growth, but in the structure of industry and distribution. As the economist Albert Fishlow, former U.S. Deputy Assistant Secretary of State, has pointed out, the purchasing power of wages was forced down, [13] One of the major successes which the military dictatorship claimed as its own was the taming of inflation. A close inspection of the anti-inflation program of the military regime suggests that it was more successful in depressing the living standard of the working class than in stabilizing the price level.

A major qualitative change occurred in the political environment of Peru during the period under review, though there is some controversy over its character. [14] The controversy arises in part over the extent to which the post-1968 military government fostered any significant popular participation, and whether this led to significant changes in income distribution. What is true is that the real or illusory changes implemented from 1968 to 1975 affecting popular participation and income distribution have subsequently been reversed. While the coup of 1968 changed the class nature of the Peruvian state, this resulted in no increase in popular participation, except inadvertently by raising the consciousness of the working class and peasantry. [15]

While in Chile, Brazil, and Peru major political events occurred that significantly altered the balance of class power in these societies, this is not the case in Mexico, Nicaragua, and Venezuela, except insofar as the political relationship between classes is always in flux in the process of economic development. [16] The shift in form from dictatorship to formal democracy in Venezuela in 1958 was a major event, but did not seem to carry the same epoch-making significance as the coups in Chile, Brazil, and Peru. The last 25 years of Somoza rule in Nicaragua and the PRI government in Mexico represent continuations of particular types of unrepresentative regimes, the latter being more benign than the former. In each of these countries save Nicaragua (where there are no reliable data), the evidence indicates that distribution of income became more unequal over time, differences in levels of development, economic structure, and political institutions notwithstanding.

The Brazilian situation is perhaps the best documented, with the increase in inequality being quite substantial from 1960 to 1970. [17] The summary statistic in the last row of Table 2, the Gini coefficient, rose from .53 to .62, a change bordering on the astounding. The poorest 40 percent of the population received 10.3 percent of national income in 1960 and 8.1 percent in 1970. Morever, the incomes of this 40 percent grew at 3.7 percent, while the incomes of the richest 5 percent grew at almost twice that rate (7.3 percent). When one accounts for population growth, income per head for the bottom 40 percent grew at less than one percent per annum, while for the richest 5 percent at over four times this rate. There is little doubt that since 1970 distribution has become more unequal, for the purchasing power of wages has been stable at best. [18] In summary, one can say that the aggregate growth performance of the Brazilian economy over the last 25 years was sufficient to make possible a dramatic reduction in poverty; however, the evidence indicates that little has occurred to reduce poverty and, indeed, it may have gotten worse.

The situation of the poor in Brazil has been the subject of extensive debate. In response to Albert Fishlow's conclusions that there was a substantial increase in poverty between 1960 and 1970, [19] Gary Fields attempted to prove that the standard of living of the poor improved dramatically in absolute terms. [20] Fields is particularly concerned with demonstrating that although income distribution may worsen in a period of economic growth, frequently the poor will benefit from that growth. While this may be true, Fields' conclusions about improvements in the situation of the poor in Brazil have been refuted by a series of articles which show that his argument is fallacious on arithmetic, technical, and theoretical grounds. [21] Albert Fishlow, in his comment on Fields' article, states that if there was a decline in absolute poverty in Brazil, it was minimal. He concludes:

> The relative deterioration in income distribution during the decade prevented economic growth from significantly alleviating the burden of crushing absolute poverty that afflicted a third of Brazilian families, and a still larger proportion of the population. [22]

Of all the countries we are considering, Chile had the least unequal distribution of income in the 1960s as measured in Table 2. [23] In 1968, 13 percent of income was received by the poorest 40 percent, almost three percentage points more than in Mexico for 1969, and five more than Brazil in 1970. Available evidence indicates a drastic worsening of income distribution after the Allende period, as shown in Table 3. In 1974, the Gini index of inequality was well below that for 1968 (.48 compared to .52). A survey of the redistributive policies of the Allende government suggests that they largely account for the improvement in income distribution. In fact, it is reasonable to assume that distribution was even more equal in 1973 than in 1974, for unemployment doubled in the space of 12 months. Under the military dictatorship, inequality continued to rise in 1975 and 1976, then remained more or less the same, slightly above the 1968 level. International comparisons of inequality indicate that Chile in the 1960s and 1970s was in the per capita income range in which inequality declines as economic growth continues. [24] The so-called free market policies of the military dictatorship seem to have reversed any such tendency.

In Mexico, Peru, and Venezuela inequality of incomes distribution increased in the 1960s. In each of these countries the income share of the poorest 40 percent fell during the period of comparison, and the share of the richest 5 percent rose substantially. In Peru, the income share of every quintile fell except for the highest. Indeed, the income share of the wealthiest 80–95 percentile groups also fell, with only the top 5 percent gaining relatively. Only in Mexico did the share of the poorest 20 percent rise, but the shares for the next three quintiles all declined.

For Brazil, Mexico, Nicaragua, Peru, and Venezuela, aggregate economic growth was sufficiently rapid to allow for significant reductions in poverty. However, distribution of this growth was such that it was not realized. In the case of Chile growth was quite slow, even before the economic crisis of 1973 and thereafter. From 1968 to 1973 a substantial shift toward greater equality of distribution occurred and with it a reduction in poverty. This was reversed after 1973.

TABLE 3: Measures of Income Inequality in Chile, 1968-1976

	Gini Coefficient	Share of Top 20%
1968	.51	55.8%
1974	.46	---
1975	.47	53.9
1976	.53	60.3
1978	.52	58.6

Source: United States Embassy, Santiago, "Chile: Economic Outlook Report" (December 1979), p. 9.

TABLE 4: Indices of the Purchasing Power of Blue-Collar Wages in Peru, Mexico, Chile, and Brazil, 1960-1978

	Peru [a]	Mexico [b]	Chile [c]	Brazil [b]
1960	91.9	71.3	87.3	---
1961	95.0	72.5	---	---
1962	101.5	78.2	---	---
1963	101.5	92.1	88.2	---
1964	104.2	95.1	84.3	---
1965	100.0	100.0	100.0	---
1966	102.8	103.7	111.8	100.0
1967	101.7	107.2	130.3	110.0
1968	90.2	109.9	135.5	106.0
1969	96.0	113.3	145.6	110.0
1970	89.3	111.3	161.1	109.0
1971	104.0	115.0	192.4	---
1972	112.6	116.2	181.8	---
1973	123.7	116.5	152.5*	---
1974	122.3	120.5	115.3	---
1975	102.8	118.7	106.4	---
1976	90.3	131.2	117.6	---
1977	73.4	130.7	145.7	---
1978	53.6	---	169.0	---

*64.4 for the last 3 months of 1973

[a] Private employment, blue-collar, in Lima

[b] Manufacturing only

[c] National index, deflated by official cost of living index until 1970; University of Chile index from 1970 upwards

Source: John Weeks, "The Distribution of Income and the Role of the State in Peru," in Frances Stewart, ed., *Distribution of Income and Systems of Payment* (London: Macmillan, forthcoming); and United Nations, *Monthly Bulletin of Statistics*, various issues.

Tables 4 and 5 indicate the gains or lack of gains experienced by the working class in various countries. In Peru, the purchasing power of blue collar workers was more or less constant from 1960 to 1971, which is consistent with a worsening size-distribution of income from 1962 to 1972. That is, blue collar earnings were below average earnings per member of the labor force. For a brief period, 1971 to 1974, real wages rose substantially, but subsequently fell over 50 percent. At the same time, unemployment rose, primarily in Lima. Less unemployment as compared to Chile, reflects the lower level of development of the Peruvian economy, and the presence of low-income "informal" urban activities for the unemployed. The drop in real incomes reflects the extreme labor surplus conditions which do not show up in the unemployment rate.

TABLE 5:   Unemployment in Selected Latin American Countries,
1968-1978

	Chile[a]	Peru[b]	Venezuela[b]	Nicaragua[b]
1968	6.0%	5.4%	5.5%	---
1969	6.2	5.9	6.7	---
1970	7.1	4.7	6.2	3.7%
1971	5.5	4.4	5.9	3.6
1972	3.8	4.2	5.5	6.0
1973	4.6	4.2	5.8	9.1
1974	9.7	4.0	6.1	7.3
1975	16.2	4.9	7.2	---
1976	16.8	5.2	6.0	---
1977	13.2	5.8	5.0	---
1978	13.7	6.2	---	---

[a] Santiago only.   [b] National rates.

Source: United Nations, *Monthly Bulletin of Statistics*, various
issues, and Jeffrey Hart, "Industrialization and Fulfillment of
Basic Human Needs in Venezuela," in John G. Ruggie, ed.,
Alternative Conceptions of World Order (forthcoming).

Blue collar real wages rose quite rapidly in Chile in the 1960s and
early 1970s, at 7.4 percent per annum from 1960 to 1971. There was
a 6 percent fall in 1972, and for the last three months of 1973 (the
coup was in September) the index of real wages was 36 percent of the
average for 1972. Declines continued in 1974 and 1975, and real wages
rose subsequently. Though real wages rose after 1975, the working
class continued and continues, to bear a crushing burden of unemployment. In 1975 and 1976, one out of every six members of the Santiago
labor force was completely unemployed, and in 1978 it was still one
out of seven. Some perspective is given on this if we realize that since
the end of the post-World War II reconstruction in Europe and Japan,
no industrial country has recorded an unemployment rate of as much as
ten percent, save England. Even in a major urban area this is rare, and
associated with very short-term recessions in particular industries, as in
Detroit.

The patterns of unemployment and real wage changes in Peru
and Chile reflect countries at two levels of development. In Chile, where
the labor movement is stronger, real wage cuts could be resisted more
successfully, so the burden of the economic crisis was more weighted to
unemployment, over which the working class has no control, except
through the state. In Peru the workers' movement is weaker and the
catastrophic fall in real wages during the current economic crisis reflects

that. Both situations indicate a substantial increase in poverty, particularly urban poverty, in the 1970s. [25]

The data on wages in Brazil, although quite fragmentary, indicate stagnation in purchasing power from 1967 to 1970, years during which real GDP grew at 9.3 percent per annum. The deterioration in the size distribution of income noted above should come as no shock. Real wage movements in Mexico were very similar to those in Peru over the years 1965 to 1974—initial slow growth followed by stagnation. A single-step increase occurred in 1976, but even with this real wages grew at only 2.3 percent per annum from 1965 to 1977, while GDP grew at 5.6 percent.

For Venezuela and Nicaragua we have only unemployment rates as an indicator of the position of urban workers, though official Venezuelan sources estimate that real wages in manufacturing have grown at about 2.4 percent for 1961 to 1974. [26] This would be about the same as the rate of growth of per capita income. [27] Data in Table 5 indicate that unemployment has not increased, so one can conclude that the relative position of urban workers probably did not decline in the 1970s. The information on Nicaragua is very limited and no firm conclusions can be drawn, except to note that measured unemployment doubled from 1970 to 1974.

In this section we have not considered rural workers separately. Since wage data for such workers is either not available or irrelevent, as in the case of peasant farming, more indirect measures are required. In general, the aggregate economic performance of the countries under review has been quite impressive but available evidence indicates that this has had little impact on reducing poverty; quite the contrary in some cases.

II. SOCIAL INDICATORS AS A MEASURE OF ABSOLUTE POVERTY

Poverty can be viewed from two perspectives: relative or absolute. Throughout the 1960s the poor in Brazil, Mexico, Peru, and Venezuela were becoming relatively poorer, and in the 1970s the inequalities in income distribution were sharply accentuated in Brazil, Chile, and Peru. [28] While this may suggest that there has been scant amelioration of material poverty, in reality it tells us little about the concrete conditions of the poor, for poverty is a material phenomenon which must be measured absolutely. The recognition and application of this is one of the unique contributions of the basic needs strategy. [29] Therefore, in order to analyze what different patterns of economic development have accomplished vis-a-vis the alleviation of poverty, analysis of income distribution cannot be relied on; rather an attempt, must be made to examine the material conditions of life.

Attempt is stressed since any comparative study of the quality of life must rely on data which are often problematical. Data on health, nutrition, education, or housing, referred to as social indicators, are frequently difficult to compare because the methodology for their collection is not uniform and rigorous. This is in part due to the somewhat subjective nature of what is being measured, as well as to the obstacles which must be confronted when compiling data on social welfare. Another problem in the use of social indicators is that such data are not collected frequently; hence instead of having yearly indicators, which commonly exist in the case of macroeconomic data, social indicators may be available for only several years for each country, thus making comparison more difficult. [30]

But this is not to suggest that the aforementioned problems with the data make comparison either impossible or invalid. The data are frequent and accurate enough to enable us to make valuable comparative estimates. But it is necessary to recognize that problems exist, and that the statistics must be viewed in the light of this reality.

As indicated, it is difficult to quantify the quality of life. Yet within the development literature on basic needs there is a consensus that basic needs fall primarily into five categories: nutrition, health, housing, water and sanitation, and education. The satisfaction of these basic needs in our sample of six Latin American countries will be compared in light of their record on economic performance.

Life Expectancy.   Life expectancy is often used as an indicator of the overall satisfaction of basic needs. [31] In Table 6 the six-country sample shows that a higher per capita income is, more or less, conducive to a longer life expectancy. The only exception is Mexico, where life expectancy ranks it second. The relatively rapid rate of change in life expectancy in Mexico from 1960 to 1975 (0.93 percent per annum) helps to account for Mexico's comparatively better record. If life expectancy in these six countries is compared to life expectancy in the 63 middle-income countries in the world, life expectancy in four out of the six countries is lower than what would be expected given their respective per capita income levels. Simmons and Burki demonstrate that in Venezuela, Peru, and Nicaragua there are substantial relative deficits in the life expectancy which would be predicted given per capita income.

The assumption that a higher per capita income leads to a longer life expectancy is called into question by the case of Venezuela. For its

TABLE 6:   Life Expectancy at Birth in 1975 of 6 Countries Ranked by Per Capita Income

	1975 Income	*Life Expectancy*	*Annual Change* [a]	*Relative Deficits* [b]
	dollars	*years*	*percent*	*years*
Venezuela	1,032	66.4	0.0	-4.6
Chile	736	62.5	0.73	+1.3
Mexico	718	64.7	0.93	+3.5
Brazil	525	61.4	0.71	-0.1
Peru	500	55.7	0.93	-2.2
Nicaragua	490	52.9	1.01	-4.3

[a] Percent of annual change, 1960–1975.

[b] The difference between the actual values and expected values is predicted by regression analysis comparing per capita income to life expectancy in 63 middle–income countries.

Source: Wilke and Reich, *Statistical Abstract of Latin America* and Burki, "The Performance of Middle-Income Countries on Basic Human Needs."

level of per capita income in 1976, life expectancy in 1975 was far below the norm for the 63 middle-income countries. [32]

Infant Mortality.   Another indicator which is frequently used to describe general health conditions is infant mortality, since this is dependent upon the overall health and nutrition of women of child-bearing age, as well as the health care delivery systems and general sanitary conditions. It is notable that the infant mortality rate in Brazil, considered the most industrially advanced country in Latin America and frequently described as soon to join the ranks of the developed world, is the highest in the sample, and more than twice that in Nicaragua, Mexico, and Venezuela (Table 7).

The relative commitment to improving the health and nutritional levels of the population, as reflected in the infant mortality rate, can be compared by looking at the cases of Chile and Brazil. Brazil experienced a 4.81 percent improvement per annum from 1960 to 1975 in the infant mortality rate, which corresponds closely with its annual growth in per capita income of 4.3 percent for this same period. Chile experienced a similar improvement in the infant mortality rate, 4.28 percent, at the same time that its per capita income growth was only one percent annually. It is obvious, therefore, that the governments of Chile from 1960 to 1973 devoted more resources to improvements in

TABLE 7:   Infant Mortality in 1975 of 6 Countries Ranked by Per Capita Income

	Infant Mortality [a]	Annual Change [b]	Absolute Rank [c]
Venezuela	53.0	-0.13%	22
Chile	71.0	-4.28	30
Mexico	52.0	-2.68	21
Brazil	110.0	-4.81	39
Peru	65.1	-3.52	26
Nicaragua	46.0 [a]	---	19

[a] Figures are given for the infant mortality rate (deaths per 1,000 live births) in 1975. The figure for Nicaragua is from four separate sources: *Statistical Abstract of Latin America;* United Nations, *Population and Vital Statistics Report* (New York, 1978) Series A, 30, 3; United Nations, *Demographic Yearbook,* 1977 (New York, 1978); and Simmons and Burki. Despite this, the data seem unlikely to reflect reality given other data on health and nutrition for Nicaragua. Most probably this figure represents a case of extreme inaccuracy in the compiling of statistics.

[b] Percent of annual change, 1960–1975. Based on each country's standing among 54 middle-income countries in 1975.

Source: Wilke and Reich, *Statistical Abstract of Latin America* and Burki, "The Performance of Middle-Income Countries on Basic Human Needs."

the health of the population than did those in Brazil. The greatest improvement in Chile occurred in the early 1970s, during the Popular Unity government, when the infant mortality rate fell from 86.5 per thousand in 1970 to 69.2 in 1973. [33] This is an impressive decline, especially when we consider that the last four months of 1973 saw a stark retrenchment of the social welfare programs of the government. Even with sharp cuts in central government expenditure on health after the coup, in 1975 the Chilean government spent 3.1 percent of its total current expenditure on health, as compared to the 0.8 percent by the Brazilian government.

An index of Venezuela's commitment to meeting the basic needs of its population is seen in its record on infant mortality. Although Venezuela's per capita income far exceeds that of any other country in the sample, it ranks second in its infant mortality rate and (leaving Nicaragua aside) has a higher rate than Mexico—which has a per capita income which is one-third lower. In addition, the improvement in the infant mortality rate has been exceedingly slow (0.13 percent per annum from 1960 to 1975).[34] If we look at Venezuela in relation to the other middle income countries we see that while Venezuela ranks fifth from highest in per capita income, it ranks 22 (out of 54 countries) in infant mortality.

Health Care.   Other social indicators which focus on health are the number and distribution of physicians relative to the population. With the exception of Chile, in 1975 the number of physicians in these six Latin American countries correlates closely with the per capita income (Table 8). Although Chile ranks second in per capita income, it ranks fifth in population per physician. From 1969 to 1973 the ratio of inhabitants to physicians remained stable (1,842 inhabitants per physician in 1969 and 1,836 inhabitants per physician in 1973). In 1975 the ratio had deteriorated to 2,020 inhabitants per physician. Only three other middle-income countries experienced a deterioration in the population/physician ratio during the period from 1960 to 1975, and two of these are also in Latin America: Paraguay and the Dominican Republic.

Viewed in the context of the middle income countries as a whole, the six Latin American countries under review have population/physician

TABLE 8:   Number and Distribution of Physicians in Population of 6 Countries Ranked by 1975 Per Capita Income

	Population Per Physician 1975[a]	Annual Change 1960–1975[b]	Distribution of Physicians[c]
Venezuela	910	-3.03%	1.4
Chile	2,020	0.35	1.5
Mexico	1,480	-1.94	2.5
Brazil	1,650	-2.26	2.4
Peru	1,800	-1.33	3.2
Nicaragua	2,080	-1.99	3.1

[a] Figures are for 1975 or latest available.

[b] Percent of annual change in population/physician ratio.

[c] Physicians in cities of over 100,000 inhabitants divided by total number of physicians, multiplied by the total population, divided by the population in cities of over 100,000 inhabitants.

Source: Wilke and Reich, *Statistical Abstract of Latin America* and Burki, "The Performance of Middle-Income Countries on Basic Human Needs."

ratios which approximate what would be predicted, given their per capita incomes. As in all national statistics, however, this hides regional disparities, especially those between urban and rural areas. In these six Latin American countries the distribution of physicians favors the urban areas, with the greatest urban concentration of physicians in Peru and Nicaragua. In these two countries, cities of over 100,000 inhabitants had more than three times the number of physicians per unit of population in 1975 than the less populous regions (Table 8). In Peru in 1978 there were 15.74 physicians per 10,000 inhabitants in Lima, while there was less than one doctor (0.71) per 10,000 people in the southern highlands. [35]

In regard to the basic health needs of the population, especially of the poor, preventive health care provided via local health clinics is more important than curative medicines. Preventive health care can be adequately provided by primary health workers, rather than by physicians. Thus, more instrumental in providing health care for the poor are large numbers of health workers who are readily accessible to the population— not physicians or specialists who are concentrated at large hospitals in urban areas, and who tend to provide relatively sophisticated care for the upper strata of the population. The literature on the implementation of the basic needs strategy from agencies like the World Bank, USAID, and the ILO stresses the need for health delivery systems which focus on preventive care and are staffed predominately by paramedical personnel.

Despite this, with the exception of Venezuela and Mexico, each of the countries in the sample had a significantly smaller number of health workers per inhabitant than physicians (Table 8 and 9). In 1975 Chile had by far the fewest paramedics per inhabitant, and this ratio deteriorated significantly from 1960 to 1975 (Table 9). In fact, Chile's paucity of health care workers is outstanding not only within the context of the sample, but also as compared to the 63 middle-income countries. The deterioration in the ratio of health workers per inhabitant was sharper than in any of the other middle income countries, giving Chile a rank of 63 in percentage change. And although Chile ranks 21 in per capita income, it ranks 61 in population per health worker. From the available data it is impossible to determine exactly when this deterioration occurred, but it would not be unreasonable to assume that a substantial portion of it took place in 1974 and 1975, when the military government greatly reduced the resources allocated to health care facilities. Table 11 shows that government expenditure on health fell dramatically in 1974, more so in 1975, and remained low through 1977 (the last year for which data are available).

TABLE 9:   Population in 1975 Per Primary Health Worker
(Excluding Physicians) for 6 Countries Ranked by
Per Capita Income

	Population Per Health Worker[a]	Annual Change[b]
Venezuela	430	0.0%
Chile	5,170	0.43
Mexico	1,620	-5.43
Brazil	2,920	---
Peru	2,970	-1.67
Nicaragua	4,120	-1.89

[a] Figures are for 1975 or latest available.

[b] Percent of annual change, 1960-1975.

Source: Wilke and Reich, *Statistical Abstract of Latin America* and Burki, "The Performance of Middle-Income Countries on Basic Human Needs."

The other countries in the sample are also distinguished by a scarcity of paramedical health workers. Table 10 demonstrates that while all of the countries in the sample are in the top half on per capita income, with the exception of Mexico and Venezuela, they are clustered at the

TABLE 10:   Comparison of 6 Latin American Countries to 63
Middle-Income Countries, and Population Per Primary
Health Worker, 1975

	Per Capita Rank[a]	Population Rank[b]
Venezuela	5	12
Brazil	16	54
Mexico	17	36
Chile	21	61
Peru	29	53
Nicaragua	32	56

[a] The ranking on 1975 per capita income differs here from our other ranking since we are using the data of Simmons and Burki (see end of this chapter, Note 2).

[b] Per non-physician, primary health worker ratio to general population in 63 countries in 1975.

Source: Simmons and Burki, p. 65.

TABLE 11:   Chilean Government Expenditure on Health in U.S. Dollars, 1970–1977

	Total in Millions	Expenditure Per Inhabitant
1970	$154	$16.4
1971	212	22.2
1972	253	26.0
1973	244	24.0
1974	198	19.7
1975	134	13.1
1976	133	12.8
1977	145	13.7

Source: *Sobre la Desnutrición en Chile* (Santiago, 1978).

bottom in their ranking on population per health worker. In the cases of Mexico and Venezuela they, too, have few health workers, relative to their per capita income.

Examining the number of physicians as a percentage of total medical personnel, it is clear that in Venezuela, Peru, and Nicaragua physicians comprised just under one-third of the health workers, while in Brazil 60 percent of all medical personnel are doctors (Table 9). In those Latin American countries, while there are a sizable number of physicians relative to the other middle-income countries, there has been little emphasis on the training of other health workers. This would indicate that there are minimal health facilities, especially preventive clinics, which are readily accessible to the poor.

TABLE 12:   Incidence of Disease, in 6 Countries Ranked by Per Capita Income, 1975

	Incidence of Typhoid[a]	Incidence of Dysentery & Amoebiosis[b]
Venezuela	6	163
Chile	45	41
Mexico	96	10
Brazil	4	---
Peru	101	168
Nicaragua	17	234

[a] Per 100,000 inhabitants, 1974.   [b] Per 100,000 inhabitants, 1975

Source: Simmons and Burki, p. 63.

TABLE 13:   Number of Reported Cases of Typhoid in Chile,
             1969–1977

Year	Reported Cases	Year	Reported Cases
1969	5,358	1974	4,655
1970	5,344	1975	6,110
1971	4,784	1976	7,800
1972	4,527	1977	10,000*
1973	3,688		

*Based on data for first six months.

Source: *Mensaje* 26 (July 1977):309.

The incidence of disease is another indicator of health conditions for which some relatively reliable data exist. The diseases which account for the high rate of mortality and morbidity in these countries are primarily those transmitted by human feces, and the spread of these diseases is greater in areas without clean water facilities. Table 12 indicates the incidence of dysentery and typhoid. Brazilian data on the incidence of dysentery are unavailable, but Brazil appears to have the lowest incidence of typhoid (4 cases per 100,000 people). However, some caution is necessary in light of the recent publicity surrounding the deliberate falsification in the reported number of cases of polio.[36] Chile ranked fourth in 1975 in incidence of typhoid, but there was a substantial decrease in typhoid from 1970 to 1973, followed by an increase of more than 170 percent from 1973 to 1977 (Table 13).

Every country in the sample has a relatively high incidence of fecal-related diseases. Compared to other middle income countries, Peru, Venezuela, and Nicaragua are among those countries with the highest incidence of diarrheal diseases. In Venezuela the monthly incidence among preschool age children is between 40 and 50 percent.[37] In Brazil this disease group is responsible for over 50 percent of the deaths of children under five years old in the Northeast.[38]

Nutrition. Malnutrition and disease reinforce each other, i.e., each augments the pathological effects of the other. Malnourished individuals are more likely to contract infectious diseases, to suffer severe cases, and to die from them. In malnourished children infections especially have severe effects. In a third to a half of deaths of children due to disease, malnutrition is a contributing cause. Not surprisingly, calorie deficiency is a key determinant of life expectancy and of both child and infant mortality.[39]

In every country in our sample, a major portion of the population suffers from significant malnutrition. Extreme inequalities in the distribution of income lead to wide divergencies in food consumption. This, coupled with inequalities in nutritional requirements and the distribution of food within the family, require that a country's per capita supply of calories be approximately 150 percent of the average daily requirements in order to assure adequate nutrition of all sectors of the population. The excess in the per capita calorie supply which is necessary varies with particular social, economic, and political conditions.

In Peru and Venezuela the per capita supply of calories for the country as a whole is below the average daily requirement (Table 14), suggesting severe malnutrition of a significant portion of the population. An index of Venezuela's lack of commitment to the satisfaction of the basic needs of the poor is the fact that although Venezuela enjoys the highest per capita income in the sample, it has the lowest per capita supply of calories. Venezuela's performance on per capita supply, as demonstrated in its relative deficit (−29), approaches the worst among all middle-income countries (exceeded only by Iran and Iraq).[40] In 1977 43.8 percent of all children from the ages of one to six years suffered from some form of malnutrition.[41] In Peru in 1974 and 1975, although the per capita suply of calories was below minimum requirements, that was probably close to a peak period for food consumption. Since that time the average caloric intake of not only the lowest strata, but of the middle strata in Lima has declined precipitously (Table 15).

Keeping in mind that the average requirement of 2,400 calories per day is itself too low (see note to Table 14), combined with fact that the FAO categorizes as severely malnourished any person who consumes less than 70 percent of his or her daily calorie requirement, there is substantial evidence that there was widespread malnutrition to the point of starvation in both the middle and low economic strata in Lima in 1977 and 1978. It appears that there has been further deterioration, as food consumption declined in 1979.[42]

In Peru the regional disparities are stark between the metropolitan areas, primarily Lima, and the highlands and jungle. While it is clear that a substantial portion of the population of Lima is now severely malnourished, average food deficiency in the highlands is even more severe (Table 16).

During the presidency of General Juan Velasco Alvarado (1968–1975) basic food stuffs were subsidized by the government, and there were large-scale imports of food (i.e., rice, wheat, etc.), primarily to meet the needs of urban workers. This was done in part because the

TABLE 14:   Per Capita Supply of Calories as Percent of Average
Daily Requirements in 6 Latin American Countries
Ranked by Per Capita Income, 1975

	Average Per Capita Caloric Intake	*Percent of Average Daily Requirements* [a]	*Annual Change* [b]	*Relative Deficits* [c]
Venezuela	2,422	98%	0.79%	−29
Chile	2,825	109	0.98	− 6
Mexico	2,725	117	0.64	+ 1
Brazil	2,515	115	0.66	− 2
Peru	2,359	99	0.14	−11
Nicaragua	2,387	109	1.45	+ 0.3

[a] Per capita caloric supply as a percent of average daily requirements is calculated from data based on an FAO (UN Food and Agriculture Organization) guideline of an average requirement of 2,400
calories per day. This figure is generally believed to be too low
for the population as a whole since sizeable portions of the population (e.g., adult males, pregnant and lactating women, etc.) have
significantly higher requirements. "Energy and Protein Requirements," Report of a Joint FAO/WHO Expert Group, FAO, Rome,
1972.

[b] Percent of annual change, 1960–1975.

[c] The difference between the actual values and expected values as
predicted by regression analysis comparing per capita income to per
capita supply of calories in 63 middle-income countries.

Source: Wilke and Reich, *Statistical Abstract of Latin America* and
Burki, "The Performance of Middle-Income Countries on Basic Human
Needs."

agrarian reform program initiated in 1969 resulted in a precipitous
decline in food production, which coincided with a major expansion in
industry and in the wage labor force. One of the primary aims of the
government was to encourage industrial expansion and this was facilitated
by making basic foods more accessible to workers. [43] Despite this policy,
average food consumption in the middle and lower strata in metropolitan
Lima in 1972 was considerably below the average daily requirements
(Table 15).

By 1976 Peru was clearly in the throes of an economic crisis,
whose symptoms included a substantial deficit in its balance of payments
and a huge debt whose payments it was unable to meet. In order to
renegotiate its debt, the Peruvian government adhered to a stabilization
program imposed by the International Monetary Fund. This necessitated
greatly restricting imports while encouraging exports, removing the

TABLE 15:   Decline of Average Caloric Intake in Metropolitan Lima from 1972 to 1978

	Economic Strata	Caloric Intake	Percent of Average Daily Requirements
1972	Medium	2,113	88%
	Low	1,907	79
1977 [a]	Medium	1,455	60
	Low	1,749	73
1978 [b]	Medium	1,578	66
	Low	1,490	62

[a] December data.   [b] March data.

Source: *Actualidad Económico* 1 (December 1978):11.

subsidies on food products, which caused prices to soar and holding down wages. These measures caused the consumer price index to increase to 876 in December 1979 (from 100 in 1973), and the real wages of blue collar workers in 1979 to fall to 50 percent of what they had been in 1973.[44] These measures, which were not unwelcome to a portion of Peru's local capitalist class, especially exporters, were partially responsible for the decline in the consumption of food, in the satisfaction of other basic needs, and in the standard of living in general in Peru not only among the poor, but among a large section of the middle class as well.

Food consumption in Chile has declined substantially since September 1973 and appears to be considerably lower than it had been 15

TABLE 16:   Deficiency of Average Food Consumption in the Peruvian Highlands, 1978

Category of Food	Degree of Deficiency	Category of Food	Degree of Deficiency
Meat/Fish	37%	Oil/Fats	82%
Fruit	70	Sugar	18
Eggs	78	Root Crops	74
Milk [a]	89		

[a] Includes milk products.

Source: *Actualidad Económico* (December 1978):11.

TABLE 17:   Decline in Total Food Consumption in Chile

Year	Growth Rate	Year	Growth Rate
1965-69	3.1%	1973	-9.3%
1970	3.7	1974	-4.8
1971	6.2	1975	-14.8
1972	4.7		

Source: Wilkie and Reich, *Statistical Abstract of Latin America,* p. 22.

years earlier. In 1960, 34 percent of the population consumed less than 2,000 calories per day, while in 1975 this group had grown to 85 percent. [45] In other words, more than 85 percent of the population was not consuming the standard daily calorie requirements. Table 17 shows the dramatic decline in total food consumption in Chile between 1973 and 1975.

Although per capita income in Brazil has grown at 8 percent in the last 15 years, malnutrition is common. In 1975 only 37 percent of Brazil's population had adequate calorie intake, with 26 percent having deficits of up to 400 calories per day and 37 percent suffering deficits above 400 calories per day. First degree malnutrition [46] affects 17 percent of infants from birth to six months, and increases to 40 percent by the age of two years. Only 47 percent of all children aged 1 to 17 years reach their normal weight. Specialists agree that Brazil is currently capable of providing adequate nutrition for the entire population, but this would conflict with other development priorities such as improving the balance of payments situation. The government of Brazil faces a trade-off between domestic food needs and the need to generate agricultural exports. In the past 15 years attention has turned away from domestic food production toward soybeans, cocoa, and fruit juices for export. This has resulted in internal food prices rising faster than the general price index and a falling per capita supply of some basic foods. [47]

In only two countries in our sample, Mexico and Nicaragua, is average calorie supply higher than would be predicted given per capita income (Table 14). This is not to be confused with adequate calorie supply for all segments of the population, but it does indicate that perhaps these governments have a greater commitment to meeting the nutritional needs of the population. These conclusions are tentative since this relatively better performance may have little or no impact on the poor because of inequalities in the distribution of food. An example is the case of Mexico, where the rural Indian population's average calorie intake is 85 percent of the average for the urban population. [48]

Housing.   Health is directly related not only to nutrition, but to general sanitary conditions which are associated with housing facilities. Primary among these are safe water and sanitation services which are important in providing a disease-free environment. The World Health Organization considers the provision of a safe and convenient water supply to be "the single most important activity that could be undertaken to improve the health of people living in rural areas." [49] This is because diarrheal diseases which spread rapidly through the use of contaminated water not only cause frequent illness among adults, but are one of the major cause of fatalities among infants and children.

When analyzing safe water and sanitation services, the dichotomy is great between conditions in urban and rural areas. Nicaragua is the best performer in terms of access to safe water in urban areas, where 100 percent of the population had access to drinkable water in 1975 (Table 18). However, its record is less impressive in the rural areas, where only 14 percent of the population had access to drinkable water, and from 1970 to 1975 there was a 3 percent annual decline in access. It becomes even more unimpressive in light of the fact that in 1975, 50 percent of Nicaraguans lived in rural areas (areas with less than 20,000 inhabitants).

In Brazil and Mexico the yearly percentage change from 1960 to 1975 in access to safe water in urban areas is substantial (22.51 percent and 10.07 percent, respectively). In Mexico this was complemented by a significant positive change in rural areas as well (11 percent), and the highest degree of access to safe water in rural areas among the six countries (49 percent). These statistics indicate a serious commitment on the part of both the Mexican and the Brazilian governments to provide drinkable water.

The percentage of the urban population with access to pure water declined both in Chile and Peru (Table 18). This can be accounted for primarily by large rural-urban migrations. In both countries in the rural areas the yearly growth in access to safe water was relatively high from 1970 to 1975. Without other evidence it is impossible to know whether to ascribe this to an active policy of providing safe water in rural areas, or to migration to the cities (i.e., the opposite side of the coin from the decline in access in urban areas).

Sewage disposal is as important as pure water in limiting the spread of disease. Again, a striking disparity exists between urban and rural areas in the provision of sewage services. Given the available

TABLE 18:   Percent of Population with Access to Safe Water in 6
Countries Ranked by Per Capita Income, 1975

	Urban Population[a]	Annual Change[b]	Rural Population[a]	Annual Change[c]
Venezuela	92%	0.61%	38%	0%
Chile	78	- 1.90	28	17
Mexico	70	22.51	49	11
Brazil	87	10.07	28[d]	0.0
Peru	72	- 1.70	15	13
Nicaragua	100	1.83	14	- 3

[a] 1975 data or latest.

[b] Percent of annual change, 1960-1975.

[c] Percent of annual change, 1970-1975.

[d] Data for 1970.

Source: Wilke and Reich, *Statistical Abstract of Latin America* and Burki, "The Performance of Middle-Income Countries on Basic Human Needs."

data, it appears that Brazil performs the best with 85 percent of the urban population and 24 percent of the rural population having access to sewage disposal (Table 19). It is somewhat surprising to note (given the available data), that in 1975 Chile had the least extensive access to sewage disposal, with a low of 36 percent in urban areas and 11 percent in rural areas (Table 19). The urban shortage may be correlated to the general shortage and rising cost of housing in Santiago. According to the *Banco Central de Chile,* in 1975 Santiago had a shortage of 478,556 housing units, and this shortage increased to 571,560 units by

TABLE 19:   Percent of Population with Access to Sewage Disposal in 6 Countries Ranked by Per Capita Income, 1975

	Urban Population	Rural Population	Total Percent
Venezuela	---	45%	---
Chile	36%	11	32%
Mexico	---	14	---
Brazil	85	24	58
Peru	52	16	36
Nicaragua	---	24	---

Source: Wilke and Reich, *Statistical Abstract of Latin America* and Burki, "The Performance of Middle-Income Countries on Basic Human Needs."

1977. [50] This shortage is combined with a dizzying rise in the cost of housing, approximately 460 percent from 1972 to November 1975 Table 20).

Venezuela also has a severe shortage of urban housing. This is hardly surprising since a scarcity of adequate housing exists in nearly all urban centers in Latin America. What is surprising, however, is that state-supported low income housing has actually declined since the oil boom of 1973. In the five years prior to 1973 the state subsidized the construction of 177,329 housing units, whereas in the five years subsequent to the boom of 1973 it has subsidized the construction of only 148,870 units. [51]

Excluded from the analysis is any cross-country comparison of those housing facilities which provide piped water, toilets, and electricity. This is done because we do not consider them basic needs, especially in the context of the six-country sample. They are, of course, of great convenience and improve the quality of life; but given the social realities, most particularly, in the rural regions of Latin American countries, we cannot describe them as basic needs.

Education. It is generally recognized that important linkages exist in the provision of basic needs, that is, the satisfaction of any one of the basic needs is conducive to the satisfaction of each of the others. Within this, many scholars and policy makers involved in implementing a basic needs strategy now believe that education is the key link. This is because a more educated population will understand the advantages, and consequently will more readily make use of basic goods and services

TABLE 20:   Cost of Housing in Santiago, Chile, from 1967 to 1975

[December 1974 = 100.]

Date	Index	Date	Index
1967	0.96	1973	8.97
1968	1.20	1974	56.90
1969	1.51	1974[a]	88.20
1970	1.90	1974[b]	100.00
1971	2.22	1975[c]	413.40
1972	2.83	1975[d]	461.60

[a] November 1974.   [c] September 1975.

[b] December 1974.   [d] November 1975.

Source: Banco Central de Chile, cited in Cassese, p. 69.

which may be accessible, such as a health clinic, pure water, and more nutritious foods.

If this is true, then it is appropriate to be somewhat pessimistic about the possibilities for major short-run improvements in the satisfaction of basic needs in each of the six countries in the sample. This is because in the area of education these countries perform quite poorly relative to the other middle-income countries. The relative deficits of Nicaragua, Mexico, and Brazil (—26, —34.5 and —40 percent, respectively) of students completing primary school as a percentage of those who enter, rank these three countries at the bottom compared to 35 other middle-income countries. Peru, the only other country in the sample for which data are available also has a large relative deficit (—13 percent; see Table 21). In terms of absolute ranking according to primary school completion, out of 50 middle-income countries every country in our study ranks in the bottom half, with Brazil and Nicaragua exceeded only by Panama in their primary school dropout rate (Table 21). Comparing statistics from one source with statistics from another, it would appear that in Venezuela the percentage of students who complete primary school relative to those who enter has declined from 1975 to 1978. In 1975 66 percent of the entering students completed primary school whereas in 1978 only 60 percent did. [52]

We must also keep in mind that these are national statistics, and in countries like Brazil and Peru where there are extreme regional disparities, educational performance in rural areas is far worse. For example, 47 percent of the entering students in Brazil in rural schools drop out between the first and second year of primary school, and only one rural child out of 100 will finish the sixth grade. [53]

Data on primary school completion is more significant than data on enrollment because: 1) enrollments can be high but not reflect actual attendance, and 2) enrollments tell us little about students who completely drop out of school after one or two years. Still the statistics on enrollment are somewhat interesting since they indicate not only that Nicaragua, Venezuela, and Brazil have the lowest number of children enrolled in our sample (65, 81, and 86 percent, respectively), but also that the percentage of students enrolled has actually declined in Nicaragua and Brazil, while remaining constant in Venezuela (Table 22). [54] The data on primary school enrollment and completion clearly demonstrates that Venezuela, despite its relatively high per capita income, was not committed until quite recently to primary schooling, and Brazil, despite its rapid rate of growth, has also failed to demonstrate a significant commitment to primary education.

Analysis of the data on enrollment and completion reveals slightly

TABLE 21:   Students Completing Primary School as a Percentage
of Those Who Enter in 6 Latin American Countries,
1975

[Countries are ranked by 1975 per capita income. When 1975 data
are unavailable, the latest available are used. Absolute rank is based on standing among 50 middle-income
countries.]

	Completing Students	Relative Deficit[a]	Absolute Rank[b]
Venezuela	66%	---	30
Chile	55	---	37
Mexico	65	-34.5	32
Brazil	28	-40.0	48
Peru	66	-13.0	29
Nicaragua	28	-26.0	49

[a] The difference between the actual values and expected values as·
predicted by regression analysis comparing per capita income to
students completing primary school as a percentage of those who
enter, in 35 middle-income countries.

[b] When two countries have the same incidence of completion their
relative rank is determined by their past performance.

Source: Simmons and Burki, p. 13 and p. 46.

better performance on primary education in Chile, Mexico, and Peru.
In these countries it appears that most children of school age at one time
attend school (Table 22), and of these, 55, 65, and 66 percent, respectively complete primary school (Table 21). It is only within the context of the six-country survey that these performances may be deemed
fair, because compared to the other middle income countries they are
remarkably low.

Adult literacy is a major indicator of the general level of education
and is of extreme importance in terms of facilitating the satisfaction of
basic needs. Chile is the only country in the sample with a respectable
performance in terms of its adult literacy rate, which is above what
one might predict given per capita income (Table 23). In comparing
the absolute percentage of literate adults, as well as the annual change
from 1960 to 1975, Brazil's lack of commitment to general education
is again manifest. Although Mexico, Peru, and Brazil all had similar
literacy rates in 1960, only Mexico and Peru demonstrate significant
yearly rates of improvement (1.58 and 1.11 percent respectively), so
that by 1975 over 70 percent of their adult populations were literate.

TABLE 22:   Primary School Enrollment in 1975 for 6 Latin American
Countries of Children in 7 to 13 Year Age Bracket

[Countries are ranked by 1975 per capita income, and percent of
annual change is from 1960 to 1975.]

	Percent Enrolled [a]	Annual Change
Venezuela	81%	0.0%
Chile	119	0.6
Mexico	112	2.3
Brazil	86	-0.6
Peru	111	2.0
Nicaragua	65	-0.1

[a] Figures over 100 percent indicate that persons not in the 7 to 13
year age bracket attend primary school.

Source: Simmons and Burki, p. 68.

Brazil had the worst record in terms of improvement (0.48 percent
annually), and in 1975 was second only to Nicaragua in the percentage
of illiterate adults (Table 23). Nicaragua was characterized by the most
widespread adult illiteracy both in 1960 and in 1975, but it is significant
to note that it also had the most rapid rate of improvement (3.17 percent
per annum) in this period (Table 23).

Given the generally low performance on educational indicators by
the countries in the sample, it is hardly surprising to discover that the
percentage of public expenditure devoted to education was extremely

TABLE 23:   Adult Literacy Rates in 6 Latin American Countries
Ranked by 1975 Per Capita Income

	Adult Literacy, 1960	Adult Literacy, 1975	Annual Change, 1960–1975
Venezuela	65%	82%	1.95%
Chile	84	90	0.69
Mexico	62	76	1.58
Brazil	61	64	0.48
Peru	61	72	1.11
Nicaragua	38	57	3.17

[a] Latest data are used when 1975 are unavailable.

Source: Simmons and Burki, p. 48.

TABLE 24:   Total Public Expenditure Devoted to Education in 6
Latin American Countries Ranked by 1975 Per Capita
Income

	Public Expenditure, 1975[a]	Annual Change, 1960-75	Absolute Rank[b]
Venezuela	19.9%	3.3%	19
Chile	12.5	2.2	43
Mexico	12.0	0.0	47
Brazil	14.4	5.7	46
Peru	21.7	-3.7	12
Nicaragua	14.2	-1.0	40

[a] Or latest available data.   [b] Based on 56 middle-income countries.

Source: Simmons and Burki, p. 69.

low compared to other middle-income countries. In 1975 out of 56 middle-income countries, Chile, Mexico, Brazil, and Nicaragua ranked in the lowest quartile in percentage expenditure on education (Table 24).

Brazil's generally poor record on general education is partly due to the fact that in 1975 not only did it have the second lowest percentage expenditure on education in the sample, but that even this low level of expenditure (12.4 percent) was a great improvement over 1960. In that year only 7.5 percent of total government expenditures was devoted to education (Table 24). Further evidence of the lack of commitment by Brazil's military government to primary education is the fact that, of those funds which were devoted to education, the bulk was earmarked for higher education. In 1971, 70.8 percent of public capital expenditure on education was devoted to higher education, whereas only 2.6 percent went to primary, and 10.8 percent to secondary levels. [55]

Chile's overall fair record on education and good performance on adult literacy can possibly be attributed to the fact that its extremely low government expenditure on education was a relatively recent phenomenon. In 1971 and 1972 the Chilean government spent almost twice as much on education as it spent in 1975 (Table 25).

Peru's performance on education was good relative to the other five countries, and surprising in light of Peru's low per capita income. Historically, the government of Peru has devoted a fairly large share of its budget to education (26.2 percent in 1960; 21.7 percent in 1975) which has contributed to its high incidence (relative to the other five countries) of primary school enrollment and completion.

TABLE 25:   Chilean Government Current Budgetary Expenditure on
Education, 1971–1976

[Expenditures are in thousands of constant 1969 pesos.]

Year	Expenditure	Year	Expenditure
1971	4,364	1974	3,229
1972	4,116	1975	2,429
1973	2,586	1976	1,920

Source: Cassese, p. 70.

CONCLUSION

This comparative analysis of economic performance and the satisfaction
of basic needs indicates that neither a high per capita income nor a
rapid rate of growth necessarily results in improvements in meeting
basic needs. The case of Venezuela is illustrative of a country that has
the financial resources to satisfy the basic needs of all of its people. The
rise in petroleum prices that took place beginning in the fall of 1973
and the associated increase in fiscal revenues and foreign exchange earning caused Venezuela, a country of 12 million people, to have monthly
foreign exchange earnings of U.S. $8 million. The foreign exchange
earnings of the country quadrupled in one year, and the government of
Carlos Andrés Pérez had more financial resources at its disposal than
all previous governments since 1900 combined.

While only preliminary data are available to demonstrate the
effect of this relative wealth on the basic needs of the population, most
indicators suggest that in general improvements in the standard of living
of the mass of Venezuelans have been minimal. In spite of certain
gains, especially in the fields of education and health, as seen in a
declining infant mortality rate, little progress has been made in the
important areas of nutrition and housing. Notwithstanding Venezuela's
formal democracy, there has been relatively little emphasis by the state
on improving the overall standard of living of the poor, and this has
aggravated existing social problems.

Although Brazil has experienced a growth rate that has been
acclaimed as miraculous, the country has shown little overall improvement in meeting the basic needs of the poor. At the same time as the
Brazilian government allocated considerable resources to higher education, its commitment to basic education, while increasing, remained
limited. While there are many highly trained physicians to provide
sophisticated curative health care to the upper income strata, there are

very few paramedics to administer preventive health care to the mass of the population. The absence of a widespread health care delivery system results in an exceedingly high infant mortality rate and a relatively low life expectancy.

The survey also indicates that a rhetorical concern with basic needs has little correspondence with their fulfillment. This can be seen in the case of the Velasco government in Peru from 1968 to 1975. Despite an officially stated commitment to the poor, especially to the rural poor, the level of nutrition, health, safe water, and sanitation remained generally low. And although there is little data to highlight regional disparities, the data available indicate that the quality of life in rural areas was considerably worse than in the urban regions and characterized by little improvement. By 1977 concern for the basic needs of the poor was eschewed as the Peruvian government attempted to assuage the severity of the economic crisis by attacking the living standards not only of workers and peasants, but also of large parts of the so-called middle class.

The socioeconomic rights of the population of a country may be violated without a corresponding obvious attack on civil and political rights. Since 1975, through a series of increasingly severe austerity measures the Peruvian government has driven down the standard of living of the lower and middle income strata. Not only has there been widespread malnutrition and starvation in both urban and rural areas, but the infant mortality rate has soared and life expectancy declined. This has occurred simultaneously with a return to civilian rule carried out through democratic elections. While violations of the person in the traditional sense (torture, disappearance, summary execution) have not occurred, for the most part, the high level of unemployment and the halving of real wages from 1973 to 1979 have caused violations to the person to be perpetrated against the majority of Peruvians. Because this has not been accompanied by flagrant acts of violence, as in the cases of Chile and Argentina, the denial of human rights in Peru goes almost unnoticed on the international level.

It appears from the data that the satisfaction of the basic needs of the poor is primarily dependent on two variables: 1) the actual material commitment of a government to meeting basic needs, and 2) a more equal, or perhaps it would be more appropriate to say less unequal, distribution of income. Despite economic stagnation, the Unidad Popular government of Chile from 1970 to 1973 was able to achieve substantial improvements in the quality of life of the poor, especially in the areas of health and nutrition. The succeeding military government rapidly reversed these achievements, and from 1974 to 1976, the date of most of the available data, there has been a sharp deterioration in living standards of the poor.

A ranking of five of these countries on income distribution [56] would be very similar to their ranking according to the general satisfaction of basic needs. Although Chile experienced the slowest rate of growth, it had the least unequal distribution of income, and until 1974 perhaps the best overall relative record on the satisfaction of basic needs. Mexico ranks second on income distribution and again has a fair record on basic needs. That is, Mexico is distinguished by neither its relative failure nor success. Brazil's generally poor showing on basic needs, despite good economic performance, is characterized by the most unequal distribution of income in the survey. And although Venezuela has the highest per capita income and a wealth of financial resources, it has to date demonstrated relatively little commitment to improving the standard of living of the masses of people. This perhaps is correlated to its regressive income distribution, second only to Brazil in the survey, which appears to be worsening. [57]

This comparative analysis has demonstrated that the level of the satisfaction of basic needs is not high in any of these six Latin American countries and that relative to the other middle income countries their overall performance on basic needs is remarkably low. For want of adequate data the regional disparities within each of these countries could not be satisfactorily analyzed. If this were done, a picture of stark inequality would be revealed, where the satisfaction of basic needs in rural areas was far inferior to that which exists in the urban centers in Latin America.

In summary, this survey suggests that while rapid economic growth, a relatively higher per capita income, and democratic institutions may indeed facilitate the fulfillment of basic needs, they are neither necessary preconditions nor guarantees of improvements in the standard of living of the poor. A government's political commitment to meeting basic needs emerges as the key element in promoting the well-being of the lowest income strata in a society.

NOTES TO CHAPTER 5

1. We would like to thank George Rogers for his help in gathering the data on which this paper is based.

2. In this chapter the term basic needs is used to refer to the physical requirements for human life. These fall primarily into five categories: nutrition, health, housing, water and sanitation, and education. Their satisfaction requires that the prerequisites for self-reliance and/or effective political and economic participation to insure the physical requirements for human life be met. There have been a good number of attempts to define basic needs, measure their satisfaction, and explore their relationship to the enjoyment of

civil/political rights. Among the most useful are John P. Langan's "Defining Human Rights: A Revision of the Liberal Tradition," and Drew Christiansen's "Basic Needs: Criterion for the Legitimacy of Development," in Alfred T. Hennelly, S.J. and John P. Langan, S.J. *Human Rights in the Americas: The Struggle for Consensus.* One innovative measure of basic needs fulfillment is the Physical Quality of Life Index (PQLI) developed by Morris D. Morris in conjunction with the Overseas Development Council. The rationale for this particular approach is detailed in Morris D. Morris, *Measuring the Condition of the World's Poor: The Physical Quality of Life Index,* Pergamon Policy Studies, No. 42 (New York: Pergamon Press, 1979). All such measures have limitations due to variations and omissions in the relevant available data. Nevertheless, there are sufficient data to engage in comparisons such as the present study.

3. See, for example, John Simmons and Shahid Javed Burki, "The Performance of Middle-Income Countries on Basic Human Needs," World Bank Background Paper (Washington, D.C.: January 1979).

4. The World Bank categorizes 63 countries as middle income; i.e., those with per capita incomes between $260 and $3,900 in the mid-1970s. Countries with populations of less than one million are excluded.

5. The figures used from the United Nations and the *Statistical Abstract of Latin America* indicate a per capita income for Brazil in 1976 which ranks Brazil fourth in per capita income in the sample. However, Simmons and Burki, taking their data from tne *World Development Report 1979,* indicate a per capita income for Brazil which is considerably higher relatively, and would rank Brazil second to Venezuela in the six-country sample. This is a clear indication of the problems inherent in indicators such as per capita income.

6. James W. Wilkie and Peter Reich, eds., *Statistical Abstract of Latin America* (Los Angeles: University of California, Latin American Center Publications, 1978), Vol. 19, p. 241.

7. For example, in 1975–1977 almost one-third of Mexico's merchandise exports were manufactures, excluding refined sugar, while for Chile before the coup of 1973 noncopper related manufactured exports were about 5 to 7 percent. Manufactured exports from Peru in the 1970s, excluding fishmeal and refined sugar, were an even smaller proportion.

8. See the forthcoming World Bank country report on Nigeria.

9. North American Congress on Latin America, *Chile: Recycling the Capitalist Crisis* (1976).

10. See Chapter 3, "National Security Ideology and Human Rights."

11. If the period 1965 to 1974 is taken, the "miracle" looks more impressive—an annual growth rate of 9.6 percent.

12. The difference is slightly higher if one chooses 1974, when the growth rate began to decline.

13. Albert Fishlow, "Inflation without Tears?," *Economic Activity* (1972): 293–321.

14. See Elizabeth Dore and John Weeks, "The Intensification of the Attack Against the Working Class in 'Revolutionary' Peru," *Latin American*

Perspectives 3, 2 (Spring 1976): 55–83; and, for a contrary view, Giorgio Alberti et al., *Estado y Clase: La Comunidad Industrial en el Perú* (Lima: IEP, 1977).

15. See the special issue of *Latin American Perspectives* on Peru, 4, 3 (Summer 1977).

16. Obviously, a major change has occurred in Nicaragua, but it is too recent for treatment with the economic data available to us. The discussion refers to the pre-1979 period.

17. Albert Fishlow, "Brazilian Size Distribution of Income," *The American Economic Review* LXII (May 1972) 2: 391–402 and "Brazilian Income Size Distribution: Another Look," MS, 1973.

18. For example, "the working time required to acquire basic foodstuffs in a given month in São Paulo increased from 87 hours in December 1965 to 155 hours in July 1974." Howard Stein, "The 'Brazilian Miracle,' A Tarnished Image," *Latin American Perspectives* 6, 4 (Fall 1979): 45; Marcos Arruda et al., *Multinationals and Brazil: The Impact of Multinational Corporations in Contemporary Brazil* (Toronto: Brazilian Studies, 1975).

19. Fishlow, "Brazilian Size Distribution of Income," and Fishlow, "Brazilian Size Distribution of Income: Another Look."

20. G. S. Fields, "Who Benefits from Economic Development?—A Reexamination of Brazilian Growth in the 1960s," *American Economic Review* 67 (September 1977): 570–582. Fields stated that the average income of the poor in Brazil grew by some 63 percent in real terms between 1960 and 1970.

21. Montek S. Ahluwalia et al., "Who Benefits from Economic Development?: Comment," *American Economic Review* 70, 1 (March 1980): 242–245; Albert Fishlow, "Who Benefits from Economic Development?: Comment," *American Economic Review* 70, 1 (March 1980): 250–256; and Paul Beckerman and Donald Coes, "Who Benefits from Economic Development?: Comment," *American Economic Review* 70, 1 (March 1980): 246–249.

22. Fishlow, p. 256.

23. The Chilean data covered households, while the Peruvian and Brazilian data (and Venezuela in 1971) covered income receivers. It is generally the case that household distribution is more equal than that of individuals.

24. Felix Paukert, "Income Distribution at Different Levels of Development: A Survey of Evidence," *International Labour Review* 108 (August-September 1973): 1–33.

25. For an elaboration of this point, see Dore and Weeks, pp. 55–83.

26. Jeffrey A. Hart, "Industrialization and the Fulfillment of Basic Human Needs in Venezuela," in John G. Ruggie, ed., *Alternative Conceptions of World Order,* forthcoming. Hart estimates that manufacturing wages rose 6.2 percent per annum between 1964 and 1976.

27. The source for the wage trend estimate is unpublished World Bank estimates.

28. No data on income distribution are available for Nicaragua.

29. For an analysis of two views of poverty and of the importance of measuring poverty absolutely rather than relatively, see Chapter 4, "Basic Needs: Journey of a Concept."

30. These are problems particular to the comparative analysis of social indicators and they are compounded by many of the same problems which must be faced when using macroeconomic data, which are discussed above.

31. Norman Hicks and Paul Streeten, "Indicators of Development: The Search for a Basic Needs Yardstick," (Washington, D.C.: World Bank, 1978); Simmons and Burki, p. 7 ff.

32. According to statistics from CORDIPLAN (the Venezuelan National Planning Agency), life expectancy rose to 68.1 in 1977. Interview between Terry Karl and officials of CORDIPLAN, Caracas, Summer 1979.

33. Wilke and Reich, p. 95; *Population and Vital Statistics Report,* p. 14.

34. CORDIPLAN's statistics on infant mortality differ from those of the *World Development Report* and Wilkie and Reich. According to their data, there was a substantial improvement in the infant mortality rate from 43.8 in 1975 to 35.6 in 1978. Personal communication from Terry Karl, 8 July 1980.

35. *Actualidad Económico* 2 (August 1979): 18.

36. Dr. Albert B. Sabin disclosed that statistics given the World Health Organization by Brazilian authorities had been falsified to show a decline of eight-six percent in the incidence of polio at a time when outbreaks were on the rise. Dr. Sabin said, "judging from my studies, I think that there is at least ten times more polio in Brazil than is being reported by the health officials." Warren Hoge, "Brazil Slams the Door on Sabin after Polio Disclosure," *The New York Times,* 17 April 1980, p. A3.

37. Simmons and Burki, p. 30.

38. Ibid.

39. Nutrition, Basic Needs and Growth," (Washington, D.C.: The World Bank, February 1979), p. 3.

40. Simmons and Burki, p. 13.

41. Instituto Nacional de Nutrición, *Encuestra de Malnutrición: 1977* (1978).

42. *Resumen Semanal* 3 (Lima: Desco, March 22–28, 1980): 63.

43. John Weeks, "Crisis and Accumulation in the Peruvian Economy: 1967–1975," *The Review of Radical Political Economics* 8, 4 (Winter 1976): 46–72.

44. *Actualidad Económico* 3, 25 (1980): 5.

45. International Committee on Nutrition for National Defense, "Chile Nutrition Survey," 1960; and "Nutritional Study in Schools," assisted by CARE and JNAEB, 1975. Both studies are cited in *Sobre la Desnutrición en Chile* (Santiago de Chile: December 1978).

46. This concept is derived from the Gómez malnutrition index in which first degree malnutrition results in children attaining 76 to 90 percent of normal weight for age, second degree malnutrition results in children attaining 61 to 75 percent of normal weight for age, and third degree mal-

nutrition results in children attaining 60 percent or less of normal weight for age.

47. Simmons and Burki, p. 23.

48. Ibid., p. iv.

49. "Village Water Supply" (Washington, D.C.: World Bank, March 1976), p. 5.

50. Antonio Cassese, ed., "Study of the Impact of Foreign Economic Aid and Assistance on Respect for Human Rights in Chile" (United Nations Economic and Social Council, Commission on Human Rights, August 1978), p. 69.

51. CORDIPLAN, Interview by Terry Karl, Summer 1979.

52. CORDIPLAN, Interview by Terry Karl, Summer 1979.

53. Simmons and Burki, p. 51.

54. Statistics obtained from CORDIPLAN indicate that there has been a considerable improvement in enrollments at the primary level from 1975 to 1978. These statistics indicate that 91 percent of children ages 6 through 13 are enrolled in primary school. CORDIPLAN, Interview by Terry Karl, Summer 1979.

55. The other 15 percent was not allocated by level. Wilkie and Stern, *Statistical Abstract of Latin America*, p. 133.

56. The income of people in the poorest 40 percent of the population as a percentage of total income. There are no data on Nicaragua (Table 2).

57. CORDIPLAN, Interview by Terry Karl, Summer 1979.

John A. Willoughby

6. International Capital Flows, Economic Growth, and Basic Needs

INTRODUCTION[1]

During the 1970s the explosion in the value of North-South private capital flows, the rapid growth in the Gross Domestic Product of certain so-called Third World states and the continuation of mass poverty in the Third World despite this accelerated production have resulted in substantial soul searching within both the radical and orthodox schools of development economics. On the one hand, the data challenge orthodox theorists' hope that expanded commodity production would at least slightly improve the material conditions of the vast number of absolutely poor in the Third World.[2] On the other hand, some dependency theorists' prediction that industrialization in the periphery of the capitalist world system is unlikely to occur has been called into question by the apparently successful establishment of manufacturing enterprises in Mexico, Brazil, and certain Southeast and East Asian territories.[3]

This chapter examines the connection between economic development and international capital flows during the 1970s. After describing recent trends in North-South financial relations, the perspectives of orthodox diffusionist and radical dependency economists are compared. With this empirical and theoretical background clarified, two separate but interrelated questions remain to be considered. Does foreign capital penetration encourage or impede capitalist growth in the Third World? Does foreign capital encourage or impede the development of programs that can meet the Third World population's basic needs?

This essay shows that during the 1970s most Third World countries received an increased share of finance from private capital sources, while official bilateral development assistance decreased. Multilateral lending institutions during this period substantially augmented loans to the poorest nations. Credit extended by metropolitan financial markets grew more rapidly than direct foreign investment or export-linked loans. This, together with the hardening of financial market loans, caused a sharp decline in the grant element of loans to Third World countries and an upsurge in debt service payments. Inflation, continued access to financial markets, and expanded trade have, however, all helped avoid defaults in interest and principal payments. Nevertheless, the increased dependence on private capital does limit the possibilities of growth with equity for the Latin American nations. This is particularly true in countries where the basic needs of the laboring force are not a prime criteria in the determination of economic policy. Until such time as labor unions, peasant associations and workers groups increase their participation in economic decision making, this will probably continue to be the case. There are, nevertheless, some possible reforms in the international financial system that could stimulate more equitable growth in the Third World. These are suggested in the conclusion of this chapter.

I. INTERNATIONAL CAPITAL FLOWS IN THE 1970s

First to be examined will be the change in the relative importance of aid versus finance capital flows, and then the structure of these private capital movements. This empirical groundwork will allow for the analysis of the impact of these developments on the production of basic needs.

The Decline of Public Aid.   Since the end of the Marshall Plan, it has been a generally accepted liberal principle that the developed countries—the United States and the other nations of the Organization for Economic Cooperation and Development (OECD)—should extend both generalized soft financing and project-specific technical assistance to the developing nations of the Third World.[4] This commitment was certainly not disinterested; the Alliance for Progress launched by the Kennedy Administration, for instance, was stimulated by fear that the Cuban experiment would spread and turn the Caribbean into a "red sea."[5]

This intense fear of Communism forced Washington policymakers in the early 1960s to confront the social consequences of economic inequality. In South America Alliance for Progress nations were supposed to institute reform programs to encourage the creation of an entrepreneurial class which would seriously undertake investments to raise land and labor productivity. It was hoped that a more egalitarian social structure combined with infusions of technical and financial assistance would accelerate development and thus improve the living standards of the urban and rural population.[6] This early concern with what today we would call growth with equity never was consistently expressed in the Alliance for Progress programs: few noticeably-successful land reforms

TABLE 1:   The Ratio of Total Net Official Development Assistance
to Total Net Financial Flows, 1969–1975

	All Developing Countries	Per Capita Income			
		$265 or less.	$266 to $520	$521 to $1,075	Over $1,075
1969	0.48	0.89	0.62	0.43	0.18
1971	0.46	0.86	0.64	0.39	0.19
1973	0.38	0.79	0.60	0.21	0.21
1975	0.35	0.71	0.51	0.17	0.18

Source: OECD, *Geographical Distribution of Financial Flows to Developing Countries* (Paris: OECD, 1977), pp. 170–277.

were ever undertaken, and funding for the South American aid package became, over time, more difficult to obtain from Congress.[7]

One can trace the decline of U.S. public economic assistance from the failures of the Alliance for Progress. While it is outside the scope of this chapter to explain why the advanced capitalist countries now give a smaller proportion of their GNP in foreign aid than they did in the 1960s,[8] the data in Table 1 clearly show that private capital flows have become a progressively more important component of North-South financial relations.

By the mid-1970s, the poorest Third World nations still received a high proportion of their foreign finance in the form of soft loans and grants. Even in this category, however, the importance of Official Development Assistance has diminished. Table 2 indicates that these poverty-stricken economies are increasingly dependent on multilateral lending institutions such as the European Development Fund, the regional development banks, and the World Bank. While the nominal value of private capital flows to the more advanced commodity producing Third World

TABLE 2:   The Ratio of Multilateral to Bilateral Official Development
Assistance for Countries with a Per Capita Income of
$265 or Less

[Incomes are given in 1975 U.S. dollars.]

1969	1971	1973	1975
0.15	0.16	0.30	0.48

Source: OECD, p. 270.

countries tripled between 1969 and 1975, multilateral assistance to Fourth World nations expanded more than fivefold.

With the exception of Haiti, the Latin American countries are in the second and third per capita income categories. Thus, as suggested by Table 1, private metropolitan capital has played an increasingly important role in the financial flows received by Latin American countries. The data presented in Table 3 demonstrate that Brazil and Peru, in particular, have turned to private capital sources, while Mexico's and Venezuela's utilization of subsidized funds has dwindled to almost insignificant proportions. It is more difficult to discuss with any precision trends for Nicaragua. The continued heavy reliance of the Somoza regime on foreign aid throughout the early 1970s may be a commentary on the character of "Somocismo," which failed to guarantee even transnational capital an attractive return for its investments.

The Chilean case is far more complex. Despite the extremely harsh austerity measures of the Pinochet regime, only U.S. bilateral aid of $82 million, German assistance of $20 million, and a $14 million soft loan from the Inter-American Development Bank made it possible for the Chilean authorities to counteract partially the net withdrawal of approximately $231 million in private capital in 1975. On the other hand, in 1974, the year after the fall of the Marxist-oriented Unidad Popular government of Salvador Allende, the structure of financial flows was reversed; the value of net metropolitan private capital flows was $305.1 million, while bilateral and multilateral Official Development Assistance totaled only $24.4 million.[9] The data presented in Table 3 indicate that private loans to Chile carried relatively short maturities. Thus, it is likely that the bank's initial presence in Chile after the ouster of Allende put added pressure on the multilateral institutions to bail out the Pinochet government.

TABLE 3:   The Ratio of Net Official Development Assistance to Net Total Financial Transfers in 6 Latin American Countries

	1969	*1975*
Brazil	0.38	0.06
Chile	0.40	-1.24[a]
Mexico	0.15	0.04
Nicaragua	0.66	0.57
Peru	0.58	0.13
Venezuela	0.07	0.03

[a] Total financial flows were negative.

Source: OECD.

Clearly, the relation between private and public capital flows is a complex one. Despite the claims of some radical analysts, [10] business has never been a strong supporter of foreign aid. Even during the Marshall Plan, some business lobbies opposed U.S. aid to Europe on the grounds that private capital would be supplanted by state intervention. [11] One probusiness rationale for Official Development Assistance is that once aid has developed a country so that its economy can attract large amounts of capital, there is no need for metropolitan subsidization to continue. Radicals would add that aid ties countries to the world capitalist system and thus guarantees a wider field for metropolitan capital penetration.

Today, multilateral aid institutions are following the policies suggested by this corporate rationale. The Inter-American Development Bank and the World Bank prohibit concessional lending to Brazil, Mexico, and Venezuela. [12] The historical record suggests that Official Development Assistance will continue to dwindle. The industrialization of certain key nations of the Third World, the inability of metropolitan countries to quiet Third World demands for a New International Economic Order, the chronic metropolitan business dissatisfaction with foreign aid programs, and the lack of domestic political appeal of foreign aid in the United States will likely combine to end development assistance as a significant component of financial flows.

The Changing Structure of Private Capital Flows.   In order to reach a better understanding of the significance of the growing importance of private finance for developing countries, it is necessary to specify more precisely how the structure of finance capital flows has evolved during the 1970s. To simplify the discussion, it is convenient to divide this capital into three categories. To finance trade, or the movement of commodities as capital, exporters often grant credit to the buyers of their goods or services. In the World Bank literature, this is called export supplier credits. This specific, trade-linked lending should be seen as distinct from the general lending of money from financial markets. Banks can lend funds to Third World governments so that they can undertake a specific development project, or they can extend credit so that nations can continue to finance their international trade. Furthermore nations, agencies that are government owned, or private firms can float bonds in order to obtain the necessary foreign exchange for their development projects. In any case, both the direct granting of loans by private banks and the obtaining of finance through the selling of bonds are viewed by the World Bank as credits obtained from financial markets. In other words, the extension of credit for general financing of development projects is separated from lending which facilitates the movement of specific commodities. [13]

The third major category of capital which developing nations receive from the metropolitan states can be labeled Direct Foreign Investment. This category refers to the establishment of subsidiaries by corporations whose headquarters tend to be in the advanced industrial capitalist nations. In Marxist terms, the preponderance of Direct Foreign Investment would be considered as part of a process which internationalizes productive capital. [14] Activities which create commodity-producing subsidiaries generate a complex network of productive operations under the ownership and control of one central headquarters, more likely than not lodged in New York, London, Frankfurt, Paris, or Tokyo.

Keeping these three categories in mind, the extension of credit to facilitate the movement of commodity capital, the extension of money capital in general, and the extension of productive capital, what has been the evolution of financial flows during the 1970s? One striking result indicated in Table 4 is that credit extended from financial markets has grown more rapidly during the 1970s than has any other aspect of capital export. Many commentators have argued that the 1970s was a time in which transnational corporations increased dramatically their domestic foreign investment. [15] In fact, it may be more accurate to argue that during this decade there was a consolidation of the importance of transnational financial institutions. While column 1 indicates the growing importance of debt owed to private capital, columns 2 and 3 demonstrate that metropolitan financial institutions have come to extend relatively more capital than export suppliers or direct foreign investors.

The Rise of Financial Markets and the Change in the Structure of Debt.   To assess how the increased reliance on borrowing from private sources has affected the development prospects of Latin American countries, it is essential to describe how debt has changed over this decade. If loans carry terms which require their relatively prompt payment at market rates—assumed by the World Bank [16] to be 10 percent —then it is clear that the developing nations which receive this credit are required to devote a portion of their production for exports. Without some indication that the nation has the capability to earn foreign exchange through trade, it would be difficult for any developing economy to continue to attract foreign capital. Thus, the first aspect of debt to examine is whether or not the terms of the loans are easy or hard. Additionally, the export-oriented posture of a country's development policies does have an impact on whether or not a nation will be able to meet the basic needs of its population.

TABLE 4: Debt and Private Capital Flows in 96 Developing Countries in World

	Debt Owed to Private Capital[a]		Debt Owed to Financial Markets[b]		Debt Contracted Through Financial Markets[c]
	1972	1978	1972	1978	1973-1977
96 Developing Countries	34%	52%	144%	456%	
Latin America & the Caribbean	53	74	109	709	257%
Brazil	55	81	158	430	190
Chile	44	57	92	254	326
Mexico	64	86	779	5,300	825
Nicaragua	40	46	1,417	8,260	---
Peru	54	53	68	316	116
Venezuela	71	93	232	5,215	147

[a] Owed as a percentage of total debt.

[b] Owed as a percentage of debt to export suppliers.

[c] Owed as a percentage of capital expenditures by U.S. foreign-owned subsidiaries.

Source: The debt data for private capital and financial markets were obtained from World Bank, *World Debt Tables,* 2 vols. (Washington, D.C.: World Bank, 1979). Data on the capital expenditures by U.S. foreign-owned subsidiaries were obtained from U.S. Department of Commerce, *Survey of Current Business* (Washington, D.C.: Dept. of Commerce, various editions).

Two concepts are needed to evaluate the type of loan which developing countries presently are receiving from the industrial capitalist nations. In the first place, it is necessary to determine whether or not the loan has been extended at average market rates. To the extent that the interest on loans lies below average interest, one can speak of the credit carrying a grant element.[17] Finally, irrespective of the interest rate which a given credit carries, it is necessary to examine the maturity of the loan; i.e., the length of time over which the credits have to be paid off. To the extent that the maturity structure of the loans is short, developing nations will be under more pressure to assure lenders that it is possible for the Third World economies to export and earn foreign exchange.

The switch to financial markets for credit has led to a decline in the grant elements of the loans which developing countries receive. In other words, interest on all the loans which developing economies have received has tended to approach market rates, although the payoff period is not shorter. Thus, more than ever, the economies of the Southern Hemisphere have to assume an export-oriented posture.

Table 5 shows that the terms of private loans have become progressively harder. The grant element of the average private loan to the 96 developing nations in the World Bank's sample has declined from 10.9 percent to 1.7 percent. On the other hand, there is no evident trend in the maturity structure of private credits. The major reason for this shift in the grant elements of the loans is that financial market credits have become progressively harder (although with fluctuation), while there has been a dramatic turn to financial markets for loans.

Because of the greater than average reliance of Latin American countries on these markets, the hardness of loans has risen even more sharply. Table 6 shows that the grant element of private loans to Brazil, Peru, and Chile is lower than the average grant component in these loans for all developing countries. Furthermore, the maturity length of private

TABLE 5:   Average Terms of Loan Commitments by Private Creditors to Developing Countries, 1972-1978

	1972	1974	1976	1978
Total Private Lenders:				
Amount ^{a}	$ 8.8	$19.8	$31.7	$49.8
Interest Rates	7.3%	9.7%	7.9%	9.4%
Maturity ^{b}	8.9y	10.1y	8.1y	8.9y
Grant Element ^{c}	10.9%	0.9%	7.5%	1.7%
Export Suppliers:				
Amount	$ 2.4	$-5.5	$ 5.9	$ 6.1
Interest Rates	7.0%	7.8%	7.9%	7.9%
Maturity	9.4y	10.4y	9.8y	10.3y
Grant element	11.4%	8.8%	7.9%	7.5%
Total Financial Markets:				
Amount	$ 6.4	$14.3	$25.7	$43.8
Interest Rates	7.4%	10.5%	7.9%	9.6%
Maturity	8.7y	9.9y	7.6y	8.8y
Grant element	10.7%	-2.1%	7.5%	0.9%

^{a} Billions in U.S. dollars.

^{b} Given in years.

^{c} Reckoned as a percentage of the total loan.

Source: World Bank, *World Debt Tables,* 2 vols. (Washington, D.C.: World Bank, 1979), I:194.

TABLE 6: Average Terms of Loan Commitments for Selected Latin

	1972	1974	1976	1978
BRAZIL				
Official Creditors:				
Amount [a]	$1,012	$ 777	$1,946	$1,137
Maturity [b]	19.6 y	14.6 y	16.3 y	14.9 y
Grant Element [c]	19.9%	15.9%	12.4%	13.0%
Private Creditors:				
Amount	$1,213	$2,247	$3,700	$9,478
Maturity	7.8 y	9.6 y	7.0 y	11.3 y
Grant element	8.9%	-9.1%	6.7%	-0.9%
CHILE				
Official Creditors:				
Amount	$ 176	$ 446	$ 208	$ 135
Maturity	16.1 y	14.2 y	16.8 y	17.9 y
Grant Element	45.8%	13.9%	21.8%	19.9%
Private Creditors:				
Amount	$ 159	$ 305	$ 275	$1,568
Maturity	10.5 y	8.0 y	5.2 y	6.4 y
Grant Element	10.6%	9.3%	1.9%	-3.5%
MEXICO				
Official Creditors:				
Amount	$ 409	$ 522	$ 860	$ 965
Maturity	20.1 y	20.7 y	17.1 y	16.5 y
Grant Element	20.1%	19.2%	9.4%	12.2%
Private Creditors:				
Amount	$ 827	$2,694	$4,887	$7,539
Maturity	10.4 y	9.2 y	5.1 y	5.1 y
Grant Element	12.7%	-1.8%	5.2%	4.5%

[a] Millions in U.S. dollars.

[b] Given in years.

[c] Reckoned as a percentage of the total loan.

credits is shorter than the average for Chile, Mexico, and Peru. Given fluctuations in the interest rates placed on loans to developing countries and the resulting volatility of the grant element data, it is difficult to come to firm conclusions on the basis of this information. On the other hand, the increased reliance of Latin American nations on private capital borrowing does at least indicate that their national economies are becoming more tightly integrated into the capitalist world economy.

Payments of Debt.   One direct result of both the increased Third World reliance on private capital markets and the progressive hardening

American Countries, 1972-1978

	1972	1974	1976	1978
NICARAGUA				
Official Creditors:				
Amount	$ 49	$ 58	$ 75	$ 66
Maturity	24.7 y	32.7 y	24.4 y	25.0 y
Grant Element	25.1%	53.9%	35.6%	37.0%
Private Creditors:				
Amount	$ 59	$ 125	$ 101	N.A.
Maturity	8.5 y	12.0 y	7.9 y	N.A.
Grant Element	4.3%	-10.4%	6.1%	N.A.
PERU				
Official Creditors:				
Amount	$ 200	$ 593	$ 932	$ 326
Maturity	17.1 y	14.1 y	15.3 y	10.7 y
Grant Element	27.9%	19.1%	28.3%	23.1%
Private Creditors:				
Amount	$ 247	$ 725	$ 930	$ 646
Maturity	7.6 y	9.5 y	7.2 y	6.9 y
Grant Element	7.7%	-4.1%	7.1%	-9.3%
VENEZUELA				
Official Creditors:				
Amount	$ 115	$ 31	$ 31	N.A.
Maturity	12.4 y	11.5 y	10.3 y	N.A.
Grant Element	16.4%	12.9%	3.5%	N.A.
Private Creditors				
Amount	$ 469	$ 95	$1,131	$2,730
Maturity	9.3 y	4.9 y	7.2 y	9.8 y
Grant Element	12.7%	-2.1%	9.6%	9.4%

Source: World Bank, World Debt Tables, 2 vols. (Washington, D.C.: World Bank, 1979), 1:203-207.

of loans from these sources is that the annual debt service payments which Third World nations must make to their funding sources have increased dramatically. Debt service refers to interest and principal payments on loans; these obligations contracted from past borrowing must be paid if a nation is to maintain its credit standing. Thus, debt service represents a powerful claim by foreign capital on a portion of the annual material production of a nation.

The data presented in Tables 7 and 8 indicate that these metropolitan claims on Third World output have risen during the 1970s. With the exception of Peru and Venezuela within our Latin American

TABLE 7: Debt Service in Millions of U.S. Dollars, 1972–1978

	1972	*1974*	*1976*	*1978*
96 Developing Countries	$8,610	$14,157	$18,767	$37,642
Latin America & the Caribbean	3,056	5,348	8,015	17,518
Brazil	627	1,016	1,922	3,934
Chile	98	278	757	1,064
Mexico	853	1,196	2,304	6,088
Nicaragua	32	49	79	133
Peru	182	432	454	748
Venezuela	213	506	407	750

Source: World Bank, *World Debt Tables,* I:158–159.

sample, debt service payments from 1972 to 1978 grew more sharply than the amount of new debt contracted during this period. Only the value of Brazil's exports has increased faster than its debt service. In no case has the nominal value in dollars of GDP kept pace with this explosion in interest and principal payments.

This information does not in itself prove that the Latin American nations must in the near future face acute foreign exchange crises. Even though exports and foreign direct investment have not increased at a fast enough pace to provide the foreign exchange necessary for the debt service payments, it is possible to roll over a good portion of debt by borrowing even more funds from the financial markets. This "robbing Peter to pay Paul" strategy makes good sense in an inflationary environment. Every year borrowers can expect the real value of their liabilities to erode at high rates. It has been estimated that inflation wiped out approximately 40 percent of the value of loans between 1973 and 1976. [18] The observed increase in the ratio of debt service payments to exports is not necessarily a sign of increasing financial difficulties; such shifts in a nation's debt exposure may also represent a rational response to changing global economic conditions.

Summary of Third World Aid in the 1970s:

1. Bilateral Official Development Assistance declined in importance. Nearly all Third World nations received an enlarged share of

finance from private capital sources. In addition, multilateral lending institutions greatly increased their loans to the poorest nations of the world economy.

2. Of all types of private capital export to Third World nations, credit extended from metropolitan financial markets has grown more rapidly than direct foreign investment or export-linked loans.

3. As a result of this trend and the hardening of financial market loans, the grant element of loans received by Third World countries has declined sharply.

4. The resulting explosion of debt service payments does not in itself suggest that Third World countries are on the verge of international bankruptcy. As long as inflation continues, financial markets remain open, and world trade does not collapse, it should be possible for most Third World nations to avoid any defaults in interest and principal payments.

This last conclusion should not be a source for great optimism. The stability of the world economy seems more tenuous than ever, and avoiding a collapse in international trade is not the same as developing a country so that its basic needs are met. Overall, the increased reliance on private capital could harm the growth with equity prospects of the Latin American nations.

TABLE 8:   Percentage Increases in Debt Service, Debt Contracted, GDP, and Exports, 1972-1978

	Debt Service	Debt Contracted	GDP	Exports
96 Developing Countries	337%	246%	N.A.	N.A.
Latin America & the Caribbean	473	319	N.A.	N.A.
Brazil	528	426	182	850%
Chile	986	69	-1	77
Mexico	614	526	75	251
Nicaragua	316	298	147	133
Peru	311	412	11	66
Venezuela	252	381	144	161

Source: The debt data in columns 1 & 2 are taken from World Bank, *World Debt Tables*, I; the data in columns 3 & 4 are computed from International Monetary Fund, *International Financial Statistics* (Washington, D.C.:   IMF, September 1979).

II. ADAM SMITH AND THE EVOLUTION OF LIBERAL AND DEPENDENCY DEVELOPMENT THEORIES

Before assessing how the penetration of private, finance capital has affected the ability of Latin American countries to meet the basic needs of their populations, it is important to situate the issue of development in a broad theoretical context. A review of Adam Smith's thought reveals the origins of both the liberal, laissez-faire theories of the development banks and the radical dependency theories that have critiqued the role of international financial capital in the Third World. Determining the validity of these rival development perspectives can only be undertaken by uncovering their basic theoretical assumptions.

Adam Smith wrote *The Wealth of Nations* in order to attack the state's control over private economic activity. In his analysis of the Americas, Smith argued that where government controls over capitalism were most intense, economic development was stunted, and the masses of people lived in poverty. [19] The assumption behind this laissez-faire contention was quite simple: left to their own devices, entrepreneurs would exploit the comparative resource advantages of their regions and expand the number of people engaged in productive labor. Smith himself did not foresee this new economic system leading to any sustained increase in the peoples' standard of living, but modern advocates of this thesis have not hesitated to claim that liberalized economic relations will eventually lead to considerable improvement in the material life of the masses. [20]

While *The Wealth of Nations'* advocacy of free international trade, as originally stated by Smith, is still being argued today, there is another part of his analysis which appears to contradict the promotion of this particular development policy. In Book 3 of his massive work, Smith writes that the natural path of growth which any society undertakes is first, to develop its agriculture; second, to produce for the urban market; and third, to produce for international trade. It seemed self-evident to Smith that a precondition for development was the destruction of the feudal elite and the replacement of this unproductive class with sober, industrious farmers who would first demand goods from and supply goods to small-scale agricultural marketing centers. Only after the hinterland had developed extensive commodity production would entrepreneurs begin to undertake riskier, long-distance trade. Thus, the development of a national and world market should naturally come only after the emergence of a relatively egalitarian capitalism in the rural areas. [21]

Many radical critics of liberal international economic policies share with Smith the fear that an export and urban-oriented policy emphasis which does not first transform rural economic life will eventually lead to a truncated development. They believe that a limited domestic consumption base and monopolistic restrictions on capital accumulation will prevent the trickling down of the benefits of material production to the masses.

For Smith, the enemies of true economic development were the feudal lords, the monopoly merchant class, and the mercantilist state. For modern, radical dependency theorists, such as André Gunder Frank, the social forces whose power must be destroyed are quite similar: the landed oligarchs, the bourgeoisie tied to international capital, and the authoritarian, capitalist state necessary to hold this unstable social system together. In addition, however, Frank pinpoints the transnational corporation, or international monopoly capital, as the agent which is ultimately responsible for dependency, or the development of underdevelopment. [22]

It is useful to consider more specifically why many modern radical theorists have argued that strengthened international financial arrangements among center and periphery countries have frustrated most Third World nations' attempts to meet the basic needs of their populations. The classic work on this subject is Cheryl Payer's *The Debt Trap*. [23] Payer argues that a precondition for attracting finance is that the recipient nation must show itself able to meet future debt obligations without threatening its position in the international financial system. Macroeconomic budget austerity is the only major option for Third World countries which are in chronic balance of payments difficulties. To control trade and capital flows directly would call a nation's commitment to liberal economic relations into question. Thus, the state must restrict imports and make room for exports by restricting the domestic consumption base of the economy.

To the extent that nations are forced to control the money supply tightly and attempt to balance the budget, it is easy to see how debt problems prevent the implementation of policies which create jobs and expand the living standards of the poorest members of society. Payer argues further that the IMF's insistence on lowering trade barriers forces Third World states to rely on the traditional exports of raw materials, their one area of comparative advantage in international trade. Not only does the present international economic order doom states to economic stagnation, but it perpetuates a division of labor that inhibits the production of mass consumer goods in the Third World nations themselves. While orthodox theorists argue that aid and private capital flows provide basic resources and skills which the Third World country could not generate internally, dependency theorists claim that the free market in reality perpetuates the multinationals' monopoly control over the peripheral economies and relegates much of the world's population to, at worst, economic stagnation or, at best, dependent material development which robs the masses of Third World people of their rights to economic and political self-determination. [24]

Even if the orthodox, diffusionist theorists are correct in claiming that capitalist development in the Third World is a likely outcome of pursuing the free trade policies which the IMF recommends, it is by no means obvious that expanded commodity production will improve the living standards of the majority of people. As Albert Fishlow has shown, the huge growth in Brazilian GNP has been accompanied by a worsening income distribution and a deteriorating absolute standard of living for many. [25] Furthermore, Dore and Weeks demonstrate in Chapter 5 of this volume that the meeting of basic needs in Latin America is not directly dependent on the GDP level.

To assess the connection between international finance capital and basic needs, two questions must be answered: 1) Has the present international economic order seriously hampered the capacity of Third World countries to expand material production? 2) If not, has the international monetary system prevented the emergence of a social dynamic which would allow the increased production of wealth to be shared more equitably?

Adam Smith clearly assumed that the free mobility of resources would break up monopoly control and thus simultaneously promote a more rational division of labor and a more egalitarian society. Today, it may no longer be possible to assert that capital mobility must promote the interests of all. Thus, while some dependency theorists' blanket assertion that international monopoly leads to economic stagnation may be wrong, their point that the world's poor can no longer benefit from capitalist growth may be correct. Disentangling these two aspects of development requires more than observing broad economic data; one must also engage in a complex estimation of the social forces involved in the development process. In particular, it is essential to determine how social formations respond to the inevitable crises generated by capitalist growth. In other words, class analysis must be integrated with more traditional economic investigation.

III. DOES METROPOLITAN CAPITAL PENETRATION BREED ECONOMIC STAGNATION?

If Payer's analysis were completely accurate, there would be two regularities in the statistical data: GDP would stagnate for those countries particularly dependent on foreign debt, and the trading structures of these economies would be immutable. Tables 9 and 10 examine the

TABLE 9:   Growth Rates of GDP in 6 Latin American Countries

	1965–1970	*1970–1975*	*1972–1978*
Brazil	38%	67%	182%
Chile	21	-3	-1
Mexico	40	31	75
Nicaragua	21	30	147
Peru	23	30	11
Venezuela	25	26	144

Source: Columns 1 & 2 are computed from OECD, *Geographical Distribution of Financial Flows;* column 3 is computed from IMF, *International Financial Statistics.*

first of these hypotheses by counterposing GDP growth rates (from 1965 to 1975) with the evolution of debt service ratios during this period.

Payer's contention that debt breeds economic sluggishness for the less developed nations clearly does not stand up to an examination of the data. Although Mexico experienced the highest debt exposure over the 1965–1975 decade, it was the second most rapid growing Latin American economy in the sample. Furthermore, Brazil's debt service increased in nominal terms by more than 304 percent between 1968 and 1974 and yet its debt service ratio dropped because the value of Brazil's exports rose even faster.

Despite this rapid growth, one might still be able to argue that the classic international division of labor still rules the world economy and that the Latin American economies have failed to diversify their economic activity. If this were true, then it would be possible to claim that the rapid growth which many Latin American states experienced during the late 1960s and 1970s will prove to be ephemeral in the long run.

TABLE 10:   Debt Service Ratios in 6 Latin American Countries

[Interest and Principal Payments/Total Exports.]

	1968	*1971*	*1972*	*1973*	*1974*	*1975*	*1976*
Brazil	15.6	17.1	15.9	12.6	10.0	14.6	14.8
Chile	19.9	21.5	9.8	10.9	11.7	28.4	
Mexico	26.5	23.3	22.8	24.3	19.2	25.9	
Nicaragua	7.6	13.3	10.3	17.4	10.2	11.3	
Peru	15.0	19.6	18.3	31.7	23.9	23.4	21.6
Venezuela	1.9	3.5	5.3	5.2	3.2		

Source: Various supplements to World Bank, *World Debt Tables.*

Once again, this simple dependency argument is not verified by the data. Those countries whose exports have diversified the most dramatically during the last 15 years have been especially dependent on foreign finance. Of the five Mexican exports whose value rose the most sharply between 1965 and 1975, three of them were industrial commodities (road motor vehicles, clothing, and textile yarn and thread). [26] Furthermore, Mexico's rapid expansion of internationally competitive vegetable production is an indication of a thriving capitalist agricultural sector. Indeed, it is now possible to compare the production techniques of Mexican agriculture with California agribusiness. Recently, Mexico has decided to export oil. While this new policy may lead to an expansion of traditional raw material exports, this development would certainly not indicate a lack of dynamism or diversity in the Mexican economy.

Brazil's export experience is similar to Mexico's. Footwear; non-electric power-generating machinery; road motor vehicles; oil seeds, nuts, and kernel; and office machines were the five most rapidly growing commodity exports. At the other end of the scale, coffee exports grew in value by only 2.8 percent between 1965 and 1975. What is new about the decade of the 1970s is the emergence of manufactured commodities as leading exports of the most dynamic capitalist economies of Latin America.

Another way to examine whether or not metropolitan capital export serves to perpetuate an international division of labor, which forces Third World countries to specialize in raw material exports, is to investigate the pattern of foreign investment to these countries. Multinational capital undoubtedly diverts domestically generated savings, and the technological superiority of advanced capitalist nations also frustrates the ability of national private capitalists from creating industries that can effectively compete with U.S., European, or Japanese businesses. Thus, if capital is flowing into the traditional extractive sector, one would expect that historical patterns of economic relations would be retained.

Table 11 provides confirmation that one cannot make any general statement about the impact of bank and productive capital export on the ability of Third World nations either to grow rapidly or to diversify their economic production. Foreign capital certainly does not prevent capitalist growth, and the evidence on foreign investment suggests that it can actually contribute to a nation's efforts to develop new productive and trading capacities. Having said this, it is important to note that Payer's debt trap hypothesis still has some relevance. After the 1973 fall of the Unidad Popular government in Chile, foreign investment both expanded and oriented itself toward the traditional extractive industries. There is also little evidence that the multinational penetration of Peru has contributed to a diversified industrial or agricultural base. On the

TABLE 11: Percentage Distribution of U.S. Direct Foreign Investment in 5 Latin American Countries

[Millions are given in U.S. dollars.]

	Total in Millions	Mining & Smelting	Petroleum	Raw Material Processing a	Machinery & Equipment b	Other Manufacturing	Total Manufacturing
BRAZIL							
1971	$ 362	1%	7%	19%	25%*	4%	74%
1973	688	--	2	27	25*	**	83
1975	1,033	--	2	35	30	10	77
1977	970	1	3	30	38	6	75
MEXICO							
1971	$ 204	4%	--	42%	21%	4%	69%
1973	247	3	--	40	30	2	74
1975	335	2	--	45	24	3	74
1977	339	1	--	49	24	2	77
CHILE							
1971	$ 4	--	--	--	25%	25%	75%
1973	2	--	--	--	50	--	100
1975	16	--	6%	18%	6	12	37
1977	17	11%	23	17	--	--	35
PERU							
1971	$ 83	53%	15%	6%	--	--	9%
1973	217	**	45	1	--	--	2
1975	475	**	38	4	--	--	4
1977	90	**		8	--	--	8
VENEZUELA							
1971	$ 330	--	71%	6%	2%	6%	17%
1973	328	--	50%	14	3	--	27
1975	217		8	30	8	22	62
1977	335	0%	3	49	8	8	67

a Paper, chemicals, rubber, primary and fabricated metals.   *Data withheld from the Transportation Equipment sector.
b Equipment for the Transportation sector.   **Data withheld.
Source: U.S. Department of Commerce, *Survey of Current Business*, various editions.

other hand, the Venezuelan data provide dramatic evidence that foreign capital export can aid in expanding a developing nation's industrial structure.

IV. DOES METROPOLITAN CAPITAL PENETRATION FRUSTRATE THE MEETING OF BASIC NEEDS?

The previous section has shown that the assertion by orthodox economists that reliance on foreign capital can stimulate capitalist growth and thus lead to an expansion and diversification of commodity production has validity for some countries but not for others. Indeed, this growth in material production is one of the characteristics of the recent historical experience of Brazil, Mexico, and Venezuela. On the other hand, the "trickle-down" argument that prolonged expansion must eventually improve the living standards of the poorest members of these societies is made problematic by the imprecision of the world "eventually."

If placed in historical perspective, this should not be surprising. Economic historians have for years wondered whether or not the living standards of the English proletariat expanded between 1790 and 1850, the heyday of the first industrial revolution. Some scholars have claimed that the new patterns of consumption and savings which emerged prove that industrial growth enhanced the material position of a significant number of the producing class. Challenging this is the argument that the first half of the nineteenth century produced a new professional middle class, but did not improve the lives of the agricultural and industrial proletariat. While the debate has been inconclusive, the mere fact that scholars argue about the impact of capitalist growth in England illustrates the tenuous nature of the "trickle-down" hypothesis. [27]

What then are the conditions which permit economic expansion to generate a significant improvement in living standards for a majority of the population? To answer the question quite simply, in addition to economic growth, the peasantry and industrial work force must be able to mobilize political-economic power if their living standards are to be improved in the course of sustained capitalist expansion. [28] Historically, this has not necessarily meant that the working class always had to possess strong trade union organization. In late nineteenth century England, for example, the competitive structure of the British economy permitted a substantial increase in real wages even though growth slowed and the trade union movement had not attained the institutional maturity of the twentieth century. [29]

Given the present monopolistic structure of modern capitalist economies, however, it is less likely that this historical experience will be repeated. The response by multinationals to sagging demand and/or profits is much more likely to lead to a crisis in production and rising unemployment. The likelihood of the poor protecting themselves during these periodic slumps depends on their ability to place social demands on the government and economic demands on private capital. If this analysis is correct we must ask whether dependence on foreign capital weakens the ability of the working class and peasantry to build social-democratic institutions which can contribute to the meeting of basic needs.

Any crisis in capitalist production will place pressures on the government to lower the living standards of the working population. The expectation of "acceptable" profit rates is a necessary condition of a healthy free enterprise system, and if output is stagnating or falling, entrepreneurs need to be especially assured that they will not experience "unwarranted" cost pressures. Even more important is the assurance that any new reorganization of production will not be resisted by a work force experiencing an erosion of their traditional working conditions. Whether or not foreign capital is present, one would expect that economic instability would continually challenge the organizational integrity of trade unions and peasant associations.

To specify the connection between basic needs and foreign capital, it is necessary to examine more precisely the nature of economic instability in Third World countries. The World Bank provides us with a clue to the chronic problems of Third World growth when it stresses the overriding importance of developing a flexible export structure that can respond to sectoral slumps and booms in the demand for exportable commodities.[30] Economic crises in Third World countries almost always entail foreign exchange crises, and the conditions for receiving loans that can roll over debt obligations inevitably require the pursuit of stabilization policies of economic austerity. These programs are discussed in Richard E. Feinberg's essay in this volume.

It is important to note that macroeconomic policies implemented within the context of an open world economy which attempt to restrict consumption in order to make room for exports nearly always erode the strength of labor and peasant organizations. To the extent that an atomized population is a condition for the participation of foreign capital in the growth process, capitalist development makes it more difficult for a society to meet the basic needs of its citizens. The examples of Chile, Argentina, and Brazil all illustrate the connection between political-economic repression, foreign capital penetration, and capitalist growth. In all three cases, the fulfillment of basic needs and the level of real wages of the organized working class have deteriorated.[31]

The effect of foreign capital on the living standards of the agricultural population, where the problems of absolute poverty are most severe, is more difficult to interpret. On the one hand, dramatic changes in social structure are necessary if backward methods of subsistence agricultural production are to be eliminated; the reorganization of society is a precondition for improved agricultural production. [32] On the other hand, land reform which creates an entreprenurial, capitalist class simultaneously forms a landless protetariat. In England, this process, which stretched over centuries, directly eroded the living standards and economic security of marginal farmers. [33] The same process seems to have occurred in the Green Revolution areas of India and Mexico. The recent experience of Chile also provides a stark illustration of the attempts by the Pinochet regime to create a capitalist farming class: the government's efforts have successfully stimulated an export-oriented farming sector in the northern part of the country, but at the cost of a sharply worsening distribution of income in the countryside and a decline in the production of basic foodstuffs. [34]

One final point needs to be made on the subject of foreign capital and basic needs: beyond the atomizing effect of capital penetration and the pressure on states in foreign exchange difficulties to cut back on consumption and erode the power of workers' and peasants' organizations, it is necessary to note that past reliance on foreign capital makes it more difficult for reformist governments to attempt to build a more "self-reliant" economic order. Foreign capital penetration necessarily entails the creation of an international division of labor. This specialization in economic activities does not necessarily imply that Third World countries are doomed to raw material production. Nevertheless, any attempt to break from the international economic order necessarily entails a period of austere readjustment as the nation develops the capacity to produce commodities that it previously obtained through trade or direct foreign investment. During these periods of readjustment, the interdependence basic to the capitalist world economy can create problems of dependence for a Third World nation. In other words, past economic relations can directly frustrate attempts by states to reorient their economies so that they more directly meet the basic needs of their citizens. The debt trap does not necessarily block economic growth; it can prevent, however, the peaceful transition to a more egalitarian economic order.

CONCLUSION

Global corporations and banks are political opportunists. As long as they are provided some security, they can operate in almost any contemporary economic system. In some cases the enormous expansion of metropolitan capital into Latin America via growth in loans and direct foreign investment has been associated with the rapid expansion of commodity production. Substantial increases in material production have taken place within both liberal (Venezuela, Mexico) and authoritarian (Brazil) political environments. In other cases, the intensified entry of foreign capital has been associated with a stunning decline in the living standards of workers and peasants (Chile and Argentina). These different results correspond to the more general theoretical discussion of the original Smithian underpinnings of dependency and orthodox development theory. The precise role that metropolitan capital can play in meeting the basic economic needs of a particular underdeveloped country ultimately depends on the internal environment of that country.

The problem is more complex than this last statement implies, however. Multinational corporations and banks always attempt to fashion an international framework which guarantees the free mobility of their capital, and this effort influences every nation in the world economy. Any Third World country facing a foreign exchange crisis, for instance, will have to respond to demands by metropolitan capital to restructure the domestic economy in order to guarantee the security of metropolitan investments.

It is in this context that the data presented in the first section of this paper should be interpreted. Third World nations' reliance on foreign capital to maintain economic stability has increased during the 1970s, and Latin American states in particular presently face acute contradictions stemming from this trend. To the extent that these infusions of finance promote the rapid development of commodity production, social demands of the poor are bound to intensify. On the other hand, dependence on metropolitan capital may make it more difficult for the states to accede to proposals for the redistribution of income and the improvement of production conditions. Unlike the Northern industrial countries, the newly emerging industrial powers of the South will not be able to displace the contradictions of industrialization by seizing cheap raw material sources or by securing captive markets.

In interpreting recent efforts to reform the world financial system, it is important to keep in mind the problematic role of foreign capital in development. If the New International Economic Order (NIEO) proposals to forgive debt, ease credit terms, and limit the economic power of global corporations were implemented, it might be possible to weaken the necessity of Third World countries to introduce macroeconomic stabilization policies. In this sense, the NIEO could contribute to the production of basic needs.

The possibility of achieving these reforms through negotiations within the United Nations, however, is not good. Furthermore, the partial implementation of the NIEO proposals may be harmful rather than helpful. If only the most nationalistic Third World states attempt to place restrictions on foreign capital, metropolitan capital might withdraw from these nations, thus severely harming their development prospects. Or, if the North and South ratified only a watered-down reform program, the resulting compromise might not fundamentally change the ability of Third World states to modify the deleterious impact of multinational corporations on the economies of the periphery.

Because of the doubtful impact of these grand international economic negotiations, it makes more sense for human rights activists in the advanced capitalist nations to concentrate their demands for the reform of the world economic system on their own governments. To the extent that metropolitan states bend to internal pressure and begin to redirect financial assistance to those countries attempting to boost the social and economic positions of the poor, the relatively stable consensus among governments in the North to promote and protect the investments of metropolitan capital could begin to break down. It might then be possible to force banks to withdraw finance from those states which can only support their position in the world economy by stripping the poor of organized political-economic power. It might then be possible for metropolitan states to supplant private capital if it withdraws support from a socialistic government.

A basic question still remains: How can a movement to change the present economic order be mobilized in the metropolitan world? It is beyond the scope of this chapter to provide answers to this question. It can only be suggested that the internal expansion of capital does not uniformly benefit all sectors of the metropolitan population. In an economy experiencing chronic unemployment, workers will be particularly resentful of attempts by businesses to shut down factories and offices in order to move them to lower wage areas. In addition, human rights groups have already attempted to link demands for loans to low income communities with demands against loans to repressive regimes. Domestic movements to restrict the economic freedom of large corporations and banks within the industrial capitalist countries are still small and particularistic; some also contain within them an isolationist perspective which is not sympathetic to the concerns of Third World peoples. Nevertheless, it is in these struggling attempts to preserve some economic stability for the workers of the metropolitan nations that lies the best hope for human rights organizations working in the metropolises of the world economy.

It is useful in closing to remind ourselves that no restructuring of the world economy can guarantee by itself the meeting of basic needs of the masses of people in the world today. Nevertheless, international finance plays a major role in shaping each nation's economic prospects.

Our challenge is to persuade the citizens of the advanced industrial world that reform of the international economic order matters.

NOTES TO CHAPTER 6

1. I would like to thank Meg Crahan, Liz Dore, Richard Feinberg, Brian Smith, and John Weeks for their support and critical assistance in preparing this essay. This paper has also greatly benefited from the theoretical and editorial advice of Micaela di Leonardo. Throughout this chapter, as in the rest of the book, Brazil, Chile, Peru, Venezuela, Nicaragua, and Mexico are used most frequently as examples.

2. As a World Bank study notes, "In sum, the growth record is encouraging. There has been an appreciable improvement in living standards. Many countries have been able to participate successfully in international trade. But in another sense, the record is quite discouraging. The low income countries have lagged seriously behind and large numbers of people still live in extreme poverty." The World Bank, Development Policy Staff, *Prospects for Developing Countries, 1978–1985* (Washington, D.C.: World Bank, 1977), p. 12.

3. For an account of the emergence of manufacturing exports, see Martin Landsberg, "Export-Led Industrialization in the Third World: Manufacturing Imperialism," *Review of Radical Political Economics* 11 (Winter 1979): 4.

4. For an account of the developing consensus among OECD nations which led to the decision to attempt to coordinate and promote foreign aid, see the various OECD publications entitled either *Development Assistance* or *Development Cooperation*.

5. In a very interesting pamphlet published in 1963, Dr. Edmundo Flores made the following point: "Fidel Castro has claimed to be the indirect promoter of the *Alianza;* and there is some truth in his boast, since without the Cuban Revolution, Latin America would not be in the headlines today. . . . Without Castro, few outside Latin Americans would care about the region's economic stagnation, its political instability, or its undeniable ability to upset the balance of power in the cold war." Edmundo Flores, *Land Reform and the Alliance for Progress* (Princeton: Center for International Studies, Woodrow Wilson School of Public and International Affairs, Princeton University, 1963), p. 3.

6. Lincoln Gordon, the U.S. ambassador to Brazil during the early 1960s, described the goals of the Alliance for Progress in this way: "The Charter of Punta del Este, in its Title I, sets broad goals in terms of overall economic growth: more equitable distribution of national income; balance and diversification of economic structures; accelerated industrialization; improved agricultural productivity and output; agrarian reform; broader and

modernized provision for education, public health, and low-cost housing; price stability; Latin American economic integration; and improved stability of foreign-exchange earning." Lincoln Gordon, *A New Deal for Latin America: The Alliance for Progress* (Cambridge, Mass.: Harvard University Press, 1963), p. 34.

7. Of four major Latin American agrarian reforms analyzed by the noted Brazilian economist Celso Furtado, only one was in any way connected with the Alliance for Progress. Chilean reforms were initiated in 1962, but as Furtado notes: "The 1962 law was little more than a tactical diversion, a formal undertaking within the framework of the Alliance for Progress." *Economic Development of Latin America* (Cambridge: Cambridge University Press, 1976), p. 273. The more far-reaching agrarian programs of the Christian Democratic and Popular Unity governments were a product of internal conflict rather than U.S. pressure. Major reforms in Bolivia (1952), Mexico (1930s) and Peru (1969) were also a result of intense social unrest. Ibid., pp. 251–277.

8. In 1976, bilateral Official Development Assistance was only 0.33 percent of the OECD nations' GNP. The corresponding figure in 1961 was approximately 0.63 percent. See Development Assistance Committee, *Development Assistance* (Paris: OECD, 1968); and Development Assistance Committee, *Development Cooperation* (Paris: OECD, 1977).

9. OECD, p. 48.

10. For the classic radical statement on the uses of foreign aid, see Teresa Hayter, *Aid as Imperialism* (Middlesex, England: Penguin Books, 1971).

11. For an interesting account of the political difficulties in getting the Marshall plan underway, see Joyce and Gabriel Kolko, *The Limits of Power: The World and United States Foreign Policy, 1945–54* (New York: Harper & Row, 1972), pp. 359–383.

12. I am grateful to James Bass of the Inter-American Development Bank for pointing this out to me.

13. For an account of these distinctions, see the World Bank, *World Debt Tables*, 2 vols. (Washington, D.C.: The World Bank, 1979), 1: 3–12.

14. Christian Palloix, 'The Self-Expansion of Capital on a World Scale," *Review of Radical Political Economics* 9 (Summer 1977): 2.

15. Richard J. Barnet and Ronald E. Mueller, *Global Reach* (New York: Simon & Schuster, 1974).

16. The World Bank, *World Debt Tables*, 1: 11.

17. The grant element is the face value of the commitment minus the discounted present value of the future flow of repayments of principal and payments of interest as a percentage of the face value of the commitment. This concept is used by the World Bank to assess the relative hardness of public and private loans.

18. Gordon W. Smith, "The External Debt Prospects of the Non-Oil-Exporting Developing Countries" in William R. Cline, ed., *Policy Alternatives for a New International Economic Order.* (New York: Praeger, 1979), p. 291.

19. Adam Smith, *The Wealth of Nations,* 2 vols. (Chicago: University of Chicago Press, 1976), 1: 82, 388.

20. Hollis Chenery and Morses Syrquin, *Patterns of Development 1950–70* (London: Oxford University Press, 1975), pp. 60–63. Chenery and Syrquin do not deny that income distribution may worsen during the initial stages of growth. They predict, however, that eventually income distribution would improve as a country continues to develop.

21. Adam Smith, 1: 399–446.

22. André Gunder Frank, *Capitalism and Underdevelopment in Latin America* (New York: Monthly Review Press, 1969). It is at this point that Smith and the modern dependency theorists part company. While Smith believed that the unleashing of capitalism would erode monopolistic privilege, the radical dependency theorists maintain that it is capitalism which has created monopolistic control over Third World economies. With these arguments, Frank tends to follow Marx's assertion that accumulation breeds monopoly. Recently, some Marxists have stated that this interpretation of Marx is based on a misconception. Dore and Weeks, in particular, have persuasively argued that Marx envisaged the simultaneous intensification of competition and the centralization of capital. This view is the basis of a new Marxist critique of dependency theory. See John Weeks, "Marx's Theory of Competition and the Theory of Imperialism," paper presented at the Union for Radical Political Economics (New York, 1977).

23. Cheryl Payer, *The Debt Trap* (New York: Monthly Review Press, 1974).

24. Dependency theorists no longer unanimously claim that development is impossible in the Third World. Cardoso and Faletto, for instance, have argued that dependent industrialization is a characteristic of contemporarary center-periphery relations. It is unclear whether these theorists believe that the basic material needs of the masses of Third World people can be met under capitalism. For a schematic summary of the various stands of dependency theory, see Steven Jackson, Bruce Russett, Duncan Snidal, and David Sylvan, "An Assessment of Empirical Research on Dependencia," *Latin American Research Review* 14, 3 (1979): 7–28.

25. Albert Fishlow, "Brazilian Size Distribution of Income," *American Economic Review* 62 (May 1972): 392.

26. The trade data are taken from: United Nations, *Yearbook of International Trade Statistics, 1977* (New York: United Nations, 1978).

27. E. J. Hobsbawm and R. M. Hartwell, "The Standard of Living during the Industrial Revolution," *Economic History Review,* 2nd Series, 15 (August 1963): 2.

28. Ben Fine, "On the Origins of Capitalist Development," *New Left Review,* 109 (May–June 1978).

29. S. B. Saul, *The Myth of the Great Depression, 1873–1895* (London: Macmillan, 1969).

30. The World Bank, Development Policy Staff, *Prospects for Developing Countries, 1978–1985* (Washington, D.C.: The World Bank, 1977), p. 27.

31. This argument does not imply that foreign capital penetration must inevitably breed political repression. The cases of Mexico and Venezuela demonstrate that no single factor is responsible for the erosion of democratic institutions. It is probably no accident that both of these "liberal democracies" are able to rely on oil production to maintain a degree of domestic economic stability.

32. Robert Brenner, 'The Origins of Capitalism: A Critique of Neo-Smithian Marxism," *New Left Review* 104 (July–August 1977).

33. Phyllis Deane, *The First Industrial Revolution* (Cambridge, England: Cambridge University Press, 1969).

34. Joseph Collins, "Agrarian and Counter-Reform in Chile," *Monthly Review* 31 (November 1979): 6.

RICHARD E. FEINBERG

7. The International Monetary Fund and Basic Needs: The Impact of Stand-By Arrangements

INTRODUCTION

Because the International Monetary Fund has so frequently become involved in countries at crucial moments in their histories, it has attracted considerable attention and criticism. In Brazil in the mid-1960s, in Bolivia in the early 1970s, and in Chile, Argentina, and Uruguay in the mid-1970s, the Fund signed stand-by arrangements at critical junctures.[1] In Peru and Mexico, IMF stand-bys were signed as populist periods (the presidencies of Velasco Alvarado and Echevarría) were giving way to the governments of Bermúdez and López Portillo. Most recently, the IMF has found itself enmeshed in politically convulsed Nicaragua and Jamaica. In Latin America, one could say that the International Monetary Fund has been the midwife of change.

Observers who have identified with those social forces that did poorly during these historic conjunctures have tended to place considerable blame on the IMF. Most notably, the IMF has been accused of imposing severe austerity programs on weak developing countries. In fact, an IMF agreement cannot proceed without the approval of the government in question, which, however unpopular, usually reflects the predisposition of important societal interests. Moreover, in many cases, overheated economies living beyond their means had no remaining options but to depress living standards to seek to adjust their external and internal financial accounts to sustainable levels. The issue cannot be framed in terms of whether or not to adjust. Rather, what requires examination is which societal groups bore the heavier burdens of adjustment, and whether the adjustment was carried out efficiently, i.e., at minimum loss of output and employment.

Another way to analyze the division of the burden of adjustment is to examine the impact of stabilization programs on the basic needs of the poor. Both absolute and relative measures of poverty are relevant.[2] A decline in absolute standards of living at the depth of the adjustment period is insufficient evidence to prove that the poor suffered disproportionately. When severe adjustment is required, an equal sharing of the burden of adjustment can still leave the poor absolutely worse off. This chapter first describes the short-term and longer term "structural" components of IMF stand-bys, and then relates them to a basic needs approach to stabilization and development. The various economic instruments that typically are employed in an IMF stabilization program are scrutinized for their potential impacts on income distribution, when viewed in isolation and when implemented as a package. The implications for basic needs of the Fund's preference for market mechanisms over official intervention are also discussed. An attempt is made to offer some explanations as to why IMF programs have so frequently failed to meet their own stated goals, and in the process proved more costly than necessary. Finally, corrective policy recommendations are offered.

The likelihood that the IMF will become even more important in the near future makes an examination of these issues especially pressing. The looming recession in the industrial countries, skyrocketing oil prices, and burgeoning debt burdens inflated by high interest rates will increase the developing countries' demand for external financing at the very moment when the commercial banks are expressing growing concern about their extensive overseas exposure, and New International Economic Order (NIEO) proposals for a rapid and massive expansion of development assistance appear to be floundering. In these circumstances the International Monetary Fund will be standing by as a major source of balance-of-payments financing. Once the currently programmed increase in quotas is completed, the Fund will have 58 billion ($75 billion) in Special Drawing Rights (SDR) of normal quota resources to lend, plus another $10 billion in the special Supplementary Financing Facility (Witteveen Facility). The oil importing developing countries will potentially have access to approximately one-fourth of these resources.

Basic needs are generally discussed in the framework of development strategy. Some might contend that, since the division of labor of the Bretton Woods institutions has traditionally placed the IMF in charge of short-term financial stabilization and given the World Bank jurisdiction over longer term development matters, the World Bank, and not the IMF, should be concerned with basic needs. (Indeed, this essay ought never to have been written!) In reality, this sharp dichotomy between the short term and the long term, between stabilization and development, is obscured in concrete cases.

An IMF stabilization program involves a comprehensive package of measures which go well beyond merely seeking to control the money supply, and seeks to alter fundamentally the structure of the economy. If successful, these changes set the parameters within which development planners will have to operate. The blending between stabilization and development has been implicitly recognized by the IMF in its establishment in the mid-1970s of the Extended Fund Facility (EFF). Under an EFF, a country has three years rather than the normal one year to undertake the necessary adjustments, to allow time for "structural" changes. Among the structural issues that the EFF addresses are food and energy supplies, typically considered priority development problems. At the same time, seeing some of its own projects threatened by immediate financial squeezes, the World Bank has begun to offer quick-disbursing "program loans" for balance-of-payments assistance.

Fortunately, the IMF itself has begun to recognize the inevitable repercussions of stabilization programs on income distribution, and at least two staff studies have been written. [3] The Fund has not yet, however, begun to integrate systematically this incipient concern for basic needs into its routine procedures for drawing up stand-by arrangements.

I. IMF STRUCTURALISM

In recent years, the IMF has attempted to negotiate stand-by arrangements with numerous Latin American and Caribbean countries, including Argentina, Bolivia, Chile, Costa Rica, the Dominican Republic, El Salvador, Guyana, Haiti, Jamaica, Mexico, Nicaragua, Panama, Peru, and Uruguay. In some cases no agreement was reached, or the program was abandoned before complete disbursement. While the particular conditions of each case were, of course, different, the Fund's analysis and prescription generally bore important similarities, [4] and might be paraphrased as follows. Persistent balance of payments deficits resulted from internal inflation and overvalued exchange rates. Inflation was caused by excessive domestic demand, the product of government budget deficits financed by borrowing from the banking system, i.e., printing money. Excess demand both raised domestic prices and increased the demand for imports, and the overvalued exchange rate further reduced the relative profitability of exports. Confronted with a deteriorating balance of payments and vanishing international reserves, desperate governments resorted to import controls and the rationing of scarce foreign exchange through multiple exchange rates or direct administrative allocation.

In many cases, while widening fiscal deficits and rising aggregate demand were viewed as the immediate causes of the balance-of-payments crisis, the Fund saw deeper causes, the products of years of mistaken economic management in pursuit of policies associated with import substitution industrialization. Beginning in the late 1930s, and intensifying after the Second World War, many Third World governments attempted to speed national industrialization by overvaluing the exchange rate, subsidizing capital investment, and stimulating aggregate demand through public sector spending and, sometimes, increasing the earnings of the urban work force. Official controls over foreign exchange allocation, administration of the prices of many commodities, and public sector ownership of key industries often accompanied the drive to establish a domestic industrial base.

The Fund's prescription involves a two-pronged approach, one to deal with the immediate external and internal financial imbalances, and a second structural one to halt the imposition of exchange and trade controls and, preferably, to move toward dismantling these and other elements of the skeleton of import-substitution industrialization strategies. The immediate disequilibria are normally dealt with by increasing the profitability of the export and import-competing sectors through currency devaluation and the wringing out of "excessive" demand, by closing the budget deficit, controlling wages, and restricting credit. The Fund's emphasis on controlling the money supply, as a principal instrument to squeeze out excessive demand, has earned it the label monetarist, but it would be a major mistake to believe that the Fund is only or even primarily concerned with tracking the monetary aggregates. The Fund's vision of an efficiently functioning economy encompasses a much broader range of variables.

The Fund will frequently take advantage of a country's immediate financial difficulties to press for deeper structural reforms. A stand-by arrangement is the product of often prolonged negotiations between the Fund and the government of the member country. When the Fund feels that an important segment of local opinion shares its views, or that the country's desperate need for foreign exchange leaves it with few options, it will press hard for structural reforms. These are often already being advocated by some within the government, and the entrance of the Fund strengthens their hand.

Without demanding perfection, the Fund will propose at least a partial removal of such restraints on the free movement of goods and capital, as, for example, important licensing systems, import quotas, multiple exchange rates or other more direct means of allocation of foreign exchange. [5] The Fund does not limit itself to policy instruments that directly affect its official purpose of restoring equilibrium to a member's balance of payments. While a stand-by may contain only four or five explicitly quantified "preformance criteria" (usually targets deal with the size of the government deficit, the rate of growth of domestic credit and the money supply, and the amount of new external borrowings and/or other balance-of-payments tests), the accompanying documents will detail a much wider plan that will be taken into account when the Fund determines, at quarterly intervals, whether preformance has been satisfactory enough to warrant further disbursements.

This detailed plan generally concentrates on stimulating private capital formation by offering adequate incentives to savers and producers, and by creating a general atmosphere of business confidence. The efficient allocation of this capital will best be guaranteed by allowing price signals to be set by the free market. This logic, in turn, reinforces the view that government controls over relative prices (other than wages) should be removed. In many cases, the Fund also advocates that the relative size of the state sector itself be reduced, to reserve a larger proportion of economic activity and of available credit to the private sector.

Beginning with the mandate, enunciated in its *Articles of Agreement,* to help restore a balance of payments equilibrium, the Fund moves from a concern to reduce imports to controlling aggregate demand, from the need to expand exports to the wisdom of reducing the size of the state sector in order to stimulate private investment in exportables. The involvement goes deeper and deeper, as controlling aggregate demand leads to establishing ceilings on wages, to curtailing fiscal expenditure, and to eliminating subsidies on particular items such as bread or bus fares.

The profound implications of this two-pronged approach of financial stabilization and structural reform explain the heatedness of the controversy in Latin America over Fund policies. The inevitable discontent generated by austerity measures is amplified by policies which attack a development model erected over two generations.

II. THE IMF AND BASIC NEEDS

In the pursuit of external balance and financial stability, the IMF becomes involved with a wide range of problems. The basic needs of the poor, however, are not a direct concern. Some measures may indirectly benefit the poor, such as the creation of employment in export-oriented industries that are also labor intensive, and steadier prices, if applied to essential consumer items, which halt the erosion of workers' purchasing power. In essence, however, the Fund adheres to the trickle-down approach whereby aggregate growth in GNP is thought to lead to full employment and rising real incomes.

The Fund's emphasis on the free market and a circumscribed public sector biases it against official provision, whether through subsidies or directly, of five basic needs—food, health care, education, shelter, and water and sanitation. Moreover, the Fund tends to view such budgetary allocations for "consumption expenditures" as expendible, as it concentrates on laying the foundations for savings and investment in physical capital. This focus contrasts sharply with the World Bank's increasing emphasis on human resource development, for investment in human capital, as central to improving labor productivity and generally fostering development. [6] While the IMF tends to see expenditures on basic needs as postponable, the World Bank now views them as foundation-laying investments.

While not generally made explicit, the Fund's belief in the market carries with it all the assumptions that lie behind the neoclassical paradigm, including an acceptance of given or market-determined factor endowments (assets and income), consumer sovereignty and the non-comparability of consumption between individuals. If a basic needs approach implies that the consumption levels of the better off ought to be restrained until the basic needs of all or nearly all of society are being met, then the Fund's basic philosophy would place it in opposition.

The Fund is not alone among economic institutions in viewing both production and consumption as aggregates, while a basic needs approach is, by definition, taking a disaggregated view that confers priority on particular goods and services. The Fund seeks to create an economic environment that fosters aggregate growth, with the market determining the mix of production. In such a paradigm, the issue of basic needs does not arise.

III. STABILIZATION MEASURES AND INCOME DISTRIBUTION

Although the Fund does not routinely worry about basic needs, its stabilization programs can significantly alter both the relative and absolute income levels of the poor. Analyzing these effects involves several hazards. Unfortunately, comprehensive income data to compare distribution before and after the program is rarely available. Resort must often be made to less disaggregated statistics on functional or urban-rural distribution, or to data across productive sectors. The results may be contradictory. For example, as one study found in the case of Peru, while functional data on urban wages and profits suggested an increasingly skewed distribution of income, rising food prices may have benefited the rural population where many of the poor are concentrated. [7] More generally, the impact of changing relative prices may be marginal on subsistence farmers less integrated into the monetary economy. An additional hazard involves the choice of timeframe: the differential impact on incomes of a stabilization program during its first year or two may be misleading. Finally, whereas some variables (e.g., wage controls, selective credit allocation) have a direct effect, many others have indirect distributional results that are harder to trace.

Notwithstanding these caveats, considerable evidence suggests that under many IMF-supported stabilization programs the wealthy elites have fared better than the rest of the population, and significant sectors of the poor have suffered disproportionately.[8] To date there is no in-depth study which argues that IMF programs have actually improved income distribution. These findings are generally based on the cumulative effect of the stabilization package. It would not be inconsistent to discover that particular policies may have had a more ambiguous or even positive impact on income distribution. The disaggregated analysis which follows is intended to elucidate the potential distributional effects of policies commonly employed in IMF stabilization programs. *Ceteris paribus* conditions are invoked for simplicity and space allows for only a suggestive treatment of each variable. The cumulative impact of packages of measures will then be considered.

Devaluation. Devaluation can effect income distribution in numerous ways. Consumers find imported goods to be more costly, but the composition of a nation's imports will determine the relative effect on different social groups. If luxury goods are a major component, the wealthier classes may suffer more, but if food is a major component the impact may fall most heavily on the poor. Devaluation renders exports more profitable and, if effective, will move more resources into the export sector. In the Argentine case, where agriculture remains the major export and where land tenure is concentrated, devaluation has historically benefited the landed elite and hurt the urban workers who had to pay more for foodstuffs.[9] However, where export agriculture is potentially labor intensive, the introduction of new labor-using technology allows both for the possibility of higher real wages and for increased rural employment. Mexican agriculture might fit this mold. Devaluation also affects holders of cash balances; holders of foreign currency gain relative to holders of local currency, thereby altering the value of assets within the monied classes. Also, foreign investors suddenly find assets priced in local currency relatively cheaper to purchase.

The Relaxation of Exchange Controls. The relaxation of exchange controls will adversely affect those groups that benefited from the existing exchange regime. If controls were administered with a high degree of corruption and official favoritism of the wealthy, unification of exchange rates and reduced administrative allocation of scarce foreign exchange might actually improve income distribution. Thus, in the case of the ill-fated stand-by with Nicaragua in the spring of 1979, the Fund's insistence on the elimination of advance import deposits and deposits for obtaining foreign exchange, and injunctions against any further official restrictions on international transactions, might have reduced at least one avenue whereby the Somoza regime funnelled privileges to its adherents. On the other hand, Jamaica maintained a dual exchange rate system as a means of holding down the prices of imports consumed by low-income groups. The Fund prevailed on Jamaica to unify the exchange rate in 1978.

Credit Restrictions.   Squeezing credit to the private sector, in the absence of selective controls, would most likely harm those smaller firms that lack privileged access to banking institutions. In the absence of controls over private foreign borrowing, larger firms may also use their access to international credit in order to offset domestic restrictions.

Easing of Price Controls.   Releasing price controls, while generally increasing the return to capital unless wages keep pace, may redound to the benefit of the rural poor if internal terms of trade are administered to benefit urban food consumers, and if the revenues from higher prices reach the small farmers and landless laborers. However, in the presence of structural tendencies for internal terms of trade to move against agriculture, the removal of price controls may ultimately harm the rural sector.

Elimination of Interest Rate Ceilings.   Removing interest rate ceilings, and the creation of domestic capital markets with positive real rates of return, if resulting in efficient capital markets, can benefit small savers (but not the very poor, who do not have financial assets) by offering higher rates of return on deposits. However, very high rates of return on financial instruments, and excessive spreads between rates paid to lenders and borrowers, can divert resources into speculation and away from more productive, employment-creating investment. This adverse effect of a liberation of capital markets in the absence of a healthy climate for productive investment seems to have occurred during the stabilization processes in both Chile [10] and Argentina [11] in the mid-1970s. The holders of the speculative assets, and owners of the financial intermediaries, benefit, while the other sectors, including workers left without jobs for lack of investment in real capital, lose.

Wage Controls.   Notwithstanding occasional disclaimers to the contrary, IMF stand-bys frequently establish ceilings on wage increases significantly under the projected rate of inflation. If certain assumptions regarding quickly adjusting labor markets hold, new hirings could offset some of the adverse effect of decreased real wages on income distribution. This is unlikely to occur, however, in the context of falling aggregate demand and sluggish investment. The partial incomes policy of the IMF, whereby wages but not other prices are controlled, is designed to increase the return on capital to stimulate savings and investment. The immediate effect on the functional distribution of income is to reduce labor's share of national income. [12]

Budget Restraint.   The impact of budget restraint naturally depends upon whether fiscal balance is sought by increased taxes or reduced expenditures, and the incidence of such measures. While the Fund will sometimes recommend selective tax increases, the emphasis is generally on expenditure reduction. In that case, the burden may fall on public-sector workers whose wages or numbers decrease, on consumers who lose their subsidies, and on workers who had planned to work on investment projects that were postponed.

Limits on Public-Sector Enterprises.   In its drive to reduce state subsidies, the IMF sometimes advocates the transference of state-owned enterprises to the private sector. This transfer could allow for reduced taxation and more efficient production, and thereby benefit the entire society. However, if this transfer occurs at bargain prices, as appears to have occurred in the Chilean case, then the new owners can look forward to very high rates of return on their investments. [13] The Fund tends to look askance at the forced redistribution of assets within the private sector or from the private sector to collective ownership. Land reform would generally be seen as prejudicial to investor confidence. President Luis Echevarría's dramatic gestures favoring land redistribution toward the end of his term were viewed as contributing to the drop in private investment in Mexico preceding the 1976 stand-by arrangement. In the Peruvian case, the Fund regarded the watering down of the industrial community law, whereby labor was to be given increasing equity and a commensurate voice in management, as conducive to business confidence. [14]

Redistribution of land is obviously an explosive political subject with ramifications well beyond the scope of this paper. A recent World Bank staff study, however, concluded that, among eight middle-income, semi-industrialized countries examined, a key factor in determining income distribution was the distribution of land. [15] The poor showings of Brazil and Mexico were partly attributed to this variable. Of special relevance was the conclusion that, in the cases of more even income distribution, agrarian reform had occurred before the period of accelerated growth. This finding would appear relevant to stabilization programs which are attempting to lay the foundations for future growth with equity.

Stabilization and Inflation.   The main stated objective of a number of these stabilization measures—restricting credit, fiscal restraint, controlling wages—is to reduce inflation.[16] It is frequently assumed that inflation harms the weaker, generally poorer, sectors most. The prices of basic needs may rise especially fast and the poor are less able to defend their wage levels. Inflation also allows a government considerable leeway to alter relative prices. The Brazilian government consciously adjusted certain wage scales by less than the actual inflation rates. This partial indexation was intended both to decelerate inflation and to hold down real labor costs. As Barbara Stallings has shown in the case of successive regimes in Chile, different governments adjusted wage levels with respect to inflation depending upon their respective sources of political support.[17] Governments representative of business interests (e.g., the administration of President Jorge Alessandri 1958–1964) turned the functional distribution of income against labor, whereas the prolabor government of Salvador Allende (1970–1973) favored its constituents.

Social Costs of Stabilization Policies.   This discussion suggests that the distributional impact of particular stabilization measures is not at all obvious. Within a generally declining national income, certain sectors may actually benefit while others will suffer disproportionately. An important factor is the nature of the governments that preceded and are implementing the stabilization program. In the presence of a new government concerned with income distribution that had recently displaced a corrupt or elite-oriented regime, selective and carefully targeted implementation of some of the above measures could actually advance income distribution. The removal or modification of administrative controls and other fiscal policies that primarily benefited the ruling elite could assist the poor in the short and long run. More generally, a government concerned with income distribution, but forced by circumstances to undertake a stabilization program, can consciously select measures to reduce the burden on the poor. For example, in determining the depth of a devaluation, the capital-labor ratios in the most affected productive sectors could be considered. Tax increases and expenditure cuts could be made with income distribution effects in mind.[18] Public-sector enterprises should be sold off only at prices that reflect their future productive worth. As certain restraints on capital markets are removed, nonproductive speculation should be discouraged. Where otherwise desirable measures unavoidably cut more deeply against the poor, offsetting subsidies would be in order.

Less effort, however, is required in implementing orthodox stabilization measures that avoid considerations of income distribution. Under such circumstances, it is easy to envision the poor suffering both in absolute and relative terms. At the disaggregated level of individual stabilization measures, the above analysis indicated numerous possibilities for measures impinging most severely on the poor. Devaluation or the removal of multiple exchange rates can raise the price of imported foodstuffs. The removal of price controls may work to the detriment of real wages and to the benefit of producers. The reduction of fiscal expenditures will harm those more who depend upon official subsidies to obtain the basic services. High interest rates will, in absolute terms, benefit large owners of financial assets the most.

Perhaps most devastating on the poor is the cumulative and reinforcing nature of these stabilization measures. Although it is true that in perfectly functioning markets adjustment would occur through relative price changes under continuing full employment, in reality adjustment occurs through price increases and rising unemployment. The real wages of the workers fall, while the unemployed may find their unemployment benefits reduced if they exist at all. The IMF will typically restrain the hand of a government considering using administrative controls over prices or resource allocation to ameliorate these adverse consequences.

From a basic needs perspective, even a strictly proportionate distribution of the economic burden is not sufficient. The wealthier have a thicker cushion on which to lean before their access to basic needs is affected, while the poor may have no cushion at all. A basic needs approach to stabilization would argue for shifting the burden disproportionately onto the wealthier groups (although the longer run economic impact of such measures would have to be taken into account). A government especially sensitive to the needs of the poor might attempt such basic needs strategy, but the political obstacles—namely, the ability of the wealthier groups to resist—are likely to be effective constraints in most cases. It would be a major step forward for the IMF to strive consciously for a proportional distribution of the burden of adjustment.

IV. THE PREFERENCE FOR THE MARKET AND BASIC NEEDS

While it would be an exaggeration to claim that the IMF's ideal economic system would be one in which the government consisted only of a central bank maintaining a steady and slowly increasing money supply, imbedded in an otherwise smoothly functioning market system fully integrated in world commodity and capital markets, it is certainly true that the Fund views many administrative interventions as inefficiently disrupting a more perfect market mechanism. In the Latin American case, this predisposition has pitted the Fund against the import-substitution industrialization (ISI) policies mentioned earlier. While ISI policies may at first have stimulated employment for a rapidly growing urban work force and created the conditions for initial industrialization and the welfare state, a near consensus has developed among economists over the last decade that further progress on job creation and meeting basic needs requires modifications in economic policy.[19] For example, the maintenance of certain protectionist measures benefits the ensconced industrialists and relatively high-wage labor to the detriment of the under and unemployed and the rural areas. To this extent, the Fund's critique can assist those local forces attempting to remove outmoded policies protecting strong vested interests.

While the World Bank is also a critic of ISI policies, it still sees the need for an interventionist state. The Bank officially recognizes that the development of a capital goods sector, in countries that have already passed through the lighter manufacturing stage that ISI policies were designed for, may require some protective tariffs or other modes of subsidization. Moreover, the Bank argues that:

> the indivisible nature of investments in the sectors using capital goods, and the need for correspondingly large and discontinuous expansion in the capital goods-producing sector itself, justify some degree of indicative macro-economic planning in order to reduce uncertainty and avoid costly errors.[20]

In other words, since the assumptions required for the free market to function efficiently may not hold, an active state role may be necessary.

For countries that have attained a semi-industrialized status, including much of Latin America, the World Bank is even more insistent on an activist role in providing jobs and services to the poor. To eliminate poverty and meet basic needs, the World Bank now advocates such measures as: expanded public investment to increase the productivity of labor and land; the elimination of dualistic agricultural structures where an impoverished peasantry lacking minimal resources co-exist with large, modern farms, by land reform if necessary (citing specifically Brazil, Colombia, and Mexico); and an expansion and more equal distribution of public services, including a restructuring of health systems in favor of preventive health care.[21] The state, in short, is awarded an activist role in supply management of the basic necessities for the poor. In many countries, the Bank concludes, larger public sectors will be required to meet these pressing needs.

Of course, these recommendations may fall on deaf ears, and any increase in public revenues may be spent in the traditional patterns benefiting the middle and upper urban sectors. In such cases, the Fund at least has an arguable case in favor of maintaining or increasing the proportion of goods and services distributed by the market.

In countries where the government is already attempting to follow policies consistent with these World Bank guidelines, the IMF may find itself at odds with those genuinely concerned with basic needs. During recent attempts to negotiate a stand-by with the Fund, President Julius Nyerere feared that Fund recommendations endangered his egalitarian development strategy, and told diplomats in Dar es Salaam:

> Tanzania is not prepared to devalue its currency just because this is a traditional free market solution to everything and regardless of the merits of our position. It is not prepared to surrender its right to restrict imports by measures designed to ensure that we import quinine rather than cosmetics, or buses rather than cars for the elite.
>
> My government is not prepared to give up our national endeavour to provide primary education for every child, basic medicines and some clean water for all our people. Cuts may have to be made in our national expenditure, but WE will decide whether they fall on public services or private expenditure. Nor are we prepared to deal with inflation and shortages by relying only on monetary policy regardless of its relative effect on the poorest and less poor. Our price control machinery may not be the most effective in the world, but we will not abandon price control; we will only strive to make it more efficient. And above all, we shall continue with our endeavours to build a socialist society. [22]

The IMF and the World Bank are "sister" institutions physically located directly across the street from each other in Washington. In recent years, their official policies have been drifting apart as the World Bank evolves toward urging a more direct attack on basic needs. As stabilization policies significantly affect basic needs in both the short and long term, closer coordination between the Fund and the Bank is essential if the two Bretton Woods Institutions are to avoid working at cross purposes.

V. THE EFFICIENCY OF FUND STABILIZATION
   PROGRAMS

Stabilization programs that succeed in their stated objectives of restoring external and internal financial balance with as little loss in output and income as feasible will, within a given income policy, minimize the burden on the poor. Unfortunately, in recent years the record of IMF stand-bys when judged on their own terms of restoring financial equilibrium, has been disappointing. A Fund study of 21 upper tranche stand-bys undertaken between 1973–1975 found that only seven could be judged successful in the sense that the performance criteria of the stand-by were broadly achieved. [23] The Fund has offered various explanations for these failures, including the difficult global environment of the period, the inadequate responsiveness of performance criteria to changing conditions, the disruptive effects of unanticipated price increases, and the reluctance of governments to resist political pressures, including those opposing reductions in real wages. More recently, at least in Latin America and the Caribbean, the IMF's record has, at best, been mixed.

Recent stand-by agreements in Latin America and the Caribbean have persistently encountered three problems worthy of elaboration: a costly and disruptive underestimation of inflation; the presence of unaccounted for political realities and psychological expectations which upset projections of economic behavior; and the hesitancy of countries to undertake IMF stand-bys until their economies had reached advanced stages of disequilibria.

Why does the Fund, with its expertise on monetary matters, so frequently miscalculate inflation rates? The reasons are multiple. First, some of the Fund's assumptions about the structure of an economy may be invalid. For example, markets may adjust more slowly than anticipated, oligopolistic structures may permit cost-plus pricing, the velocity of circulation may change more rapidly than expected, and supply may respond more slowly than hoped. Secondly, the stand-by arrangement may fail to take sufficiently into account inflationary psychology, and overestimate the ability of the monetary authorities to control the money supply. Third, the stand-by may call for budgetary cuts or other inflation-fighting fiscal measures that prove politically infeasible. Fourth, policy measures that the Fund itself had advocated often have an inflationary impact. Devaluation, higher producer prices, and positive real interest rates can have cumulative effects on prices which produce the inflationary "bubble" associated with many IMF stand-bys. Finally, the Fund may purposely underestimate inflation, for two main reasons: to deflate potential criticism of its inflationary measures and to discourage catch-up wage demands.

Unanticipated inflation throws off most of a stand-by's quantitative targets, and is severely disruptive of a program intent upon restoring financial stability. If it is true that inflation hurts the poor more, from a basic needs perspective, stand-bys must either do better at slowing price increases, or else anticipate them more accurately and provide compensating measures to reduce the burden on the poor.

The Fund is obviously operating in the realm of political economy, but it vigorously maintains that its technocrats are apolitical. The failure to factor in political variables correctly while devising a stand-by, especially in moments of great domestic strife, can prove fatal to the most elegant adjustment model. The 1977–1979 stand-bys in Jamaica, and the 1978 stand-by with Nicaragua are cases in point.

The Jamaican stand-by assumed that government measures designed to restrain consumption, restore financial stability, and increase the return to capital would automatically stimulate domestic investment and restore Jamaican access to international capital markets. Neither occurred, because regardless of what particular measures he might have taken, investors did not trust Prime Minister Michael Manley and the more leftist wing of his party, and because investors sensed that Manley's reformist rhetoric correctly reflected underlying social tensions. The slump in domestic demand—itself a success of the stabilization program—also contributed to sluggish investment.

The signing of the stand-by with Nicaraguan President Somoza, just days before the final insurrection against him in 1979 got fully under way, provides the most glaring example of the fallacy of attempting to divorce a program from the political environment. The stand-by's success depended upon increased fiscal revenues and the termination and then reversal of capital flight at the very moment when the regime was about to face a second, prolonged, and ultimately decisive, general strike, and when many of the wealthy were fleeing not only with their capital but with their families. Even if Somoza had prevailed militarily, he could not have convinced the hostile private sector to resume investing. Yet the success of the Fund program required the restoration of business confidence. To argue, as the Fund did, that the stand-by was "technically sound," despite the admitted risks, is to imagine an environment of statistics and behavioral relations without real-world actors.

In October 1978 the IMF signed an Extended Fund Facility with Haiti. The main element of the program was the centralization of government revenue into the budget and the abolition of the tax assessment and collection functions of the infamous Régie du Taboc. In other words, the intention was to eliminate the personal slush funds, such as the Régie, of the ruling family, and to terminate the spending of revenues that were not accounted for adequately. This attempt to introduce a minimal level of probity into fiscal management was a clear threat to the *modus operandi* of the Duvalier regime. Other donors conditioned their assistance upon compliance to the stand-by criteria. Acting in consortia, and organized behind an IMF program, the bilateral donors sought to increase their own and the Fund's leverage.[24] Nevertheless, by 1980 the refusal of the regime to implement these reforms had led to the suspension of the IMF program.

Confronted with equally frustrating political realities in Zaire, the Fund has actually placed its own expatriate appointees in key governmental positions. Even then, a handful of foreigners will have great difficulty controlling a bureaucracy so thoroughly ridden with patronage and corruption.

The Fund often attributes the severity of its stand-bys to the fact that countries come to the Fund only after their economic crisis is so deep that all their foreign exchange resources are depleted and no alternative sources remain. For example, the Peruvian government avoided an IMF agreement during more than two years of economic crisis, and finally negotiated accords in 1977–1978 only after all other avenues were closed.[25]

Why is it that countries are so hesitant to enter into a stand-by arrangement? The Fund would blame the member governments for lacking the political will or technical wisdom to adopt prompt corrective measures. While this is often the case, the preceding discussion suggests additional explanatory factors. The combined impact of unanticipated inflation and less-than-predicted private, foreign, and domestic investment can result in more lost output and employment than necessary, in an "overshooting" of stabilization requirements, and an unwarranted deprivation of basic needs. Unanticipated inflation, in the context of restrained wages and tight fiscal and monetary policies, squeezes demand, which in turn depresses investment. The Fund's often unwarranted optimism regarding the likelihood of a quick restoration of investor confidence—when judged outside of the relevant political context—is thus further compounded. The resulting disappointing performance of private investment is especially devastating where governments have a strong bias against public-sector investment. Southern cone stabilization experiences, especially in Chile, exemplify such low aggregate capital formation. In the cases of Chile, and especially Argentina, the rapid accumulation of foreign exchange reserves was one indication that the sharp reduction in demand—for both investment and consumption—overshot the mark.[26]

If rapid inflation and low capital formation have frequently compounded stabilization woes, another reason governments avoid IMF stand-bys is the fear of imposing measures designed to attain financial stability *and* structural reform at the same time. In those country cases where, as Nyerere argued, the Fund's quest for more market-oriented structures harms the poor, their adaptation at a time of generally falling incomes is especially burdensome.

Finally, the Fund has long been accused of pursuing a "shock" treatment approach rather than a generally less costly gradualism. [27] If an economy has simply run out of foreign exchange, the stabilization program may necessarily have to seek rapid adjustment. In other cases, however, the choice of the proper speed of adjustment may hinge on a political judgment: are the authorities likely to weaken gradually as political discontent mounts, so that it is better to implement most of the tough measures immediately, while the iron is hot? This political judgment can only be made on a case-by-case basis, but the Fund's normal reflex is to press for adjustment immediately. If, in fact, a more gradual adjustment were feasible, the costs incurred may have been greater than necessary.

The Fund, then, is partially responsible for countries avoiding stand-bys until they have no other choice. Ironically, the Fund itself bears some of the burden for the tendency of developing nations to postpone adjustment.

VI. POLICY RECOMMENDATIONS

To soften the burden of adjustment on the poor, and to foster a general improvement in the efficiency of its stabilization programs, the IMF should consider adopting the following policies:

1) The IMF has begun to investigate the distributional aspects of stabilization programs, and should pursue this work with greater intensity. In designing stabilization programs, the impact of particular measures, as well as their cumulative effect, on income distribution and basic needs should be carefully analyzed. Member governments should be informed of the likely consequences of recommended stabilization programs on income distribution, and be given assistance in devising measures attentive to such concerns if they so request, including measures to offset the adverse distributional consequences of otherwise desirable policies. The IMF and the World Bank should encourage governments to improve their collection of income distribution data.

2) Despite assurances from the IMF and the World Bank that existing informal cooperation is sufficient, their increasing divergence on central philosophical issues suggests a need for much closer coopera-

tion. If the IMF is not to be working against the World Bank's basic needs strategies, it will have to give greater priority to human capital formation and allow for a more active public-sector role in supplying basic needs. A desirable innovation would be the creation of a joint office, containing officials from both institutions, which would seek to coordinate activities in specific countries.

3) If the Fund is to attract countries at an earlier stage, before the crisis becomes severe, it should take a closer look at why countries are so hesitant. Greater restraint and flexibility is needed in dealing with countries who fear the combined effects of a simultaneous adoption of measures designed both to restore financial balance and reform fundamental structures. The Fund should be less dogmatic in its negation of administrative instruments to offset adverse income distribution consequences of adjustment measures. In predicting inflation rates and private investor behavior, the Fund should refrain from unwarranted optimism, and avoid an overshooting of deflationary targets which increases the cost of adjustment. If private investment is likely to be slow to respond, greater public-sector investment should be programmed. Finally, gradualism is preferable to "shock" treatment if economic and political conditions permit.

Such measures cannot entirely shelter the poor during periods of austerity, but they could contribute to a more equal sharing of the burden of adjustment. When local governments are not themselves concerned with protecting "basic needs" in moments of slowed growth, the Fund's ability to materially bend the stabilization program will be very limited. But where important segments of the government are so concerned, the Fund should be supportive of their efforts.

NOTES TO CHAPTER 7

1. A stand-by arrangement is a written promise by the IMF to provide a determined amount of credit conditioned upon the country fulfilling specified performance criteria. The amount of credit depends upon a member's quota, the seriousness of the problems, and the Fund's judgment regarding the member's willingness to accept rigorous performance criteria, and thereby be worthy of "upper tranche" drawings.

2. For a discussion of these two measures of poverty, see John F. Weeks and Elizabeth W. Dore, "Basic Needs: Journey of a Concept," Chapter 4 in this volume.

3. For a published example, see Omotunde Johnson and Joanne Salop, "Distributional Aspects of Stabilization Programs in Developing Countries," *IMF Staff Papers,* 27, 1 (March 1980).

4. For a general description of stand-bys, see Omotunde Johnson, "Use

of Fund Resources and Stand-By Arrangements," *Finance and Development,* 14, 1 (March 1977): 19–21.

5. In justifying an attack on such practices, the Fund often refers to its founding document, the *Articles of Agreement,* which charge the Fund to foster international trade and orderly and stable exchange arrangements. However, the *Articles* could be read with a different emphasis, to permit official practices consistent with "the primary objectives of economic policy," namely, "the promotion and maintenance of high levels of employment and real income." IMF, *Articles of Agreement* (Washington, D.C.: IMF, 1978), p. 2.

6. World Bank, *World Development Report, 1980* (Washington, D.C.: World Bank, 1980).

7. W. R. Cline, "Economic Stabilization in Peru, 1975–78," in W. R. Cline and Sidney Weintraub, eds., *Economic Stabilization in Developing Countries* (Washington, D.C.: The Brookings Institution, 1981). In the abstract, rising incomes for the rural sector as a whole create the possibility, but do not guarantee, that landless laborers will benefit. Cline did not present disaggregated data on income distribution patterns within the Peruvian countryside.

8. There is a growing number of case studies of Latin American and Caribbean stabilization programs. In addition to studies cited elsewhere in this paper, recent works include: on Argentina, Roberto Frenkel and Guillermo O'Donnell, "The 'Stabilization Programs' of the International Monetary Fund and their Internal Impacts," in Richard R. Fagen, ed., *Capitalism and the State in U.S.-Latin American Relations* (Stanford: Stanford University Press, 1979); on Brazil, Edmar L. Bacha, "Issues and Evidence on Recent Brazilian Economic Growth," *World Development* (January–February, 1977); on Chile, Joseph Ramos, "Inflación persistente, inflación reprimida e hiperstagflación: lecciones de inflación y estabilización en Chile," *Desarrollo Económico,* 18, 69 (April–June 1978); on Jamaica, Adlith Brown, "Economic Policy and the IMF in Jamaica" (Kingston: ISER, University of the West Indies, 1980); on Mexico, Carlos Tello, *La Política Económica en México, 1970–76* (Mexico City: Siglo XXI, 1979); on Peru, Daniel Schydlowsky and Juan Wicht, "The Anatomy of an Economic Failure: Peru, 1968–78," Boston University Center for Latin American Development Studies, Discussion Paper Series No. 31 (February 1979); and on Uruguay, "Uruguay: en el Círculo Vicioso del Estancamiento y la Inflación," *Economía de América Latina: Papel de las Políticas de Estabilización* (Mexico City: Centro de Investigación y Docencia Económica, 1978).

9. Carlos Díaz-Alejandro, *Essays on the Economic History of the Argentine Republic* (New Haven: Yale University Press, 1970); and Aldo Ferrer et al., "Devaluación, Redistribución de Ingresos, y el Proceso de Desarticulación Industrial en la Argentina," in *Los Planes de Estabilización en la Argentina* (Buenos Aires: Paidos, 1969), pp. 13–30.

10. Alejandro Foxley, "Income Distribution and Employment Programmes: Stabilization Policies and Stagflation: The Cases of Brazil and Chile," Working Paper No. 81 (Geneva: ILO, 1979), pp. 70–75.

11. Carlos Díaz Alejandro, "Southern Cone Stabilization Plans," in Cline and Weintraub.

12. See Elizabeth W. Dore and John F. Weeks, "Economic Performance and Basic Needs: The Examples of Brazil, Chile, Mexico, Nicaragua, Peru, and Venezuela," in this volume for evidence that worsening functional income distribution in Chile and Peru, following IMF stand-bys, contributed to a decline in the poor's calorie intake, as an indicator of a general deterioration of "basic needs" provision.

13. Foxley, p. 68.

14. Rosemary Thorp, "Inflation, Stabilization, and Attempted Redemocratization in Peru, 1975–79," paper presented at the Smithsonian Institution, Woodrow Wilson Center, Latin American Program, June 21–23, 1979. For a discussion of the evolution of the industrial community law, see Alfred Stepan, *The State and Society: Peru in Comparative Perspective* (Princeton, N.J.: Princeton University Press, 1978), Chapter 7.

15. Joel Bergsman, "Growth and Equity in Semi-industrialized Countries," World Bank Staff Working Paper No. 351 (Washington, D.C.: The World Bank, 1979). The countries examined were Argentina, Brazil, Mexico, Taiwan, South Korea, Yugoslavia, Turkey, and the Philippines.

16. The adverse impact of at least mild inflation on growth has probably been exaggerated, and countries like Brazil and South Korea have enjoyed periods of high growth with significant ongoing inflation. If the antiflation battle is pursued more vigorously than necessary, the sacrifice in output and employment may be an avoidable tax on basic needs provision. The efficiency of IMF programs is discussed later in this chapter.

17. Barbara Stallings, *Class Conflict and Economic Development in Chile, 1958–1973* (Stanford, Calif.: Stanford University Press, 1978).

18. For a survey of ways to bring about a fairer distribution of the tax burden in developing countries, see Arnold C. Harberger, "Fiscal Policy and Income Distribution," in Charles R. Frank, Jr. and Richard E. Webb, eds., *Income Distribution and Growth in the Less-Developed Countries* (Washington, D.C.: The Brookings Institution, 1977), pp. 259–280.

19. For an early exposition of this argument, see I. M. D. Little, T. Scitovsky, and M. Scott, *Industry and Trade in Some Developing Countries: A Comparative Study* (London: Oxford University Press, 1970).

20. The World Bank, *World Development Report, 1979* (Washington, D.C.: The World Bank, 1979), p. 96. Unofficial backup studies are: Armeane M. Choksi, "State Intervention in the Industrialization of Developing Countries: Selected Issues," World Bank Staff Working Paper No. 341 (Washington, D.C.: The World Bank, 1979); and Jayati datta Mitra, "The Capital Goods Sector in LDC's: A Case for State Intervention?," World Bank Staff Working Paper No. 343 (Washington, D.C.: World Bank, 1979).

21. The World Bank, *World Development Report, 1979,* Chapter 7.

22. Julius Nyerere, speech at the Kilimanjaro Hotel, Dar es Salaam, January 1, 1980.

23. T. M. Reichmann, "The Fund's Conditional Assistance and the

Problems of Adjustment," *Finance and Development*, 15, 4 (December 1978): 38–41.

24. For a discussion of the limited leverage of AID when acting alone, see Constantine Michalopoulos, "Basic Needs Strategies: Some Policy Implementation Issues of the U.S. Bilateral Assistance Program," Chapter 8 in this volume.

25. Barbara Stallings, "Peru and the U.S. Banks: Privatization of Financial Relations," in Fagen, pp. 217–253.

26. Foxley, 'Income Distribution," and Carlos Díaz Alejandro, "Southern Cone Stabilization Plans," in Cline and Weintraub.

27. One recent overview of IMF stand-bys cites several country cases where the Fund was "unreasonably severe in its demands," including Brazil (1964), Colombia (1966), and Peru (1977–78). John Williamson, "Economic Theory and IMF Policies," in U.S. Congress, House Subcommittee on International Trade, Investment and Monetary Policy, Committee on Banking, Finance and Urban Affairs, *To Amend the Bretton Woods Agreements Act to Authorize Consent to an Increase in the United States Quota in the IMF*, 96th Congress, 2nd sess., February–April, 1980, pp. 236–238.

PART III

United States Policies

*Basic Needs Strategy: Some Policy Implementation
Issues of the U.S. Bilateral Assistance Program*

*U.S.-Latin American Military Relations Since
World War II: Implications for Human Rights*

*The Carter Administration and Human Rights
in Latin America*

CONSTANTINE MICHALOPOULOS [1]

8. Basic Needs Strategy: Some Policy Implementation Issues of The U.S. Bilateral Assistance Program

INTRODUCTION

Support of developing countries' efforts to address the basic needs of their poor, through U.S. economic assistance programs, was a key theme of the Carter Administration's U.S. assistance policy from its earliest days. The United States, through various actions by the Executive Branch and Congress, made its basic policy on this issue abundantly clear. For example, a Presidential directive in late 1977 mandated that Congressional assistance would be provided to meet the basic needs of poor people, primarily in low income countries. The Foreign Assistance Act of 1979 stated that "development assistance shall be concentrated in countries which will make the most effective use of such assistance to help satisfy human needs of poor people through equitable growth."

While the basic policy thrust and objectives of U.S. foreign assistance programs had been made explicit, various ambiguities, issues, and problems arose in attempting to implement this policy in practice. The purpose of this chapter is to examine some of the issues that arose in implementing a U.S. foreign assistance policy whose key, but not sole, objective was to assist developing countries in their efforts to better fulfill the basic needs of the poor. These issues can be divided into three groups:

First, there were conceptual issues having to do primarily with the optimum developing-country strategy for promoting basic needs objectives. Second, there were programmatic issues which had to do with the focus and mode of operations of specific assistance projects and programs that could be used to implement the policy. Third, there were issues involving the relationship of assistance policy to other U.S. objectives and international economic policies which affect our relations with developing countries. There are many such objectives and policies. Two interacting issues will be singled out for particular attention: the link between basic human needs and human rights objectives and the link between basic needs and U.S. international trade policy. Although some issues of bilateral-multilateral program interaction will be addressed, the focus in most of the discussion will be AID's bilateral development assistance program which has been the main instrument through which the policy has been implemented.

The multiplicity of problems raised here should not give the impression that there is no sympathy for the objectives pursued by the policy. The purpose is to clarify the issues somewhat so that ways can be found to resolve them. Also, the purpose is to outline a pragmatic view of what can be accomplished through such a policy so that the policy is not discredited by the setting of unrealistic goals.

I. POLICY BACKGROUND

The U.S. and the Developing Countries.   The magnitude of the main components of U.S. concessional economic assistance is presented in Table 1. Bilateral assistance accounted for $5.2 billion or 77 percent of the total for the 1982 fiscal year. Within bilateral assistance, development assistance programs amounted to $1.7 billion, while food shipments under PL 480 amounted to $1.0 billion. The Economic Support Fund (ESF) accounted for the rest. This fund is administered by AID and involves economic assistance which has important developmental effects, but the primary justification for the assistance is the pursuit of broad U.S. foreign policy objectives. The bulk of this assistance (over 75 percent) is extended to Israel and Egypt. The bilateral development assistance program and, to a lesser extent, PL 480 have been the main instruments for the promotion of the U.S. strategy to support basic needs objectives in developing countries.

Policy implementation becomes confused when the analytical underpinnings of the policy are ill defined, controversial, or logically flawed. In the case of assistance policies aimed at helping developing countries better address their basic needs, there has been considerable confusion between basic human needs as an objective of development strategy, pursued by developing countries, and basic needs as an objective of U.S. assistance programs.

Helping address the basic needs of the poor in low income countries seems to have become a U.S. assistance objective before the development strategy that developing countries could pursue to attain basic needs objectives was fully articulated and understood, and despite the fact

TABLE 1:   U.S. Bilateral and Multilateral Assistance to Developing
Countries

[Budget authority is given in millions of U.S. dollars.]

	FY 1980 Actual	FY 1981 Estimate [a]	FY 1982 Request [a]
Development Assistance	$1,602	$1,712	$1,691
Economic Support Fund	1,942	2,104	2,548
PL 480	886	1,229	1,023
Sub-Total	$4,430	$5,045	$5,190
International Organizations and Programs (UN/OAS)	$ 260	$ 262	$ 189
MDBs [b]	2,568	1,266	1,579
Sub-Total	$2,828	$1,538	$1,768
Total	$7,258	$6,583	$6,958

[a] October 1981 estimate.

[b] Includes International Development Association, International Bank
for Reconstruction and Development, International Finance Corporation, Asian Development Bank, Inter-American Development Bank,
African Development Fund, African Development Bank, International
Fund for Agricultural Development paid-in; excludes callable capital.

that developing countries on various occasions have been openly hostile
to making such objectives the main basis for international cooperation.
This occurred in good part because of the fundamental humanitarian
appeal of an assistance strategy aimed at addressing the basic needs of
the poor to a small but important and vocal group of supporters of the
U.S. bilateral assistance program such as the private voluntary organizations, the Overseas Development Council, and specific supporters in
Congress, especially on the House Foreign Affairs and the Senate Foreign
Relations Committees.

Problems arose, because basic needs as an assistance policy objective
resting primarily on humanitarian considerations caught on quickly, and
ahead of intensive analysis of the development strategies that would best
achieve basic needs objectives in individual country settings.

Within bilateral development assistance, emphasis was placed on
programs and instruments which aimed at increasing directly the supply
of and access to goods and services consumed by the poor which appeared
essential to meeting their basic needs. These needs were assumed to
consist primarily of food, shelter, health, and education.

Projects in these sectors, often labeled "basic human needs projects," became the main U.S. assistance instrument for furthering the policy. This was facilitated by congressional support for existing bilateral programs which had already been focusing on agriculture, education, health, and family planning—sectors [2] called "direct impact sectors." These are all sectors whose output under certain conditions could be easily demonstrated to help relieve the worst aspects of human deprivation.

AID programmatic emphasis in these sectors antedated the development of the basic needs policy. Helping developing countries reach their basic needs objectives provided an explicit and easily comprehended rationale for continuing efforts in these areas. While Agency policy had for some time stressed the importance of increasing incomes and employment of the poor, this was fundamentally pursued only through activities in the aforementioned sectors.

Developing countries have had decidedly mixed responses to basic needs as a development policy in international forums. At the 1976 Conference on Employment, Growth, and Basic Needs of the International Labor Organization (ILO), there was ample support both for the promotion of basic needs objectives and for domestic and international policies that would further their achievement. At the Colombo Plan meeting in 1978 this support was reinforced. Similarly, individual countries implicitly or explicitly introduced such objectives in their own planning, and—with varying degrees of commitment and success—pursued supportive policies.

In various other international forums, however, including the United Nations and the UN Conference on Trade and Development (UNCTAD), developing countries were vocal in opposing basic needs objectives as something which they, with the support of the international community, would wish to achieve. Some were suspicious that the U.S. intention was to sidetrack discussion of issues that focus on the international distribution of income in favor of issues pertaining to internal distribution of income. Most developing countries consider the former an appropriate subject for international discussion and cooperation, but view the latter as undue intervention in sensitive domestic social areas. Still others viewed the emphasis on basic needs objectives as a desire on the part of the United States to promote a pattern of development that emphasized an essentially rural and backward production structure at the expense of industrialization and modernization. Thus they considered the basic human needs (BHN) policy as irrelevant at best and as undermining their own stated development objectives at worst.

Several other donors supported the U.S. assistance policy thrust more because they felt that, due to Congressional support, such a policy had a good chance of raising U.S. bilateral assistance levels, an important objective to them, and less because they were convinced that such an approach or objective was the most appropriate way to promote development.

Some Conceptual Considerations. Over time, some of the confusion pertaining to concepts, objectives, ends, and means seems to have been resolved.

It has always been clear that developing countries, themselves, must decide what their development objectives are, what weight they wish to place on enabling the poor to meet their basic needs, and over what time frame. The bulk of the resources that would be required to attain these development objectives would have to come from the developing countries themselves, for external assistance can play but a small part. Finally, developing countries' broad economic and social policies and institutional capabilities play a determining role in their success in attaining basic needs objectives.

What has become clear is that the strategy a developing country might follow to attain basic needs objectives would be quite complex and likely to vary from country to country. It certainly cannot be considered to be limited to policies aimed at increasing the supply of and access of the poor to goods and services which, when consumed, would result in a better satisfaction of basic needs. While the details of the development strategy that would best enable developing countries' governments to promote the achievement of basic needs objectives in individual settings are not well defined, some consensus has developed on a few key ingredients of such a strategy.

Perhaps the most important realization has been that fulfillment of basic needs objectives not only has to take place within a climate of overall economic growth, but also that a particular pattern of growth is desirable. This is a growth pattern that:

1) significantly increases the earned income of the poor over time, at least absolutely and possibly relatively;

2) results in increased overall supplies of goods and services that the poor consume, and which are essential to better meeting their basic needs;

3) requires that the poor obtain access to productive assets as well as to the increased supply of essential goods and services. [3]

Some corollaries can be derived from these key ingredients: the degree to which an internal redistributive process, i.e., internal transfers in cash or in kind, can be relied upon to promote the attainment of basic needs objectives would vary significantly from country to country. In the low income countries of Asia and Africa where the bulk of the poor are, such transfers cannot be relied upon to a significant degree. The countries are frequently too poor and the administrative mechanisms for the transfers are adequate. As a consequence, increasing the productive assets and incomes of the poor, whose main asset is their own labor, would require a growth process that provides increased and more productive employment. Furthermore, such a process would require that developing countries place relative emphasis on labor-intensive sectors and techniques of production.

In more advanced countries, especially in Latin America, there is a potential to redistribute assets and income, in the sense that income levels are relatively higher and the distribution of assets and income is skewed. But here the political structure sometimes does not permit such redistribution. At the same time, the same power structures which inhibit redistribution may also make the adoption of labor-intensive growth processes more difficult.

While increased supply of goods and services, critical to the satisfaction of basic needs, is a necessary ingredient, it is not sufficient to assure the success of the strategy. Increased output in a variety of other sectors which would increase overall income and employment of the poor is also necessary. This is true for a number of reasons:

1) The sectors whose output may need to expand to increase the supply of goods and services consumed by the poor, e.g., agriculture, while providing a significant source of income and employment for the poor, cannot usually absorb productively the currently unemployed and underemployed workers as well as future increases in the labor force;

2) Expansion of output even along this narrow set of sectors requires significant output increases in a variety of others sectors providing capital and intermediate inputs, e.g., road network, power, fertilizer.

3) If increased supply of goods and services consumed by the poor is not accompanied by increased employment and incomes for the poor, income redistribution policies will not be adequate to permit them to obtain the bundle of goods and services that would result in better satisfaction of their basic needs.

Some of this consumption of essential goods and services can be more accurately characterized as investment in human capital through better education, nutrition, and health, which contributes to longer term GNP growth through increased labor productivity. Moreover, when the poor obtain additional income, they may not necessarily use it to obtain goods and services which planners (or worse, foreign aid agencies) consider essential to the satisfaction of their basic needs. To obtain these objectives, both additional mobilization of internal and external resources as well as better allocation of resources would be required.

Assistance Program Implications.   This brief discussion of the key ingredients of a development strategy that could contribute to better satisfaction of basic needs demonstrates the complexities of the problem, and gives rise to a number of issues as to the proper focus on U.S. assistance programs aimed at supporting developing countries' efforts:

(a) Since no sector can be excluded a priori as a legitimate target of assistance, it is not possible to assert that the most effective way to help developing countries is to provide them with assistance in agriculture and rural development, health, and population—the direct impact sectors which also have been the sectors of emphasis in the AID program. Whether a given sector turns out to be a suitable target for economic assistance depends on how substantial are the linkages between the sector and achievement of basic human needs objectives, compared with alternative uses of assistance.

Agriculture is obviously important as a sector, especially in low income countries, because expanded production, when undertaken in small farmer-owner settings, raises both incomes of the poor and the supply of the main staple that they consume. However, all sectors employ labor. While most of the poor, especially in low income countries, are located in rural areas and depend directly or indirectly on agriculture for their livelihood, there is no presumption that agriculture is the only productive sector worthy of assistance. Policies and programs that increase productivity of the poor engaged in agriculture through the introduction of labor-intensive technologies are only one approach to the employment problem. Labor-intensive industry is another sector whose expansion tends to promote a substantial expansion in employment, especially where a larger portion of the poor is likely to be located in urban areas, and hence, not directly served by an emphasis on agricultural employment.

Furthermore, activities that provide productive employment depend on various types of infrastructure. Improving infrastructure, which ultimately makes a significant contribution to productive, labor-intensive activities, may need to be included among foreign assistance activities that receive top priority.

Achieving adequate supplies of food, housing, health, and education in the direct impact sectors is likely to depend on the availability of various materials, inputs in the form of public services, e.g., agricultural research and extension, credit facilities, and trained personnel (teachers, paramedics). AID programs already do a great deal of this. However, foreign assistance is needed in a variety of other sectors as well. In some countries the least costly approach to assure adequate food supply (or fertilizer supply) may be to produce and export some other goods and then import food consumed by the poor. This simple comparative advantage principle has often been lost sight of in drives toward self-sufficiency in food. While it is true that in many LDCs there are significant food distribution problems and increasing food production may provide more security in raising nutritional levels, opportunity costs of production should not be ignored in connection with basic needs strategies.

It is conceivable that a thorough overall assessment of a particular developing country's problems and prospects would reveal that U.S. development assistance should be allocated in the direct impact sectors for a number of reasons, including that the developing country or other donors are addressing effectively the employment problem outside agriculture. Indeed, an important component of AID's rationale for placing emphasis on these sectors had been that, given its size and the kind of programs other donors and the developing countries were undertaking, the sectoral emphasis discussed above is appropriate. But it is not legitimate to assume automatically that assistance extended to the direct impact sectors is in some ways superior to assistance extended in other sectors with respect to achievement of recipient's basic needs objectives.

b) AID's relative emphasis on activities in such service sectors as health and education has led to some criticism that such activities are nonproductive and welfare oriented.

If developing countries' governments are not willing to make the commitment that they continue support of such activities through the future allocation of their own resources in these sectors, such activities may indeed not be productive. On the other hand, properly conceived programs in these areas could be critical to the long-term human resource development of a recipient.

More generally, the point needs to be made that while it is proper to place emphasis on economic assistance activities that add to a recipient's productive capacity, there is always room for activities directed at current consumption because of their impact on future production. Future productivity can increase, e.g., by increased current nutrition of children, implemented by raising current food availabilities through PL 480. Indeed, if aid activities are undertaken only when they apparently add to investment instead of current consumption, the whole PL 480 program, which accounts for about one-third of U.S. bilateral assistance, would have to be questioned. But this is not the issue. The issue is the proper mix of activities in support of individual developing countries' policies, programs, and objectives.

c) Developing country macro and sectoral policies pertaining to budgetary allocation, prices of factors and products, and asset distribution have a direct and important bearing on the contribution that any individual assistance project can make, and have to be assessed prior to the undertaking of any aid activity. If these policies are incompatible with the achievement of the recipient's basic needs objectives, it is necessary to influence recipient government policies. For example, raising food production cannot be accomplished if prices to farmers are kept at depression levels to benefit the urban poor. Efforts to direct investment to labor-intensive activities will founder if domestic prices are distorted and/or the trade regime favors capital-intensive sectors or technology. Land tenure systems pose constraints both on increasing efficiency of production and improvements in income distribution. Moreover, progress in increasing supply of goods and services must be carefully balanced with efforts to raise the employment and income of the poor; otherwise supply may remain underutilized, or services may be co-opted by the rich or, if income gains outstrip the supply response, prices of goods may be forced up, resulting in no real change in consumer welfare. All this implies that adoption of a development strategy in pursuit of basic needs objectives will tax significantly the planning and implementation capacity of many developing countries, as well as donors' capacity to monitor, assess, and influence such a strategy.

d) In countries where the needs of the poor are great, but the existing power structure offers little opportunity for future improvement in their status, serious dilemmas arise. How does the United States design assistance programs that would have a lasting impact on the poor under the circumstances? Does the United States stay out of assistance completely despite the obvious needs of a significant segment of the population? One answer is to rely on direct impact activities and direct transfer programs. But while such programs may provide short-term remedies, they offer few prospects for lasting impact.

This discussion suggests that a proper interpretation of the development strategy that can promote the attainment of basic needs objectives requires a thorough assessment of the effectiveness of developing countries' policies, institutions, and commitment in support of basic needs objectives, prior to deciding what sectors to assist and how, and in which direction to influence recipients' policies. Program implementation issues thus arise at both the macro planning level and at the project level in connection with activities in the direct impact as well as other sectors.

II. PROGRAM IMPLEMENTATION ISSUES

Macroeconomic Policies, Planning, and the Role of Foreign Assistance Instruments. Better achievement of basic needs objectives depends primarily on a complex set of economic and social policies by the recipient, the development of appropriate institutions, and a political process that permits allocation of resources in ways that promote realization of these objectives. Assistance by any donor has to fit into and be supportive of developing countries' efforts. The particular aid program must be chosen from among alternative sectors and different potential interventions; effectiveness in promoting basic needs objectives can never be assumed. But chances of success are considerably enhanced if the macroeconomic policies and planning of the recipient are supportive. This is all perfectly obvious and applicable no matter what the particular thrust of the aid program. However, a number of policy implementation problems do arise.

Neither AID nor any other part of the U.S. government possesses a staff with the analytical capability to evaluate adequately development strategies, macroeconomic policies in aid recipient countries, and the optimal types of intervention that would promote the attainment of basic needs objectives by the recipients. Over the years, as the capacity of the developing countries to plan and execute broad development policies and programs has increased, the capacity of AID to interact at the national level with recipient governments has declined.

This has been recognized as a problem for some time. The previous response had been that AID would rely on the World Bank's (IBRD) macroeconomic policy judgment in individual countries and focus its attention on sectoral policies. Two problems stemmed from this:

1) A sectoral policy focus alone cannot substitute for a capacity to analyze macroeconomic effects of policies on the incomes of the poor, which play a critical role in the attainment of basic needs objectives.

2) The particular emphasis and policy concerns of the IBRD may well not be the same as those of AID.

Pari passu with the decline in the capacity to analyze developing country policies, and perhaps an important reason for it, came a decline in the aggregate size of development assistance programs. This decline was masked by the fact that supporting assistance programs, extended primarily to bolster short-term political security objectives—first in Vietnam and then in Israel and Egypt—have been rising in recent years relative to a decade ago. The average size of a country development assistance program in 1976–1978 was $10.1 million compared to $22.3 million in 1966–1968. If one takes account of developing countries' growth and inflation, the real size of the average program relative to the economies the United States assists is even smaller. [4] By contrast, the average size of supporting assistance activities over the same period more than doubled from $49.1 million to $117.7 million. [5] The decline in size in development assistance programs in turn implies a decline in capacity to affect developing country policy and resource allocation. Size alone is not a guarantee for influence or aid effectiveness. The most critical element is to have some useful advice. Also, the capacity of the United States or any other donor, including the IBRD, to induce significant policy or resource allocation changes in recipients is limited. At most, resource allocation can be influenced at the margin; and, given often competing policies and groups within recipient governments, it may be possible to strengthen the hand and support the policies of those groups most interested in pursuing policies that would better enable the poor to improve their living standard. It is this inability to influence macro and even sectoral policy at the margin which was lacking. The easy rationalization is that "AID was no longer in the business of making resource transfers" and that "this has to be left to the Bank."

There are a number of problems with this view: First, it is quite clear that, no matter what AID does, it makes resource transfers to developing countries. Thus, the question is the form and size of the transfers. Given that the size is relatively small, it may make sense to try to address critical institutional and technological constraints, rather than, for example, to support import programs whose impact on the poor may be indeterminant, especially since we do not have the capacity to assess the overall effectiveness of recipients' policies. However, larger size would obviously make it more possible to affect both policy and resource allocation of the recipient. Second, in the absence of U.S. ability to influence overall policy and allocation, there is no assurance that the impact of particular projects would not, in fact, be negated by overall developing policies. Third, even if AID were able to succeed in establishing particular activities which tend to increase output or services consumed by the poor, e.g., health, their long-term viability depends heavily on developing country commitment to channel resources to these institutions or sectors on a more permanent basis. This is especially important because the ratio of recurrent costs in some of these activities is quite high; hence they are not often self-sustaining and, therefore, require future budgetary allocations. In the absence of such policy commitment, which cannot be easily obtained, the long-term effect of such activities on the welfare of the poor may be indeed negligible.

It is thus ironic that the United States moved strongly to support basic needs objectives in developing countries at the very time when the bilateral resources it could bring to bear had shrunk in relative terms, and when both large additional resources and significant developing country policy changes were required to achieve these objectives.

Direct Impact Sector Issues.   In recent years the bulk of AID assistance has been provided through individual projects, focused on well-identified, specific problems in the areas of agriculture and rural development, education, health, and population. The process of implementation involved first, the identification of a problem; second, the provision of enough resources to address the problem in a particular locality; and, third, an effort to obtain commitments from the recipient government to replicate the activity on a larger scale. The sectors on which emphasis was placed were those which could increase the supply of goods and services important to the satisfaction of basic needs. They form the core of what AID does now and were considered the main thrust of the U.S. bilateral effort in support of basic human needs.

There are two types of implementation problems that arose with these traditional direct impact programs:

1) Inadequate Levels of Appropriate Staff. These activities usually require meticulous identification of social, cultural, economic, and political interrelationships which are commonly quite different from those of the donor. It was also felt desirable that target groups participate in defining their own objectives, though in practice such a collaborative approach has not been extensively used. To the extent that these objectives differ from those of the national government or the donor, delicate design and program compromises are needed. Similarly, this type of assistance frequently is intended to introduce technologies and/or values alien to local systems. Extreme care must be exercised in both the design and implementation phases to enhance prospects for a successful project. For all these reasons, it was necessary to employ highly qualified and trained staff, especially in the social sciences, to implement aid activities. AID had very limited numbers of such staff.

A related problem was that such projects not only required a staff different from that previously employed in the Agency, but also required more staff because the amount of analytical input per dollar outlay in aid funds is significantly higher than that required to implement a large capital-intensive hydroelectric project or a program heavy in commodity imports. However, there were significant constraints on increasing staff. Both the Executive Branch and Congress were wary of personnel increases, irrespective of program justification. Furthermore, Congress had imposed ceilings on Agency operational costs. This posed a constraint on moving more Agency personnel to field missions to design and implement projects, since it is far more expensive to maintain personnel in the field than to keep them in Washington, and gave rise to the need to reevaluate the overall system of Agency program implementation.

2) Lengthy Implementation Periods. The period of implementation is the time it takes to design, obtain congressional approval, negotiate agreement with the recipient, and fully disburse program funds. Projects of this type would appear to have significantly longer implementation periods. Often the design and execution phases blend into each other, since such projects require continuous refinement procedures. [6] If the projects require institution building of some sort, the process will be even slower. AID generally considers a minimum of five to eight years necessary to launch successfully an institution with outreach at the local level.

Some projects with immediate and direct impact on local population do disburse rapidly. Examples have been vaccination and fertilizer projects or other activities involving financing of imported inputs. In general, however, project activities have taken a long time to implement. AID experience in the last ten years shows that the average total time for fully implementing a project loan was 46 to 52 months. On the other hand, "Program" and "Sector" lending typically has been implemented in about a third less total time. To the extent that direct impact project activities account for a larger portion of the current AID portfolio, implementation periods in the future may well rise.

Constraints on the speed of the program implementation, combined with constraints on the kind of activities and sectors that can be supported, having given rise to a further problem: assistance is increasingly being sought and extended through the Economic Support Fund rather than the Development Assistance program in countries requiring significant amounts of external support across a broad development front, as well as where it is desirable to address quickly foreign exchange constraints that are limiting long-term development. While such aid is also, to the extent possible, supposed to help recipients address basic needs, there tends to be generally less rigorous economic conditioning because, presumably, assistance from ESF is designed primarily to promote U.S. political security objectives. This has contributed to the present situation where the size of the bilateral assistance program under ESF is significantly higher than under the Development Assistance program.

Finally, a few words should be added on a topic which has been identified as a potentially serious issue, but which, to my mind, is not a substantial problem. The concern has been that foreign donors would substitute their preferences of what constitutes basic needs for the preference of the ultimate beneficiaries of the assistance—the poor in developing countries. Others have been concerned with the same issue but from the opposite perspective. The poor in developing countries, perhaps due to ignorance of the existence or the impact of alternatives, have a disconcerting habit of spending their meager incomes in ways which do not maximize nutritional values or meet health or other standards. A number of writers have argued that under such circumstances it is appropriate for developing countries' governments, and presumably donors, to provide or help provide some so-called "merit goods" gratis or at a reduced cost in order to increase information through demonstration and thus ultimately "improve" the consumption patterns of the poor. [7]

The broad issue then has been how much should the developing countries' governments, and donors, interfere with the present market allocation system to affect consumption patterns in general, and of the poor in particular. This is a thorny issue which gives rise to many specific problems: How does one evaluate consumer preferences when informational systems are inadequate? How does one treat services normally supplied through the private market? What is the role for government intervention in each? How does one increase participation of the poor in the decision-making process, so that their interests will be respected in public resource allocation which directly impinges on their welfare?

This has not been a problem for the U.S. bilateral assistance program because the program is typically so small that it alone does not tend to affect existing patterns of consumption for better or for worse. Its usual demonstration-experimental nature means that it is up to the recipient to pick up on a large scale or abandon. It is the responsibility of the recipient government to determine whether it meets the needs of its poor or not and how the poor could let their government know about their needs and affect its decisions on what to do about them.

However, the PL 480 program is often significant enough to affect consumption patterns and dietary habits. This program has tended generally to have a beneficial impact on nutrition standards. The problem that can arise results primarily not from a conflict between the United States and the developing country's views of what is better for its poor to consume, but rather between our interest in expanding exports and the recipient's consumption and production patterns. This problem, however, seems to arise less frequently in recent periods when development concerns have been more explicitly introduced in the PL 480 program.

Indirect Program Approaches. Outside of the agriculture sector, which is very important in low income countries, AID has limited recent experience with activities aimed at addressing basic needs indirectly, through means that increase income and employment of the poor. There have been some efforts in Latin America to promote agribusiness activities as well as rural public works programs, but these have been limited in scope. AID has had extensive experience in infrastructure support, but such activities have been questioned by Congress unless they seem to be closely related to activities which directly influence agricultural production by low income farmers. As a result, a good deal of AID's involvement in infrastructure has been limited to construction of secondary rural roads.

There is a fundamental implementation problem for activities outside the traditional sectors; many in Congress, and some in AID, do not believe that such activities can be useful in promoting developing countries' basic needs objectives, or that the U.S. bilateral program should be involved in them even if the ultimate payoff in terms of jobs or productivity is high. One of the reasons appears to be the belief that there is more certainty in dealing with direct impact programs. In other programs, the links to basic needs are not obvious, cannot be easily demonstrated, and work through the entire economic system, which AID has limited capacity to analyze.

The second implementation problem is that the Agency has limited experience in developing activities aimed at increasing employment in industry. Thus, even if the necessity to generate increased employment through a variety of means has become generally accepted, there is little that AID has to offer. This is a particularly acute problem because there is evidence that some of the technology needed to increase agricultural yields per acre, especially in grains, which AID is helping introduce, is actually less labor intensive than traditional forms of subsistence farming. As a result, serious unemployment problems can be expected to continue and perhaps even increase in severity, unless systematic efforts to increase employment opportunities are undertaken, both in the rural and urban sectors. [8]

III. INTERACTION ISSUES

Human Rights.   During the Carter Administration it was U.S. policy to give special consideration in the allocation of economic assistance to countries with a good or substantially improving record on human rights and less favorable consideration to countries with a poor or deteriorating record. Thus, there was supposedly a symmetry in the treatment of good performers and bad performers. The way this policy worked in practice was as follows: on the positive side, a government's commitment to promotion of basic needs was viewed as support for one element of human rights—that which pertains to basic economic and social rights. AID took this into account in its process of allocating development assistance. Thus, there was a clear link between support of basic needs development objectives and human rights; and it was argued that the United States positively encouraged observance of rights, especially economic rights, through its normal aid allocation policy. But this positive encouragement received less attention than the negative U.S. response in cases of violation of human rights. In these instances, the rights involved are primarily personal and political, e.g., the right of the individual to be free from government violation of the person; the right to enjoy freedom of thought, religion, assembly, or speech.

Foreign assistance legislation calls for the United States to withhold assistance from developing countries which are judged to violate flagrantly the human rights of their citizens, unless the assistance involved activities that "will directly benefit the needy people." Thus, the reaction was not entirely symmetrical. The United States did little positively to promote personal and political human rights through assistance; it did so primarily through denial of assistance in cases of violations. But with respect to economic rights the U.S. response was symmetrical by incorporating commitment to basic needs objectives as part of its regular development assistance allocation. Moreover, it continued to extend assistance, on strict humanitarian grounds, through direct impact programs even when there were violations of political and personal rights.

This policy has come under considerable criticism from a variety of directions. Some viewed it as hypocritical, because human rights considerations were given short shrift when other U.S. interests were important. Others viewed it as detrimental to U.S. interests because it tended to introduce what they considered extraneous ethical considerations into the realpolitik of international relations.

There are many problems, ambiguities, and issues and a lot of room for clearer understanding, especially of the linkages between developing countries' policies on personal and political rights and policies affecting economic rights. One of the problems is that the policy of denying assistance was more symbolic and less a deterrent which seriously affected economic prospects of recipients. This was true for two reasons: first, the U.S. bilateral program was and is typically too small to affect materially overall economic prospects; second, the multilateral institutions programs are usually larger, but given the voting structure of these institutions, our opposition usually is not sufficient to prevent the programs from going through. However, one should not underestimate the cumulative and, one hopes, consistent effect of symbolic gestures in exerting international pressure.

Another issue concerns the possible differences in developing country commitment to different types of human rights. The most common divergence occurs in countries which may have a significant commitment to addressing basic needs through a variety of policies, but whose support of political and personal rights is suspect. An example is Korea. There may be others and more may exist in the future. Some would argue that this divergence is not possible, and that economic rights will only be safeguarded if individuals are free to participate fully in the political process and there are adequate safeguards of personal freedom. And yet there are problems since few countries, even those with laudable performances on political and personal rights, have attained the type of equitable growth patterns characterized by Korea under a regime whose practices on human rights have often been questioned.

A further issue arises in the context of providing exceptions to violators of political and personal rights if the "aid activities directly benefit the needy people." The problem is the following: a development strategy has many components, of which policies and programs that directly impact on the welfare of the poor are a part. It is quite possible that general policies of a government negate the effects of aid aimed at directly helping the poor. On the other hand, it is conceivable that the best way of helping the poor may be through indirect programs and policies aimed at providing increased employment and incomes. If the overall economic policy structure would permit the poor to benefit from such programs there may be a case for continuing assistance.

During the early stages of implementing human rights policies, an effort was made to identify the type of basic needs projects that would qualify for aid, even when there were other human rights violations. Fortunately, this effort was abandoned when it became clear that projects and programs must be viewed in the total context of the recipient's economic, social, and political policies.

There is no easy substitute for intensive analysis of individual countries. However, the basic human needs project syndrome is difficult to get away from. In implementing policies toward multilateral development banks, the United States repeatedly voted against certain projects in individual country settings because the countries had been suspect on human rights grounds. At the same time, the United States provided bilateral assistance through the ESF because of the importance of these countries to the United States in a total foreign context.

International Trade.   The link between basic needs strategies and U.S. international trade policy is employment in labor-intensive export industries of developing countries. Increased developing country employment is a key element in the success of a basic needs strategy. In turn, employment increases in developing countries can be promoted by outward-looking industrialization strategies. A series of case studies undertaken under the direction of Anne Krueger provides abundant recent evidence in support of the traditional hypothesis that export industries in developing countries are more labor intensive than competing import activities; and that developing country trade and domestic policies that encourage, or do not discourage, exports can play a role in expanding their total employment.[9] Thus, U.S. support for developing country policies that encourage exports of labor-intensive goods can be a significant means for promoting the attainment of basic needs objectives.

Herein lies the policy problem and dilemma that faced the United States in the recent past. The U.S. government has been under significant pressure from both industry and labor to protect U.S. industries, especially from labor-intensive imports of developing countries. A large portion of U.S. industry demands for tariff protection as well as action on counter-vailing duties has been focused on labor-intensive products from develop-ing countries. The countries whose trade is most frequently challenged are Taiwan, Korea, Mexico, Brazil, and India. These are all countries which have either made significant progress in promoting employment through an export orientation, or, as in Mexico and India, in which it is in the U.S. interest to promote employment, both in pursuit of basic needs objectives and in order to relieve pressure on immigration to the United States. Other countries further down the industrialization ladder will soon follow.

The U.S. response to such pressure has been mixed. Only a limited number of the requests for protection has been granted. On the other hand, there are nontariff barriers to expansion of developing countries' trade in textiles and shoes. And while the average tariff level on develop-ing countries' products is only about four percent, there is tariff escalation and the nominal tariffs on individual countries such as Taiwan and Korea are higher (11 percent and 13 percent, respectively).

The United States has traditionally avoided integrating its develop-ment and its trade policies. The former have been usually addressed through foreign assistance instruments. The latter have been funda-mentally guided by other principles although their impact on development is frequently much larger than that of development assistance.[10] It is quite clear that a policy that supports developing countries' exports of labor-intensive manufactures is in the U.S. domestic interest and also supports the attainment of basic needs objectives. While imports of labor-intensive products do cause some domestic adjustment problems, there is strong evidence that these problems are miniscule in comparison to the problems of adjustment due to technological and demand changes faced by U.S. industries. This is particularly so of those competing with de-veloping countries' labor-intensive imports.[11] A key challenge to the United States in the future would be whether it will be able to resist domestic protectionist pressures and in so doing promote broad U.S. economic interests, as well as support developing countries' efforts to address their basic needs.

CONCLUSION

This general review of issues that arose in implementing a U.S. assistance policy supportive of basic needs concludes with policy suggestions. These focus on the limitations of past policy and how, given these limitations, it could have been pursued more effectively.

1) Given present and likely levels of U.S. economic assistance, the impact that the United States can make in helping developing countries

promote their basic needs objectives is decidedly small. Thus, we should guard against undue raising of expectations that are implied by such goals as eliminating poverty, or eliminating hunger by the year 2000. Such goals are not and cannot be the goals set for the development assistance program.

2) The obstacles that need to be addressed require both significant policy changes on the part of developing countries and significant additional resources, most of which have to be provided by the developing countries. The present U.S. bilateral program is often too small to exert a policy influence or to have an impact on developing country resource allocation. While we should not exaggerate the importance of constraints arising from overall lack of resources, at the same time larger volumes of aid, and perhaps higher concentration of resources, will make us better able to pursue these objectives.

3) Increased assistance levels need to be complemented with appropriate policies in other spheres, especially trade, whose impact complements and frequently may be even more important than that of economic assistance.

4) The development strategy that is appropriate for individual developing countries in pursuit of their particular objectives is varied and complex. Thus, there are no easy answers, nor are there any easily identifiable lists of sectors that best promote these objectives.

5) The U.S. bilateral program should develop more flexibility in terms of the forms of assistance used—project vs. sector vs. program lending—as well as with respect to the areas of concentration. Program type assistance may well be very appropriate for countries in which we are quite convinced that both their overall policy commitment and their institutional development are helpful in addressing their basic needs objectives. Limiting assistance to basic human needs sectors or projects reflects a narrow view of the development process, and will have increasingly undesirable results. Given likely constraints in total staff size, it might become more and more difficult to implement and disburse quickly a rising level of assistance commitments. In light of the obvious needs of developing countries in a variety of sectors and the rigidities inherent in the current program, it is likely that pressure will increase for additional aid resources to be allocated to the Economic Support Fund. The economic impact of aid from this fund can be potentially as great as that from the Development Assistance program, but in practice this is not the case. In implementing ESF activities there are considerable political pressures to commit aid resources to particular activities, irrespective of the economic policies of the recipient and the contributions of the aid to the attainment of basic needs objectives.

6) Increased flexibility does not imply that aid should be provided

for all types of activities regardless of the capacity of the United States to provide it. We may still wish to concentrate on particular sectors in which we have the ability to assist more effectively, e.g., agriculture, but such decisions must be made on the basis of a thorough examination of alternative interventions, after detailed analyses of developing countries' overall policies and prospects. There are significant personnel constraints which limit AID's capacity to undertake both the broad-gauged macro-economic policy analysis and the intensive microanalysis needed. It is urgently necessary to address these personnel needs in order to improve the effectiveness of our assistance policy.

7) Assistance policy that aimed at helping developing countries better meet basic economic needs was an important part of U.S. human rights policy. While a number of policy conflicts arose in implementing these policies, the United States has been making slow but steady progress in integrating human rights concerns in the pursuit of its overall foreign policy. The issues that did arise result from the complex relationships between developing countries' commitment to economic rights, on the one hand, and political and personal rights, on the other. Given the complexity of individual situations, great care is needed to undertake intensive analysis of these relationships prior to taking any actions to support or withhold assistance from any country.

Notes to Chapter 8

1. The author wishes to acknowledge helpful comments by Charles Paolillo, Antonio Gayoso, and Michael Crosswell on an earlier draft of this paper. This paper, however, expresses solely the personal views of the author. Nor does it necessarily reflect policy of the U.S. Agency for International Development.

2. A distinction needs to be made between assistance activities to Less Developed Country (LDC) sectors whose output can have a *direct impact* in expanding supplies of goods and services the poor consume and *direct transfer* activities which involve transfering the output itself, e.g., food. AID does the former; PL 480 involves primarily the latter.

3. For a detailed discussion of these issues, see Michael Crosswell, "Basic Human Needs: A Development Planning Approach," AID Discussion Paper No. 38, October 1979.

4. AID's bilateral assistance can be divided into Development Assistance and Supporting Assistance (now called Economic Support Fund). Only about half of the development assistance is in country programs. The other half goes for worldwide technical assistance activities (including some for population), operating expenses, and other noncountry-oriented activities. The average country program figures understate slightly the actual AID in-

volvement in individual countries. However, this does not materially affect the conclusions either about the absolute size or the trend in the size of the program over the last decade.

5. The decline in the average size of development assistance programs occurred despite an increased concentration. In 1966–1968, 82 countries received development assistance compared to 55 in 1976–1978. By contrast, the number of countries receiving supporting assistance remained constant at 15.

6. This discussion draws heavily on Antonio Gayoso's "Aid Instruments—A Review of their Implications for Speed of Program Implementation," AID, December 1978.

7. See Danny Leipziger and Maureen Lewis, "The Basic Human Needs Approach to Development." Paper presented at the Western Economic Association Meetings in Hawaii, June 1978; also Paul Streeten, "The Distinctive Features of a Basic Needs Approach to Development," Basic Needs Paper No. 2, IBRD, August 1977.

8. See John Mellor, *The New Economics of Growth* (Ithaca, N.Y.: Cornell University Press, 1976).

9. Anne Krueger, "Alternative Trade Strategies and Employment in LDCs," *American Economic Review* 68, 2 (May 1978): 270–275.

10. An interesting case of policy integration occurred in Korea. Korea was asked to "voluntarily" reduce its exports of textiles in exchange for receiving a significant amount of PL 480 assistance. In Sri Lanka on the other hand, AID had been strongly supporting the local government's efforts to increase employment while other parts of the U.S. government were considering steps aimed at curbing the expansion of Sri Lanka's textile exports to the United States, which perhaps offer the best prospects for increasing Sri Lanka's urban employment opportunities.

11. See Anne Krueger, "LDC Manufacturing Production and Implications for OECD Comparative Advantage," paper prepared for the Conference on Prospects and Policy for Industrial Structure Change in the U.S. and other OECD Countries, Department of State, Washington, D.C., January 1979.

BRIAN H. SMITH

9. U.S.-Latin American Military Relations Since World War II: Implications for Human Rights

INTRODUCTION

The purpose of this chapter is to analyze major aspects of U.S.-Latin American military relations since World War II and their impact on human rights observance in the hemisphere. To accomplish this, major ideological and policy objectives of U.S. strategy will be traced, indicating how they differed or coalesced with Latin American military and development goals, and assessing to what extent U.S. military assistance and training programs have helped or hindered the promotion of human rights in the Americas.

The essay is divided chronologically according to major time spans so as to ascertain shifts in emphases and tactics of the United States: 1) pre-World War II, 2) immediate postwar years, 3) Cold War period—1947–1960, 4) the era of the Alliance for Progress—1961–1968, 5) the Nixon years—1969–1974, and 6) new congressional and presidential initiatives between 1974 and 1980.

Throughout, three recurring themes are highlighted as underlying U.S. policy:

1. U.S. security interests in Latin America since World War II have always been heavily influenced by the global strategic concerns of this country, namely, the containment of communism, the maintenance of close military relationships with Western allies, the enhancement of conditions favorable to U.S. private investments, and U.S. access to raw materials in the Third World.

2. Human rights objectives that have been given emphasis in recent years have roots in earlier concerns in U.S. dealings with

Latin America—official U.S. preference for formal democracies in the Americas, a desire for limits on the sale of sophisticated weapons, and encouragement to Latin governments not to divert resources away from economic development to arms production and purchases.

3. Seldom over the past 35 years has there been a consensus within the U.S. Government (among State, Defense, Congress, and the Office of the President) as to what should be the priorities in our Latin American policy, and current disagreements among these departments over human rights objectives are affected by these perennial differences.

I. PRE-WORLD WAR II PERIOD (1890–1940)

For 50 years prior to World War II, Germany and France were the major foreign influences on Latin American military thinking and training. Beginning in the late nineteenth century and the early part of the twentieth century, German military missions were invited to several Latin countries—Chile, Argentina, and Bolivia—to train the various branches of the armed forces in these countries. The French performed the same function in Peru and Brazil, particularly after World War I.[1] The skills and technology provided by these German and French missions helped to professionalize the Latin American military. The missions emphasized in their training that military men were morally superior to civilians and that they had a major political and economic role to play in the development of their countries.

During this period German and French military strategists developed theories of geopolitics in their own military schools and transmitted to Latin America many of these ideas—namely, that defense required development of economic, political, and social resources, that the state was a living organism constantly growing and in need of geographical space, and that civilian populations must be organized effectively to meet the ends of the state and the nation.[2] None of these ingredients of continental geopolitics placed emphasis on the civil and political rights of citizens. They also inculcated a strong sense of nationalism among the Latin military and inspired them with a vision of their own importance as leaders for the integration of their societies. Such perspectives and strategic thinking continue to shape the attitudes of the Latin military and form an important part of current national security doctrines taught in Latin American military academies.

United States military presence was concentrated primarily in the Caribbean in the period after the Spanish American War of 1898. It was closely associated with the promotion and protection of North

American business interests, especially in countries such as Nicaragua, Panama, Haiti, Cuba, and the Dominican Republic. In each of these countries, U.S. troops engaged in various types of expeditionary missions and also had a major role in training national guard and police units. [3] Such incursions by U.S. military forces ceased during the first Franklin Roosevelt administration in the mid-1930s, when a Good Neighbor policy of mutual respect and nonintervention was emphasized by the United States regarding Latin America. [4]

During World War II close working relationships between U.S. and Latin American military representatives were established. Bilateral military defense agreements between the United States and Latin American nations included lend-lease agreements of $450 million in arms and equipment for seven countries, the inauguration of U.S. training missions for military personnel from a number of republics, and U.S. support for the construction of air and naval bases in 16 countries that were to be utilized by the United States during the war [5]

From the Latin American side large quantities of strategic war materials were provided to U.S. wartime industries, and Latin America sent more than 50 percent of its exports to the United States during World War II. A 25,000-member Brazilian expeditionary force served in the European theater in close collaboration with allied military forces, and a series of high-level meetings were held just prior to and during the war by foreign ministers of the American republics to coordinate efforts against Nazi agents and prepare for a possible Axis invasion of Brazil. [6] All Latin American states entered the war on the side of the Allies, although Argentina waited until 1945.

By the time the war began, all U.S. expeditionary forces in the Caribbean had been withdrawn and there was greater mutual public respect between Latin America and the United States. By 1941 all Axis military advisory missions in the Americas had withdrawn. In their wake the United States established bilateral security relationships with most Latin American countries and in return received important strategic support from them during the conflict.

II. IMMEDIATE POST-WORLD WAR II PERIOD (1945–1946)

In the immediate post-World War II period strong differences of opinion emerged within the U.S. government regarding the strategic importance of Latin America to North American security. With the defeat of the Axis powers, the President and his national security advisors paid little attention to Latin America. In their perspective, U.S. hegemony was secure and there was no danger of any foreign interference in the hemisphere. The Defense Department, however, wanted to transfer its surplus weapons to Latin America and thus standardize armaments throughout the Americas. Furthermore, 100,000 military and civilian personnel from the United States had been diverted to Latin America to coordinate united defense efforts during the war. The U.S. military now wanted to withdraw some of these personnel for more crucial security work elsewhere and prepare the Latin military to take over their own defense against any future external threat. The State Department opposed such strategies, arguing that arms shipments to Latin America would drain Latin resources away from economic development and also help keep authoritarian rulers (such as Trujillo in the Dominican Republic and Perón in Argentina) in power, thus hindering the chances for democracy. Because Latin America was a low security priority, and because State and Defense disagreed, Congress took no action on the proposed Inter-American Military Cooperation legislation of 1946. [7]

III. COLD WAR PERIOD (1947–1960)

Although long-standing U.S. concerns about Russian communism were submerged during the war efforts against the Axis powers, by the late 1940s all major decision-making centers in the U.S. government became increasingly preoccupied with the emerging Cold War and the threat of further Soviet expansion in Europe. The first priority of defense was Western Europe, but Latin America came to be seen as an important piece of this overall strategy to contain communism. Within the U.S. government there was a desire for a united hemispheric defense against possible external attack, particularly from Russian submarines. In such a context, the State Department's objections to the transfer of weapons to Latin America were subordinated to the Department of Defense's desire for uniformity of arms and technology throughout the hemisphere and for an expanded capacity for Latins to defend their coasts.

Two major meetings took place among representatives of the American republics in the late 1940s—the Rio Conference in 1947 and the Ninth International Conference of American States in Bogotá in 1948. It was clear, however, that at both of these gatherings the objectives of the U.S. representatives differed from those of the Latins. In each instance, it was evident that the Latin delegates had as their major goal the establishment of effective regional mechanisms which would both limit U.S. dominance in military affairs, thus preventing future U.S. military intervention, and serve as a means of channeling public resources from the United States into economic development in Latin America on a large scale. Security concerns and the containment of communism were not their major preoccupations. Rather they wanted something like a Marshall Plan for Latin America.

U.S. representatives, however, refused to grant massive economic aid, given the postwar belt-tightening in the United States and its commitment of several billion dollars to the reconstruction of Europe. President Truman at Rio de Janeiro and Secretary of State Marshall at Bogotá both stressed the importance of private domestic and foreign investment as a better means to engineer development in Latin America. The United States also opposed a defense system in the hemisphere which functioned collegially, preferring to establish bilateral agreements for arms transfers and training between itself and each Latin country. [8]

The U.S. perspective prevailed, since the resources for both military and economic programs would have to come from Washington. At Rio the Inter-American Treaty of Reciprocal Assistance was signed which established the principle that an external attack on one member nation would be considered an attack on all. No effective multilateral structures for collective military action were established, however. At Bogotá the following year the Organization of American States was formed to provide ongoing exchanges of information and opinion on a regular basis among foreign ministers of member nations, but the United States gave no guarantees for major economic assistance. Resolution XXXII of the Final Act of Bogotá, moreover, declared that "by its interventionist tendency, the political activity of international Communism or any totalitarian doctrine is incompatible with the concept of American freedom . . . ," and encouraged each member state to adopt measures "to eradicate and prevent activities directed, assisted, or instigated by foreign governments, organizations or individuals." [9]

Hence, in the late 1940s the Latin Americans sought to prevent future U.S. military intervention in their countries as had transpired during the interwar period, and wanted substantial foreign public support to speed up national economic development in their societies. The United States, however, was more concerned with security agreements against possible outside intervention into the hemisphere by the Soviet Union and with guarantees for private investment opportunities throughout the Americas.

Different priorities characterized these respective positions. For the Latin Americans national political sovereignty vis à vis U.S. hegemony and state-supported economic growth were of great importance. For the United States democratic governments and free enterprise were paramount. These different emphases have continued to affect inter-American relations and they help explain some of the present disagreements between Latin American military governments and the United States regarding human rights. [10]

With the outbreak of the Korean War in 1950 the United States began to establish bilateral agreements with several Latin countries for military assistance. The rationale in the Office of the President and in the Defense Department was that while the United States was engaged in police action in Asia, it needed to protect the safety of Latin American raw material supplies for its own war efforts, and it had to help Latin military organizations perform tasks the United States would otherwise have to carry out in the hemisphere. The Mutual Security Act of 1951, therefore, authorized $38 million for the fiscal year (FY) 1952 to set up military assistance programs (MAPs) for Latin America. This aid included grants of arms and equipment, credits for purchasing weapons and technology, and U.S. Army, Navy, and Air Force missions to train Latin American forces. Such assistance did not include tanks, jets, and large naval vessels. These were needed in Korea and in Europe, and the State Department opposed the transfer of such items to Latin America for fear of stimulating a competitive arms race among neighboring countries. [11]

After the Korean War the Defense Department proposed that such arms transfers and training for the Latin American military continue. New arguments were made to Congress which included the need for the United States to obtain missile tracking stations in Latin America and the desirability of preventing Latins from purchasing new weapons elsewhere as post-World War II vintage U.S. equipment (previously given or sold to them) became obsolete. The Pentagon also claimed that U.S. training of Latin American officers, in Panama and in the United States, could help to inculcate democratic attitudes and promote respect for civilian governments. Military regimes in Argentina, Venezuela, and Colombia had all handed over power to civilians in the late 1950s and the Pentagon knew that Congress, State, and the Office of the President all wanted to reinforce such movements toward constitutional government.

Finally, the Defense Department said that ongoing military assistance could protect internal security within these nations and also guarantee U.S. access to needed raw materials. [12] The military assistance to Latin America was renewed each year by Congress in the 1950s and by the end of fiscal year 1959, 20 countries had received a total of $317 million, and approximately 9,000 Latin American personnel had received some form of training from the United States. [13]

With the ebb of Cold War hostilities by the late 1950s, however, congressional opposition to military aid to Latin America increased and strong arguments were made by some senators, particularly Wayne Morse and Frank Church, that such assistance only helped to promote dictatorial forms of government and repress civilian opposition to such regimes. Morse was instrumental in putting into the Mutual Security Act of 1958 a clause that explicitly rejected granting military aid to promote internal security in any Latin American nation. It stated that: "Internal security requirements shall not normally be the basis for military assistance programs to American Republics." [14] Senator Morse and Congressman Charles Porter, however, were unsuccessful in getting Congress to pass a concurrent resolution in 1959 to give military assistance only to those Latin countries having representative governments. [15]

Amidst this mounting criticism of continued military aid, President Eisenhower appointed a blue ribbon committee, composed mainly of active and retired military personnel, to study the pro's and con's of such assistance to third world countries. In 1959 this group, known as the Draper Committee, published its recommendations, strongly in favor of continuing military assistance programs. The Committee argued that for economic development to occur, order and stability were essential. For the first time in U.S. public policy, a close link between security assistance and economic progress was made, thus rejecting positions previously espoused in the State Department that these were virtually incompatible. The Committee advocated an expansion of U.S. training of Third World military personnel, and concluded that to abandon the program, for mistakes in execution or for any other reason, would be to abandon the Free World and to lose the Cold War. [16]

Parallel to this new emphasis by the Draper Committee on the link between security assistance and economic development was a similar but more sophisticated trend among several Latin American military establishments. War colleges or institutes in Argentina, Brazil, and Peru, founded in the late 1940s and early 1950s, were reinforcing some of the themes that had been part of their education during the 51-year period when German and French military advisors were training their officers.

The course of studies in these institutions by the mid-1950s included not only military strategy and tactics, but also economics, political science, management, and industrial planning. The rationale was that national defense had to be coordinated with, and include, development of all sectors of the country needed to support potential war efforts. Furthermore, these academies taught that in order to prevent communist mobilization of the poor in their societies, major reforms were needed in banking, industry, agriculture, education, and politics, and that the military might very well be superior to civilian leaders in accomplishing these needed structural changes. In some cases, civilian students were admitted with military officers into these classes (Brazil), while in other cases (Peru) civilian economists and political scientists with reformist (and sometimes anticapitalist) attitudes actually taught courses to the military. [17]

Although the United States through its MAP program gave some initial advice and technical assistance in setting up the Brazilian Escola Superior de Guerra (ESG) in 1949, its influence in developing the type of security doctrine emphasized in the courses was not preponderant. The chief strategist of the ESG, General Golbery do Couto e Silva, drew heavily upon French and German writings published during the pre-World II period and during the Indochina and Algerian struggles. He also modified and adapted this body of literature to the Brazilian situation, emphasizing such uniquely Brazilian problems as development of the Amazon region. [18]

Furthermore, in Peru at the Centro de Altos Estudios Militares (CAEM), founded in 1950, no U.S. military advisors had a hand in the establishment of the school or in the development of the curriculum. General Marcial Romera Pardo, the professor of CAEM most influential in the elaboration of its theories in the 1950s, had studied at the Superior War School of Paris and drew heavily upon French geopolitical writings in his teaching. Under his tutelage in the 1950s CAEM emphasized the importance of eliminating illiteracy, sickness, and hunger among the rural poor in Peru so as to strengthen the nation's moral and physical resources for defense. The goal was integral security, which linked adequate military strength to the provision of social and economic needs of the poor. Running through the courses at CAEM were strongly nationalistic currents highly critical of foreign private capital and dependent economic relationships that limited the rights of the Peruvian state to determine its own course of development. [19]

French military advisors began teaching at the Argentine Escuela Superior de Guerra in 1957, preceding by several years U.S. military instructors. At the Centro de Altos Estudios (CAE) for Argentine colonels (founded in 1943), emphases on current social, economic, and political problems appeared in the curriculum by the 1950s.

Hence, by the end of the decade three of Latin America's largest military establishments in Brazil, Peru, and Argentina had begun to develop their own security doctrines. While some U.S. influence was having a reinforcing impact, especially the Cold War emphasis on anti-communism, much of the ideology was a mixture of the old German and French geopolitics, nationalism, anticommunism, and a desire on the part of the military to make a contribution to economic development. Well before the Alliance for Progress and the expanded training of Latin American military personnel by U.S. officers to take part in civic action programs, the Latin military themselves were doing serious thinking about their future role as managers of national development. While some emphasis on social and economic rights was included in this strategic doctrine, particularly by the Peruvians, much more priority was given to the rights of the state to expand its field of competence and act as an autonomous arbiter of national development.[20] National security doctrine prominent today in the Southern Cone region of Latin America, as described in Chapter 3 in this volume, was well underway 20 years ago and not simply created by the U.S. Department of Defense.[21]

IV. ERA FOR THE ALLIANCE FOR PROGRESS (1961–1968)

When John Kennedy began his presidency, Latin America was one of the first priorities on his foreign policy agenda. Castro's successful insurrectionary war in Cuba, and his subsequent option for an alliance with the Soviet Union, sent political and emotional shock waves throughout the hemisphere. It was a clear sign that North American economic and military hegemony could no longer be guaranteed effectively by the transfer of conventional weapons to Latin America along with traditional training of Latin officers and enlisted men to fight external invasions. In addition, many Latin Americans felt that the Eisenhower years were a period of neglect, and there was growing resentment of U.S. values and power, dramatically expressed in Caracas in 1958 when Vice President Nixon was stoned by an angry crowd.

When Kennedy took office, he and his advisers quickly sought a new aproach in order to prevent proponents of revolution in Latin America from capitalizing on discontent, chronic poverty, and growing animosity toward the United States. Within two months of his inauguration the president announced plans to begin an Alliance for Progress throughout the Americas which would entail the transfer of large amounts of U.S. capital and technology for development projects in Latin America. It would encourage governments to undertake major internal structural reforms within a democratic framework so as to make this outside aid an effective catalyst for change on behalf of the poor.

Simultaneously, the State Department prepared a policy paper entitled "Internal Development and Defense," which laid out a strategy to involve military forces in Latin America intimately in the development process. The paper argued that in order to combat wars of insurrection, counterinsurgency tactics had to be taught to Latin armies and police forces. It also proposed that these same groups be employed in civic action programs in the countryside, building roads, schools, clinics, and improving communication networks. Three goals would thus be achieved: 1) important infrastructures necessary for development and private investment would be established; 2) basic services would be provided for the poor, thus diminishing their potential support for revolution; 3) the energies of the military would be channeled into useful development programs and civilian-military relations would thereby be enhanced. Counterinsurgency campaigns again communist or nationalist guerrillas in the Philippines, Indonesia, and Malaya had all pointed to the necessity of removing the causes of insurrection, such as poverty, and of winning the support of the civilian population both for the government and the military establishment. [22]

Behind this thinking at State (and the Pentagon) was the belief that for the Alliance for Progress to succeed, internal stability and the prevention of guerrilla war were essential. The earlier suggestions and arguments of the Draper Committee were now accepted as policy. The Department also hoped that by enabling the Latin American military to become more professionalized and technically competent, with a special role of their own in the development process, they would become less interested in intervening in politics and less inclined to carry out coups against civilian governments. It was assumed that this policy would not only help defeat guerrillas, create publicly funded infrastructure for private investments, and provide social services for the poor, but would also inculcate democratic attitudes and support for civilian government among the Latin American military. [23]

Thus, the same objectives of U.S. foreign policy in Latin America expressed in the late 1940s—security against communism, hegemony of private investment, and the promotion of democratic governments—were all reinforced by the Alliance for Progress and by the concept of internal development and defense. The major differences in the Kennedy strategy were that more U.S. government economic grants and loans would be given to promote these objectives and that the Latin American military could be incorporated into achieving such goals.

For the first time since World War II there was a strong executive coalition—Office of the President, the State Department, and the Department of Defense—joined by a Congress acquiescent to a consistent U.S. policy toward Latin America. Economic loans and grants were significantly increased as a result, [24] and new equipment for counterinsurgency efforts (helicopters, trucks, jeeps, light arms, communications technology) were transferred to Latin America. Training programs for Latin military personnel were also greatly expanded, including preparations for riot control, intelligence gathering, surveillance techniques, and psychological warfare. By the mid-1960s there were over 1,300 U.S. military personnel in Latin America (as compared to 800 in 1959), providing training and advice for Latin military, and two-thirds of the MAP program proposed for 1967 ($48 million of $71 million) was directed to internal security or civic action activities. [25]

The total expenditures for training Latin American military personnel between 1951 and 1967 reached $91 million. Over 36,000 officers and enlisted men from 20 different countries received some form of training during this 16-year period, with approximately half of them being educated in Panama and the rest in various installations inside the continental United States. The countries with the largest number of personnel in this program (IMET) include Brazil (5,518), Peru (3,751), Colombia (3,133), Nicaragua (3,044), Ecuador (3,042), and Chile (2,882). [26] In addition to training, between 1963 and 1967 $421 million in arms grants and sales were provided to countries throughout the hemisphere, with Brazil ($110 million), Argentina ($70 million), Peru ($49 million), Colombia ($44 million), Chile ($43 million), and Venezuela ($43 million) receiving 75 percent of the total. [27]

The concept of defense in the Americas quickly shifted away from preparations against an external invasion or coastal attack to strengthening internal security and development. The Morse amendment in the Mutual Security Act of 1958 against such a rationale for military aid was put aside. [28] The dominant feeling both in Congress and in the State Department was that the armed forces in Latin America were not threats to democracy, but rather immediate bastions against radical revolution as well as nation builders through their contribution to economic development.

The U.S. Army Caribbean School at Fort Gulick in Panama, founded in 1949, changed its name in 1963 to the U.S. Army School of the Americas to reflect its wider scope of interest in the hemisphere. It also significantly expanded its Latin American enrollment and reoriented its curriculum to offer training in rural counterinsurgency and civic action. [29] In 1962 the Inter-American Defense College was founded at Fort McNair in Washington, D.C., offering annual ten-month courses for 40–60 colonels, lieutenant colonels, and some civilians, focusing on strategic, economic, social, and political problems of Latin American republics. In the same year the International Police Academy was begun in Washington and offered training to Latin American police personnel including techniques in counterinsurgency warfare and surveillance. [30]

In addition to the transfer of new types of technology and training to Latin American military personnel, networks of communication and cooperation were also expanded. In 1963 the Central American Defense Council (CONDECA) was established to provide a structure of continuing coordination of regional defense efforts among all five Central American countries with U.S. military installations in Panama. The

Permanent Commission of Inter-American Military Communications (COPECOMI), set up under U.S. aegis, provided more effective radio communication among all military installations in the hemisphere, closely tied to the Panama Canal Zone. Mobile Training Teams (MTTs) of U.S. military personnel were authorized to train Latin American forces in their own countries in counterinsurgency tactics, and one such mobile team assisted the Bolivian army in successfully eliminating a guerrilla force led by Che Guevara in that country in 1967. [31]

There is no evidence that this expanded military aid and network under U.S. tutelage included methods of torture or other inhumane techniques to control the civilian population. Nor is there any proof that U.S. military officers training or advising the Latin Americans during the 1960s actively encouraged them to intervene in politics or overthrow civilian governments. Three things, however, are true: 1) the course content of training programs involved a high degree of anticommunist indoctrination; [32] 2) the organizational skills and managerial capabilities of the Latin American military vis à vis civilians were significantly upgraded; and 3) the type of technology and arms the Latin American military received from the United States significantly increased their ability to wield potentially repressive power inside their own countries. [33]

U.S. military training in the 1960s, therefore, reinforced currents already present in the security doctrines of several Latin American military establishments—mounting antipathies toward those espousing radical or Marxist solutions to societal injustices, predilections toward an expanding role for themselves in guiding their countries, beliefs that they were equally if not more competent than civilians to manage the complexities of development. These reinforced attitudes, along with sophisticated techniques and technologies which the United States provided to control the civilian population, contributed to a type of professionalization that was conducive to a more active political role for the military in Latin American society. [34]

What is also fact is that not only did military forces in Latin America during these years carry out a series of coups against civilian governments (Peru, 1962 and 1968; Guatemala, 1963; Ecuador, 1963; Honduras, 1963; Dominican Republic, 1963 and 1965; Argentina, 1962 and 1966; Brazil, 1964; Bolivia, 1964; Panama, 1968), but that a new style of military intervention was emerging in several of these countries by the mid-1960s. Unlike traditional Latin American coups that resulted from infighting within the armed forces or strong urging by civilians in opposition parties (and which tended to be short-term in duration), the coups that occurred in Brazil in 1964, Argentina in 1966, and Peru, in 1968 were different in purpose and style. In each of these cases the military acted as a relatively unitary force and avoided promises of prompt elections and a return to civilian government. In all of these instances the military announced that civilian politicians were no longer capable of directing the process of national development and that they themselves planned to stay in power for some time in order to insure stable and equitable economic growth.

Structural crises precipitated these military coups, brought on by rapidly rising demands for a more equitable share of wealth and power by workers and peasants; refusal on the part of many landed, industrial, and financial groups to accept economic changes benefiting the poor; mismanagement of reform efforts by some civilian politicians; and expanded activities by guerrilla movements. In such circumstances, the security doctrines developing inside war colleges and institutes of advanced military studies in countries such as Brazil, Argentina, and Peru provided important legitimation for a new style of military intervention in government. Those who engineered coups in these countries argued that effective internal security required efficient mobilization of all critical sectors of the economy and population under centralized control. They also claimed that they themselves, due to their experience in managing complex organizations and carrying out development projects in the interior of their countries, were the most qualified persons to oversee this process of centralized control. Normal civilian procedures and constitutional mechanisms, they argued, were inefficient, corrupt, or infiltrated by Marxist ideas. [35]

Concomitant with this new trend in civil-military relations in the mid and late 1960s in several of the larger military establishments in Latin America, was the development once again of contingency plans by U.S. military personnel for possible intervention in Latin countries should crises be too much for national military establishments to handle on their own. Such plans were elaborated for Colombia during unrest there in 1962. In Brazil in 1964, U.S. troops stood ready to assist in the coup if necessary. [36] In 1965 U.S. armed forces did intervene in the Dominican Republican to help crush a popular revolt against a military regime on the grounds that the insurrection was controlled by communists, although subsequent evidence did not substantiate this conclusion. [37]

By the end of the Johnson administration in 1968 the threat that rural guerrillas would overthrow existing governments had substantially subsided in Latin America. The scenario of other Cuban type revolutionary movements coming to power was more remote, although for a time urban guerrilla movements caused considerable concern by carrying out bank robberies, kidnappings, and terrorist activities in Brazil and the Southern Cone region. Efforts by the United States to encourage major structural reforms by democratic governments in the hemisphere, however, had met with mixed success. Furthermore, counterinsurgency training and experience in civic action by military forces in several countries had not reduced the likelihood of coups but rather had expanded the capability and inclination of military officers to take a more active and directive role in the political process of their countries.

Finally, networks of communication and collaboration between U.S. and Latin American military representatives were not contributing to greater support for civilian governments, nor to greater noninvolvement in domestic Latin affairs by the U.S. government. While the use of torture was not yet widespread nor the effect of greater military involvement in the development process on socioeconomic rights yet clear, confidence in civilian government and constitutional procedures by many Latin American officers had diminished considerably.

V. THE NIXON YEARS (1969–1974)

With the decline of the threat of successful guerrilla wars spreading throughout Latin America, with several stable military governments in place in the hemisphere, and with U.S. involvement in Vietnam at its peak, the Nixon administration took a rather pragmatic approach to Latin American relations, giving them a low priority among its foreign policy concerns. A study group headed by Nelson Rockefeller visited several Latin American countries during Nixon's first year in office and concluded that "the question is less one of democracy or the lack of it than it is simply of orderly ways of getting along." Their final report suggested that a new brand of military was emerging in Latin countries that was reformist and should be supported by the United States as the best way of preserving stability and preventing a reemergence of a communist threat. Finally, the group recommended that the United States continue to give security aid to military governments along with weapons, on the grounds that other countries would do so if the United States decreased its assistance. [38]

Important members of Congress did not agree with this approach, however. As congressional criticism of the Nixon administration's escalation of the Vietnam war increased, so did its opposition to the president's easy acceptance of military governments in the hemisphere. Senator Church conducted an extensive review of U.S. military aid programs for the Foreign Relations Committee in 1969, challenging the Rockefeller Report's recommendations for continued security assistance to military governments in the hemisphere. Some of the former arguments against military aid from the 1950s reappeared in Congress, namely, that such assistance merely encouraged authoritarian governments and thereby went against fundamental democratic principles and constitutional government espoused by this country. [39]

In congressional hearings during the late 1960s and early 1970s, administration spokespersons (civilian and military) disagreed. They claimed that continued military assistance was necessary to insure stability in the hemisphere, to maintain influence with Latin military leaders and keep open the lines of communication with them now that they were important political actors running their countries. This argument was made particularly in reference to Chile after the election of Salvador Allende in 1970, when U.S. military argued before Congress that it was important for them to solidify lines of communication with the Chilean military to promote U.S. interests against a Marxist government. [40]

Congress was reluctant to accept these claims, however, and a series of amendments was added to foreign assistance legislation just before or during the first Nixon Administration limiting military aid and arms sales. The Conte amendments to the Foreign Assistance Act of 1967 prohibited the United States from transferring sophisticated weapons systems (e.g., missiles, jets) to any underdeveloped country, and called for reduction in economic assistance to any poor nation by the amount spent by its government on such arms. The Fulbright amendment (1967) placed an annual ceiling of $75 million on military grants and sales from the U.S. government to Latin America. The Symington amendment (1968) cut military sales to countries that diverted excessive resources to defense spending. The Reuss amendment (1972) disapproved of all military sales that would strengthen dictators who were denying the growth of fundamental rights or social progress to the people. [41]

The results of these congressional efforts, along with a desire on the part of the administration to take a lower profile in Latin America and therefore to withdraw many of the U.S. military advisors in the hemisphere, was that the military grant assistance program (MAP) fell from $75 million annually in 1966 to $6 million in 1971. However, during the same period the administration sold more nonsophisticated weaponry to Latin American military forces that were useful for maintaining internal security and controlling civilian populations. In 1966 foreign military sales from the U.S. government totaled $85 million, whereas in 1973 they reached $150 million. [42]

After 1968 there was undeniable evidence from Brazil that some of this nonsophisticated technology being sold by the U.S. government or by private U.S. businesses was being used by the Brazilian military to engage in systematic violations of the personal rights of their citizens. In 1971 a Senate investigation found that not only were repressive measures increasing in Brazil, but that U.S. training programs and technology transfers included censorship methods, clandestine operations, defoliation, electronic surveillance, use of informants, espionage and counterespionage, interrogation of prisoners and suspects, and undercover operations. An Amnesty International report in 1972 on the state of human rights in Brazil concluded that systematic use of torture was widespread in that country, and suggested that U.S. police training and technology had contributed to the apparatus being used to carry out such repression. [43]

What also was becoming clear by the early 1970s was that the new economic model of development under way in Brazil that had produced an annual growth rate of 9 percent between the 1964 coup and 1971, and which was being watched closely by other Latin American military for possible adaptation in their own countries, was placing a great burden on the poor. During this seven-year period, despite impressive gains in overall production and in controlling inflation, real purchasing power of workers declined, peasants and Indians were being deprived of land and employment in favor of large agribusinesses, and basic social services were not being provided to large sectors of the population by the government. Not only were civil and political rights being violated systematically but socioeconomic rights were not being fulfilled for large numbers of people. It was becoming clear that political repression was essential in order to sustain such a model of development. [44]

The reaction of Latin American military to a decreased interest in Latin America manifested in the executive branch, to congressional criticisms of internal domestic policies in their countries, and to the new limits on the amount and types of weapons they could purchase from the United States, was a mixture of bewilderment and annoyance. In some cases (Uruguay, Argentina, Brazil, and Central America) military leaders believed that guerrilla activities and the threat of an eventual communist takeover were still very real. They had been encouraged and trained by the United States to fight counterinsurgency war and argued that they still needed the arms and technology to do so. Even in cases such as Peru, Bolivia, Venezuela, and Colombia, where the possibility of armed revolution had been eliminated or significantly reduced by the late 1960s, the military continued to search for a new justification to modernize and maintain their expanded installations and technology. Civic action and counterinsurgency activities did continue, but new arguments for arms and training were based on general national defense, border protection, and preparations for conventional war. [45]

Behind these arguments were resentments by the Latin American military of technological dependency on the United States. By the late 1960s and early 1970s, the geopolitical thinking in advanced colleges and institutes of war in Argentina, Brazil, Peru, and Chile as well, was stressing the importance of national autonomy, or at least flexibility, in maintaining a sound defense policy. Too heavy a dependence on one source of weapons or technology was regarded as a severe limitation for fighting a war, especially if that source of supply—the United States—refused to grant or sell all the equipment which the Latin military considered essential for their security. These criticisms were strongly voiced by both Argentine and Peruvian military representatives in Caracas in 1973 at the Tenth Conference of American Armies. They called for more tolerance within the hemisphere, especially by the United States, for the respective security interests of each nation as defined by its own leaders. [46]

Between 1968 and 1972 both Brazil and Argentina launched substantial programs for domestic arms production with increased federal allocations for such efforts and with assistance from private business firms and investors from abroad. By the mid-1970s both of these nations were in a position to export some of these weapons to other Latin countries and to the Middle East (Iraq and Libya), including ammunition, vehicles, and planes. [47] During this same period the Latin American military increased arms purchases from Europe, [48] thus diminishing their traditional dependence on United States suppliers. Table 1 gives a comparative overview of the amount and percentage of weapons imported by Latin American countries from various nations in the North Atlantic region.

This policy of neglect toward Latin America by the Nixon administration, combined with mounting congressional criticisms of arms transfers and training programs, made Latin military establishments more intent on seeking aid elsewhere. It also had no effect on reducing their propensity to overthrow constitutional government or refrain from

TABLE 1: Arms Transfers to Latin America Valued at $1.627 Billions, 1968–1972

[Amounts given in millions of U.S. dollars.]

	Amount	Percentage	
United States	$334	20.5%	
Great Britain	548	33.7	
France	441	27.1	
Canada	145	8.9	79.5%
West Germany	105	6.5	
Italy	54	3.3	

Source: U.S. Congress, House, Committee on Foreign Affairs, *Hearings, Mutual Development and Cooperation Act of 1973*, 93d Cong., 1st sess., 1973, pp. 147, 197–198.

regressive tactics. Military coups continued to occur during the early 1970s throughout the hemisphere, in Bolivia (1971), Ecuador (1972), Uruguay (1973), and Chile (1973). In all of these interventions except Ecuador, new military regimes engaged in systematic violation of civil and political rights of citizens.

Moreover, the brunt of the oppression was felt most directly by those groups that had been most active and outspoken in proposing more equitable distribution of income and resources in favor of the poor in their respective societies—labor leaders, organizers of peasant coopera- tives, reformist party representatives, and students. While arguments were made, especially in Uruguay and Chile, that strong repressive measures and a suspension of constitutional guarantees were necessary in order to prevent an imminent Marxist takeover of these countries by force, the extent and prolongation of the repression and the harsh economic measures that followed in the wake of these military interventions were an indication that the armed forces had something more in mind.

In the case of Chile the military were determined to change the trends in economic development of the past decade and wanted to over- turn many of the reforms begun in the Frei administration in the 1960s and accelerated by the Allende government in the early 1970s. After September 1973 public expenditures for such basic human needs as health care, nutrition, and education were curtailed, prices were allowed to rise at a much faster rate than wages, publicly owned enterprises were sold to private speculators, and land reform ceased, with many cooperatives given back to the original private owners or divided up into inefficient and unviable plots for small farmers. Repression of civil and political rights continued long after any possible danger of armed insurrection was eliminated and became an integrally necessary part of inaugurating a style of development that violated the social and economic rights of the poor. [49]

By the end of the Nixon administration, therefore, it was evident that many of the assumptions of both the Alliance for Progress and the Rockefeller Report regarding the Latin American military were incor- rect. U.S. training in counterinsurgency tactics, civic action programs, and greater exposure to U.S. military personnel had not professionalized the Latin armed forces in the style of U.S. military behavior—namely, made them more respectful of democratic values and procedures and also less inclined to intervene in politics.

Except in Peru,[50] no other Latin American military government in the late 1960s or early 1970s carried out economic or social changes that directly benefited workers, peasants, or other low income sectors of their societies. Furthermore, freedom and privileges for U.S. private investments in lucrative extractive industries were not guaranteed by the coming to power of these governments. In the case of Peru, Ecuador, and Chile the military inaugurated or continued policies of nationalization of enterprises engaged in extracting and developing critical natural resources such as copper and oil.

The only assumption on the part of U.S. policymakers that proved to be correct was that, by increasing military aid and arms transfers and training, communist and leftist movements in the hemisphere could be eliminated or substantially brought under control. Once this limited objective was achieved, however, and the United States began to focus its security concerns and assistance on other parts of the world (Southeast Asia, the Middle East), the expanded military machines that it had helped to create in Latin America did not atrophy. The proportions of national budgets devoted to defense remained fairly constant or in some cases increased, [51] and other Western arms suppliers proved most eager to take up where the United States had left off in supporting Latin American armies.

Furthermore, it was clear that some Latin military leaders had definite plans to continue in power for some time in countries such as Brazil, Peru, Bolivia, Ecuador, Uruguay, and Chile. The role expansion and institutional growth of the military that had occurred during the Alliance for Progress, along with the continual development of security doctrines—reinforced in part by U.S. training—that gave them a rationale for managing the development process, had led to some perhaps unforeseen negative consequences for both civil and political and socioeconomic rights in the hemisphere.

VI. NEW CONGRESSIONAL AND PRESIDENTIAL CONCERN FOR HUMAN RIGHTS (1974–1980)

After 1973 new coalitions within the Congress, the State Department, and the Office of President emerged to make human rights concerns a major priority in evaluating military assistance programs and arms transfers to Latin America. Many of these concerns were rooted in perennial preoccupations with promoting democratic forms of government in the hemisphere, dating back to the post-World War II period in the State Department and Congress. There was, however, some uneasiness with these policies among U.S. military leaders, some of whose arguments were rooted in traditional U.S. security priorities regarding hemispheric strategy—standardization of weapons, defense against Communism, access to raw materials, ongoing communication, and cooperation among military leaders throughout the hemisphere.

Opposition to congressional and presidential emphases on human rights as a condition for further military assistance also arose among

Latin military leaders themselves, and these too were in continuity with what Latins, both civilian and military, have been saying for well over 30 years: U.S. interventionism in the domestic affairs of Latin America is wrong and Latin Americans have the right to determine their own course of economic and political development.

Beginning in 1974, Congress began to focus attention on rights violations in several parts of the world, but Latin America was a major area of concern due to the proximity of the region and the publicity which repression in several Latin countries was receiving in the U.S. media. Pioneer work in heightening congressional awareness of the human rights issues in the Americas was done by Congressman Donald Fraser and his staff on the Subcommittee on International Organizations of the House Committee on International Relations. In late 1973 and throughout 1974 the Subcommittee held hearings on rights violations in Chile and Brazil. In 1975 similar hearings were conducted on Uruguay, and in 1976 on Nicaragua, Guatemala, El Salvador, Paraguay, and Argentina.

In those countries where the military had just recently come to power (Chile, Uruguay), or had returned to power after a brief civilian interlude (Argentina), or had engaged in new forms of repression after having been in power for some time (Paraguay, Brazil, Nicaragua, Guatemala, El Salvador), the patterns seemed to be the same: communist subversion, real or potential, was being used as a justification for systematic torture, murder, arbitrary detention, and disappearances. Civilians in labor unions, opposition parties, peasant leagues, and student movements were suffering the brunt of this repression, and economic measures placing a low priority on basic services for the poor were being imposed.

As a result of the information gathered in these hearings, congressional support was marshaled to place further restrictions on military aid, in spite of opposition from the White House. The International Security and Arms Export Control Act of 1976 stated as a "principal goal of the foreign policy of the United States" the promotion of "increased observance of internationally recognized human rights." The act further stated that U.S. military aid programs should be administered in ways which both "advance human rights and avoid identification of the United States, through such programs, with governments which deny to their people internationally recognized human rights and fundamental freedoms." The legislation therefore forbade, except where the president believed the national security of the United States required otherwise, any security assistance to a government which has a "consistent pattern of gross violations" of such rights. It also mandated an annual report to Congress from the State Department on the status of human rights observance in all countries receiving U.S. security assistance, and established in the Department a Coordinator for Human Rights and Humanitarian Affairs. [52]

In 1977, after Congress enacted specific legislation that suspended security assistance to Uruguay and Chile, Brazil, Guatemala, and El Salvador all announced that they would not accept further U.S. security assistance. Tying military aid to a positive human rights report card, they argued, was an unjust interference in the domestic affairs of their societies and a violation of national sovereignty. [53]

The election of President Carter in late 1976 gave an impetus to congressional critics of U.S. military aid and arms sales to Latin America since the new chief executive made human rights the cornerstone of his foreign policy. He also announced in May 1977 that the curtailment of the sale of conventional arms to foreign countries was a major goal of his administration and that such sales and transfers could no longer be considered a means to achieve diplomatic ends. One of the functions of the new Cordinator for Human Rights and Humanitarian Affairs which the Congress established in 1976 inside the State Department was to assist in reviewing requests from private U.S. companies wishing to make arm sales to Latin American countries and to evaluate these in terms of what impact such technology could have on furthering repression against civilians.

After President Carter took office, the Congress began to move against private arms sales abroad. It imposed new legal limits on the commercial export of technology directly associated with repression. The State Department also ceased giving licenses to private U.S. companies to sell napalm, incendiary munitions, flame throwers, silencers, radiological weapons, or delayed action explosives in Latin America. [54]

With the dramatic decline of military grants, credit sales of arms, and training available for Latin American military from countries with serious rights violations, the number of U.S. military personnel serving in advisory capacities in Latin America was substantially reduced. In 1968 there were 769 U.S. military advisors stationed in Latin America, whereas in 1979 there were fewer than 100. [55] The number of Latin American officers, cadets, and enlisted men receiving training at the U.S. Army School of the Americas in Panama also diminished substantially in the late 1970s. In 1976 there were 1,777 in the School, but in 1979 only 782, and in early 1980 under 600. [56]

One result of this steady decline of U.S. security assistance and training was that Latin America, which accounted for over 7 percent of total U.S. military aid in 1967, dropped to 4.8 percent in 1977 and to 1.3 percent in 1979. After 1974, however, European, Israeli, and Soviet arms sales increased steadily, along with domestic production and exports in both Argentina and Brazil. As of 1979, the U.S. share of arms transfers to Latin America was down to about 15 percent of the total. Moreover, the Brazilians, Argentines, Peruvians, and Chileans all were providing more training for military officers and personnel from Central American countries, as well as for Ecuador, Bolivia, and Paraguay. This not only helped to offset the decline of aid and training formerly available from the United States, but also provided important export earnings as well. [57]

Thus, Latin American military leaders in the late 1970s were pursuing objectives in line with security doctrines emanating from their own war colleges—namely, elimination of heavy dependence on sole sources of supplies, promotion of national sovereignty and independence from outside intervention in domestic affairs of their countries, and significant military involvement in the process of economic and social development. Military establishments in several countries have become more independent of U.S. control, and have found more than willing sources of arms and technology elsewhere.

Criticisms of the current restrictions on military assistance voiced by the Pentagon also have roots in longstanding objectives of the U.S. military in the hemisphere—namely, access to raw materials, communication with allied military leaders, elimination of communist influence, and control over the style and amount of weapons flowing into the region. Testifying before a House subcommittee in 1978, Admiral Gordon Schuller stated that long-term U.S. interests in Latin America were not being given sufficient attention. He stated that:

> Our security interests in Latin America are high and we must not lose sight of the fact that sea lines of communication which connect NATO and the Middle East pass through the South Atlantic. The state of our security relationships with Latin America impact on our ability to effectively control these sea lines of communication. Therefore, our U.S. military objectives are to preclude the establishment of military power bases hostile to U.S. interests, maintain access to regional resources, avoid intraregional hostilities, and maintain secure lines of communication. [58]

While stating that he was in favor of the human rights policy of the United States, he also claimed that he did not always agree with the manner in which it has been carried out. [59]

Other spokespersons for the Pentagon and the State Department argued before Congress in early 1980 that a renewal of U.S. training programs and military sales and credits for Latin America were needed at the time to re-establish friendship bonds with Latin American military leaders, to check the influence of third country supplies of arms and training in the region, and to influence positively the attitudes of Latin American junior officers in favor of U.S. values and interests. Strong arguments were also made to renew both IMET and FMS programs in El Salvador, Guatemala, Honduras, and in the eastern Caribbean to strengthen the capacities of the military in these countries to maintain internal security and thus offset what the Pentagon believed to be growing Marxist-oriented insurrectionary or political movements. [60]

The Office of the President supported this position. In the aftermath of developments in Iran and Afghanistan in 1979, the administration did not want in 1980 (an election year) to be accused of "losing" additional countries to U.S. influence, especially those bordering on the Caribbean basin close to our shores. It was also concerned about what it first believed to be significant Cuban support for guerrilla movements in Central America, although no solid proof was given to Congress to substantiate this charge. Moreover, the administration was reluctant to stand back and watch other Central American and Caribbean countries follow in the socialist-oriented path of Nicaragua for fear of the restrictions on U.S. private investments that this might entail. [61]

Under the Reagan administration, several of the global strategic and economic considerations that have perennially affected U.S. security policies toward Latin America are once again prominent factors shaping the positions espoused by the Office of the President, the Department of Defense, and the State Department. The perceived threat of communism, the desire for continued contact and communication with military allies, the preoccupation with securing access to raw materials, and the desire to promote stable investment opportunities for the export of U.S. capital have all re-emerged as major considerations.

It is not yet certain what congressional reaction will be in the decade of the 1980s to these arguments from the executive for renewal or increased security assistance to Latin America. It is clear, however, that the momentum of 1976 and 1977 to give human rights priority over security issues in U.S. foreign policy toward the Americas had dissipated by early 1980.

VII. THIRTY-FIVE YEARS OF U.S.-LATIN AMERICAN MILITARY RELATIONS: IMPLICATIONS FOR HUMAN RIGHTS

The previous historical analysis of U.S.-Latin American military relations since 1945 indicates that simplistic judgments about past correlations between security assistance and human rights in the Americas are impossible. The following observations do seem to be in order, however, and are based on the evidence that exists. They are also necessary to clarify projected future impacts of U.S. security assistance on human rights in the hemisphere.

1) Despite the stated intentions of U.S. policymakers to make Latin American military more apolitical and more respectful of democratic values, security assistance to date has not contributed to this objective nor is it likely to in the future. U.S. training and technology have enabled many Latin American military organizations to become more professionalized and more effective in curbing insurrectionary movements. Such assistance has also contributed to an upgrading of managerial skills and development techniques and to an increased capacity to exercise coercive power against civilians.

None of these skills nor the exposure to U.S. military officers, however, has led to a decline of intervention into politics on the part of Latin American officers. Such assistance and interchanges have also not induced a greater respect on their part for democratic processes and civilian-controlled government. In fact, in several countries in the hemisphere the military have used equipment and techniques previously provided by U.S. security assistance to violate internationally recognized human rights of their fellow citizens.

The U.S. government is therefore responsible for some of these negative consequences of its previous security assistance on human rights observance in Latin America. Moreover, arguments proposed by some U.S. policymakers for renewed military aid in the future so as to positively influence younger Latin American military officers in favor of democratic and humane values are on weak ground. Past experience indicates that the possibility of affecting attitudinal changes among Latin American military men by U.S. training and interchanges are minimal. No solid evidence exists to indicate that future attempts will prove otherwise. [62]

2) Very different rights priorities have long characterized U.S. policymakers and Latin American military leaders. These are not likely to change quickly, nor to be affected significantly by either the granting or the withholding of security assistance in the future. When U.S. government leaders have taken human rights into account in past statements and policy formulations involving Latin America, they have emphasized the importance of civil and political rights. This has been due in large part to the priority these rights have in U.S. cultural and political traditions. The Latin American military, however, have been far more concerned wtih the rights of the state to pursue societal goals of internal security, economic growth, and national autonomy.

While these latter sets of rights are not necessarily incompatible with the former, the way in which highly nationalistic Latin American military leaders perceive the nature of threats to such societal goals has led to their adoption of measures which violate or limit civil and political rights of citizens. These perceptions are due in large part to social and political crises in their countries and to the nature of the national security doctrines taught in their own academies that give priority to the rights of the state over those of individuals.

These different emphases are also due to the measures they have chosen to pursue economic growth—suppression of union activities, limits on wages and salaries, curtailment of public spending on social services. Such policies have been necessitated in part by demands of foreign creditors, private banks and international public lending institutions, such as the International Monetary Fund,[63] that Latin American countries control inflation, increase exports at comparative advantage, and improve balance of payments.

While such austerity measures please large landholders, industrialists, and financiers in Latin America, they cannot satisfy the basic needs of the majority of workers and peasants. Limitations on civil and political rights are seen by the Latin American military as essential to prevent sustained opposition by these latter groups to unpopular methods that are damaging their own survival. Were the military in Chile, Brazil, Argentina, Paraguay, Uruguay, and Guatemala to accede to U.S. pressures for open and free elections, multiparty competition, and complete freedom for the media, the pursuit of economic growth at the cost of not meeting the basic needs of the poor would be much more difficult.

The military in such countries, therefore, resent emphases on civil and political rights by many U.S. government spokespersons and the curtailment of U.S. military assistance until these rights are restored. They consider this both a lack of sensitivity to their internal security problems as they perceive them and a misunderstanding of the costs of economic growth—a type of growth which is sustained by, and is a benefit to, many economic interests in the United States.

Regardless of the correctness of the perceptions of Latin America military about the range of political and economic options available to them, the different emphases on rights priorities between themselves and U.S. policymakers are real and long-standing. Neither granting nor withholding security assistance by itself is going to reconcile these differences. Other critical factors would first have to change, e.g., the viability of insurrectionary movements, emphases in Latin American national security doctrines on the rights of the state over those of the individual, austerity-inducing policies of international private and public lending institutions, and more equitable sharing of the costs of development by all social classes in Latin American society.

3) It is not self-evident that curtailing U.S. security assistance has led to an improvement in human rights observance nor to a decrease

in arms transfers and military training opportunities in Latin America. It has, however, helped to disassociate the United States from governments which violate the rights of their citizens. According to the State Department, some of the more brutal violations of individual rights (torture, disappearances, arbitrary arrests, and long-term imprisonment) declined in 1978 and 1979 in countries such as Brazil, Chile, Argentina, Uruguay, and Paraguay. [64] While a denial of U.S. security assistance continued in all of these countries, other critical factors were also at work, e.g., decline in the viability of insurrectionary movements, mounting internal opposition to authoritarian rule, diplomatic representations by foreign governments, pressures of international public opinion, and limitations on bilateral public economic aid from several Western nations.

It is difficult to assess, therefore, what positive impact cuts in U.S. military assistance had in this process of decompression in comparison to other converging factors. In some cases (Argentina, Brazil, El Salvador, and Guatemala) denial of security assistance precipitated strong denunciations, and probably made military leaders in these countries less, not more, disposed to U.S. views on human rights. [65]

Moreover, it is clear that third-country suppliers of arms and training (France, Great Britain, West Germany, the Soviet Union, Israel, Italy, Spain, Brazil, and Argentina) have quickly filled the gap left by a decline in U.S. security assistance. The type of weapons provided by such suppliers has undermined previous U.S. efforts to limit the flow of expensive and sophisticated weapons into the region. There is also no reason to believe that the form of training given by countries such as Brazil, Argentina, and France (especially to the police forces) is any less repressive in its potential for violating personal rights of civilians than that once offered by the United States, and may very well be more so.

Hence, just as the United States cannot be exonerated from some responsibility for the repressive tactics used by several Latin American military establishments in the past, it cannot by itself curb arms buildups, defense spending, or potentially repressive military training in the hemisphere in the future. So long as there are demand and willing suppliers elsewhere, this trend will continue.

Denial of U.S. security assistance to countries with poor human rights records in the hemisphere, however, has contributed to one important purpose articulated in the International Security and Arms Export Control Act of 1976, namely, avoiding "identification of the United States through such [military] programs with governments which deny to their people internationally recognized human rights." [66] In the legislation this goal is placed on an equal par with the other objective, the positive advancement of human rights. Even if the latter goal has not been clearly enhanced by denial of U.S. security assistance, the former objective has, and this is frequently overlooked by critics of U.S. human rights policies who are unfamiliar with the wording of the legislation. While more limited in scope than the latter, its symbolic importance is significant since at least some legitimizing support by the United States for repressive Latin American regimes was reduced. Moreover, official U.S. contributions to human rights violations by Latin American military are less now than prior to the 1976 legislation.

4) Although recent emphases on human rights in security assistance decisionmaking have roots in traditional U.S. foreign policy objectives in the hemisphere, other perennial U.S. concerns are of equal importance in the minds of U.S. policymakers and often take precedence. Congressional limitations on U.S. security assistance to Latin America in the mid- and late-1970s as a sign of disapproval of human rights violations were consonant with previously stated U.S. foreign policy goals in Latin America—promotion of democratic processes and constitutional government, limitations on the amount and type of weapons available in the hemisphere, preference for economic as opposed to defense programs in Latin American budget allocations.

Nevertheless, other priorities have traditionally competed with the pursuit of such goals in the past and at times have overshadowed them in U.S. security assistance decisions, e.g., containment of communism, U.S. access to raw materials in Latin America, protection of stable environments for U.S. private investments, and ongoing contact and communication with allied military leaders in the hemisphere.

Moreover, in the past 35 years, whenever the Office of the President, the Department of Defense, the State Department, and the Congress have felt that this latter set of objectives was being threatened, concern about democratic processes, civilian government, and human rights has not been given priority in decisions about security assistance. Regardless, therefore, of some past U.S. responsibility for repression in Latin America because of the uses to which its security assistance was put, and despite moral gains from a self-distancing by the U.S. government from several brutal regimes in the hemisphere in the late 1970s, the trend of denying military aid on humanitarian grounds is reversible. Early indications are that this is occurring under the Reagan administration.

This judgment is not meant to justify de-emphasis on human rights in U.S. foreign policy. Nor does it mean that renewed U.S. security assistance to repressive military establishments will actually stop the threat of communism, protect U.S. access to raw materials, and secure stable markets for U.S. investments. What this analysis is meant to convey is that when leading U.S. policymakers, civilian and military, perceive that these security and economic interests are in proximate jeopardy because of insurrectionary movements, they are likely to favor an increase of military aid and underestimate the consequences for human rights in Latin America.

Notes to Chapter 9

1. By World War I Chilean officers, once trained by Germans, were sending their own military missions to Colombia, Ecuador, and El Salvador. They also were educating cadets and young officers from Central America, Venezuela, and Paraguay in Santiago. See Chapter 2, "The Evolution of the Military in Brazil, Chile, Peru, Venezuela and Mexico: Implications for Human Rights."

2. For an overview of German and French geopolitical thinking in this period and how it continues to shape much of Latin America military ideology, see Chapter 3, "National Security Ideology and Human Rights"; and Genaro Arriagada, "Ideology and Politics in the South American Military: Argentina, Brazil, Chile and Uruguay," paper presented in a colloquium in the Latin American Program, The Wilson Center, The Smithsonian Institution, Washington, D.C., March 21, 1980.

3. Willard Barber and Neale Ronning argue that in these five Caribbean countries between 1912 and 1934, U.S. expeditionary forces trained local militia and/or police in order to make them more professional (and thus less interested in interfering in politics), to encourage them to engage in civic action programs (similar to the U.S. Army Corps of Engineers), and to encourage them to respect constitutional and democratic government—all of which were to characterize the rationale for U.S. military aid to Latin America in the 1960s. Barber and Ronning conclude that, while the immediate results of these earlier training expeditions were positive, the long-term consequences were not. In each of these five countries the security forces expanded their managerial capacities and skills, but also continued to intervene in politics, in some cases creating very repressive and long-lived dictatorships in the 1940s and 1950s. *Internal Security and Military Power: Counterinsurgency and Civic Action in Latin America* (Columbus: Ohio State University Press, 1966), pp. 58–63. See also Clyde H. Metcalf, *A History of the U.S. Marine Corps* (New York: Putnam, 1939); Dana G. Munro, *Intervention and Dollar Diplomacy in the Caribbean, 1900–1921* (Princeton, N.J.: Princeton University Press, 1964).

4. Frederico G. Gil, *Latin America-United States Relations* (New York: Harcourt Brace Jovanovich, 1971), pp. 154–168.

5. Ibid., pp. 176, 177, 183.

6. Ibid., pp. 180–183. No contingency plans for joint multilateral or bilateral action against such an invasion were ever agreed upon by these foreign ministers. It was not until a series of documents in the U.S. National Archives were declassified in 1973 that it became public that U.S. military leaders had developed a series of contingency plans for unilateral invasion of critical Latin American areas during the war (particularly Brazil, Central

America, and Mexico) in the event that the Axis powers threatened to invade the northeast of Brazil or attack the Panama Canal. John Child, "From 'Color' to 'Rainbow': U.S. Strategic Planning for Latin America, 1919–1945," *Journal of Interamerican Studies and World Affairs* 21, 2 (May 1979): 233–259.

7. For a summary and analysis of these differences within the U.S. government in 1945 and 1946, see Stephen S. Kaplan, "U.S. Arms Transfers to Latin America, 1945–1974," *International Studies Quarterly* 19, 4 (December 1975): 407–410.

8. Roger R. Trask, "The Impact of the Cold War on United States-Latin American Relations, 1945–1949," *Diplomatic History* 1, 3 (Summer 1977): 272–282; Gil, pp. 196–200.

9. Trask, p. 281.

10. Delegates at the Bogotá meeting in 1948 did reach a formal legal consensus on the wording of the American Declaration of the Rights and Duties of Man, which emphasized the importance of both sets of rights, civil and political as well as socioeconomic and cultural. This document, however, skirted other politically sensitive issues, such as national sovereignty and publicly supported economic development. No international mechanism was established to enforce the American Declaration within the boundaries of a nation and no obligations were placed on governments to fulfill the economic rights of citizens. These were left to individual initiative and private enterprise. Lawrence J. Le Blanc, "Economic, Social and Cultural Rights and the Interamerican System," *Journal of Interamerican Studies and World Affairs* 19, 1 (February 1977): 63–71.

11. Kaplan, pp. 412–413; J. Lloyd Mecham, *The United States and Inter-American Security, 1889–1960* (Austin: University of Texas, 1961), p. 337; Michael J. Francis, "Military Aid to Latin America in the U.S. Congress," *Journal of Interamerican Studies* 6, 3 (July 1964): 390–391.

12. Kaplan, p. 413; Francis, pp. 397–399. There is evidence that perhaps this preoccupation by the Defense Department for continued access to raw materials in Latin America overshadowed concern for promoting democratic attitudes among Latin American military officers. In a letter to Congressman Charles Porter in July 1957, the Department said: "The requirements of the defense effort of the United States for strategic raw materials and location of military facilities, in peace and war, bear no relation to the type of government which rules the nation capable of contributing to these requirements." *Congressional Record* 103 (August 1, 1957): 13408.

13. Mecham, pp. 338; 340–341.

14. *Mutual Security Act of 1958, Statutes at Large,* vol. 72 (1958), p. 262.

15. Francis, p. 401.

16. U.S. President's Committee to Study the Military Assistance Program, *Composite Report,* 2 vols. (Washington, D.C.: The Committee, August 17, 1959).

17. For an account of the founding of these schools and an analysis of the emphases in their respective curricula, see Chapter 2 in this volume and Alfred C. Stepan, *The Military in Politics: Changing Patterns in Brazil*

(Princeton: Princeton University Press, 1971), pp. 172–187; Victor Villa-nueva, *El CAEM y la revolución de la fuerza armada* (Lima: Instituto de Estudios Peruanos, 1972); Robert A. Potash, "Argentina," in Lyle N. Mc-Alister et al., *The Military in Latin American Sociopolitical Evolution: Four Case Studies* (Washington, D.C.: Center for Research in Social Systems, 1970), pp. 99–100.

18. One of the major sources for the ideology of Brazil's ESG is Golbery's *Planejamento Estratégico* (Rio de Janeiro: Biblioteca do Exército Editora, 1955). Golbery was one of the first of the geopolitical strategists in the Southern Cone region to emphasize (early in 1959) that Communist advances in the Americas would not be made through frontal and external attacks, but indirectly by capitalizing on local discontent and frustrations arising from misery and hunger. He also underscored the need for the study of counterinsurgency tactics from the Philippines, Malaya, Indonesia, Indo-china, and Algeria. Stepan, pp. 179–180.

19. Villanueva, pp. 55–63. Villanueva also argues that CAEM was not set up to fight communism or to train soldiers in counterinsurgency tactics. Such goals, he claims, were later emphasized in the 1960s by the United States during the Alliance for Progress. In fact, according to Villanueva, some of the ideas promoted by the Alliance for Progress were first suggested by Peruvian military officials. For example, as early as 1958 Peruvian repre-sentatives on the Inter-American Defense Council proposed that military forces in Latin America engage in civic action projects in the interior regions of their respective countries. They reasoned that building roads into the Amazon could have an important strategic significance if, in the event of war, the Panama Canal was blocked by the Soviets and it was necessary to transport goods over land between the two oceans. Ibid., pp. 35–36.

20. In some cases explicit criticism of certain expressions of civil and political rights was included in military lectures and wrtings during the 1950s. The Brazilians by the middle of the decade were complaining that political parties were too personalistic and dominated by local concerns to give coherent leadership for national development plans. Attention was given by the Brazilian military to the desirability of setting limits to the number of parties allowed to compete in electoral politics. There was little praise among them for pluralism, civic participation, or mobilization politics, while the necessity for hierarchy, efficiency, and control in government was a frequent theme articulated at the War College. Stepan, pp. 181–182.

21. A personal on-site examination I made in February 1980 of course descriptions, lesson plans, bibliographical lists, and library materials used in the U.S. Army School of the Americas in Panama during the 1950s con-vinced me that the type of national security doctrines taught in Brazilian, Peruvian, and Argentinian military academies did not originate in U.S. training programs. The Army School of the Americas at that time modeled its courses on those offered to U.S. military personnel in the continental United States. They emphasized technical training in armaments, automotive materials, communications, military engineering, food services, military police, elementary and advanced tactics, and the functioning of command at

different levels of responsibility. *The U.S. Army Caribbean School Catalog, 1958–1959.*

22. This policy paper is discussed in detail in John Child, "The Inter-American Military System," Ph.D. dissertation, American University, 1978, pp. 367 ff.

23. This belief that greater professionalization of the military in developing countries would make them less inclined to intervene in civilian politics was defended by Samuel Huntington, "Civilian Control of the Military: A Theoretical Statement," *Political Behavior: A Reader in Theory and Research,* eds. Heinz Eulau, Samuel Eldersveld, and Morris Janowitz (New York: Free Press, 1956), pp. 380–385; Samuel Huntington, *The Soldier and the State: The Theory and Politics of Civil-Military Relations* (New York: Random House/Vintage, 1964). Huntington was a professor at Harvard, where many of Kennedy's advisers were educated or had taught, and his views were well known in the Kennedy administration.

24. In 1961 Congress authorized an initial amount of $2.4 billion for the Alliance for Progress for its first three years of operation. This amount, however, was $600 million less than what President Kennedy had requested for the period. In addition, Congress stipulated that the administration would have to request appropriations annually, making it difficult for recipient countries to formulate long-range programs that depended on U.S. assistance and putting pressure on U.S. administrators to use up funds by the end of each fiscal year. By 1969, total U.S. public economic aid to Latin America during the first decade of the Alliance amounted to $10.2 billion, or approximately one-half of what the U.S. delegation had promised Latin America at the Punta del Este meeting in 1961 that launched the program. Congressional support for the Alliance was important, but less generous than the Kennedy administration had originally wished. Jerome Levinson and Juan de Onís, *The Alliance That Lost Its Way: A Critical Report on the Alliance for Progress* (Chicago: Quadrangle Books, 1970), pp. 15, 65–66, 114–115, 138.

25. U. S. Congress, House Committee on Foreign Affairs, "Statement of Vice Admiral L. C. Heinz, U.S. Navy, Director of Military Assistance, Office of the Assistant Secretary of Defense for International Security Affairs," *Hearings, Foreign Assistance Act of 1966,* 89th Congress, 2d sess., 1966, Part II, p. 237.

Admiral Heinz in his presentation indicated that Latin America would receive 7 percent of all U.S. military aid worldwide in 1967, and that the purpose of this assistance was threefold: 1) to develop Latin American forces capable of maintaining security against threat of violence and subversion, whether communist inspired and supported or 'home grown'; 2) to encourage the armed forces of Latin America to support democratic institutions in their countries and undertake civic action projects, thereby contributing to economic development and improving civil-military relations; and 3) to develop peace-keeping units for the Organization of American States.

26. Robert P. Case, "El entrenamiento de militares latino-americanos en los Estados Unidos," *Aportes* 6 (October 1967): 55.

27. "La dependencia militar latinoamericana," *Cuadernos Semestrales, Estados Unidos: Perspectiva latinoamericana* 4 (1978): 334.

28. Lt. General Andrew P. O'Meara, Commander in Chief for the Caribbean, told the Congress in 1963 that the Morse amendment was obsolete since "every day we are trying to convince our friends and allies that their principal problem is internal security, but our laws say otherwise." U.S. Congress, House Committee on Foreign Affairs, "Statement of Lt. Gen. Andrew P. O'Meara, U.S. Army, Commander in Chief, Caribbean," *Hearings, Foreign Assistance Act of 1963,* 88th Congress, 1st sess., 1962, p. 924.

Accordingly, the Congress changed the wording of this amendment in 1963, making the restriction much broader and giving the appearance that U.S. military aid could be used against all kinds of revolutions:

> Except (1) to the extent necessary to fulfill prior commitments or (2) to the extent that the President finds, with respect to any Latin American country, that the furnishing of military assistance under this Act is necessary to safeguard the security of the United States or to safeguard the security of a country associated with the United States in the Alliance for Progress against overthrow of a duly constituted government, and so informs the Congress, no further military assistance under provision of this Act shall be furnished to any Latin American country.

Foreign Assistance Act of 1963, Statutes at Large, vol. 77 (1963), p. 384.

29. "U.S. Army School of the Americas," *Military Review* 50, 4 (April 1970): 88–93.

Between 1949 and the end of 1961, the School trained 11,351 Latin American officers, enlisted men and cadets. In 1962 alone, however, 1,200 more Latin Americans graduated, and by the end of 1967 the total number of trainees from the time the School began reached 22,800. *U.S. Army School of the Americas Catalog, 1963,* p. vi; *U.S. Army School of the Americas Catalog, 1969,* p. i.

In 1963 (and thereafter throughout the 1960s) the six major purposes of the School, as listed in the preface to the annual catalogue, were as follows: 1) support U.S. army missions, attaches, military assistance advisory groups (MAAGs) in Latin America by instructing Latin military and paramilitary personnel in U.S. military technical skills, leadership techniques and doctrine covering military actions during peace and war; 2) augment efforts of other U.S. agencies in fostering of friendly relations with Latin American countries; 3) instill in Latin American personnel present at the school a further appreciation of the ideals of democracy and the American way of life; 4) translate into Spanish selected training publications; 5) provide selected training material in support of mobile training teams as required; and 6) provide quarters, appropriate administration and discipline, and logistical support to Latin American students attending the U.S. Army School of the Americas.

Counterinsurgency and civic action training at the school emphasized the importance of military units expanding their reach to rural areas. In 1963, 8 of the 25 courses taught at the U.S. Army School of the Americas included counterguerrilla and/or civic action techniques to improve conditions in the countryside. *U.S. Army School of the Americas Catalog, 1963.* By 1967, 34 of 47 courses emphasized aspects of one or both of these new trends in training. *U.S. Army School of the Americas Catalog, 1967.*

30. "The Inter-American Defense College," *Military Review* 50, 4 (April 1970): 20–27; Child, pp. 389–393.

In 1962 the Office of Public Safety (OPS) within the Agency for International Development was expanded and reoriented to upgrade police skills in developing countries. Between 1962 and 1974 (when it was terminated by Congress) the OPS program channeled $56.6 million to Latin American police forces to modernize their respective intelligence, communications, and mobility capacities for combating urban guerrilla movements. During this 12-year period these funds provided training for 3,800 Latin American police officers at the International Police Academy in Washington, and supported U.S. public safety advisors operating in police headquarters throughout the Americas. The program also involved direct grants of equipment to Latin American police units, including riot gear, communications technology, jeeps, and computers. Michael T. Klare and Cynthia Arnson, "Exporting Repression: U.S. Support for Authoritarianism in Latin America," *Capitalism and the State in U.S.-Latin American Relations,* ed. Richard R. Fagen (Stanford, Calif.: Stanford University Press, 1979), pp. 152–153.

31. Child, pp. 395, 403, 409–410; John Saxe-Fernandez, "The Central American Defense Council and Pax Americana," *Latin American Radicalism,* eds. Irving Louis Horowitz, Josué de Castro, and John Gerassi (New York: Random House, 1969), pp. 75–101.

32. Miles Wolpin's analysis of the courses offered at the U.S. Army School of the Americas led him to the conclusion that by the end of the 1960s ideological indoctrination accounted for from 2 to 4 percent of enlisted trainees' time, and from 15 to 20 percent for the officers. Wolpin claims, for example, that by 1969 approximately one-half of the 41 courses listed in the catalog dealt with some aspect of communist doctrine or practice. Miles Wolpin, *Military Aid and Counterrevolution in the Third World* (Lexington, Mass.: D. C. Heath, 1972), pp. 78–80.

My own content analysis of the catalogs and lesson plans for courses offered during the 1960s parallels Wolpin's findings. In 1963, 15 of the 25 courses offered in the School (including those for officers, enlisted men, and cadets) treated aspects of communist ideology or systems of government. Only 3 of the 25, however, made any mention in the course descriptions of democratic values and processes. In 1967, of the 47 courses presented, 21 included communism as a theme, whereas only 13 dealt with democracy. *U.S. Army School of the Americas Catalog, 1963 and 1967.*

Although one of the six main missions of the School was to "instill in Latin American personnel . . . a further appreciation of the ideals of democracy and the American way of life," apparently much more effort was placed on discrediting communism.

33. The technology and training, while not in itself an encouragement to repression or violations of citizens rights, included many skills and materials that could be used for repressive purposes. The program at the U.S. Army School of the Americas in the mid-1960s, for example, taught the following techniques: procedures of military intelligence and counter-intelligence, tactical operations against dissident groups, police functions as coordinated in counterinsurgency operations, psychological operations, interrogation of criminal suspects, surveillance and undercover police investigation, crowd and mob psychology, riot control formations, use of chemicals and gas, countersabotage, irregular warfare operations in urban areas, propaganda analysis and counterpropaganda planning, correctional administration, and the use of religion as a therapeutic aid in the rehabilitation of prisoners. *U.S. Army School of the Americas Catalog, 1963,* pp. 15–19, 24–30, 35–38; *U.S. Army School of the Americas Catalog, 1967,* pp. 52–60, 101–104.

An assistant to the Commandant of the School stated that none of these techniques emphasized inhumane use of force against civilians and was, in fact, the same type of training that U.S. military personnel receive in continental United States. He acknowledged, however, that what Latin American officers and enlisted men did with such techniques once they returned home and were subject to the orders of others in a different context, was clearly beyond the control of the United States. Interview with Major James Pitts, U.S. Army School of the Americas, Fort Gulick, Panama, Feb. 25, 1980.

34. Alfred Stepan argues, on the basis of evidence from Brazil and Peru, that a new type of professionalism emerged among Latin American military units, in large part due to sophisticated training for, and experience in, both counterinsurgency and civic action. These new skills and experiences did not, however, lessen their interest in politics, as Huntington and others had hypothesized, but actually led to an expansion of their political roles and functions. Such training and experience, Stepan claims, also contributed to the judgment by some military leaders that they were more competent than civilians to direct the process of development and provide efficient, stable leadership for their nations as well. "The New Professionalism of Internal Warfare and Military Role Expansion," *Authoritarian Brazil: Origins, Policies and Future,* ed. Alfred C. Stepan (New Haven, Conn.: Yale University Press, 1973), pp. 51–53; 57; 61–62.

For other studies that reach similar conclusions about the positive correlation in Latin America between increased professionalization of the armed forces and more institutionalized patterns of military intervention in politics, see Chapter 2 in this volume and Guillermo O'Donnell, *Modernization and Bureaucratic Authoritarianism: Studies in South American Politics* (Berkeley: Institute of International Studies, University of California, 1973), pp. 154–165; Richard Maullin, *Soldiers, Guerrillas and Politics in Colombia* (Lexington, Mass.: Lexington Books, 1973), pp. 111–118; John Samuel Fitch, *The Military Coup d'Etat as a Political Process: Ecuador, 1948–1966* (Baltimore:

The Johns Hopkins University Press, 1977), pp. 136–145, 162–164; Brian Jenkins and Caesar D. Sereseres, "U.S. Military Assistance and the Guatemalan Armed Forces," *Armed Forces and Society* 3, 4 (Summer 1977): 587–588; Charles Corbett, "Politics and Professionalism: The South American Military," *The Politics of Anti-politics: The Military in Latin America,* eds. Brian Loveman and Thomas Davies (Lincoln: University of Nebraska Press, 1978), pp. 20–21.

35. See Chapter 2 in this volume and José Enrique Miguens, "The New Latin American Military Coup," *Militarism in Developing Countries,* ed. Kenneth Fidel (New Brunswick: Transaction Books, 1975), pp. 99–123; Stepan, pp. 57–58, 61–62; *The State and Society: Peru in Comparative Perspective* (Princeton, N.J.: Princeton University Press, 1978), pp. 117–157; Carlos Astiz, "The Argentine Armed Forces: Their Role and Political Involvement," *Western Political Quarterly* 22, 4 (December 1969): 862–878.

36. Child, p. 407; *Washington Post,* Dec. 29, 1976, p. 1; Vernon A. Walters, *Silent Missions* (Garden City, N.Y.: Doubleday, 1978), pp. 374–406.

Walters claims that the United States did not engineer the 1964 military coup in Brazil, but that U.S. military officers were in close contact with leaders of the Brazilian armed forces before and during the intervention, and were ready to provide direct assistance if necessary. General Walters was sent to Brazil just before the coup, and had close contacts with several Brazilian officers (including its leader, General Castello Branco) based on cooperation during World War II when a 25,000-member Brazilian expeditionary force participated with allied forces in the invasion of Italy. Walters claims that upon arrival in Brazil in early 1964 he was given three instructions by U.S. Ambassador Lincoln Gordon: 1) I want to find out what is going on inside the Brazilian armed forces; 2) I may want to influence the outcome through you; and 3) I never want to be surprised by events. Ibid., pp. 374–375.

37. The best documented account of the Dominican Republic episode in 1965, and of the weakness of Marxist groups in the popular uprising attempt to restore civilian government, is Piero Gleijeses' *The Dominican Crisis: The 1965 Constitutional Revolt and the American Intervention,* trans. Lawrence Lipson (Baltimore: The Johns Hopkins University Press, 1978).

38. *The Rockefeller Report on the Americas* (Chicago: Quadrangle Books, 1969). The Report acknowledged the danger of the new military becoming too authoritarian (and therefore repressive of civil and political rights), or too nationalistic (and therefore a threat to U.S. private investments). It concluded, however, that one important influence counteracting these dangers was the exposure to the "fundamental achievements of the U.S. way of life that many military from the other American countries have received through the military training programs which the United States conducts in Panama and in the United States." Ibid., p. 32.

39. U.S. Congress, Senate, Foreign Relations Committee, *U.S. Military Policies in Latin America,* 91st Congress, 1st sess., 1969, pp. 1–2, 8, 24–25.

40. U.S. Congress, House Committee on Foreign Affairs, *Hearings, Foreign Assistance Act of 1969,* 90th Congress, 2d sess., 1968, pp. 645, 662;

U.S. Congress, House Subcommittee on Inter-American Affairs of the Committee on Foreign Affairs, *Cuba and the Caribbean,* 91st Congress, 2nd sess., 1970, p. 92; U.S. Congress, House Committee on Foreign Affairs, *Hearings, Foreign Assistance Act of 1971,* 91st Congress, 2d sess., 1970, pp. 420–421.

41. Luigi Einaudi et al., *Arms Transfers to Latin America: Toward a Policy of Mutual Respect* (Santa Monica, Calif: Rand Corporation, 1973), pp. 71–73.

42. Several factors contributed to this shift from grants to sales: the growing scarcity of Korean War surplus equipment, the expansion of U.S. involvement in Vietnam, and an emerging balance of payments problem for the United States in world trade. Between 1963 and 1967, of the $421 million in U.S. military aid to Latin America, only 36.1 percent was in the form of sales and the rest were grants. Between 1968 and 1972, however, 82 percent of the $316 million in military assistance was transferred through sales. Einuadi et al., p. 13.

For an analysis of the various reasons for the shift in U.S. security assistance worldwide from grants to sales in the late 1960s, see David J. Louscher, "The Rise of Military Sales as a U.S. Foreign Assistance Instrument," *Orbis* 20, 4 (Winter 1977): 933–964.

43. U.S. Congress, Senate Subcommittee on Western Hemisphere Affairs of the Committee on Foreign Relations, *U.S. Policies and Programs in Brazil,* 92nd Congress, 1st sess., 1971, p. 89; *Human Rights and the U.S. Foreign Assistance Program, Fiscal Year 1978, Part I—Latin America* (Washington, D.C.: Center for International Policy, 1977), p. 26.

44. One of the first North Americans to criticize the "Brazilian miracle" for placing great burdens on the poor (and thereby requiring political repression) was Albert Fishlow, "Some Reflections on Post-1964 Brazilian Economic Policy," *Authoritarian Brazil,* pp. 69–113. See also Chapter 5 in this volume and Shelton H. Davis, *Victims of the Miracle: Development and the Indians of Brazil* (New York: Cambridge University Press, 1977); São Paulo Justice and Peace Commission, *São Paulo Growth and Poverty* (London: Catholic Institute for International Relations, 1978); Edmar L. Bacha and Lane Taylor, "Brazilian Income Distribution in the 1960s: 'Facts,' Model Results and the Controversy," *Journal of Development Studies* 14, 3 (April 1978): 271–297.

45. Child, p. 452.

General obsolescence and dilapidation of weapons acquired from the United States and Great Britain after World War II and the Korean War became major problems for Latin American military by the late 1960s. Modernization of weapons systems to be used in possible conventional wars reemerged as a preoccupation of the six largest military establishments (Argentina, Brazil, Chile, Peru, Colombia, and Venezuela) right at the time when the United States was refusing to sell them sophisticated arms. Not only did they consider modernization important from a strategic perspective; it was also, as Luigi Einaudi has observed, a significant "symbol of national prestige" since "armaments embody national dignity" in the minds of many citizens. Einaudi has further emphasized that "no military branch wants to be saddled with old or obsolete equipment," particularly "highly visible weapons as tanks, jets, and destroyers," since this "reflects adversely on the dignity of the service." Einaudi et al., pp. 23, 27–28.

46. Child, pp. 462, 473.

In 1967 the United States military, acting under congressional restrictions, refused to sell such sophisticated weapons as napalm and F-5 supersonic jets to the Peruvians and tanks to the Argentines. This aroused great consternation in the minds of the military in both of these countries, and feelings of national pride were seriously wounded. They, and other Latin American military, began at this time to look toward Europe as an alternate source of arms. Joseph Novitski, "Latin Lands Turning to Europe for Arms," *New York Times,* May 4, 1971, pp. 1, 7; David Ronfeldt and Caesar Sereseres, *U.S. Arms Transfers, Diplomacy, and Security in Latin America and Beyond* (Santa Monica, Calif.: Rand Corporation, 1977), pp. 5–12.

Antidependency arguments were also used by Latin American military to justify the development of autonomous local defense industries, for example, by General Edgardo Mercado Jarrín, a leading Peruvian military strategist and former Prime Minister, "La política nacional y la estrategia militar en Peru," *Estrategia* (Buenos Aires), 27 (March–April 1974): 16–29. For another strongly critical appraisal of U.S. restrictions on arms transfers to Latin America based on antidependency arguments (and written by a former lecturer at the *Instituto Argentino de Estudios Estratégicos y de las Relaciones Internacionales*), see Horacio L. Veneroni, *Estados Unidos y las fuerzas armadas de América Latina: La dependencia militar* (Buenos Aires: Ediciones Periferia, 1973).

47. Child, p. 474; Ronfeldt and Sereseres, pp. 14–19; "Argentina: Defense Industry Changes," *Weekly Reports on Strategic Latin American Affairs* 6, 1 (Jan. 10, 1980): 1–2; "Brazil-Iraq: Arms Bartered for Oil," *Weekly Reports on Strategic Latin American Affairs,* 5, 29 (July 26, 1979): 1–2.

48. The six largest Latin American military establishments accounted for 96 percent of these arms imports: Brazil (36 percent), Argentina (18 percent), Venezuela (13 percent), Peru (12 percent), Chile (11 percent), and Colombia (6 percent). Over four-fifths of the dollar value of these weapons was constituted by jet aircraft (46 percent) and heavy war ships (35 percent). Einaudi et al., pp. 10–11.

49. Bernardo Elgueta, et al., *Five Years of Military Rule in Chile, 1973–1978* (New York: Earl Coleman, 1980); Fernando Dahse, *El mapa de la extrema riqueza* (Santiago: Editorial Aconcagua, 1979).

50. In the first few years following the 1968 military coup in Peru, some significant structural reforms were initiated to reduce the power of traditional landed elites and to provide increased employment opportunities in industry and food subsidies for urban workers. By the mid-1970s, however, advances in meeting basic needs of the poor were reversed due to declining food production and substantial deficits in balance of payments. See Chapter 5 in this volume and John Weeks, "Crisis and Accumulation in the Peruvian

Economy: 1967–1975," *Review of Radical Political Economics* 8, 4 (Winter 1976): 46–72.

For other assessments of the successes and failures of the Peruvian military regime's reformist efforts, see: Abraham F. Lowenthal, ed., *The Peruvian Experiment: Continuity and Change in Military Rule* (Princeton, N.J.: Princeton University Press, 1975); E. V. K. Fitzgerald, *The State and Economic Development: Peru Since 1968* (London: Cambridge University Press, 1976); Pierre L. Van Den Berghe and George P. Primov, *Inequality in the Peruvian Andes: Class and Ethnicity in Cuzco* (Columbia: University of Missouri Press, 1977); Alfred C. Stepan, *The State and Society: Peru in Comparative Perspective* (Princeton, N.J.: Princeton University Press, 1978).

51. While the overall average of central government expenditures devoted to defense in Latin America declined slightly from 15.4 percent in 1967 to 14.7 percent in 1974, total arms imports in the region rose from $269 million to $492 million. Furthermore, in some countries with large military establishments, such as Brazil and Peru, defense spending remained higher than the regional average (18.8 percent and 18.9 percent, respectively), and in the case of Chile increased dramatically (rising from 8.5 percent in 1967 to 19.5 percent in 1974). During this same seven-year period, per capita military expenditures (in constant dollars) increased from $14 to $20 in Brazil, from $24 to $29 in Peru, and from $15 to $45 in Chile. Heliodoro González, "U.S. Arms Transfer Policy in Latin America: Failure of a Policy," *Inter-American Economic Affairs* 32, 2 (Autumn 1978): 73–74.

52. *International Security and Arms Export Control Act, Statutes at Large,* vol. 90 (1978), pp. 748–750.

For a summary of other legislative initiatives on human rights enacted since 1973, see Congressional Research Service, Library of Congress, *Human Rights and U.S. Foreign Assistance: Experiences and Issues in Policy Implementation (1977–1978),* Report prepared for the Committee on Foreign Relations, U.S. Senate (Washington, D.C.: Government Printing Office, 1979), pp. 16–24.

53. "The Foreign Assistance and Related Programs Appropriations Act, 1978 prohibited foreign military sales to Brazil, El Salvador, and Guatemala. These countries, along with Argentina and Uruguay, had rejected further U.S. military assistance following the publication in 1977 of State Department's reports on the status of human rights in those countries." Congressional Research Service, *Human Rights and U.S. Foreign Assistance,* p. 106.

In the case of Brazil, the rejection of U.S. military assistance also came in the aftermath of U.S. behind-the-scenes efforts to stop West Germany from selling them nuclear technology as a means of limiting nuclear proliferation. This particularly angered the Brazilians, perhaps even more than the U.S. human rights policy, since the Nixon administration had given Brazil favored nation status in U.S. foreign policy considerations. The new administration did not consult Brazil before putting pressure on the West Germans on an issue considered crucial by Brazil for its national development.

54. González, p. 88. Loopholes continue to exist, however, in both commercial and government export laws that permit continued flow of repressive technology to Latin America, especially to police forces. For example, as of 1980 shock batons, thumb screws, and leg irons were not outlawed as items for sale abroad. Moreover, although the Congress in 1974 terminated assistance programs for foreign police forces, the International Narcotics Control program (INC) closely resembles the old Office of Public Safety (OPS) since it provides similar equipment and training to police, ostensibly for the purpose of stopping drug traffic. Between 1973 and 1980, the INC granted $125.9 million to Latin American police agencies. This provided them with: 1) small arms and equipment, such as helicopters, light planes, jeeps, motorcycles, computers, communications, and surveillance devices; 2) training at special schools in the United States; and 3) U.S. instructors and advisors stationed in their own local headquarters. Michael T. Klare, *Supplying Repression: U.S. Support for Authoritarian Regimes Abroad* (Washington, D.C.: Institute for Policy Studies, 1977), p. 25.

Although these INC funds were intended exclusively for drug enforcement units, a 1976 General Accounting Office report to Congress revealed that the program in some countries was used to support other police functions unrelated to control of the drug traffic. It also concluded that sometimes "commodities previously furnished to police units under the public safety program are now being provided to the same units under the narcotics program." Comptroller General of the United States, *Stopping U.S. Assistance to Foreign Policy and Prisons* (Washington, D.C.: Government Printing Office, 1976), p. 22.

55. U.S. Congress, House Subcommittee on Inter-American Affairs of the Committee on International Relations, "Statement of John Bushnell, Deputy Assistant Secretary, Inter-American Affairs, Department of State," *Arms Trade in the Western Hemisphere,* 95th Congress, 2d sess., 1978, p. 7.

56. Curriculum Development Office, U.S. Army School of the Americas, Fort Gulick, Panama.

57. Argentina imported approximately $3 billion worth of arms between 1977 and 1980 from France, Italy, Spain, and other European countries. Argentina and Brazil also developed state-owned industries which produce light trainer and attack planes and counterinsurgency aircraft for both domestic use and foreign export. Both of these countries, under a series of coproduction licensing agreements with U.S., British, German, and Italian companies, have manufactured aircraft, ships, and missiles on their own soil. Klare and Arnson, p. 164.

Brazilian arms sales abroad for 1979 totaled $800 million, and included shipments to countries such as Bolivia, Uruguay, Paraguay, Chile, Guatemala, and El Salvador. Some estimates in 1979 predicted that Brazil would shortly become one of the leading arms manufacturers in the Third World, with exports reaching $1 billion by the early 1980s. "Brazil: Arms Study Published," *Weekly Reports on Strategic Latin American Affairs* 5, 42 (October 25, 1979): 1–2; "Brazil: T-27 Test Flights," *Weekly Reports on Strategic Latin American Affairs,* 5, 24 (June 21, 1979): 1.

The Brazilian National Police Academy for some time has been training police personnel from all over the continent. Moreover, by the late 1970s there were over 100 military advisors from Argentina, Brazil, France, the United Kingdom, and Israel stationed throughout Latin America. Klare and Arnson, p. 164; U.S. Congress, House Subcommittee on Inter-American Affairs of the Committee on International Relations, "Statement of Rear Admiral Gordon J. Schuller, Director for the Inter-American Region, Office of the Assistant Secretary of Defense for International Security Affairs," *Arms Trade in the Western Hemisphere,* 95th Congress, 2d sess., 1978, p. 32.

58. Ibid., p. 33.

59. Ibid., p. 30.

60. U.S. Congress, House Subcommittee on Inter-American Affairs of the Committee on Foreign Affairs, "Statement of Franklin D. Kramer, Principal Deputy Assistant Secretary of Defense for International Security Affairs," and "Statement of John Bushnell, Deputy Assistant Secretary, Inter-American Affairs, Department of State," *Hearings, Foreign Assistance Act of 1981,* 96th Congress, 2d sess., February 1980.

61. "Carter Warns of Cuba as Caribbean Threat," *Washington Post,* April 10, 1980, p. A27.

In early 1980 President Carter also established a new organization, known as Caribbean-Central American Action, aimed at stimulating more economic development programs by private U.S. institutions (business, labor, churches) in the region. Subsequently, the Reagan administration proposed increased economic aid and private investment to help combat communist influence in the area.

62. A seminar including social psychologists and civilian and military policymakers on the potential impact of the International Military Education and Training Program (IMET) on human rights attitudes of foreign military officers, sponsored by the Congressional Research Service in 1979, concluded that even a carefully designed program would be unlikely to generate more than a five percent change in trainees' attitudes. Even this slight gain would probably diminish once the trainees were reimmersed in their own culture. This conclusion was based on results of comparable educational programs for adults carried out in other circumstances. William J. McGuire, "A Social Psychologists's Perspective on Using IMET to Increase Human Rights Awareness," paper presented at the Congressional Research Service seminar, "Human Rights and the International Military Education and Training Program," Whittall Pavilion, Library of Congress, Washington, D.C., January 31, 1979; John Samuel Fitch, "Human Rights and the International Military Education and Training Program," summary paper of the seminar prepared for the Congressional Research Service, Library of Congress, Washington, D.C., February 27, 1979.

63. For a critical appraisal of the policies of the International Monetary Fund as these limit the choices of policymakers in Latin America and negatively impact on basic needs of the poor, see Chapter 7; and for a similar assessment of the activities of private banks and how they impact on basic needs in Latin America, see Chapter 6, both in this volume.

64. U.S. Department of State, *Country Reports on Human Rights Practices for 1979,* Report submitted to the Committee on Foreign Affairs, U.S. House of Representatives, and the Committee on Foreign Relations, U.S. Senate (Washington, D.C.: Government Printing Office, 1980), pp. 239–247, 262–279, 385–390, 412–421.

65. The Congressional Research Service study of the impact of U.S. human rights initiatives since 1973 concludes that:

> In Latin America . . . an attempt in the early days of the Carter Administration to reduce or terminate military assistance programs on human rights grounds . . . led to bitter denunciations of the United States and strong retaliatory action. Relations with four countries— Argentina, Brazil, El Salvador, and Guatemala . . . suddenly chilled, and though other factors may have been involved in some of the decisions, all four . . . canceled their requests for security assistance from the United States. . . .
>
> In the case of Chile, knowledgeable U.S. officials believe that Washington's vigorous investigation of the assassination of former Ambassador Orlando Letelier may have been the most effective measure employed.

Human Rights and U.S. Foreign Assistance, p. 77.

66. *International Security and Arms Export Control Act, Statutes at Large,* vol. 90 (1978), p. 748.

LARS SCHOULTZ

10. The Carter Administration and Human Rights in Latin America

INTRODUCTION

As World War II drew to a close, the U.S. government appeared ready
to make the protection of human rights an important component of its
foreign policy. The nation was at the end of a war which had been
fought in large measure to halt violation of rights, and it therefore seemed
appropriate that international efforts to forestall further infractions
should receive American support. The appointment of Eleanor Roosevelt
to the UN Commission on Human Rights underscored the nation's concern over the issue and guaranteed an energetic U.S. presence in that
forum. Under the leadership of her delegation, commission members
labored more than two years to complete their initial task, the creation
of the Universal Declaration of Human Rights. When the document
was accepted by the General Assembly in the predawn hours of December 10, 1948, the presiding officer rose to congratulate U.S. officials for
making the protection of human rights a cornerstone of American
foreign policy. The assembled representatives of the world's governments
responded with a standing ovation.

In the years between the beginning of the Cold War and the development of widespread opposition to the Vietnamese War, human
rights all but disappeared as a component of United States foreign
policy. On the domestic scene, the alleged incompatibility of human rights
conventions with existing federal-state jurisdictional boundaries and the
fears accompanying the relinquishing of the rights of domestic jurisdiction
to international bodies influenced many groups (most notably the
American Bar Association's Committee on Peace and Law through the
United Nations) to oppose U.S. participation in human rights accords. In
international relations, the issue became increasingly politicized as ideological disagreements over the definition of human rights were reinforced

by Cold War divisions. By the early 1950s, human rights had become a propaganda weapon to be pulled out of a nation's arsenal whenever strategic considerations indicated it would be useful. The coup de grâce which virtually eliminated human rights considerations from U.S. foreign policy came in 1953, when Senator John Bricker received the Eisenhower administration's commitment not to become a party to binding human rights agreements.

Throughout the 1950s and most of the 1960s the nation's few human rights activists were dismissed as unrealistic, and often unreasonable liberals, and their proposals were discarded as utopian. Gradually, however, political forces advocating a larger role for human rights slowly began appearing on the periphery of foreign policy decision making. By the late 1960s human rights had commenced its quiet resurgence as a component of U.S. foreign policy, with primary emphasis on the Third World and the Soviet bloc. During the following decade, human rights considerations were added to the list of conditions under which the United States granted economic assistance, supplied military weapons, or supported loans by multilateral development banks. To accomplish these changes, human rights activists mobilized a substantial constituency through a number of interest groups and stimulated the creation of a State Department bureaucracy dedicated to increasing the impact of humanitarian considerations in United States foreign policy.

When Jimmy Carter became president in 1977, human rights assumed unparalleled prominence in foreign policy. Human rights did not replace national security as the fundamental guiding principle of U.S. foreign policy, but where national security objectives were not threatened, human rights became a significant component. Critics have complained that the Carter human rights policy was administered inconsistently and that several of the nation's most powerful foreign policy instruments were not utilized in the effort to promote human rights. Nearly everyone agrees, however, that human rights considerations came to enjoy a substantially enlarged role in United States foreign policy in general and U.S. policy toward Latin America in particular. This essay is an analysis of that development.

I. THE NIXON-FORD YEARS, (1968–1976)

Most of the witnesses who appeared in 1973 at hearings on human rights held by Congressman Donald Fraser's Foreign Affairs Subcommittee on International Organizations and Movements noted that the policy of the Nixon administration was to discount humanitarian values in foreign policy making. Fresh from a tour as the U.S. representative to the UN Commission on Human Rights, Rita Hauser stated that "we speak out against violations of countries we are not particularly close to . . . and we are largely silent . . . when human rights violations occur on the part of all allies." Princeton political scientist Richard Falk lamented that human rights were such a low priority that they were all but excluded from consideration in foreign policy decision making. This evaluation was echoed by a specialist in international law, Tom Farer, who characterized human rights as "the stepchildren of United States foreign policy." "The best guarantor of an aborted career in the defense and foreign policy establishments," he observed "is a marked concern for the humanitarian consequences of national behavior." [1]

The issue of United States policy toward human rights violations in Latin America was never discussed directly by President Nixon. This in itself is significant, for a presidential address serves as one of the principal mechanisms by which a President informs the executive branch of the concerns he wishes to emphasize. When President Nixon did refer indirectly to human rights, he emphasized his greater interest in other potentially competing values, particularly the stability of existing relationships:

> The United States has a strong interest in maintaining cooperation with our neighbors regardless of their domestic viewpoint. . . . We hope that governments will evolve toward constitutional procedures but it is not our mission to try to provide, except by example, the answers to such questions to other sovereign nations. We deal with governments as they are. [2]

Except for this comment and a similar one near the end of his presidency, [3] Mr. Nixon was silent on the issue of human rights in Latin America.

The principal Nixon administration spokesperson on human rights was Henry Kissinger. Until 1975 he commented on the issue only in response to direct questioning. At his 1973 confirmation hearing, Kissinger was asked about the administration's intentions in light of the increasing levels of repression among U.S. allies. He responded:

> In our bilateral dealings we will follow a pragmatic policy of degree. If the infringement on human rights is not so offensive that we cannot live with it, we will seek to work out what we can with the country involved in order to increase our influence. If the infringment is so offensive that we cannot live with it, we will avoid dealing with the offending country. [4]

At the time, human rights violations in many countries with which the United States was closely allied (Chile, Indonesia, Iran, the Philippines, South Korea, Uruguay) were reaching new heights. When Kissinger and President Nixon failed to make an issue of these violations, the foreign policy bureaucracy logically concluded that the administration wished to emphasize goals other than human rights observance in its relations with repressive governments. In July 1974, the issue of diplomatic intervention on behalf of human rights appeared to be settled for the duration of the Nixon-Ford administration. In that month the American ambassador to Chile, David Popper, broached the subject of torture and other abuses during the course of a meeting with the Chilean Minister of Defense. In the margin of the cable describing the discussion Kissinger scrawled an instruction to his aide: "Tell Popper to cut out the political science lectures." [5]

Then in mid-1975 the Ford administration began to propose a change in the role of human rights in United States foreign policy. Once again, Secretary of State Kissinger was the principal spokesperson. During his final year and a half in office he asserted repeatedly that there were limits to the extent to which governments engaged in the systematic repression of their citizens' human rights could be "congenial partners" with the United States. [6] The impetus for this change is uncertain, although many factors probably contributed. Certainly congressional pressure was among the most prominent. Many observers agreed with David Weissbrodt, a legal scholar who has carefully chronicled the Kissinger human rights policy, that the Secretary's "rhetoric may not have been translated into his policies." [7] Nonetheless, the fact is that the human rights policy enunciated by the "late" Kissinger differed from that of the "early" Kissinger.

The most vivid example of this came in his June 1976 speech entitled "Human Rights and the Western Hemisphere" to the sixth general assembly of the Organization of American States (OAS) in Santiago, Chile. In it he stated: "One of the most compelling issues of our time, and one which calls for the concerted action of all responsible peoples and nations, is the necessity to protect and extend the fundamental rights of humanity." [8] There exists no parallel to this address in the first seven years of the Nixon-Ford period. The message to American diplomats was that the role of human rights as a criterion of United States policy toward Latin America had increased considerably.

It is of absolutely crucial importance to note, however, that throughout the period from 1969 to 1977 Kissinger consistently voiced his belief that human rights concerns must remain secondary to the maintenance of peace and world order. The best example of his understanding of this subordinate relationship appeared in a 1976 speech in which he acknowledged that

> it is our obligation as the world's leading democracy to dedicate ourselves to assuring freedom for the human spirit. But responsibility compels also a recognition of our limits. Our alliances . . . serve the cause of peace by strengthening regional and world security. If well conceived, they are not favors to others but a recognition of common interests. They should be withdrawn when those interests change; they should not, as a general rule, be used as levers to extort a standard of conduct or to punish acts with which we do not agree. [9]

Overall, the message from the Secretary of State was that human rights, while deserving greater attention, should not distract foreign policy officials from the pursuit of their more traditional national security interests.

Once out of office, Kissinger placed this position in sharper focus in commenting upon the obvious difference between his human rights policy and that of the Carter administration. Speaking as a private citizen in 1977, he warned the new policymakers to "maintain the moral distinction between aggressive totalitarianism and other governments which, with all their imperfections, are trying to resist foreign pressures or subversion and which thereby help preserve the balance of power in behalf of all free peoples." [10] This statement appears to confirm Rita Hauser's conclusion that during the Nixon administration the United States had friends—"free peoples" in Kissinger's lexicon—whose human rights practices were irrelevant to United States policy because these allies were engaged in a struggle to maintain a higher value, the balance of power. The human rights behavior of "aggressive totalitarianisms," conversely, was morally distinct: their abuses could not be counterbalanced by the value of maintaining freedom. It is upon this logic that U.S. policy toward the international protection of human rights was based during the Nixon and Ford administrations.

II. THE PROMISE OF THE CARTER ADMINISTRATION

Candidate Carter's first major speech emphasizing human rights and foreign policy came on September 8, 1976, during an appearance before a national convention of the B'nai B'rith:

> We cannot look away when a government tortures people, or jails them for their beliefs or denies minorities fair treatment or the right to emigrate. . . . We should begin by having it understood that if any nation . . . deprives its own people of basic human rights, that fact will help shape our own people's attitude towards that nation's government. [11]

During the second pre-election debate in October 1976, Carter accused the Ford administration of ignoring "in our foreign policy the character of the American people," and of acting "contrary to our longstanding beliefs and principles." Responding to President Ford's statement that the United States "does not condone . . . repressive measures" in South Korea, Carter noted "that Mr. Ford didn't comment on the prisons in Chile," where "his administration overthrew an elected government and helped to establish a military dictatorship."

Thereafter, statements about human rights became a prominent feature of the Carter campaign. By the time of his inauguration, no one was startled to hear him assert that "our commitment to human rights must be absolute." Perhaps the most quoted passage from his initial presidential address concerned human rights: "Because we are free, we can never be indifferent to the fate of freedom elsewhere. Our moral sense dictates a clearcut preference for those societies which share with us an abiding respect for individual human rights." [12] Even if President Carter had done nothing else on the issue, he would have been noted for bringing human rights to the center of diplomatic exchange. After January, 1977, United States diplomats knew that the value of human rights had risen dramatically in American foreign policy.

Why did the United States cease reinforcing the Somozas, Pinochets, and Vídelas of Latin America? Why in the 1970s did Congress cease writing Hickenlooper amendments to protect U.S. investors and start writing Harkin amendments to protect human rights? The answer lies in an unusual conjunction of five events which caused a breakdown in the consensus among policymakers that the core values of anticommunism and support for liberal capitalism were threatened in Latin America.

First there was the U.S. intervention in Vietnam, which undermined popular support for foreign policy in general. Vietnam labeled the United States as the primary supporter of a repressive government whose principal justification was its fanatical anticommunism. Virtually all of the human rights activists within and without the government began by challenging the Johnson and Nixon policies toward Vietnam. Having made progress on that issue, antiwar activists then searched for related questions, and became involved in the opposition to United States support for repressive Third World governments.

Watergate was the second event that increased the importance of human rights in the 1970s. The Nixon administration collapsed in August 1974, and the following November voters expressed themselves by electing an overwhelmingly Democratic Congress, 291 Democrats to 144 Republicans in the House. Among the new members were Tom Harkin, Toby Moffett, Stephen Solarz, and Paul Tsongas, all of whom worked during 1975–1976 to add human rights amendments to legislation governing aid programs. Lacking moral authority in the area of human rights, the Ford administration was unable to defeat these congressional initiatives.

The third important event was the 1973 coup in Chile, the nation that had been the pride of Latin American democracy. On nightly television the world was exposed to the brutality of the Pinochet government and a liberal Congress turned against the Nixon administration's policy of supporting the junta. Then came the revelations in Congress and the press of U.S. covert action against the Allende government and U.S. support of the junta through military aid and the Food for Peace program. Citizens who took the time to read the documents produced by congressional investigating committees were simply appalled by the behavior of the U.S. government. [13]

Although high levels of human rights violations occurred elsewhere in the hemisphere, Chile provided the one case which combined the destruction of a strong democratic tradition, followed by uncommonly widespread human rights violations and extensively documented U.S. complicity. As Chile became the focus of the human rights movement in the United States, it directed the attention of human rights activists to Latin America.

Fourth, by adopting human rights as the soul of his foreign policy, President Carter legitimized humanitarian concerns in much the same way that John Kennedy had legitimized economic aid through the Alliance for Progress. The policy strengthened State Department personnel who voiced concern over the lack of humanitarian values in foreign policy. In addition, the individuals President Carter named to direct the State Department's new Bureau of Human Rights and Humanitarian Affairs were people with strong commitments to the issue. Until 1977 the few human rights personnel in the State Department were chosen largely for their ability to counter criticism from the public and Congress. Thereafter, they were selected because they could increase the impact of human rights in foreign policy decision making.

The fifth factor contributing to an increasing role for human rights concerns in U.S. foreign policy is that during the 1970s there was no *credible* threat to United States security in Latin America. By 1975–1976 a good number of Latin American countries were dominated by repressive conservative governments. There were no Allendes or Goularts to preoccupy stability-oriented foreign policy officials. No government was threatening the continued dominance of liberal capitalism. There were only the Sandinistas in Nicaragua, with little hope in 1975 of ever overwhelming Somoza's U.S.-supplied National Guard. The assertions that United States security was threatened began to reappear only as the challenge to Somoza grew.

Once human rights came out of the closet, the question arose over their relative value. Brady Tyson, a member of UN Ambassador Andrew Young's staff, observed that "those of us who had been outside came in with lots of ideas about what was wrong and about what ought to be, but not many ideas of how to go about it." [14] Gingerly, they groped their way. At his February 8, 1977 news conference, the President noted that he was "reserving the right to speak out forcefully whenever human rights are threatened," but then he finished this sentence by adding "not in every instance, but when I think it's advisable." In contrast to his inaugural address, this suggested that President Carter had a relative rather than an absolute commitment to increasing the role of human rights considerations in U.S. foreign policy.

The question then became the same which had faced all previous administrations: How much of a commitment? The first attempt at an answer was made by Secretary of State Cyrus Vance when he appeared before the Senate Appropriations Subcommittee on Foreign Operations on February 24, 1977. He announced that the administration planned to reduce aid to Argentina, Ethiopia, and Uruguay because of their gross violations of human rights. Absent from the Secretary's statement was any suggestion that human rights had the absolute value which the President had mentioned in his inaugural address. Instead, Vance noted that while human rights considerations would receive greater attention, as with previous administrations they would be incorporated in U.S. policy on a country-by-country basis: "In each case we must balance a political concern for human rights against economic or security goals." [15] At his initial appearance before the UN General Assembly in March 1977, President Carter again expressed the relative value of human rights in United States foreign policy by asserting that human rights would not interfere with progress in certain other areas, especially arms control. The important point, however, is that the President actually addressed the issue of human rights and pledged the support of his administration for improved human rights observance.

In December 1978 the President took advantage of the 30th anniversary of the Universal Declaration of Human Rights to emphasize his commitment:

As long as I am President, the government of the United States will continue throughout the world to enhance human rights. . . . No force on earth can separate us from that commitment. . . . Our human rights policy is not a decoration. It is not something we have adopted to polish up our image abroad, or to put a fresh coat of moral paint on the discredited policies of the past. . . . Human rights is the soul of our foreign policy. [16]

From the outset of his administration, it was obvious that the President and his major advisors agreed that human rights should be given a greater relative value than they had during the Nixon-Ford years.

Once this was established, a number of ancillary issues had to be clarified before U.S. diplomats could implement the administration's policy. One such issue—the selection of the human rights to be given major emphasis—was settled by Secretary of State Vance at his Law Day speech at the University of Georgia in April 1977. The Carter administration, he declared, would concentrate first on the right to be free from governmental violation of the integrity of the person; second, on the right to the fulfillment of basic needs; and third, on the right to enjoy civil and political liberties. Nothing that problems might arise over which of these rights should be given priority, he indicated his preference for seeking "a rapid end to such gross violations as those cited in our law: torture, or cruel, inhuman or degrading treatment or punishment, or prolonged detention without charges. . . . The promotion of other human rights is a broader challenge. The results may be slower in coming. . . ." [17]

A second issue—the relationship between terrorism and human rights violations by governments—had particular significance for Latin America. It too was clarified by Secretary Vance, this time at the seventh general assembly of the Organization of American States in June 1977. In that forum Vance presented a vigorous rebuttal to the contention that human rights abuses were an unfortunate but necessary by-product of the war against terrorism. In direct contrast to the position of his predecessor, the Secretary of State rejected the legitimacy of combating terrorism with counterterrorism:

If terrorism and violence in the name of dissent cannot be condoned, neither can violence that is officially sanctioned. Such action perverts the legal system that, alone, assures the survival of our traditions. The surest way to defeat terrorism is to promote justice in our societies—legal, social and economic justice. Justice that is summary undermines the future it seeks to promote. It produces only more violence, more victims, and more terrorism. [18]

At the same meeting the United States cosponsored a resolution which deflected the Carter administration's refusal to recognize terrorism as an excuse for repression.

Finally, the manner in which the Carter administration handled four specific events in 1977 and early 1978 served to clarify the limits of the new emphasis upon human rights in United States policy toward Latin America. First, any fears that the President would project a fundamentalist view of human rights protection were put to rest in the spring of 1977. On March 8, 1977, Brady Tyson, a Methodist minister and university professor, who was serving as an aide to UN Ambassador Andrew Young, appeared at a meeting of the UN Commission on Human Rights in Geneva and expressed "our profoundest regrets" over official and unofficial U.S. involvement in the overthrow of the Allende government in Chile. He further expressed sorrow that such regrets could not "contribute significantly to the reduction of suffering and terror that the people of Chile have experienced." Tyson was immediately called home for instruction in diplomatic procedures. [19] At his news conference the following day, President Carter repudiated both Tyson and his own charge in the October 1976 pre-election debate with President Ford that the United States "overthrew an elected government and helped to establish a military dictatorship" in Chile. Between October and March he discovered the lack of "any evidence that the U.S. was involved in the overthrow of the Allende government in Chile." [20]

The second event was the September 1977 ceremonial signing of the new Panama Canal treaties, attended by nearly all of the Western Hemisphere's chiefs of state. President Carter spoke individually with each of the leaders, including Chile's Pinochet and Argentina's Vídela, thereby signaling his conclusion that the need for hemispheric solidarity on such important issues as the Panama Canal treaties overrode the earlier impulse to show official displeasure with governments causing major human rights violations.

The third event was an extraordinarily ill-timed letter sent by President Carter to Nicaraguan President Somoza in July 1978, complimenting him on making a verbal commitment to improve human rights observance. This letter was sent just two months before the beginning of the full-scale civil war which eventually toppled Somoza. It was drafted by the National Security Council staff and cabled to Managua over the strong opposition of the Department of State.

The fourth and surely the most widely received message to U.S. diplomats came in the form of a demonstration of what happened to half-hearted supporters of Carter's human rights policy. Terence A. Todman, the Assistant Secretary of State for Inter-American Affairs, initially opposed the use of public diplomacy to pursue aggressively the protection of human rights in Latin America. Upon completion of a trip to Chile in October 1977, he remarked that the Department of State was encouraged "by recent evidence that the trend away from democracy may be ending," citing as an example of this the Chilean government's "public commitment to a timetable" for elections. No such timetable existed. Within a week the State Department took the unusual step of presenting a detailed rebuttal to Todman's statement. It noted that the Assistant Secretary "has tried to emphasize the readiness of our Government to recognize progress" and "to avoid the development of a sterile adversary relationship." Nonetheless, the Department argued that "at no time did he allege that the human rights situation in the Southern Cone countries was satisfactory," and even if he did give that impression, "the Department continues to be disappointed with the lack of political freedom in Chile." [21]

Todman's second major break with the Carter administration came in February 1978 during the course of a speech at the Center for Inter-American Relations in New York. There he presented a list of ten "tactical mistakes" which the United States must avoid "if we are truly to help and not hinder the cause of promoting human rights and alleviating suffering." Among these were the practices of "condemning an entire government for every negative act by one of its officials" and of "holding entire countries up to public ridicule and embarrassment." [22] Shortly thereafter, Mr. Todman was asked to accept the ambassadorship to Spain.

The general message which emerged from these actions was that human rights would have a significant place in nearly all foreign policy decisions, but that the amount of significance would depend upon the countries involved. As it happened, many of the truly egregious human rights violators were outside the U.S. sphere of influence—the United States, for example, had no diplomatic relations with Cambodia or Uganda. Other major violators were of such importance to U.S. strategic and economic interests that administration officials concluded that human rights objectives could not be pursued vigorously. In this category were the governments of Indonesia, Iran, the Philippines, and South Korea. This left the nations of Latin America linked to the United States by two centuries of intimate intercourse and, with the possible exceptions of Brazil, Mexico, and Venezuela, lacking any of the strategic significance which exempted other nations from diplomatic pressure on behalf of human rights. Once the Carter administration recognized that a universal absolute standard of human rights would conflict with other foreign policy goals, the administration adopted a case-by-case approach to human rights abuses.

III. CONVERTING PROMISES INTO POLICY

Bilateral Diplomacy.   Within the Department of State, the two bureaus charged with implementing United States policy on human rights in Latin America are the Bureau of Inter-American Affairs (ARA) and the Bureau of Human Rights and Humanitarian Affairs (HA).

ARA's prime task is the maintenance of smooth relations with the various governments of Latin America. It is responsible for day-to-day diplomatic interaction with Latin America, the staffing of embassies and consulates, and the monitoring of developments in the region which might affect U.S. interests. Because of the nature's of the Bureau's duties, ARA officials have always been reluctant to raise publicly the issue of human rights abuses. Thus the following statement by a Nixon administration Assistant Secretary of State for Inter-American Affairs, Jack Kubisch, expresses a widely held attitude: "It is one thing for our newspapers or for private citizens to make charges or make complaints or appeal to the Chileans. It is something else for U.S. government officials or the executive branch to lean hard publicly on a regime since to do so might make them feel that they are required to dig in their heels and resist us publicly, or not have anything to do with us, or discuss the matter with us." [23]

While such a position could reflect a willingness to accept repression as an alternative to disorder and revolution, it is at least as plausible to suggest that the attitude stems from the simple perception that, as Kubisch stated, if the United States publicly presses a Latin American government too hard on a sensitive issue such as human rights, the government might indeed decide "not to have anything to do with us." Should that occur, ARA will have failed in its mission to maintain smooth relations.

Because the officials of ARA have as their principal task the preservation of effective working relationships with all recognized Latin American governments, regardless of their level of repressiveness, the Bureau has always preferred quiet diplomacy. There are, however, various types of quiet diplomacy. During the Nixon-Ford years diplomatic interaction over human rights issues was of a perfunctory nature. Secretary Kissinger's Assistant Secretary of State for Inter-American Affairs, William D. Rogers, liked to compare his marital experience and the Nixon-Ford administration's activities on behalf of human rights. He contended that he was much more willing to accept his wife's criticism of his social misbehavior if she waited until they were alone in bed rather than chastising him publicly. Following this approach, Rogers argued that he could be more successful by tactfully suggesting rather than by openly demanding that a repressive regime change. [24]

Readers will recognize that private criticism by most spouses varies widely in its intensity. The quiet diplomacy ARA had in mind under the Nixon administration was often very gentle. Take, for example, the response from William Roundtree, the U.S. ambassador to Brazil, when Senator Frank Church inquired whether ARA had expressed concern over evidence that the Brazilians dictatorship was systematically exterminating all dissent: "To the government, yes. I might say that the Department of State here in Washington has mentioned its concern to the representatives of Brazil, and the various members of the mission . . . have indicated concern regarding these stories." [25] To the Nixon-Ford administration, quiet diplomacy on behalf of human rights generally involved only the most circumspect protestations.

This style of diplomacy contrasts vividly with that practiced under the Carter administration. In 1978, for example, the Deputy Assistant Secretary of State for Inter-American Affairs, Richard Arellano, was asked the same question regarding the repressive activities of El Salvador's White Warriors Union. He responded by describing a far more aggressive form of quiet diplomacy: "Repeatedly, upon instructions from Washington, the Embassy has made formal demarches, sent protest notes and otherwise actively sought to impress upon Salvadoran authorities and others the abiding concern of the American people and Government with the human rights ramifications of developments in El Salvador." [26] It is worth noting that few of the national security concerns which might have prompted a relatively mild approach to the Brazilian government's human rights violations applied to tiny El Salvador in 1977. But in those instances where national security was a minor consideration —Uruguay in the mid-1970s, for example—the Nixon-Ford administration's form of diplomacy was also lacking in aggressiveness.

Despite these differences, it should be emphasized that under any administration ARA strives to conduct diplomatic relations in such a way that relations are not strained. While under the Carter administration the Bureau occasionally accepted the risk of straining relations, even then its opposition to the strategy was apparent. In fact, throughout the late 1970s the Bureau maintained its reputation for remitence on the human rights issue. Much of this reputation was undeserved, for it regularly used quiet diplomacy in defense of human rights. But because it was quiet, it often went unnoticed, and thus the Bureau's reputation came from its public efforts to protect existing aid programs from attacks by Congress and the Bureau of Human Rights and Humanitarian Affairs. Given its responsibility to maintain contact, access, and influence with all Latin American governments, it is difficult to imagine how the Bureau could have behaved otherwise. Its often criticized "curator mentality"— the desire to protect existing relationships—will probably never disappear. [27]

The Bureau of Human Rights and Humanitarian Affairs, the second executive branch bureaucracy responsible for implementing United States policy on human rights in Latin America, is a new organization whose present structure and functions date from early 1977. Prior to the creation of HA, responsibility for the diplomatic aspect of human rights protection rested briefly (1975–1977) with the Office of the Coordinator for Human Rights and Humanitarian Affairs and, before that, with both the Bureau of International Organization Affairs (IO) and, to a lesser extent, with the Office of the Legal Advisor. This reflected the State Department's conception of human rights questions as primarily technical: the preparation of instructions for United States representatives to international human rights commissions and the creation of policy toward international human rights agreements. At the time of the initial Fraser Subcommittee hearings in 1973, IO had assigned one foreign service officer to work full-time on human rights, assisted part-time by a junior officer. In the Office of the Legal Advisor, there was one assistant legal advisor for human rights.[28]

Soon after the hearings were completed, a human rights officer was designated in every regional bureau. It is not known whether the purpose of this move was to please congressional critics or to promote a larger role for human rights in United States foreign policy. But it is instructive to note that each of these new human rights officers was initially expected to continue with his or her previous tasks (most were labor specialists) and to perform human rights functions as well.[29] In addition to the creation of the posts of regional human rights officers. IO's human rights officer was upgraded to deputy director of the UN Political Affairs Office, and another officer was assigned to work as his assistant. Finally, in April 1975 the State Department anticipated Congress' directive and appointed a Coordinator for Humanitarian Affairs in the office of the Deputy Secretary of State.[30] In 1976 Congress changed the title of the coordinator, made the position subject to Senate confirmation, and guaranteed that it could not be abolished without congressional approval.

Despite these structural changes, human rights officials had little impact on policy determination during the Nixon-Ford administration. The initial coordinator, James M. Wilson, Jr., was noted for his low visibility during his brief tenure. Most of his first year in office was devoted to the problem of Vietnamese refugees; thereafter he spent much of his time attempting to convince Congress not to pass human rights legislation. In his only public statement on human rights and diplomacy, he offered a view of diplomatic interaction which differed not at all from that of his colleagues in ARA:

> In every instance . . . human rights problems are likely to be
> a unique result of a special set of circumstances. There will be
> few general prescriptions that will apply equally well to all coun-
> tries. A case-by-case approach . . . is essential. . . . bilateral diplomacy
> remains the basic weapon for promotion of human rights. . . . This
> requires deft diplomacy of the highest order. We have to retain
> contact and influence and yet try to persuade governments who feel
> fiercely besieged [by terrorists]. [31]

Responding to congressional demands for an activist human rights policy,
Wilson urged instead that the United States concentrate upon "quiet and
friendly persuasion" to combat human rights abuses. [32]

At the initiative of the House of Representatives, in mid-1977
Congress included in its Foreign Relations Authorization Act (PL
95–105) an amendment upgrading the position of the coordinator to
that of an assistant secretary of state, a move which was strongly en-
dorsed by the Carter administration. HA quickly became the center
of human rights activities in U.S. foreign policy, in large measure due
to its highly competent and aggressive staff. Most of HA's considerable
bureaucratic strength stemmed, of course, from President Carter's
emphasis on the international protection of human rights, an emphasis
which was most evident in United States policy toward Latin America.
Because of this commitment, HA's staff grew both quantitatively and
qualitatively. The two-person staff under the Ford administration was
augmented by five new human rights officers, and further additions were
made as needs became identified. By the end of 1978, HA had at least
one expert covering each aspect of United States policy toward Latin
America.

Two individual appointments were particularly significant. As the
first Assistant Secretary of State for Human Rights and Humanitarian
Affairs, Patricia Derian set the tone of HA's activities. A civil rights
activist, a founder of the Mississippi Civil Liberties Union, and an
organizer of the biracial Loyalist Mississippi Democratic Party which
successfully challenged the all-white Mississippi delegation for seating
at the 1968 Democratic Party convention, Ms. Derian is a person of
unusually strong will. If President Carter wanted an Assistant Secretary
who could forcefully present the case for human rights and who was
not intimidated by established bureaucratic procedures, there could have
been few better choices than Derian. [33] Her principal associate was
Mark Schneider, as Deputy Assistant Secretary for Human Rights.
Through Schneider, HA enjoyed extremely close relations with several
members of Congress who had been working for years to enlarge the

human rights component of U.S. foreign policy. A former Peace Corps volunteer in El Salvador, Schneider had worked for some years as an aide to Senator Edward Kennedy, where he performed most of the staff work which resulted in a number of Senate-sponsored hearings, resolutions, and laws on repression in post-Allende Chile.

Under Derian, HA concentrated upon building its staff and its expertise in specific policy areas such as foreign aid. Interspersed with this institution-building activity was an ongoing attempt at direct bilateral diplomacy on behalf of human rights, including a number of meetings with the leaders of Latin America's most repressive governments. Unlike officials at ARA, whose actions and private conversations expressed profound concern over human rights violations but never went so far as to offend foreign leaders, HA was willing to push the issue beyond the bounds of normal diplomatic intercourse. Derian characterized her diplomatic conversations with leaders of repressive governments as "a very serious kind of thing. It's not just talk. It is always extremely tense." [34] She was one of the few United States diplomats to elaborate publicly upon her discussions:

> What happens is that we begin a meeting, and this is at the official level, with long statements about the concern and affection and importance of human rights to the country involved. All countries say that they are great defenders of and believers in human rights. Then we have a kind of pause in the discussion and they explain whatever the crisis is in the country that causes them to violate human rights. No country really admits it is a human rights violator. All countries, or representatives of countries, profess to care as much as we do. They often hold up their own constitutions and pronounce them better than ours. Then they explain their crisis, which threatens their society, and next say that as soon as they get on the other side of this crisis they will begin to observe human rights again, but during this interval it is necessary for them to take extraordinary measures. Then I talk respectfully about what they mean by extraordinary measures. There is ordinarily a great breakthrough because I use this word "torture" in places where this is applicable, and it is applicable in far too many places. I talk about the specific kinds that they do, the names of places where people are detained, the names of people who are missing, the names of people who are no longer in detention but are not [at liberty], who have suffered various kinds of abuses and mistreatment.
>
> Then we come to a kind of reality facing. Mostly an explanation that they are not responsible, that we have to understand things

are so terrible and intense in the place that people at a lower level are moved by their own overriding emotions to take these actions on their own. Then I talk about responsibility. If you hold high office you must take the full responsibility and the blame. Then we generally start all over again and go through the whole thing again. That is generally the end of the first encounter.[35]

To Latin American leaders accustomed to exchanges with United States diplomats who emphasize the maintenance of smooth relations, Ms. Derian's brand of quiet diplomacy must have come as a surprise.

Multilateral Diplomacy.   In addition to their bilateral activities, United States diplomats worked through the United Nations and the Organization of American States to implement U.S. policy toward human rights in Latin America during the 1970s. For most of the Cold War period, however, multilateral diplomacy has not been a favored tool of American policymakers. In 1974 the legal scholar Louis Henkin lamented that

> the United States has remained largely outside the international human rights program. It has been for this country a peripheral aspect of its United Nations activities, themselves increasingly peripheral, and conducted by officials peripheral to the seats of power and the major concerns of United States foreign policy.[36]

This is not to suggest that the United States has always ignored the United Nations in addressing its human rights concerns. Indeed, the United States dominated the early human rights activities of the UN, providing the major impetus for the human rights provisions of the Charter and much of the initiative for the Universal Declaration of Human Rights and the Genocide Convention. In addition, the United States was instrumental in urging the creation of the UN Commission on Human Rights, and it has a largely unrecognized record of sponsoring improvements in the Commission's procedures. Given the Cold War attitudes of American policymakers and the decline of U.S. hegemony in the United Nations, it was probably inevitable that U.S. participation in multilateral human rights activities peaked early. Still, the decline in U.S. interest in multilateral diplomacy to protect human rights was impressive in its dimensions.[37] The nadir was reached during the Nixon administration.

The general policy of the Nixon-Ford administration toward human rights issues in the United Nations was to protect U.S. allies from criticism.[38] Since the only major Latin American human rights issue to arise in the United Nations during the 1970s was that of Chile, it is upon the U.S. position in this instance that the record of the Nixon-Ford administration stands. There is some question as to the content of that position. In his March 1976 testimony before Congress, Secretary of State Kissinger asserted that at his direction the United States "voted in the United Nations with the majority on the issue of human rights in Chile." [39] Contrary to the impression Kissinger may have left with Congress, what he must have meant by this statement is not that United States consistently voted with the majority or that it regularly voted with the majority, but that it *once* voted with the majority. The record is fairly unambiguous, and it indicates that the Nixon-Ford administration obstructed the efforts of the United Nations to assess the situation in Chile and to promote increased respect for human rights. This position appears congruent with other aspects of their policy toward post-Allende Chile.

In early 1974 the Social Committee of the UN Economic and Social Council (ECOSOC) adopted its first resolution on Chile, a mild statement calling upon the government of Chile to "restore and safeguard basic human rights." The measure passed by a vote of 41 to 0, with two abstentions: Chile and the United States. The resolution was then passed to the parent ECOSOC, where it was adopted by consensus. According to one active observer, California Supreme Court Justice Frank Newman, the contribution of the United States to the resolution "was to make it as weak as conceivable." [40]

In October 1974, the General Assembly's Social, Cultural and Humanitarian Committee voted 83 to 9 to urge the Chilean government to restore human rights and to free political prisoners. The United States abstained. The following month the General Assembly passed two resolutions on human rights in Chile. One called upon the government of Chile "to release all persons who have been detained without charge or imprisoned solely for political reasons." The resolution passed by a vote of 90 to 8. The United States abstained, calling the resolution "unbalanced." The second resolution requested freedom for Clodomiro Almeyda, Chile's foreign minister under Allende and the president of UNCTAD III. Again the United States abstained.

Finally, on November 11, 1975 the United States voted with the majority on an issue of human rights in Chile, when the General Assembly's Social, Cultural and Humanitarian Committee recommended by a vote of 88 to 11 that the General Assembly express its "profound distress at the constant, flagrant violations of human rights, including the institutionalized practice of torture" in Chile. [41] This vote occurred as part of a broader effort by the Ford administration to distance itself from the Pinochet government. The Chilean junta was a particularly vulnerable target for a variety of reasons: its unusual brutality, its 1975 decision to support (and later abstain on) the UN resolution equating Zionism with racism, its refusal to permit a UN human rights investigating team to enter Chile, and its repression of all domestic political opposition. Also relevant were the negative connotations of an association with the Chilean junta during the upcoming United States presidential contest.

Thus in his June 8, 1976 speech to the foreign ministers of the OAS, Secretary of State Kissinger addressed the subject of human rights with unusual frankness. Although he noted that the OAS's Inter-American Commission on Human Rights had concluded that "the infringement of certain fundamental rights in Chile has undergone a quantitative reduction" and that "Chile has filed a comprehensive and responsive answer [to the Commission's charges of institutionalized torture] that sets forth a number of hopeful prospects," he expressed the dismay of the U.S. government that violations continued to occur:

> In the United States, concern is widespread in the executive branch, in the press, and in the Congress, which has taken the extraordinary step of enacting specific statutory limits on United States military and economic aid to Chile. The condition of human rights . . . has impaired our relationship with Chile and will continue to do so. We wish this relationship to be close, and all friends of Chile hope that obstacles raised by conditions alleged in the report will soon be removed. [42]

Except for the periodic vilification of Cuba, this was at the time the strongest formal statement any OAS member had made against the internal human rights violations by another member government. Aside from this activity in support of human rights in Chile, however, the Nixon-Ford administration demonstrated little interest in using multilateral diplomacy to promote the observance of human rights in Latin America or elsewhere.

There were some changes during the Carter administration in the use of multilateral diplomacy as a foreign policy tool to promote human rights. In the United Nations, the major difference was in the level of rhetoric. On March 17, 1977 President Carter chose the UN General Assembly for the site of his first major foreign policy speech as President. Although he spoke on several topics, his remarks were noted for their emphasis on human rights. To demonstrate his administration's commitment, the President signed and promised to seek Senate ratification of the two UN human rights covenants, and he continued his predecessors' attempts to obtain ratification of both the Genocide Convention and the Treaty for the Elimination of All Forms of Racial Discrimination. In addition, he pledged to support efforts by the United Nations to improve its human rights machinery. Specifically, he proposed moving the UN's human rights division back to the New York headquarters from Geneva, and he promised to support efforts to establish the post of UN high commissioner for human rights.

Beyond these initial activities, the Carter administration did not emphasize the use of the United Nations to promote respect for human rights in Latin America. This reflected in part a desire to address the issue via the Organization of American States, where U.S. diplomatic power is far greater than in the United Nations. But even on non-Latin American human rights issues, the Carter administration appeared to view the United Nations as a relatively limited arena. For example, the administration continued the practice of appointing part-time representatives to the UN Commission on Human Rights. These individuals were often selected because they were underemployed party loyalists, particularly recently defeated members of Congress, rather than experts in the field of human rights or persons with a significant influence upon United States foreign policy.

Less than a month after his initial speech to the UN General Assembly, President Carter gave his first address to the Permanent Council of the Organization of American States. Unlike some of his predecessors, who had taken advantage of their initial appearance at the OAS to announce a new Latin American policy, President Carter's speech was basically a catalogue of problems affecting inter-American relations, nearly all of which were economic in their nature. Special emphasis was placed on human rights, however. He told the delegates that

> our values and yours require us to combat abuses of individual freedom, including those caused by political, social, and economic injustice. Our own concerns for these values will naturally influence our relations with the countries of this hemisphere and throughout the world. You will find this country eager to stand beside those nations which respect human rights and promote democratic values. [43]

In addition to this relatively mild statement, the President signed .the American Convention on Human Rights on June 1, 1977.

The Carter administration's use of the OAS to encourage respect for human rights can best be pictured as an extension of the policy begun in 1976 by the Ford administration. Its major effort occurred in mid-June 1977, at the organization's seventh general assembly on the Caribbean island of Grenada. The human rights issue totally dominated the meeting.

Secretary of State Vance went far beyond the Kissinger statement at Santiago in 1976, presenting a strong rebuttal to the popular contention that human rights abuses were a necessary part of the war against terrorism. In addition, the United States cosponsored, and helped obtain the necessary votes for, a resolution which states in part that "there are no circumstances which justify torture, summary executions or prolonged detention without trial contrary to law." [44] The Secretary of State then proceeded to link the provision of United States foreign assistance to the recipient's level of respect for human rights, noting that aid would be useless in an environment of extreme repression. Finally, Vance met privately with the foreign ministers of nearly all OAS member states, urging the representatives of repressive regimes to take seriously his public comments. Each of these statements was a significant extension of the human rights policy of the preceding administration.

But beyond this initial effort in 1977, multilateral diplomacy through the OAS did not become a prominent tool to implement United States policy toward human rights. OAS members soon became aware that the Inter-American Commission on Human Rights was fully supported by the United States, and that the reports of the Commission could no longer be ignored as they had been for years. The necessary resolutions and declarations were made; there was little more that the OAS could do to promote human rights. There was never a question about the possibility of the OAS punishing an individual member, for most Latin American governments have always considered the level of respect for human rights an internal political matter. In addition, many nations were understandably suspicious of the role of the United States in the human rights effort. One need not know much about U.S.-Latin American relations to recognize why Latin Americans might be wary of the motivations behind yet another United States crusade in Latin America. So while Latin America's repressive regimes could not prevent the United States and several hemispheric allies from making human rights a major issue in the OAS, they could make concrete action extremely difficult to accomplish. Recognizing this reality, the Carter administration decided to invest its diplomatic resources in bilateral efforts to promote human rights in Latin America.

IV. CONVERTING POLICY INTO ACTION

The Carter administration used principally four policy tools to encourage repressive governments to reduce their level of human rights violations: military aid, economic aid, multilateral development bank loans, and private economic transactions. The manner in which each was used reveals much about the potential and the limits of humanitarian considerations in United States foreign policy.

Military Aid. Early analyses of the Carter administration's military aid budget were uniformly negative. The Interreligious Task Force on U.S. Food Policy blasted the administration's fiscal year (FY) 1978 security assistance proposals as heavily skewed toward the most repressive governments. Brazil, Indonesia, the Philippines, and South Korea were all scheduled by the Carter administration to receive major assistance. After holding his criticism for nine months, the highly respected leader of the Friends Committee on National Leglislation, Edward Snyder, was quoted as saying that "with regard to giving military aid to repressive regimes, I see little difference between this administration and the Nixon-Ford approach." [45]

While this criticism was justified in the sense that military aid continued to flow to many repressive regimes, in the case of Latin America it was first premature and then, for a brief period, simply incorrect. It was premature because the FY 78 budget was largely the creation of the outgoing Ford administration, and incorrect because executive branch requests for military aid to Latin America dropped dramatically between FY 76 and FY 79. While worldwide military assistance expenditure requests remained roughly unchanged between FY 77 and FY 79, Latin America's share of the total dropped from 8.1 percent to 2.3 percent.

Several factors contributed to this reduction. As mentioned previously, political dissent by leftist groups in several nations (Argentina, Chile, and Uruguay) had been largely eliminated by 1977, so less aid was required to contain the political groups which had been considered threats by earlier administrations. At the same time, the level of human rights violations accompanying this political repression had risen so dramatically that Congress legislated a series of country-specific aid reductions. By the end of 1978, the executive branch could not provide certain types of military aid to Argentina, Brazil, Chile, El Salvador, Guatemala, and Uruguay. Perhaps more significantly, in order to preempt action by either Congress or human rights activists within the State Department, military aid requests were reduced for other countries with governments noted for their high levels of human rights violations. ARA decided not to request the typical $1 million to $4 million in Foreign Military Sales (FMS) credits for Somoza's Nicaragua, for example, simply because the Bureau recognized that either HA or liberal members of Congress would put up too much of a fight.

It is difficult to determine how these variables interacted, and hence to estimate the extent to which reductions in aid reflected autonomous decisions by the Carter administration to withdraw military assistance in order to promote respect for human rights in Latin America. There were some documented cases where the administration used military assistance to Latin America for this purpose. In 1977 the United States signed an FMS agreement with Nicaragua, for example, but the State Department refused to release the funds because of the Somoza government's human rights violations. The administration delayed the actual use of the money until pressure by pro-Somoza members of Congress forced a partial release.[46] Then in late 1978 the administration placed a complete ban on military aid and export licenses for Nicaragua, making Somoza's government the third in Latin America (together with Chile and Uruguay) to be totally cut off from U.S. military arms and services.

In another case, in mid-1978 the Carter administration briefly suspended military aid to Bolivia when General Juan Pereda Asbún seized power following a disputed election, and it suspended aid again when the Bolivian military launched yet another coup in July 1980.[47]

Most of the repressive regimes in Latin America were pressured from time to time by delays in the approval of military aid requests, but the U.S. military aid program to Latin America had been declining since the mid-1960s, so that by the late 1970s it had lost much of its utility as an instrument to influence the region's repressive governments. Once aid had been reduced, the Carter administration was forced to turn to other foreign policy tools, especially limitations on commercial arms sales, to promote its human rights policy. As for military aid, the administration could do little more than wait to see if the reductions were having their desired effect.

It is possible to argue that in the case of Nicaragua the effect was to contribute to the fall of Anastasio Somoza and, more positively, to the creation of a government that gave every indication of respect for human rights, including the economic and social rights to which the U.S. government had given limited attention during the Carter administration. But if such an argument is possible—and I believe it is— then it is equally possible to argue that in the case of El Salvador the effect of an increase in military aid was to shore up a government which perpetuated human rights abuse.[48] In April 1980 the Assistant Secretary of State for Human Rights and Humanitarian Affairs, Patricia Derian, attempted to assuage the concerns of a group of Latin Americanists by informing them that the administration's military aid was "to enable the Salvadoran Armed Forces to purchase communications and transportation equipment to improve its ability to control the violence." Then, in the very next sentence, she added that the level of violence in El Salvador was in part "the responsibility of undisciplined security forces in the countryside."[49]

Overall, the Carter administration's FY 1981 military aid request to Congress was a grave disappointment to human rights activists. Reflecting the general drift of foreign policy toward a renewal of the Cold War, the administration's $63.6 million request reflected a large increase (15 percent) over FY 79. Moreover, it was directed toward the Central American and Caribbean nations where civilian political forces were struggling to assert their control over public policy. Regardless of what this aid might accomplish in strengthening defenses against a real or imagined threat by Cuba, increased military aid could only strengthen the forces most closely identified with the violation of fundamental human rights in Latin America. If the military aid budget can be viewed as a reliable indicator of policy, by 1980 the Carter administration appeared to have forgotten the lesson it learned with such difficulty in Nicaragua.

Bilateral Economic Assistance.   By 1978 Congress and the executive branch had accomplished about as much as could be expected in linking human rights considerations to bilateral economic assistance to Latin America. They had reached agreement on the principle that bilateral economic aid was to be halted or reduced to Latin American countries which engaged in a consistent pattern of gross violations of fundamental human rights, unless such aid directly benefited needy people. Moreover, the two branches had agreed upon tentative definitions of the various terms of this agreement. These understandings served to accelerate the decline in the level of economic aid to Latin America which had begun in 1966. With the exception of relatively small programs to the economically least developed Latin American nations and a few projects in such showcase countries as Costa Rica, by the end of the 1970s bilateral economic aid had become a minor instrument of United States policy toward Latin America.

Multilateral Development Assistance.   In the late 1970's considerable change occurred in United States policy toward human rights and the multilateral development banks (MDBs). First, in late 1977 Congress created a law (PL 95–118) requiring the executive branch to oppose loans to governments which violate their citizens' fundamental human rights unless the funds would directly benefit needy people. This was an unusually difficult battle for human rights activists, in that they were opposed not only by the Democratic congressional leadership, a common feature of all human rights battles of the 1970s, but by the human rights-oriented Carter administration as well. Nonetheless, with the help of conservative colleagues opposed to all forms of foreign aid, liberal members of Congress produced a law which human rights activists inside and outside the government then proceeded to exploit.

Although Congress was unable to add a human rights/needs amendment to 1978 legislation governing United States participation in the Supplementary Financing Facility of the International Monetary Fund (IMF), it raised again the long-standing humanitarian concern of a relatively small number of citizens to the level of national policy debate and international diplomacy. By challenging the necessity for deprivations of basic needs which accompany IMF stabilization programs, Congress brought closer the day when the poor of the Third World will no longer be forced into even greater poverty in order to compensate for the financial mismanagement of their leaders and the negative impact of international market forces.

Second, the Carter administration adopted a policy of using its influence in the MDBs as an instrument to promote respect for fundamental human rights. The administration was vulnerable to criticisms that it did not use this power with sufficient vigor or consistency, that it approved many loans which violated the spirit if not the word of congressional directives, and that it was too quick to reward the marginal diminution in repression by approving a resumption of favorable votes. But there is no contesting the evidence that the Carter policy was a clear departure from that of its predecessors. The issue of human rights was raised in MDB councils, and while no loans were formally denied because of opposition from the United States, the Carter administration policy served to deter loan applications by Latin America's most repressive governments.

Within the U.S. government, the administration created a formal bureaucratic mechanism that served almost automatically to inject human rights considerations into any MDB loan proposal. All HA needed to do to raise a human rights issue was refuse to sign off on a loan proposal. Then the issue went to the Christopher Committee,[50] where HA won some battles and lost others. On this question the administration could be criticized for adopting a proposal-by-proposal review process, which at first simply overwhelmed officials in the newly created human rights bureau. But the administration staffed HA with energetic personnel, and the Christopher Committee provided a forum where HA could demonstrate its vigor. As a result of these changes in United States policy, in the MDBs the subject of human rights was alive and, if not well, at least doing better by 1980.

The Private Sector. An examination of U.S. government attempts to employ the linkages between the private sector and repressive

Latin American governments yielded far less encouraging results. In theory, the government had at its disposal a variety of foreign-policy instruments which could have been used to encourage improved human rights practices or, barring that, to dissociate the United States from repressive regimes. Prime among these instruments are the Export-Import Bank, the Overseas Private Investment Corporation, the American Institute for Free Labor Development (AIFLD), and commercial arms export licenses granted through the State Department's Office of Munitions Control. [51] With minor exceptions none of these instruments was used during the 1970s to promote the nation's human rights policy. Indeed, Congress passed legislation (PL 95–630) specifically prohibiting the executive branch from employing Eximbank loans and guarantees for human rights purposes.

In addition, the administration failed to exploit less formal relationships between its private sector and Latin American governments. Certain forms of cooperation are matters of public record; for example, the CIA's use of U.S.-based corporations to provide cover for its personnel and information for its analysts. It is also evident that the government on occasion asks these corporations for assistance in bringing direct pressure upon Latin American governments, as in early 1960 when Treasury Secretary Robert Anderson personally urged executives of Exxon, Shell, and Texaco not to refine Soviet crude oil in their Cuban refineries. [52] But it is not clear whether the few rather sensational public examples are typical of public-private cooperation in the pursuit of U.S. policy objectives in Latin America. Rather than dwell upon this unanswerable question, it is more illuminating to approach the issue from another perspective by looking at the potentially powerful private sector relationships which the government did *not* use during the 1970s to promote its human rights policy in Latin America.

In general, both the Nixon-Ford and Carter administrations were extremely reluctant to request private-sector cooperation in efforts to pressure repressive governments to cease their human rights violations. Since the Nixon administration placed little emphasis upon the human rights component of foreign policy, its decision not to ask private corporations for assistance seems natural; but the absence of such an effort by the Carter administration was one of the most striking characteristics of its human rights policy. After 1977 an attentive public became accustomed to verbal flourishes on behalf of human rights, to cuts in economic and military aid, to pressure through MDBs, and even to an occasional halt in Eximbank or OPIC financing. In many cases, however, for every dime halted by the U.S. government, a dollar was sent to repressive governments by U.S. corporations. This vitiated the Carter human rights policy for, as even fairly friendly critics noted, "official bilateral assistance became irrelevant when billions of dollars in private resources were available for the asking. . . . "[53] Given the prominence of human rights in the administration's policy toward Latin America, it might have been expected that policymakers would take some actions when their public goals were thwarted by private actions. Yet the Carter administration did nothing.

The case of Chile attracted the most attention. In the years immediately following the 1973 coup, private investors remained wary of sending their funds to Chile. But then as Congress and, later, the Carter administration began to halt public support of the Chilean government, U.S.-based multinational corporations stepped in. Two investments in early 1978 broke the lull which had existed since the Frei administration (1964–1970). The Exxon Corporation purchased for $107 million the state-owned La Disputada de las Condes copper complex, and Goodyear Tire purchased for $34 million the state-managed CORFO–INSA tire company. Attracted by generous incentives from the Pinochet government, U.S.-based transnational corporations slowly began to return to Chile. In mid-1979 Anaconda Copper, now a subsidiary of Atlantic-Richfield, handed the Chilean government a check for $20 million and took control of the unexploited Pelambres copper deposit. Despite the clear U.S. government policy of halting aid to Chile, business was being conducted as usual.

Even more striking than corporate investments in mining and manufacturing was the support of the Pinochet government by private multinational banks. As public sources of external aid declined, private borrowings, which had been insignificant in 1974, increased to $100 million in 1975, to $520 million in 1976, to $858 million in 1977, and to an estimated $977 million in 1978.[54] Noting that these loans exceeded by far what could have been expected from official bilateral and multilateral assistance, House Banking Committee Chairman Henry Reuss sent telegrams to six U.S. banks, suggesting that their loans "appear inconsistent" with the accepted banking policy of not interfering with U.S. foreign policy. The full explanation demanded by Reuss was never forthcoming—indeed he did not pursue the matter beyond his telegram—and the United States banking community continued to lend to Chile.[55]

Given the very energetic human rights policy of the Carter administration, it is difficult to be certain why no serious attempt was made to influence private sector transactions which supported repressive governments in Latin America. Although this means was used for other purposes ranging from the isolation of Cuba to the promotion of majority rule in Rhodesia, apparently the costs in some cases were considered too high. Facing an enormous balance of payments deficit and a highly vocal, well connected business community, the administration was extremely reluctant to halt any potential source of foreign trade or profit. Reinforced by Congress' refusal to adopt binding human rights amendments to legislation governing public support for private trans- actions, the Carter administration concluded that the financial and political costs outweighed the potential humanitarian benefits of a policy of interference.

In summary, the Carter human rights policy served to limit some- what U.S. involvement and identification with repressive governments. In addition, it is possible that several Latin American governments became less repressive sooner than they would have had the United States not adopted a human rights policy. But it is also reasonable to believe that the gross violations themselves responded to a dynamic beyond the control of Washington. The U.S. government could encourage the coming to power of repressive governments, as the examples of Brazil in 1964 and Chile in 1973 demonstrate, but it was only after the early repression subsided that the U.S. government appeared to be an effective advocate of greater respect for the physical integrity of persons and, much later and more slowly, of the process of political liberalization.

This evaluation seems particularly appropriate in the cases of Argentina, Brazil, Chile, and Uruguay, but it is a less accurate description of the impact of U.S. policy toward El Salvador, Guatemala, and Nica- ragua, where there was a rising tide of public opposition to existing repressive regimes which *coincided* with the U.S. emphasis upon human rights. This public opposition led to what appeared in mid-1980 as an authentic revolution in Nicaragua and to extraordinarily strong threats to the existing structure of privilege in El Salvador and Guatemala.

The human rights policy of the United States clearly helped to stimulate this opposition. There are no conclusive data to confirm this, but, for example, the normally critical liberal weekly *Latin America* noted that "Carter's policy (albeit unwittingly) undermined the entire *somocista* system in Nicaragua," and that "the best the Guatemalan government can hope for is a victory at next year's U.S. presidential polls for a Republican." [56] The United States encouraged opposition and resistance to repression. It is here that the policy of promoting human rights promised to leave its most lasting impact upon Latin America.

Institutional Impact of the Carter Policy. It is unlikely that we will soon witness another major period of positive human rights activity on the part of the United States government. But three structural changes in the foreign policy decision-making process which strengthen the role of humanitarian values in United States policy toward Latin America did occur in the 1970s.

First, the increased influence of interest groups promoting humanitarian values is a reality. The monopoly once held by business groups and lobbyists for Latin American governments has been broken. As a result, United States policy can no longer be made the way it once was. The day is gone when a highly competent attorney such as Monroe Leigh can quietly slip a piece of paper into the hand of a senator and expect to see it processed without opposition into law, as he did with both Hickenlooper amendments in the 1960s. The day is gone when a Latin American dictator such as Anastasio Somoza can engage in gross violations of human rights and expect to continue to nose up to the foreign assistance trough. There may be more Hickenlooper amendments, and there undoubtedly will be times when foreign policy officials feel obliged to support a repressive dictator in order to protect their vision of national security, but now these actions will be contested. This will be done, in part, by highly effective human rights lobbyists, who in the 1970s succeeded not only in influencing foreign policy but in institutionalizing themselves as well. In the struggle for support from United States policymakers, the next Somoza will be faced with a serious battle.

A second change in the policy-making process of the 1970s was the resurgence of congressional interest in humanitarian issues, which had as a natural consequence a renewed interest in selected aspects of U.S.-Latin American relations. Since about 1965, when the invasion of the Dominican Republic marked the end of a brief period of congressional concern with Latin America per se, few members of Congress have been interested in any Latin America-related issue. At the beginning of the 1980s there is still little congressional interest in Latin America. The two foreign affairs subcommittees responsible for U.S.-Latin American relations are largely composed of lawmakers without substantial knowledge of Latin America. But this condition, ostensibly lamentable, has a positive aspect. It permits eager, aggressive legislators to capture the congressional policy-making process despite their lack of strategic bureaucratic positions. Had these legislators been opposed by informed, industrious leaders of the inter-American subcommittees during the 1970s, few of the human rights proposals of Congressmen Fraser, Harkin, Koch, Drinan, Solarz and Senators Kennedy, McGovern, and Abourezk would have become law. Or, perhaps more accurately, their proposals would have been seriously weakened by amendments.

As it was, and is, virtually any member of Congress has a reasonable chance of having his or her favorite topic become part of United States policy toward Latin America. This is a two-edged sword, of course. Only in the 1970s, however, did persons concerned with humanitarian aspects of American foreign policy learn to wield it with proficiency.

The third change in the policy-making process was the institutionalization of a human rights bureaucracy within the executive branch. Created at congressional insistence in the years immediately prior to the Carter administration, this bureaucracy proved to be absolutely indispensable in implementing U.S. human rights policy toward Latin America during the 1970s. Few, if any, of the human rights initiatives of the Carter administration would have occurred without the aggressive prodding of the Bureau of Human Rights and Humanitarian Affairs. But circumstances will certainly change over time, perceptions of threats to national security will arise, and in that event any administration's concern with the humanitarian aspects of foreign policy will decline rapidly. This will obviously diminish the effectiveness of the human rights bureaucracy within the executive branch.

V. RESTRICTIONS ON U.S. HUMAN RIGHTS POLICY IN THE FUTURE

The future of human rights in U.S. policy toward Latin America will therefore depend upon the balance struck between the structural changes that reflect greater political power for human rights forces— the development of interest groups, the increased congressional assertiveness in areas related to humanitarian concerns, the institutionalization of a human rights bureaucracy in the executive branch—and the ever-changing environmental factors which cannot be expected to encourage human rights initiatives to the same extent as they did in the 1970s. At the beginning of the 1980s, the great imponderable is when and under what conditions a fairly unambiguous threat to the core security and economic values of U.S. foreign policymakers will appear again in Latin America. The course of decompression is difficult to predict, for there are many possible scenarios. They range from a continuation of the authoritarian status quo through mildly participatory democracy to violent social revolution. But some repressive governments will undoubtedly be less capable than others in controlling the decompression process, and in at least one Latin American country a popular, reform-oriented government may be created. Here, history tells us, are the makings of a threat.

Whether elected by a slim plurality or swept into office by overwhelming public support, this new government will probably be weak, administered by inexperienced personnel and buffeted by a bewildering array of long-submerged political pressures. But it will nonetheless attempt to initiate reforms that threaten to alter significantly the existing structure of socioeconomic privilege, not out of devotion to an abstract ideological model, but because the government's political base is support from citizens who desire such a restructuring. If history repeats itself, this simple fact may well be beyond the realm of comprehension of U.S. policymakers. Like the governments of Allende, Arévalo-Arbenz, and Goulart, the new popular government will nationalize property because its leaders and their followers believe that their country will be a more just and peaceful place in which to live if peasants do not work for landowners and if major productive enterprises are owned and administered by the government rather than by private corporations.

While no one can predict the results of such attempts at reform, it is far less difficult to speculate about U.S. policy toward the governments that institute them. Certainly, major socioeconomic reforms will lead some part of the public and its representatives in Congress and .the executive branch to perceive a threat to the U.S. economy, and hence its national security. These citizens will demand that their government act to neutralize the threat. The measures they suggest taking will probably differ very little from those taken in the past: covert action using contacts in the military and organized labor, an unannounced economic blockade through Eximbank, OPIC, and private sector financial institutions, a halt in economic aid, a boost in military assistance.

In policy-making councils, the opposition to these actions would logically consist of the same forces of the center and liberal left which championed human rights in the 1970s. Throughout the 1970s these forces demonstrated their ability to influence U.S. policy toward Latin America, but with the exception of Somoza's Nicaragua they never faced in Latin America a circumstance in which human rights were competing with the core values which orient U.S. foreign policy. Latin America is therefore the wrong place to assess the likely outcome of such a competition. For purposes of prediction there are instead the cases of Iran, the Philippines, and South Korea—major defeats for human rights forces during the Carter administration. Only where communism was not a perceived threat were human rights an important component of U.S. policy.

In the Nicaraguan case, human rights forces were victorious because they prevented Somoza from making a communist threat credible to more than a few policymakers. This subtle distinction between outright combat and the struggle for credibility should not be missed. So long as anticommunism remains a component of national security policy, it will always defeat humanitarian values in a straightforward struggle for control of U.S. policy toward Latin America. Once a threat to national security is perceived, officials who perceive it must act. By definition, not to act on a national security threat is to jeopardize the nation's safety, something no administration would consider. Thus the goal of forces defending a reform-oriented Latin American government from hostile acts by the United States is to break the perceptual link that permits a situation involving major structural reforms in Latin America from being defined as a shift toward communism and, therefore, as a threat to the United States. The goal is influence over the perceptions of policymakers.

This is precisely what human rights activists accomplished in the case of Nicaragua. Note, however, that by late 1978 it was relatively easy for human rights forces to influence policymakers' perceptions on Nicaragua, given the unusual repressiveness of the Somoza government. With the Nicaraguan population in armed rebellion and with such progressive Latin American allies as Costa Rica and Venezuela, in open support of the rebels, it was obvious that something more than a simple communist conspiracy was afoot. It will be a different matter entirely to convince senior foreign policy officials that the next popular, reform-oriented Latin American movement or government is not a threat to the security of the United States.

VI. STRATEGIES FOR COMPLETING AN UNFINISHED AGENDA

How does a group promoting humanitarian values influence senior foreign policymakers' perceptions? How does such a group successfully contest the assertions of rival groups, both within and outside the government, who claim to have identified a threat to the most important foreign policy value of all, national security? The 1970s' struggle over human rights contains some lessons. First, human rights activists must fight with facts. Just as they showed policymakers and the public how Anastasio Somoza maintained power through raw terror, corruption, and coercion, they now must demonstrate that the next progressive government, far from deserving hostility, merits support because it is seriously pursuing reforms designed to meet the basic needs of its citizens, reforms that the United States has proclaimed for decades as essential to long-term stability and as the basis for widespread civil and political rights. Foreign policy officials know that United States policy is to encourage stability through reform in Latin America. But they have to be reminded that what they know about social change and human needs should guide their actions, rather than what they have been conditioned to fear about communism.

This argument, however, will not convince the more enthusiastic supporters of the status quo in Latin America; in no case are facts alone sufficient. Also essential is a foundation upon which to build a structure of facts. In this context, it is extremely important to note that a major source of strength of human rights activists during the 1970s was they spoke from a position of recognized moral authority. At a time when the moral authority of the United States government had all but disappeared, human rights forces began to talk about the felicitous consequences of a policy based upon humanitarianism. They said a people imbued with anticommunism had squandered what was left of their moral legacy in the corrupt exercise of power. They said that a sobered people now needed to reclaim their principles. They spoke with certainty of how to do some limited good in a confusing world where good is difficult to find and even harder to create. They spoke of principles all citizens understand. They spoke of human rights.

There are few principles more self-evident than that which asserts the human right to be free from torture at the hands of one's government. But there is at least one. It is that people have basic needs: to eat, to have shelter, to receive medical care, to read and write. During the twentieth century these have become recognized as fundamental human rights. They are rights systematically denied to millions of Latin Americans not because they are poor, but because the human and financial resources of their societies are controlled by groups that are no more concerned with malnutrition than they are with the moral implications of torture. Yet, as we have seen, these are groups that the United States has traditionally supported, not because we stand for either malnutrition or torture, but because our policymakers believe that anything more than very modest reforms in the existing structure of privilege in Latin America will be detrimental to our national security.

There will be neither peace nor stability in Latin America until the basic needs of the people are met, not by another reformist program reminiscent of the Alliance for Progress, but by a fundamental restructuring of privilege, so that the right of the minority of Latin Americans to spend their vacations at Disney World is made subordinate to the right of peasants to eat. That is the truth with which United States policymakers must become acquainted. And that is the truth the Reagan administration has missed in formulating its Latin American policy. Instead of recognizing that political turmoil is a symptom of widespread discontent over conditions of deprivation, the Reagan policy has interpreted unrest in Latin America as a sign of Cuban and Soviet expansionism.

Thus in the battle for control over policymakers' perceptions, human rights forces have suffered a setback at the beginning of the 1980s. Following the rejection of Ernest Lefever by the Senate Foreign Relations Committee, the administration placed a neo-conservative, Elliot Abrams, in the post of Assistant Secretary of State for Human Rights and Humanitarian Affairs. The young (33) Mr. Abrams had been an aide to Senators Henry Jackson and Daniel Moynihan, where he was best known for his anti-Soviet positions. Since the beginning of the Reagan administration, he had been Assistant Secretary of State for International Organization Affairs. While in that position, he came to the attention of senior policymakers by authoring a memorandum that advocated an increased emphasis upon human rights considerations in U.S. policy: "Human Rights is at the core of our foreign policy because it is central to what America stands for," he wrote. " 'Human Rights' is not something we tack on to our foreign policy but its very purpose: the defense and promotion of freedom in the world." [57]

Despite these encouraging words, Mr. Abrams' statements during his confirmation hearing left little doubt that the human rights component of the Reagan foreign policy would focus upon our ideological adversaries. Abrams' harsh words for the Soviet Union ("an enemy of the United States") were in stark contrast to those used to describe rightwing tyrannies in Latin America. Abuses in Argentina, for example, were "largely a matter of the past;" the U.S. should support multilateral lending to Argentina, Chile, South Korea, Paraguay, and Uruguay because of improved human rights conditions in those countries; in El Salvador the human rights situation may be "very bad," but requires no more than quiet diplomacy.

The human rights record of the Reagan administration should be judged not by the statements of a young assistant secretary, however, but by the specific actions of the government. Here the record of the first year of the Reagan administration was uncommonly discouraging for human rights advocates. Eight days after the inauguration of Mr. Reagan, Secretary of State Haig announced that international terrorism would take the place of human rights in U.S. foreign policy. Then the administration took the following steps that effectively removed human rights considerations from U.S. foreign policy:

1) Certain economic sanctions against Chile are lifted and the government is invited to participate in inter-American naval exercises. (February 22)

2) Argentine President Roberto Viola is invited to make a state visit to the United States. (March 15)

3) U.S. votes against a U.N. Commission on Human Rights resolution condemning human rights violations in El Salvador. (March 11)

4) Reagan administration presents its FY 1982 foreign aid requests, increasing military aid by 27%, decreasing economic aid by 26%, and requesting repeal of the Clark Amendment prohibiting U.S. covert action in Angola and repeal of prohibitions on military aid to Argentina. (March 19)

5) National security advisor Richard Allen announces that future relations with South Africa should depend on U.S. self-interest and not on U.S. disapproval of apartheid. (March 21)

6) Mennonite Church denied license to ship milk powder to Vietnamese children—the first denial of a license to any private voluntary organization engaged in humanitarian relief. (May 1)

7) Reagan administration welcomes South African foreign minister Pik Botha, the first African foreign minister to visit President Reagan. (May 14)

8) Undersecretary of State James Buckley announces new policy on arms sales. Of the seven factors to be considered when a country requests arms, not only makes any mention of human rights. (May 21)

9) Administration circumvents human rights legislation and sends 100 jeeps, 50 2½-ton trucks, and spare parts to Guatemala. (June 5)

10) Vice-President Bush visits the Philippines and praises President Marcos for his "adherence to democratic principles and democratic processes." (July 1)

11) Administration announces that it will vote in favor of multilateral loans to Argentina, Chile, Paraguay, and Uruguay, thereby violating the specific legislation (PL95–118, Sec. 701) prohibiting positive votes on loan proposals from human rights violators. (July 1)

12) Administration brings 16 Guatemalan military officers to the United States for training, thereby violating Sec. 502B of the Foreign Assistance Act that prohibits military aid to repressive governments.

13) U.N. Ambassador Jeane Kirkpatrick visits Argentina and Chile, praises both governments for their improved human rights behavior and announces U.S. intentions to normalize relations with the Pinochet dictatorship. (August 10)

With these and other actions, the Reagan administration abandoned human rights as a criterion of United States policy toward Latin America and the Third World.

Nevertheless, of all the political groups opposed to various domestic and foreign policies of the Reagan administration, human rights activists have been perhaps the most adaptable to adversity. They have redesigned their tactics to fight a two-front war: one to force the U.S. government to cease supporting Latin American political groups that use repression to thwart change, especially in El Salvador and Guatemala; and another to protect the progressive Nicaraguan government, whose policies are designed to meet the basic needs of Nicaraguan citizens. The overall goal is not to convert the Reagan administration, but rather to limit the damage the administration does to human rights in Latin America. As with all damage control efforts, the question is not how many victories can be won for human rights, but how many losses can be avoided. This, we must remember, was how the human rights movement of the 1970s began, out of the ashes of Vietnam and Chile. In the face of considerable opposition, the activists of that decade created a period of unprecedented concern for human rights in United States policy toward Latin America. Now, in the face of equally strong opposition and circumstances that seem far less propitious, it is time to begin again.

NOTES TO CHAPTER 10

1. U.S. Congress, Subcommittee on International Organizations and Movements of the House Committee on Foreign Affairs, *International Protection of Human Rights,* 93d Congress, 1st sess., 1973, pp. 233, 250, 113.

2. U.S. Congress, Subcommittee on Western Hemisphere Affairs of the Senate Committee on Foreign Relations, *United States Policies and Programs in Brazil,* 92d Congress, 1st sess., May, 1971, p. 290.

3. U.S. President (Nixon), *U.S. Foreign Policy for the 1970s: Shaping a Durable Peace; A Report to the Congress,* May, 1973, p. 118.

4. *International Protection of Human Rights,* p. 507.

5. *New York Times,* 27 September 1974, p. 18.

6. David Weissbrodt, "Human Rights Legislation and U.S. Foreign Policy," *Georgia Journal of International and Comparative Law* 7 supplement (Summer 1977): 237–238.

7. Ibid., p. 237n.

8. *Department of State Bulletin* 75 (5 July 1976): 1.

9. *Department of State Bulletin* 75 (15 November 1976): 603.

10. *Washington Post,* 25 September 1977, p. C3.

11. In earlier speeches—to the Chicago Council on Foreign Relations on March 15, 1976, and particularly to the Foreign Policy Association of New York City on June 23, 1976—Mr. Carter emphasized the need to "restore the moral authority of this country in its conduct of foreign policy" by discarding "policies that strengthen dictators or create refugees, policies that prolong suffering or postpone racial justice." During the course of the New York speech, he advocated that the United States "take the lead in establishing and promoting basic global standards of human rights."

12. *Department of State Bulletin* 66 (14 February 1977): 121–122.

13. See U.S. Congress, Senate Committee on Foreign Relations, *CIA Foreign and Domestic Activities,* 94th Congress, 1st sess., January 22, 1975; U.S. Congress, Senate Committee on Foreign Relations, *Shlaudeman Nomination,* 94th Congress, 2d sess., May–June, 1976; U.S. Congress, Senate Committee on Foreign Relations, Subcommittee on Multinational Corporations, *The International Telephone and Telegraph Company and Chile, 1970–71,*

93d Congress, 1st sess., June, 1973; U.S. Congress, Senate Committee on Foreign Relations, Subcommittee on Multinational Corporations, *Multinational Corporations and United States Foreign Policy,* 93d Congress, 1st sess., 1973; U. S. Congress, Senate Committee on the Judiciary, Subcommittee to Investigate Problems Connected with Refugees and Escapees, *Refugee and Humanitarian Problems in Chile,* Parts I, II, and III, 93d Congress and 94th Congress, 1973 and 1975; U.S. Congress, Senate Select Committee to Study Governmental Operations with Respect to Intelligence Activities, *Alleged Assassination Plots Involving Foreign Leaders; An Interim Report,* 94th Congress, 1st sess., November, 1975; U.S. Congress, Senate Select Committee to Study Governmental Operations with Respect to Intelligence Activities, *Covert Action in Chile 1963–1973,* 94th Congress, 1st sess., 1975; U.S. Congress, Senate Select Committee to Study Governmental Operations with Respect to Intelligence Activities, *Intelligence Activities,* volume 7, 94th Congress, 2d sess., December, 1975; U.S. Congress, Senate Select Committee to Study Governmental Operations with Respect to Intelligence Activities, *Supplementary Detailed Staff Reports on Foreign and Military Intelligence,* Book IV, 94th Congress, 2d sess., April, 1976.

14. Tom Quigley et al., *U.S. Policy on Human Rights in Latin America (Southern Cone): A Congressional Conference on Capitol Hill* (New York: Fund for New Priorities in America, 1978), p. 41.

15. U.S. Congress, Subcommittee on Foreign Assistance and Related Programs of the Senate Committee on Appropriations, *Foreign Assistance and Related Programs Appropriations, Fiscal Year 1978,* 95th Congress, 1st sess., 1977, pp. 161, 196.

16. *Department of State Bulletin* 79 (January 1979): 1–2.

17. Cyrus Vance, "Human Rights and Foreign Policy," *Georgia Journal of International and Comparative Law* 7 supplement (Summer 1977): 223–224, 228; *Department of State Bulletin* 79 (January 1979): 1.

18. *Department of State Bulletin* 77 (July 18, 1978): 70; *New York Times,* 17 September 1977, p. 6.

19. The instruction consisted of a four-hour discussion with Assistant Secretary of State for International Organization Affairs Charles W. Maynes, during which Tyson steadfastly resisted Maynes' insistence that he resign.

20. For the evidence President Carter chose to ignore, see above note 13.

21. U.S. Congress, Subcommittee on International Organization of the House Committee on International Relations, *Human Rights and United States Foreign Policy: A Review of the Administration's Record,* 95th Congress, 1st sess., October 25, 1977, pp. 30–31.

22. Terence A. Todman, "The Carter Administration's Latin American Policy: Purposes and Prospects," speech at the Center for Inter-American Relations, New York, February 14, 1978.

23. U.S. Congress, Subcommittee to Investigate Problems Connected with Refugees and Escapees of the Senate Committee on the Judiciary, *Refugee and Humanitarian Problems in Chile,* 93d Congress, 1st sess., September 28, 1973, p. 41.

24. Interview with William D. Rogers, November 6, 1975, Washington, D.C.

25. *U.S. Policies and Programs in Brazil,* pp. 281–282.

26. U.S. Congress, Subcommittee on International Organizations of the House Committee on International Relations, *Religious Persecution in El Salvador,* 95th Congress, 1st sess., July, 1977, p. 34.

27. I. M. Destler, *Presidents, Bureaucrats, and Foreign Policy: The Politics of Organizational Reform* (Princeton, N.J.: Princeton University Press, 1974), p. 248.

28. *International Protection of Human Rights,* pp. 506–507.

29. As a further indication of the limited importance given to regional human rights activity, the 1975 State Department telephone directory did not list the human rights officers. Beginning in 1977, ARA's human rights officer was listed immediately after the Assistant Secretary of State, with the title of Special Assistant and Human Rights Officer.

30. State informed Congressman Donald Fraser of its intentions in August 1974. The first coordinator actually started work in June 1975.

31. U.S. Congress, Senate Committee on Foreign Relations, *Foreign Assistance Authorization; Arms Sales Issues,* 94th Congress, 1st sess., 1975, pp. 465–466.

32. Interview with James M. Wilson, December 15, 1978, Washington, D.C.; *Foreign Assistance Authorization; Arms Sales Issues,* p. 467. Wilson was never confirmed by the Senate.

33. Derian, however, was criticized at times by human rights activists for conceding on several important issues, including the 1978 military aid request for the Philippines and the 1980 military aid request for El Salvador.

34. "Foreign Policy and Human Rights," speech to the National Foreign Policy Conference on Human Rights, Washington, D.C., February 27, 1978.

35. *U.S. Policy on Human Rights in Latin America (Southern Cone),* pp. 53–54.

36. Lóuis Henkin, "The United States and the Crisis in Human Rights," *Virginia Journal of International Law* 14 (Summer 1974): 666.

37. The best analysis by far of U.S. policy toward human rights issues in intergovernmental organizations through 1970 is Vernon Van Dyke, *Human Rights, the United States, and World Community* (New York: Oxford University Press, 1970).

38. Thus, for example, in 1972 the United States, with the United Kingdom, South Africa, and Portugal opposed seven of the eight General Assembly resolutions on southern Africa and colonialism, and abstained on the eighth.

39. U.S. Congress, House Committee on International Relations, *Report of Secretary of State Kissinger on His Trip to Latin America,* 94th Congress, 2d sess., March 4, 1976, p. 20.

40. U.S. Congress, Subcommittee on International Organizations and Movements of the House Committee on Foreign Affairs, *Review of the U.N. Commission on Human Rights,* 93d Congress, 2d sess., 1974, pp. 42, 92.

41. John Salzberg and Donald D. Young, "The Parliamentary Role in Implementing International Human Rights: A U.S. Example," *Texas International Law Journal* 12 (Spring–Summer 1977): 260–261; *New York Times,* November 7, 1974, p. 6.

42. *Department of State Bulletin* 75 (July 5, 1976): 4.

43. *Department of State Bulletin* 76 (May 9, 1977): 454.

44. The resolution passed by a vote of 14 to 0, with 8 abstentions (Argentina, Brazil, Colombia, Chile, El Salvador, Guatemala, Paraguay, and Uruguay) and 3 absences (Bolivia, Honduras, and Nicaragua).

45. *Washington Post,* October 25, 1977, p. A3.

46. U.S. Congress, Subcommittee on International Organizations of the House Committee on International Relations, *Human Rights and United States Foreign Policy: A Review of the Administration's Record,* 95th Congress, 1st sess., October 1977, p. 43.

47. In the former case the suspension lasted for 25 days.

48. For an excellent interim analysis, see William Leo Grande and Carla Anne Robbins, "Oligarchs and Officers: The Crisis in El Salvador," *Foreign Affairs* 58 (Summer 1980): 1084–1103.

49. Patricia Derian, "Review of Human Rights in Latin America," speech at the Center for Inter-American Relations, April 24, 1980, New York.

50. The Christopher Committee—more formally, the Inter-Agency Committee on Human Rights and Foreign Assistance—was established in 1977 to insure consideration of human rights factors in the administration of foreign aid policy. During the Carter administration the committee was chaired by Deputy Secretary of State Warren Christopher, and gathered together representatives from nearly all State Department bureaus, the Departments of Defense, Commerce, Agriculture, and Treasury, the National Security Council, the Export-Import Bank, Overseas Private Investment Corporation (OPIC), Agency for International Development (AID), and the U.S. directors to the various multilateral development banks. The committee examined the human rights aspects of all AID budgetary program decisions and the U.S. positions on loans in the multilateral development banks.

51. The Export-Import Bank encourages the export of U.S.-made goods by financing their purchase at below-market interest rates. The Overseas Private Investment Corporation encourages the export of U.S. capital by insuring U.S. corporations against losses in Third World countries due to expropriation, war, revolution, insurrection, or currency nonconvertibility. The American Institute for Free Labor Development is an organization sponsored by the AFL-CIO to train Latin American labor leaders and, many critics assert, to undermine Latin American labor unions that advocate a policy independent from that of the United States. Charges have been made that AIFLD is linked to the Central Intelligence Agency. On this issue, see my *Human Rights and United States Policy toward Latin America* (Princeton, N.J.: Princeton University Press, 1981), Chapter 8.

52. Philip W. Bonsal, "Cuba, Castro, and the United States," *Foreign Affairs* 45 (January 1967): 272.

53. Albert Fishlow, "Flying Down to Rio: Perspectives on U.S.-Brazil Relations," *Foreign Affairs* 57 (Winter 1978/79): 395.

54. Isabel Letelier and Michael Moffitt, "Human Rights, Economic Aid and Private Banks: The Case of Chile," A Report Submitted to the Subcommittee on Prevention of Discrimination and Protection of Minorities, United Nations Commission on Human Rights, April 1978. Mimeographed, p. 14.

55. *Washington Post,* April 13, 1978, p. A19.

56. *Latin America Regional Report* RM 79-10, November 16, 1979, p. 5.

57. "Excerpts from State Department News on Human Rights," *New York Times,* November 5, 1981. See also "Human Rights Revisited," *The New Republic* (November 25, 1981), pp. 5–6.

CONTRIBUTORS

Margaret E. Crahan co-directed the Woodstock Theological Center's project on human rights and is currently Luce Professor of Religion, Power, and Political Processes at Occidental College. She is also a member of the Department of History, Herbert H. Lehman College, City University of New York. Dr. Crahan received her doctorate from Columbia University and has done field work in Peru, Colombia, Cuba, Mexico, Spain, and Switzerland on topics that span the seventeenth to twentieth centuries in Latin America. Her publications include studies of Spanish colonial administration, church-state relations, religion and politics, twentieth century Cuba, and African cultural heritage in the Caribbean. Dr. Crahan has served on the Executive Council of the Latin American Studies Association, as Vice-President of the Latin American Foundation, and on the Board of Directors of the Washington Office on Latin America. She is currently editing two books for publication in 1983: *Power and Piety: The Political Dimension of Religion in Latin America* and *Cuba: Social Transformations, 1750–1950.*

Elizabeth W. Dore is currently a consultant on basic needs at the Nicaraguan Ministry of Planning. She received her doctorate in Latin American history from Columbia University. Dr. Dore has done field research in Peru on several occasions and traveled extensively throughout Latin America. She has been the recipient of numerous fellowships, including a Social Science Research Council grant for research in Peru on economic development. From 1974 to 1976 she served as a visiting professor of economics at the Pontificia Universidad Católica del Perú and in 1978 as a consultant to the Instituto Nacional de Planificación del Perú. She has also taught at Tufts University, the New School for Social Research, the American University, and the University of the District Columbia. Dr. Dore has published a number of economic studies, including "Accumulation and Crisis in the Peruvian Mining Industry: 1968–1974" (1977) and "Social Relations and the Barriers to Economic Growth: The Case of the Peruvian Mining Industry," (1978), as well as 'The Human Rights Situation in Argentina: 1977" for the Subcommittee on International Organizations of the U.S. House of Representatives.

Richard E. Feinberg is currently a visiting Fellow at the Overseas Development Council and formerly had responsibility for international economic issues on the Policy Planning Staff of the U.S. Department of State. He is also an adjunct professor in the Landegger Program in International Business Diplomacy at the Georgetown University School of Foreign Service.

He has also worked as an international economist in the U.S. Treasury Department and been a Research Fellow in Foreign Policy at The Brookings Institution. Recently, he received fellowships from the Woodrow Wilson International Center for Scholars and the Council on Foreign Relations. Dr. Feinberg holds a Ph.D. in economics from Stanford University. His publications include *The Triumph of Allende: Chile's Legal Revolution* (New York: New American Library, 1972), *Government Banking: The Export-Import Bank in the U.S. Economy* (New York: Cambridge University Press, 1982), *Central America: International Dimensions of the Crisis* (New York: Holmes and Meier, 1982), and "Central America: No Easy Answer," *Foreign Affairs* (Summer, 1981).

Constantine Michalopoulos is Chief Economist at the Agency for International Development. He joined AID in 1969 and has since held various positions involving policy development and analysis of international economic issues. Prior to joining the Agency for International Development, Dr. Michalopoulos was Associate Professor of Economics at Clark University, Worcester, Massachusetts. He also taught at Trinity College, Hartford, Connecticut, and was a consultant to a number of UN organizations. A native of Athens, Greece, he is a graduate of Ohio Wesleyan University, Delaware, Ohio, and holds a Master's degree in International Affairs and a Ph.D. in Economics from Columbia University. He has published extensively on development issues. His most recent publication is "Institutional Aspects of Developing Countries Debt Problems" in David Denoon, ed. *The New International Economic Order: An American Response* (New York: New York University Press, 1980).

Lars Schoultz is an associate professor of political science at the University of North Carolina, from which he received his doctorate in 1973. He has done field research in Bogotá, Colombia, and Buenos Aires, Argentina on urban electoral behavior. Recently, he has been studying U.S. policy toward Latin America with special emphasis on human rights. He has also published studies of anti-United States sentiment in Latin America and of foreign aid as an instrument of U.S. foreign policy. He is currently serving as a member of the Latin American Studies Association's Task Force on Human Rights and Academic Freedom. His publications include three books—*Latin America, The United States, and the Inter-American System* (Boulder, Colorado: Westview Press, 1980), *Human Rights and United States Policy toward Latin America* (Princeton, N.J.: Princeton University Press, 1981), and *The Populist Challenge: Argentine Electoral Behavior in the Post-War Era* (University of North Carolina Press, forthcoming), plus numerous articles.

Brian H. Smith was co-director of the Woodstock Theological Center's human rights project and is assistant professor of political science at Massachusetts Institute of Technology. Dr. Smith holds a Ph.D. from Yale University, a Master of Arts in Political Science from Columbia University, and a Master of Social Theology in Social Ethics from Union Theological

Seminary. He has taught American Government and International Relations at Fordham University and has conducted field research on church-state issues in Chile. He is a member of the Task Force on Human Rights and Academic Freedom of the Latin American Studies Association, and has lectured at the U.S. Southern Command Headquarters in Panama on the relationship between U.S. security assistance and human rights observance in Latin America. His publications include: *The Catholic Church and Political Change in Chile, 1920–1980* (Princeton, N.J.: Princeton University Press, 1982) and "Churches and Human Rights in Latin America: Recent Trends on the Subcontinent," in *Churches and Politics in Latin America,* ed. Daniel H. Levine (Beverly Hills, Calif.: Sage, 1980).

John F. Weeks is currently a consultant with Financiera de Pre-Inversión in Nicaragua and professor of economics at American University. He received his doctorate in 1969 from the University of Michigan and subsequently taught at Ahmadu Bello University in Nigeria and the Universities of Sussex and London. Dr. Weeks has done field research in Africa and Latin America and served as a consultant for the International Labor Organization, the World Bank, and the Instituto Nacional de Planificación del Perú. His 30 publications deal with such issues as income distribution in peasant agriculture, wage policy in developing countries, manpower and unemployment, uneven sectoral development and the role of the state, policies for expanding employment, and foreign capital and accumulation in the manufacturing sector in Peru. His book *Capital and Exploitation* has been published jointly by Princeton University Press and Edward Arnold in 1982.

John A. Willoughby is an assistant professor of economics at American University in Washington, D.C. He received his doctorate from the University of California at Berkeley in 1979 and has an M.A. in Economics from Cambridge University. His research includes investigations of Marxist theories of imperialism and their application to modern captalism. He has been a member of North Americans for Human Rights in Argentina and has given several lectures on the relation between military repression, political democracy, and economic development. Among his writings is "Reagan's Third-World Policy: Foregoing All Pretense," *Multinational Monitor,* January 1981.